W9-BNS-756

ALSO BY JONATHAN KWITNY

The Fountain Pen Conspiracy

The Mullendore Murder Case

Shakedown (a novel)

Vicious Circles:
The Mafia in the Marketplace

Endless Enemies:
The Making of an Unfriendly World

THE CRIMES OF PATRIOTS

A True Tale of Dope, Dirty Money, and the CIA

JONATHAN KWITNY

A TOUCHSTONE BOOK
PUBLISHED BY SIMON & SCHUSTER INC.
NEW YORK • LONDON • TORONTO • SYDNEY • TOKYO

Touchstone
Simon & Schuster Building
Rockefeller Center
1230 Avenue of the Americas
New York, New York 10020

First Touchstone Edition, 1988

Published by arrangement with W. W. Norton & Company, Inc.

TOUCHSTONE and colophon are registered trademarks
of Simon & Schuster Inc.

Designed by Jacques Chazaud
Manufactured in the United States of America

10 9 8 7 6 5 4 3 2 1 Pbk.

Library of Congress Cataloging in Publication Data

Kwitny, Jonathan.
The crimes of patriots.

A Touchstone Book
Includes index.
1. Nugan Hand Bank—Corrupt practices. 2. Money laundering—Australia. 3. Murder—Australia. 4. United States. Central Intelligence Agency. 5. Narcotics, Control of. I. Title.
HG3448.N846K95 1988 364.1′0994 88-15646

ISBN 0-671-66637-1 Pbk.

In Memory of

ANNE THALER

and of *TERRI THALER*

and for their parents

Contents

Photographs appear following page 198

For some time I have been disturbed by the way [the] CIA has been diverted from its original assignment. It has become an operational arm and at times a policy-making arm of the Government. This has led to trouble and may have compounded our difficulties in several explosive areas.

I never had any thought when I set up the CIA that it would be injected into peacetime cloak and dagger operations. Some of the complications and embarrassments that I think we have experienced are in part attributable to the fact that this quiet intelligence arm of the President has been so removed from its intended role that it is being interpreted as a symbol of sinister and mysterious foreign intrigue—and a subject for Cold War enemy propaganda.

With all the nonsense put out by Communist propaganda about "Yankee imperialism," "exploitive capitalism," "war-mongering," "monopolists" in their name-calling assault on the West, the last thing we needed was for the CIA to be seized upon as something akin to a subverting influence in the affairs of other people. . . .

But there are now some searching questions that need to be answered. I, therefore, would like to see the CIA be restored to its original assignment as the intelligence arm of the President, and whatever else it can properly perform in that special field, and that its operational duties be terminated or properly used elsewhere.

We have grown up as a nation, respected for our free institutions and for our ability to maintain a free and open society. There is something about the way the CIA has been functioning that is casting a shadow over our historical position, and I feel that we need to correct it.

—HARRY S. TRUMAN, December 22, 1963

In a government of laws, the existence of the government will be imperiled if it fails to observe the law scrupulously. Our government is the potent, the omnipotent, teacher. For good or ill, it teaches the whole people by its example. If government becomes a lawbreaker it breeds contempt for law: it invites every man to become a law unto himself. It invites anarchy.

—Justice LOUIS D. BRANDEIS

Prologue

As this book goes to press, the United States Government is consumed with a foreign policy scandal. Arms were secretly sold to an Iranian government that the U.S. administration publicly preached against, and there was at least the intention to divert some of the proceeds to evade a Congressional prohibition on aiding rebels trying to overthrow the Government of Nicaragua. To keep the activity secret, the White House conducted its arms sales and Contra supply operations through a network of supposedly private citizens, most of whom had recently held jobs with the armed forces or Central Intelligence Agency.

Not only were laws broken governing the conduct of foreign policy, but private profits were evidently made in the process, of a size still being determined. There are daily expressions of shock and outrage about the "privatization" of foreign policy, and about the White House's obsession with covert activity, as if these were inventions of the Reagan Administration.

They weren't. The need, claimed by the past eight presidents, to pursue a perpetual and largely secret global war by fair means or foul against what is said to be a relentlessly expanding Soviet empire has justified gross violations of American law against the interests of American citizens for forty years. What is happening new in 1987 is that a window has suddenly been opened on this shadow world before the spooks who inhabit it could completely take cover.

By dealing with such an unreliable co-conspirator as Iran, some of whose leaders delighted in exposing the arms sales, the Reagan Administration allowed its secret operations to be blown with unprecedented prematurity. Yet it is important to keep in mind that what we are seeing is not an aberration; the aberration is only that we are seeing it, and what we are seeing is still not the most of it.

Nevertheless, some good may come from the unpleasant sight of so many greedy arms dealers and callous and bumbling ex-generals. Some good may come from the sense that all we achieved by sneaking down from the ethical high ground was to become the butt of the Ayatollah Khomeini's jokes (not to mention the killing of a lot of rag-poor Nicaraguan coffee farmers and their families). Perhaps all this will inspire the reassessment of a long-standing policy by which we have surely outwitted ourselves more often than not. That policy, not just the story of a colorful and crooked bank, is the subject of this book.

It is worth quoting again the words of Walter Lippmann, written after the failed U.S. invasion of Cuba at the Bay of Pigs in 1961: "A policy is bound to fail which deliberately violates our pledges and our principles, our treaties and our laws. . . . The American conscience is a reality. It will make hesitant and ineffectual, even if it does not prevent, an un-American policy. . . . In the great struggle with communism, we must find our strength by developing and applying our own principles, not in abandoning them."

The Crimes of Patriots was essentially finished before the Iran-Contra affair exploded. I have gone through the manuscript trying to highlight those longtime actors in the shadow world who have suddenly been catapulted onto the front pages and into the evening newscasts, and to relate their place in the Nugan Hand story to the events of the moment. Among them are air force generals Richard V. Secord and Harry ("Heinie") Aderholt, CIA-men Thomas Clines, Theodore Shackley, and Rafael ("Chi-Chi") Quintero, and even the Sultan of Brunei.

But actors come and go. It is the roles that stay, and that we need to be concerned with.

Perhaps the most surprising fact in this book is this: As of today, no one has been convicted of a crime for the activities of Nugan Hand. Only two relatively minor figures—Patricia Swan, the secretary, and Michael Moloney, the lawyer who showed up at the very end—have been charged, and only in connection with the cover-up, not with the bank's substantive work. Whether this means the others involved were innocent—or why, if any were not innocent, more charges haven't been filed—is something the reader will have to judge from the facts herein.

Jonathan Kwitny
New York City
May 1987

Cast of Characters

The Bankers

Francis John Nugan Son of a Griffith, Australia, fruitpacker; chairman and half-owner of the bank; shot dead in his Mercedes.

Michael Jon Hand Bronx-born Green Beret war hero, CIA operative, vice-chairman and half-owner of the bank, pal of dope-dealers and of retired and not-so-retired military-intelligence officials; now one of the world's most wanted men.

The Yanks in the Bank

Donald E. Beazley Florida banker, was rushed in late as president of the Nugan Hand holding company to rescue the faltering bank. The U.S. banks he ran before and after were also enveloped in scandal, but he's never been charged with anything.

General Edwin F. Black Was colleague and pal of CIA bosses Allen Dulles and Richard Helms, boasted of being involved in "right-wing" groups, ran the Nugan Hand Hawaii office.

General Erle Cocke Jr. Survived an execution, headed the American Legion, ran the Nugan Hand Washington office.

William Colby Retired as Director of CIA after a long and controversial career in clandestine services, became lawyer for Nugan Hand.

George Farris Military intelligence specialist and war buddy of Hand's, worked in the Nugan Hand Hong Kong and Washington offices, then moved into a special forces training base.

Dale Holmgren Was head of flight services for the CIA's airline, ran the Nugan Hand Taiwan office.

Maurice Bernard ("Bernie") Houghton The mysterious puppetmaster of Nugan Hand, a Texas manipulator who made money where the wars were; was he also a spy?

Robert ("Red") Jantzen Was CIA station chief in Thailand; announced as Nugan Hand officer there; inquired about drug connections, then backed out of the job.

General LeRoy J. Manor Was chief of staff for U.S. Pacific Command, U.S. Government liaison with Philippine President Marcos, ran Nugan Hand Philippine office.

Walter MacDonald Former deputy director of CIA for economic research, became consultant to Nugan Hand.

GUY PAUKER Personal advisor to Kissinger, Brzezinski, Nugan, and Hand.

ADMIRAL EARL ("BUD") YATES Was chief of U.S. strategic planning for Asia and the Pacific; president of the Nugan Hand Bank.

BILLY and GORDON YOUNG Thai-born American brothers with on-again, off-again CIA jobs for many years; helped Nugan Hand in the Golden Triangle drug zone.

THE AUSSIES (AND OTHERS) IN THE BANK

GEORGE BRINCAT The CPA who signed the phony books (but, then, so did Price Waterhouse).

JOHN CHARODY Consultant in the Sydney office; on the outside, a business associate of Sir Paul Strasser.

CLIVE ("LES") COLLINGS Headed the Hong Kong branch.

NEIL EVANS The Chiang Mai (Golden Triangle) branch representative.

JERRY GILDER Chief of the sales staff, master extractor of cash from reluctant investors.

WILFRED GREGORY Ran the Philippine office alone, then worked with General Manor; had his own ties to the Marcoses.

STEPHEN HILL The young money manager who agreed to testify to save his skin.

ANDREW LOWE Brought in Chinese customers; his commodity specialty was heroin, and his in-law ran a big Hong Kong bank that backed Nugan Hand.

JOHN MCARTHUR Worked with Collings in Hong Kong.

JOHN OWEN Was career British naval officer; ran Nugan Hand Bangkok branch while forwarding detailed reports on communist troop movements in Indochina to Mike Hand.

RON PULGER-FRAME The money courier from Deak & Company who always made it through customs.

GEORGE SHAW Link to the Lebanese money, much of it drug-related; agreed to testify despite threats to his life.

GRAHAM STEER American-educated Australian, worked under Hand in Singapore and Malaysia.

PATRICIA SWAN Nugan's secretary and executive assistant.

TAN CHOON SENG Bookkeeper-administrator Hand hired in Singapore.

OTHERS ON THE SCENE

SIR PETER ABELES Australian transportation tycoon and partner of Rupert Murdoch; his close associates employed Houghton and Hand; their close associates fixed his Mafia problem.

BRIAN ALEXANDER Lawyer for the "Mr. Asia" dope syndicate—and for Frank Nugan's brother. Mysteriously vanished.

JOHN ASTON Alexander's law partner who says he never realized there was cash in those bags he sent to Nugan Hand on behalf of clients.

THE SULTAN OF BRUNEI Nugan Hand got to him long before Oliver North did.

LEO CARTER The Australian spy chief who vouched for Houghton.

TERRY CLARK Became head of the worldwide "Mr. Asia" drug gang, after having his predecessor murdered; enjoyed chopping up bodies for multinational burials.

THOMAS G. CLINES CIA covert operations official; huddled with Hand, Houghton, and Secord on military equipment deals for Pentagon; rescued Houghton from Australia when the bank failed; later Secord's deputy running Iran-Contra covert arms network

ROBERT GEHRING Vietnam vet who worked in Houghton's operation.

PAUL HELLIWELL The CIA's drugs-and-money man for thirty years, who died, and his Caribbean bank with him, right before the rise of Nugan Hand; was it a replacement?

MICHAEL MOLONEY The lawyer Hand and Houghton brought in at the end.

KEVIN MULCAHY CIA man who blew the whistle on Ed Wilson, then wound up a corpse outside a trailer park.

KEN NUGAN Frank's brother, ran the fruit and vegetable business; the appearance of mobsters' names on his company's checks was, he assured everyone, a coincidence.

DR. JOHN K. and BARBARA OGDEN Lost their son, lost their daughter, lost every dime of their $689,000 savings entrusted to Nugan Hand.

RAFAEL ("CHI-CHI") QUINTERO CIA sabotage and assassination specialist under Clines; purged Secord's name from Houghton's travel bag. Later organized Contra arms deliveries for Secord.

MURRAY STEWART RILEY Former Australian Olympic star and cop, one of the biggest dope smugglers who used Nugan Hand, socialized with Hand.

ABE SAFFRON The Sydney vicelord Hand and Houghton dealt with.

DOUGLAS SCHLACTER "J" in the task force report, he worked for Ed Wilson and remembered Nugan Hand's help in covert arms deals.

GENERAL RICHARD V. SECORD Houghton's and Wilson's pal, introduced Houghton to Clines, later organized and ran the Iran-Contra arms network for the CIA and White House.

THEODORE G. SHACKLEY Top clandestine man at CIA, in Colby's career shadow, dealt with Hand, Houghton, and Holmgren.

SIR PAUL STRASSER Australian real estate tycoon, close friend of Sir Peter Abeles; personally hired Bernie Houghton in a coffee shop the weekend Houghton hit Australia.

FRANK TERPIL Former CIA man wanted for selling arms to lunatic dictators.

HARRY WAINWRIGHT Fugitive lawyer from San Francisco, Australian drug figure who used Nugan Hand, friend of Murray Riley's, regular chess opponent of Nugan's.

GOUGH WHITLAM Prime minister of Australia, dumped in a constitutional coup during a spat with Shackley and the CIA over exposing secrets.

EDWIN WILSON The politically influential CIA and naval intelligence operative now in prison who, while betraying the U.S. arsenal to Libya, was dealing with Shackley, Clines, Secord, and Houghton.

THE INVESTIGATIONS

CORPORATE AFFAIRS COMMISSION OF NEW SOUTH WALES Like the U.S. Securities and Exchange Commission. Final report, March 1983. Recommended further investigation.

COMMONWEALTH OF AUSTRALIA/NEW SOUTH WALES JOINT TASK FORCE ON DRUG TRAFFICKING (JOINT TASK FORCE) An elite police unit assigned by the commonwealth and state governments to investigate. Final report March 1983. Recommended further investigation.

JOHN O'BRIEN The court-appointed bankruptcy liquidator, still working on the case.

STEWART ROYAL COMMISSION Assigned by Parliament to resolve many unanswered questions of previous investigations. Final report June 1985.

HONG KONG LIQUIDATOR'S OFFICE A government agency, still working on the case.

THE CRIMES OF PATRIOTS

CHAPTER ONE

The End of the Rainbow

The Cold War strayed into the unassuming settlement of Lithgow, Australia, one Sunday morning in a Mercedes-Benz. Sergeant Neville Brown of the Lithgow Police recorded the time as 4 A.M., January 27, 1980.

"I was patroling the Great Western Highway south of Bowenfels with Constable First Class Cross," Sergeant Brown said. "We saw a 1977 Mercedes sedan, parking lights on, parked on the south side of the old highway, known as 'Forty Bends.' "

It was now three months later, and Sergeant Brown was testifying at the first day of a week-long inquest at the Lithgow courthouse. Lithgow, about ninety miles inland from Sydney, had been of little previous significance to Western civilization. Consequently, Sergeant Brown was unused to reporters in the courtroom and television cameras outside. But he maintained his official poise under the stern questioning of the big-city lawyers.

Sergeant Brown and Constable Cross had driven off the main freeway that morning, through some woods and onto the old two-lane road, which had been left open only for a few lonely homesteaders. They approached the unrecognized Mercedes. "A male person was sitting slumped over towards the center of the vehicle," Sergeant Brown testified. "He was dressed in light, bone-colored slacks, a dark blue shortsleeved shirt [January is summertime in Australia], and casual, slip-on shoes."

The reporters leaned forward intently.

"A .30-calibre rifle was held by him," Sergeant Brown went on, "the butt resting in the passenger-side floor well. His left hand held the barrel, three or four inches from the muzzle, and near the right side of his head. His right hand rested near the trigger. There was lots of blood over the console, the front seats, and front and rear floor wells. There was lots of blood on the head of the person. The rifle had a live round in the breech, one in the magazine. There was a spent cartridge in the right passenger-side floor well."

Of the throng that crammed the little courthouse that week, Sergeant Brown and Constable Cross were among the few who believed that Francis John Nugan, the man in the Mercedes, had committed suicide. In the three months since the body had been found, facts had leaked out about Frank Nugan's life that led most people to suspect, even presume, murder.

But whatever the facts of Nugan's life, the facts of his death told the local police otherwise. The autopsy had found no trace of drugs, poison, or prior injury. Nugan died of a single gunshot wound. Given the moat of undisturbed gore that surrounded his body, there seemed to be no way that someone else could have gotten into the car, killed him, and left.

Later, all this would be of great interest to politicians. But at this juncture the debate was being staged by insurance lawyers. They had been hired to try to establish facts that would relieve their clients, various companies, of responsibility under Nugan's millions of dollars in insurance policies. One large creditor had himself taken out a $1-million policy on Nugan; this policy, which Nugan's intimates weren't aware of, now stood to make the creditor rich for the first time in his life, unless it was challenged.

"Would you agree it is almost impossible to get yourself into that position?" pressed lawyer Barry Edmund Mahoney of Commonwealth Assurance Ltd.

"What position?" replied Sergeant Brown.

"The one you describe, with the head about a foot below the muzzle, which was itself being held by the left hand," said Mahoney. Then he spoke the words the gallery had been waiting for: "I suggest to you one would have to be a contortionist!"

The reporters had their lead.

Sergeant Brown, unfazed, replied, "It didn't appear to be any great distortion, viewing it." But in the newspapers his reply got second billing to the lawyer's "contortionist" remark. So did Sergeant Brown's further observation that he had plotted a trajectory from the rifle, through Nugan's head, to the bullet mark in the roof of the Mercedes. "They were all very close to being in alignment," Brown said.

That all pointed to suicide—a scenario the United States Central Intelligence Agency would be able to live with. Other aspects of Brown's testimony, however, were much more disturbing, to the CIA and others.

For example, there was a list found in Nugan's briefcase—it came to be known as "the body list"—containing scores of typed names of prominent Australian political, sports, business, and entertainment personalities. Next to the names were handwritten dollar amounts, mostly five- and six-figure sums. Were these debtors? Creditors? No one knew yet.

Then there was the Bible, a New Testament, found on the body. It bore, in Nugan's handwriting, the inscription, "I place this day my life, my work, my loved ones in the Lord's hands, He is so good and it will be a good day I believe, I believe this will be a glorious magical miraculous day, he is with me now, Jesus walks with me now. Visualize one hundred thousand customers world wide, prayerize, actualize."

Interleaved at page 252 of the Bible were two pieces of paper. One bore a telephone number in Long Beach, Florida. Nugan had just been negotiating the purchase both of a swank home near Long Beach and of controlling interest in a nationally chartered U.S. bank near there; the bank's best-known customer was the U.S. Air Force. The other piece of paper, by Sergeant Brown's description, was "what looks like the remnants of a meat pie bag." On it, Brown testified, were written "the names of Congressman Bob Wilson—and Bill Colby."

WILSON: The ranking Republican on the U.S. House of Representatives Armed Services Committee. A few weeks before Nugan's death, Congressman Wilson, his wife, fellow Congressman Richard Ichord, and their staff had been out dining with Nugan's American business partner, who had himself worked for the CIA.

COLBY: Though now a lawyer in private practice, Colby was a career professional covert operator of the highest order. A long rise through the ranks had brought him to command of the CIA's station in Saigon in the 1960s. He ran all U.S. "intelligence" operations in the Vietnam War theater, including Operation Phoenix, a Stalin-like program that fingered and assassinated an estimated forty thousand South Vietnamese civilians.* Except for the inevitable cases of wrong identification, the assassination victims were local revolutionary leaders. If left alive, they would have been predisposed to give South Vietnam some degree of independence from the Communist party of North Vietnam after the French and Americans were chased out; such an independent South Vietnam, of course, is something the United States would love to see today. The destruction by the Phoenix program of this natural barrier to North Vietnamese hegemony typifies many mistakes made in the belief that the war could be won. In retrospect, it was a colossal blunder. Colby, the man in charge of this and other blunders, was then promoted to the top of his profession—United States Director of Central Intelligence, the ultimate keeper of the secrets, guardian of the family jewels, director of the CIA, supervisor of the National Security Agency, and the voice in the president's ear. He was removed by President Ford after revelations of illegal domestic spying by the agency, four years before his name was found in Frank Nugan's Bible.

Sergeant Brown also testified that recent CIA boss Colby's calling card was in the wallet found in Nugan's right rear pocket. On the back of the card were "what could be the projected movements of someone or other," Brown testified: From January 27 to February 8, "Hong Kong at the Mandarin Hotel. 29th February - 8th March, Singapore."

William E. Colby was in those places at roughly those times.

This is not a book for people who must have their mysteries solved. It begins with unanswered questions, and it will end with them. The men this book is mostly concerned with have lived their lives in a world of spying and secrecy. Though they have been and in some cases still are paid with U.S. tax dollars, they have been trained to keep the taxpayers—among others—from finding out what they do. Compunctions about lying have seldom impeded that effort.

They entered their secret world under a cloak of patriotism. They have stretched that cloak in various ways. Claiming a patriotic duty to the United States, they have carried out unlawful and scarcely believable acts of violence against civilians in Asia, Africa, and Latin America. Like the CIA's assassinations of South Vietnamese leaders, these acts repeatedly backfired, and on the whole seriously under-

*Seymour M. Hersh, in his landmark *The Price of Power* cites South Vietnamese government statistics listing Phoenix casualties at 40,994, and concludes that the victims numbered "far more than the 21,000 officially listed by the United States."

mined the real international security and trade interests of the United States; but that's another book.*

This book is about the attempt of these men to stretch the cloak of patriotism still further, to cover civil crimes against citizens of the United States and many foreign countries. Under the cloak of patriotism, and with the help of local bankers like Frank Nugan, hundreds of millions of dollars have been stolen by fraud from innocent investors. Billions of dollars have been moved illegally about the globe, facilitating corruption and thwarting tax collectors in the United States and many countries regarded as U.S. allies. The cost of government has often been taken off the shoulders of citizens who are privileged enough to participate in such machinations, and transferred to the shoulders of citizens who aren't.

Steady, massive supplies of narcotics have been pumped into American cities for decades. As will be described in the pages that follow, the two main sources of heroin in America since World War II—the so-called "Golden Triangle" in Southeast Asia and the "French Connection" in Marseilles—were established in the course of operations by the U.S. Government's intelligence community. They have been protected by that community, ostensibly to further national security. A newer and more diffuse source of drugs, in Latin America, has often been protected similarly.

The Contra army the U.S. is now supporting to take over Nicaragua has in half a dozen documented cases made mutual-benefit pacts with big-time smugglers bringing cocaine and narcotic pills into the United States. In every case, the Justice Department has turned a blind eye to this activity. In country after country around the globe, American policy-makers have decided that an alliance with gangsters to help fight local wars against people considered Communist was worth the addiction of American youth.

The legitimate security interests of the United States certainly require a large and efficient intelligence operation. There are powerful forces that envy or oppose us, and we need constant, up-to-date information about them. But the people and organizations that make up what is called the intelligence community in the United States Government have gone far beyond the gathering of intelligence. In many cases, the word "intelligence" has been used as a cover for covert and unconstitutional acts of war and civil crime.

The CIA has often taken the rap, when things go wrong, when

*Jonathan Kwitny, *Endless Enemies* (1984).

in fact it was merely carrying out the instructions of civilian policymakers. For example, the training of Cuban expatriates and Lebanese militiamen in terror bombing, which has brought about the killing and maiming of hundreds of innocent civilian bystanders, was not a renegade act by the CIA but rather the execution of policies set by presidents from Eisenhower to Reagan.

Nor has the CIA been alone in carrying out secret plans that turned out to work against America. Other operatives, attached to the Defense Department, the National Security Agency, and the White House have also participated.

Decisions made at the highest levels of government, by our past eight presidents, have bestowed legitimacy on the stretching of the cloak: men in the government service are expected to—*ordered* to—secretly violate our laws to further national policy.

Agents operate in secrecy. Under Presidents Eisenhower and Kennedy, there are vivid examples of times the president, like some Mafia boss, was for his own protection intentionally kept in the dark about exactly what his underlings were doing. Former Undersecretary of State C. Douglas Dillon testified before the Senate Assassinations Committee in 1975 regarding the attempted murder of foreign leaders during the Eisenhower administration. He said that CIA chief Allen Dulles "felt very strongly that we should not involve the President directly in things of this nature." Eisenhower, Dillon said, would simply order "whatever is necessary" to be done, and Dulles and his organization would take it from there.

President Kennedy ordered a secret, illegal, and ultimately unwise war against Cuba, involving probably thousands of covert operatives and lasting many years beyond the public disaster at the Bay of Pigs. There's no public record on whether he specifically ordered the murder of Fidel Castro, though the CIA attempted it many times. Kennedy's closest aides in those years have argued persuasively that he wasn't aware that during one period the CIA hired some Mafia bosses to perform the Castro assassination.

What *is* clear is that the policy, and its necessarily distanced execution, resulted in setbacks both for our friendly relations throughout Latin America and for our security against criminals at home. Many of the ill-supervised operatives we hired *were* terrorists and criminals, and went on to practice their craft against civilians here and abroad while their "national security" links protected them against law enforcement. One Mafia gangster the CIA hired was actually sharing a bed partner with Kennedy at the time also, apparently without his knowledge.

One may assume that this distancing of presidential command from the invited illegal execution has continued. President Reagan became so obsessed with overthrowing governments in two relatively small and remote countries, Angola and Nicaragua, that secret operations were devised in his name to skirt federal laws that specifically banned such activity. In early 1987, the overthrow attempts appeared to be failing—in main part because of inadequate popular support in Angola and Nicaragua. Thousands of innocent Angolan and Nicaraguan civilians had been killed or wounded.

The secrecy around the attempts inevitably collapsed, greatly embarrassing the United States and perhaps mortally wounding the Reagan administration politically. In the truly important country of South Africa, the ability of future generations of Americans to trade with a black majority government was endangered by the United States's alliance with white minority South Africa over the Angolan issue.

Meanwhile, millions—possibly hundreds of millions—of American taxpayer dollars were missing and unaccounted for. As these words are written, investigations are underway to sort out what appears to be a long chain of criminal acts. Already, three senior government officials, including a general and an admiral, have invoked their Fifth Amendment right not to incriminate themselves rather than explain to the Congress what they've been doing with the money it appropriates.

Rough orders are given by presidents—prevent such-and-such from happening at all costs—and left for interpretation straight down the intelligence community's chain of command.

So when agents steal, when they facilitate drug deals, how far does the patriotic cloak granted by national policy stretch to cover them? Does it cover an agent who lines his pockets in side deals while working in the name of national security?

What are the boundaries of law and morality when it comes to helping foreigners who are regarded as our "friends," and hurting those who are regarded as our "enemies"? What acts lie beyond a presidential directive to do "whatever is necessary"? When has license been granted, and when simply taken?

Should any act, no matter how wrong, be covered up to avoid embarrassing our national security program? Who decides—the very people who run the program? And by what measure? Is the cover-up really to protect our country's security—or just to protect the politicians and bureaucrats who should be held to account?

What about the innocent people—including countless Americans—who suffer from all this? Is their only compensation to be the dubious honor of having been sacrificed to a remote battle some men chose to fight against communism? How many sins can be washed by the word "anticommunism"?

Is there a clear line at all between the authorized and the unauthorized national-security operation? Or are there men in the middle—who play both ways?

Probably the most sensational testimony at the Frank Nugan inquest came from Michael Jon Hand, Nugan's American partner. Hand identified himself to the court as chairman, chief executive, and 50 percent shareholder of Nuhan Ltd., "the major operating company of a worldwide group of companies with offices throughout the world." Most people still referred to the company by the name of its most prominent subsidiary, the Nugan Hand Bank.

In the three months since Frank died, Michael Hand had given contradictory accounts of who really owned Nugan Hand. He seemed to create whatever story suited him best at the moment. He had at times portrayed himself as merely a minority shareholder. But today, under oath, he said he and Frank Nugan had been 50–50 partners. Hand also reported that he was executor of Nugan's estate.

HAND: A highly decorated member of the Army Special Forces, or Green Berets, in Vietnam, he went on to be a contract agent for the CIA in Vietnam and Laos, training hill tribesmen for combat and seeing they were supplied. A few levels removed, Colby had been his boss. Next, Hand headed to Australia, met up with Nugan, a local lawyer, and founded Nugan Hand in 1973.

Although Hand's CIA attachment had helped lure the reporters to the inquest, thousands of people were interested in Hand's testimony for reasons that had nothing to do with the CIA or tabloid sensationalism. They, or their families or companies, had money invested with Nugan Hand. For weeks now, Hand and other officers and directors had stalled off investors who were growing increasingly itchy about their savings.

Finally, on April 10, a reporter for *Target*, a Hong Kong financial newsletter, entered the bank's Hong Kong office, was mistaken for an investor, and was told that withdrawals had been suspended for two weeks pending an audit. The next day the story spread through the international press. Still, depositors were assured, everything was all right and everyone would be paid.

Now Hand, on the witness stand, let loose the bad news—not the truth, not nearly the scope of the disaster, nor the reason for it, but the bad news. "I understand from enquiries made by me," he said, "that the company owed about $1.5 million to unsecured depositors. To my knowledge, certain of these depositors have approached the company and requested payment of their deposits, and the company has been unable to repay them and has attempted to make alternative arrangements. . . .

"The company has in excess of $5 million of secured deposits, such deposits being secured by bank-endorsed bills of exchange [like bonds] to face value. However, most of these deposits are on call, and each time a secured depositor calls a deposit, the bills of exchange have to be sold and the company is unable to meet the deficiency and pay out each secured creditor. . . ." More double-talk, but the message was clear. Even the allegedly "secured" depositors wouldn't be paid.

"I have inspected a schedule of the bills of exchange, and from enquiries made by me the drawers, acceptors and endorsers of those bills of exchange are insolvent companies, and the bills of exchange will not be met on maturity. . . ." Translation: the bonds allegedly "securing" the secured deposits were phony.

"Enquiries made by me indicate that the company owes approximately $2.8 million to its subsidiary in Hong Kong. . . . I understand from the resident director of Nugan Hand Hong Kong Ltd., Mr. John McArthur, that unless these moneys are repaid forthwith, Nugan Hand Hong Kong Ltd. will be unable to meet its obligations to depositors.

"Enquiries by me indicate [that the Hong Kong deposits] should have been secured by bank-endorsed bills of exchange, but the deposits are totally unsecured . . . The company is not in a position to repay any part of the amount outstanding." Translation: the overseas investors had been taken, too.

Actually, the unpayable claims mounted to some $50 million. And many other deposits were lost, but were never claimed, for the simple reason that the money had been illegal to begin with. Much of the money Nugan Hand received consisted of tax cheatings, dope payments, Marcos family money, and, rumored, the hoarded wealth of a few other Third World potentates—not something the losers would want to account for in an open bankruptcy court. The missing money could easily have been in the hundreds of millions of dollars.

Now, Hand, on the witness stand, laid the blame on a party who wasn't likely to object: "I have ascertained over the last two months that the late Mr. F. J. Nugan has fraudulently misappropriated a vast amount of money from the company and other companies in the group without my knowledge." The embezzled money, Hand said, was paid "to certain of his personal companies and to himself."

Hand said legal advisors had told him it would be "a long and involved process to recover these moneys, if at all."

Up to $3 million had been "loaned out to persons or companies whose identity is either unknown, or without formal documentation. . . . Prospects of recovering these moneys is extremely remote." Hand also complained that Nugan's surviving records "were incomplete and misleading." (Later, it would become clear that Hand himself played no small part in making sure the records were incomplete.)

All this embezzlement, on top of a stock fraud indictment that was pending against Nugan, might seem to create a motive for him to have committed suicide. But when lawyer Alexander Shand, representing Sun Alliance Life Assurance Ltd., repeatedly suggested as much, Hand denied it. Hand argued that his partner more likely had been murdered. "I believe that Mr. Nugan was a fighter and would have kept on going," he insisted.

In response to further questions, Hand disclosed the appallingly slipshod police investigation into Nugan's death. Hand was surprised, he said, "that the Police Department have not come down there [to the Nugan Hand office] and tried to look for his diary. . . . We certainly have not seen it. I would like to know what his last notes were, and where he has been and who he has been speaking to."

Hand said police hadn't even talked to him until two days before the inquest began, and then just to ask him "if I would be kind enough to put together a very brief and concise statement because they had a very short period of time." He said the police had never visited his office.

Before Hand was through, the lawyers made him squirm some. They revealed through their questions the fact that he had been called to testify one month earlier before an Australian royal commission looking into the drug racket. They made public certain sections of his testimony revealing that large amounts of money had been transferred by Nugan Hand from Australia to Hong Kong secretly, in apparent violation of exchange control and tax regulations.

Hand stuck by the same tortured excuses he had given to the drug inquiry. He was just following orders.

"Mr. Nugan advised me that it was part of a tax plan," Hand offered.

"And you accepted it as being part of a tax plan?"

"Certainly, sir, he was a solicitor [lawyer]."

"But now you say you regard them as improper purposes?"

"I cannot find, because I don't have adequate facts available at my fingertips to determine what in essence the purposes were of such transactions . . . Mr. Nugan would call me up from time to time or send me a note and ask me to pay a bill or to send money to a particular direction. I would have no knowledge of whether the client was in Australia or in Timbuctoo, and Mr. Nugan continually assured me that he would not breach any Reserve Bank regulations."

Hand was lying, and events would prove it. The law in Australia, and most other countries where Nugan Hand dealt, forbade the export of money. Hand himself had boasted earlier that Nugan Hand moved $1 billion a year through its magical windows. It certainly didn't do this with Reserve Bank approval.

The real questions should have been asked of the Australian security agencies: how they could have let an operation the size of Nugan Hand break the exchange laws with impunity for so many years—unless, of course, the Australian agencies were cooperating with it, or had been told that Nugan Hand had a powerful government sanction from abroad. There was reason to suspect that.

But for now, Hand was reduced to inventing new lies that the insurance lawyers in Lithgow would be unprepared to challenge. There were really two Nugan Hands, he suddenly said, one in Australia, controlled by Nugan, and one in Asia, controlled by Hand. This was certainly something the customers had never been told before. But now Hand was blaming all the problems on the Australian end of the business.

Finally, he admitted how bare the cupboard really was. He told shocked onlookers that the Nugan Hand Bank, which had believably claimed to move more than $1 billion a year, owed $20,000 rent for the Sydney headquarters "and the company is unable to pay this. . . . The company is insolvent."

There was no meat on Nugan Hand's platter anymore. But there was still plenty of spice, and Sergeant William Leslie McDonnell gave the newspapers one more thing to write about when he testified about the scene at Nugan's multimillion-dollar waterfront villa just hours after the body was discovered and identified.

Sergeant McDonnell didn't find the widow, Frank's wife Lee, at the house. Lee still hadn't returned from her home town of Nashville,

Tennessee, where she had gone with the couple's two children to live six months before. Charlotte Lee Nugan always maintained that it was perfectly natural for her to take the children to live with her parents half a world away, and that it wasn't a sign anything was wrong with her marriage. But friends assumed she just couldn't take any more of her husband's mercurial swings from a fifth-a-day Scotch habit to teetotalism, and from tireless pursuit of money to religious zealotry.

Even with Mrs. Nugan gone, however, Sergeant McDonnell found the lights on. Ken Nugan, Frank's older brother, was there with his own wife. Ken had taken over their father's fruit-and-vegetable business while Frank had gone to law school and become an international banker.

Recently, Ken had involved the fruit-and-vegetable business in a stock scandal that was getting wide publicity in Australian newspapers. The name of a prominent drug racketeer had popped up. Worse, Nugan Hand money had financed the business, and Frank had advised Ken on a scheme to block outside shareholders from taking control. As a result, a month before he died, Frank Nugan had found himself indicted with Ken on charges of stock fraud. Their name was so sullied that just before Frank's death the Nugan Hand holding company, Nugan Hand Ltd., had changed its name to Nuhan Ltd.

Ken's lawyer also was at the house the night of Frank's death—not unusual in itself, but what interested Sergeant McDonnell was the identity of the lawyer Ken had chosen. To assist him at this trying time, Ken Nugan had brought to his brother's house a solicitor named Brian Alexander. McDonnell knew that Alexander was under summons from a Commonwealth police inquiry—similar to a grand jury subpoena in the United States. He also knew that Australian customs officials wanted to talk to Alexander.

The reason for all this attention was that Alexander had become very close to a major international heroin syndicate whose members he was representing, including the leader, a man known as "Mr. Asia." The ring was British in origin, but operated in the United States, Australia, New Zealand, and, of course, southern Asia, where the heroin came from. Police had begun to suspect that Alexander himself was part of the "Mr. Asia" syndicate.

They considered their suspicions confirmed a year later when Alexander disappeared. His body wasn't found—not surprising, perhaps, since the Mr. Asia syndicate was already known to go to extraordinary lengths to disguise and hide bodies. But Alexander's car was located, abandoned, at a park overlooking the ocean near Sydney. It created a sensational news story.

The charges against which Alexander had been defending the heroin bosses included half a dozen murders of turncoat syndicate members who had been secretly talking to narcotics officers. Police were now building a case that Alexander, by bribing some corrupt Australian narcotics officers, had fingered the victims. At this point, they hadn't even come close to guessing that the widely advertised, supposedly reputable Nugan Hand operation was a vehicle for the suspected bribe money.

One might expect that the police, faced with the mysterious shooting death of the head of a large international bank, would try to seal off the house to prevent Ken Nugan and his lawyer, Brian Alexander, from removing any papers. But Sergeant McDonnell just interviewed Ken, learning that the recent indictment had "weighed very heavily" on Frank Nugan. On the other hand, Ken told McDonnell that he saw his brother hours before the shooting. Frank had just returned from Europe, where he said he sealed a big bank expansion deal. He "was quite happy and untroubled except that he was so terribly tired and suffering from jet lag," Ken told the policeman.

Though McDonnell testified that he was the chief investigating officer in the case, he said he didn't go to the Nugan Hand office. He said that a manager on the Nugan Hand staff, Graham Arthur Leighton Edelsten, had assured him that no important papers were to be found there.

Ken Nugan evidently thought otherwise. He testified that he went into the Nugan Hand office the very next morning, January 28. There were suggestions, never clearly confirmed, that Ken had obtained keys to the office from police, who had got them off Frank's body. Ken Nugan testified that he removed various documents from the office, but he assured the court that the only documents he took were from Frank Nugan's private law office, which was inside the bank. The papers concerned the brothers' joint criminal defense to the stock manipulation charges, and nothing else, Ken said.

The inquest didn't have the benefit of testimony from Patricia Swan, Frank Nugan's longtime secretary and administrative aide. But later, in a statement that was filed during the government's attempt to prosecute her, she gave a version of the looting that makes Ken Nugan's testimony seem a bit tame. That Monday, January 28, was a public holiday in Australia and all offices were closed. But Swan (according to her statement) got a call at 8:30 A.M. from Stephen Hill, a thirty-four-year-old Australian who had joined Nugan Hand six years earlier as assistant money manager and was now its vice-president and financial officer. Hill asked Swan to run in to work despite the holiday.

"I arrived at the office about 9:15 A.M. to find Steve Hill, Dennis Pittard, and Ken Nugan already in the office," she said. (Pittard was a well-known Australian football hero who, on retirement from the sport, went to work as goodwill ambassador for Nugan Hand.) Swan went on: "When I went into my office I found my desk drawers open—to my surprise. Only I and Frank Nugan had keys to those drawers. I can only assume Ken Nugan had obtained Frank Nugan's keys from the police.

"Ken Nugan was taking out of the office the masses of papers pertaining to the Nugan Group [the fruit company] litigation. He also asked me if I could find the document that Frank and he had put together, showing dates and amounts of money that Frank had advanced to Ken, and what amounts Ken had paid back. I was unable to locate this document and to my knowledge Ken Nugan did not find it.

"Steve Hill then told me to go through all the filing cabinets and drawers in my room and Frank's room and 'take out anything that might implicate you or go against you.' I asked Steve if he could be more specific, as I had no idea what I was meant to be looking for, and he just repeated what he first said.

"Not really knowing what I was looking for, I quickly went through the filing cabinets in my room—quickly, as both Ken and Steve seemed to think the Corporate Affairs [Commission, the Australian counterpart to the U.S. Securities and Exchange Commission] or the police might arrive at any moment. Steve was in his room putting papers, and I remember in particular either cash books or ledgers or journals, in cartons, and Dennis Pittard was taking them downstairs—presumably to put in a vehicle to take away."

Swan said she didn't remember taking any documents out of the office herself, and that she left with Hill, Pittard, and Ken Nugan after about an hour and a half. "The other thing I remember Ken Nugan telling me was that the next day, the first working day after Frank's death, would be horrific, that the police and Corporate Affairs would be down and things wouldn't be easy."

But the lawmen weren't nearly so diligent. They didn't even show up the next day, when the more methodical ransacking of the files took place. Present for that job was a team of former U.S. military operatives in Southeast Asia, led by former CIA-man Michael Hand and including the president of the Nugan Hand Bank, Rear Admiral Earl P. ("Buddy") Yates.

YATES: Nineteen forty-three graduate of the U.S. Naval Academy, Legion of Honor winner in Vietnam, commander of the aircraft carrier USS *John F. Kennedy,* then chief of staff for plans and policy of the U. S. Pacific Command, in charge of all strategic planning from California to the Persian Gulf, until his retirement from active service in July 1974. He became president of the Nugan Hand Bank early in 1977.

CHAPTER TWO

The Cover-Up

Attempts to sanitize the public record began almost the moment Frank Nugan's body was identified. Telephones began to ring all over the world.

One, it's now known, was on the desk of three-star General LeRoy J. Manor, Nugan Hand's representative in the Philippines.

MANOR: A much-decorated air force pilot and combat veteran, he became special assistant to the Joint Chiefs of Staff at the Pentagon for "counter-insurgency and special activities." He designed and commanded a widely publicized 1970 raid on a North Vietnamese prison camp that failed to find any U.S. prisoners. His promotions continued, however, and in 1976 he became chief of staff for the entire U.S. Pacific Command, managing and coordinating air force, navy, army, and marine corps operations "from the West Coast of the United States to the East Coast of Africa, and from the Arctic to the Antarctic." He retired full-time active service in July 1978, to undertake new duties that the air force says are so secret that it can't talk about them. These duties are generally known to have included negotiating the 1979 agreement with the Philippine Government of Ferdinand Marcos for continuation of the U.S. military bases there (which General Manor used to command), and investigating the failed hostage rescue raid in Iran in 1980—an assignment that apparently stemmed from his own raid in North Vietnam. He joined Nugan Hand's Manila office in 1979. In June 1982, the air force replied as follows to a *Wall Street Journal* request for information on Manor's official assignments: "The standard bio is good until his retirement, but as for when he was reactivated, it's basically a no-comment type of thing. It's pretty sensitive some of the stuff he might have done. He did some work for the State Department. I couldn't find out anything about the Iranian thing. As far as the Philippines goes, I'd just have to say 'no comment' on that. I'd really like to be frank on this, but they just won't let me say too much."*

According to Tony Zorilla, Nugan Hand's public relations man in the Philippines, General Manor telephoned Zorilla as soon as he learned of Nugan's death. The public relations man says Manor told him to stop the wire services from reporting the story. Zorilla says he replied that this would be unethical and impossible, and refused. "He wanted for us to see if we could persuade the Philippine media to hold off running the stories. I would not have anything to do with trying to prevent the wire services from running the story," Zorilla recalls.

General Manor acknowledges there was a conversation about the possible ill effect Nugan's death would have on the bank, but denies giving any orders to squelch the story. He says Zorilla is just angry because he later fired Zorilla, who he says wasn't working hard enough.

Of course, all the main principals (who could be located) of Nugan Hand began interviews by denying whatever they thought a reporter would be unable to prove. These denials have to be weighed against the standard denials—"honest lies"—that people in intelligence work are taught to purvey under the cloak of patriotism. Called to testify in court, even in criminal trials, CIA men have said they believe their oath of secrecy will protect them against perjury charges if they lie under another oath.

General Manor began a telephone interview with a reporter** by insisting that he "had nothing to do with the Nugan Hand Bank." When the reporter presented evidence to the contrary, General Manor said he "was brought in just to learn," and hung up. Later, confronted in person with the word of men who had served under him that he had actually enticed their deposit money on behalf of Nugan Hand—men who lost every penny—he acknowledged having done so. In fact, records show he worked and talked enthusiastically on behalf of the bank in the fall of 1979. Faced with that, he

*Interview with Peter Blume, Air Force media relations, June 21, 1982.

**The author.

explained that he was duped into doing so, and never knew that the bank was being run crookedly.

At about the time of the inquest in April, when the papers were reporting that Nugan Hand was suspending payouts and might go under, LeRoy Manor left the Philippines. Wilfred Gregory, the Nugan Hand salesman who was administering the Manila office with General Manor, says that Manor's departure was inspired by a conversation with their Manila lawyer, William Quasha. Gregory says Quasha "arranged for Manor to leave the country. He told me to go, too. He said, 'You could wind up in jail.'" The three-star general, according to Gregory, left overnight.

General Manor praises Gregory as "a real refined individual, and smart. He married a real nice girl, a society girl." But the general says he left the Philippines only because it was time for home leave, and that he would have returned except for the Iranian mission.

Of course, Gregory's word isn't necessarily trustworthy, either. Since the Philippine Government never chartered Nugan Hand as a bank, it was legally forbidden from taking deposits. Operating from a lavish suite of offices in a prestigious downtown building that also houses several U.S. Government agencies, the Gregory-Manor operation was supposed to confine itself to brokering international trade deals. It apparently never brokered a single successful transaction.

Early in an interview at his Manila office, Gregory stated flatly that the office had abided by Philippine law, and done absolutely no banking at all.

Well, maybe just a little. "I used to get involved only with Australians who were stranded here," he conceded. "They used to have deposits in Australia and come up here and need money. We used to keep a little cash in the office here [to give them]," Gregory explained. But he was very firm that "This office couldn't accept cash. . . . The law here doesn't permit you to do that. The central bank is just four blocks down. If we had done that we would have been out of business within twenty-four hours."

Faced with evidence, though, Gregory then acknowledged that, well, yes, he, like General Manor, had indeed taken substantial deposits. Told that some of the ruined depositors had actually testified about this before Australian bankruptcy officials, Gregory shook his head. "All those things were confidential," he said. "I don't know who made sworn testimony about this, but I think it's in very poor taste to reveal confidential information."

Manor and Gregory weren't the only Nugan Handers who took

deposits despite the prohibitions of Philippine law. George Shaw, a vice-president based in Nugan Hand's home office at Sydney, acknowledges that he also traveled to the Philippines to collect other people's savings. "We had a lot of clients in the Philippines," Shaw says.

One thing that might have enabled the Manor-Gregory operation to skirt Philippine law as it did was its intimate connection to the chief lawmakers at the time, Ferdinand and Imelda Marcos. General Manor had negotiated the U.S. base leases with President Marcos. Marcos's brother-in-law, Ludwig Rocka, actually shared the Nugan Hand office suite, and Rocka's International Development & Planning Corporation took over the suite after Nugan Hand's collapse. Gregory continued to work for Rocka's company after Manor departed for Virginia to help run a veterans' group.

Rocka and his wife, President Marcos's sister, Elizabeth—a provincial governor—put $3.5 million into Nugan Hand, according to records found after the collapse. Rumors that Ferdinand and Imelda moved even larger amounts through the bank remain just that—rumors.

Quasha, the Manila lawyer, says the attorney-client privilege prevents him from saying whether he told Gregory and Manor that they could get in trouble, or whether his advice had anything to do with General Manor's decision to leave in April. "I'm not confirming or denying that I gave General Manor such advice," he says. He also says, "I don't believe General Manor ever did anything wrong in his whole life." Then he adds an important qualifier: "Without believing it was right."

Michael Hand heard about his partner's death in London, where Nugan Hand was trying to buy an established bank. He had just visited Geneva, to try to enlist the help of the United Nations High Command for Refugees in a plan to move displaced Montagnard tribesmen who had fought with the U.S. side in Vietnam and Laos to an island reservation Nugan Hand was acquiring in the Caribbean.

Hand left for home that Sunday night. But instead of flying directly east to Australia, he went west, the long way around, through the United States. At some point he was joined by Admiral Yates, the bank's president. (By one account, Yates was with Hand in London when he heard of Nugan's death; by another, he was at home.)

Though the bank's main offices were in Sydney and Hong Kong, and though its official address was the Cayman Islands (because of the weak regulatory laws there), Yates lived in Virginia Beach, Virginia.

Virginia Beach was an easy hop from Washington, where Admiral Yates helped maintain a Nugan Hand office. En route to Sydney, Hand and Yates also were joined by Lee Nugan, Frank's widow, who had been with her parents in Tennessee.

Thanks to a criminal case in Australia, and the agreement of several insiders to testify, much is now known about those days that wasn't revealed at the inquest. Arriving in Sydney, Hand and Yates raced to the Nugan Hand office suites. There was sorting and sanitizing of whatever documents Steve Hill, Patricia Swan, Ken Nugan, and his lawyer Brian Alexander hadn't already made off with.

The suites occupied two floors, and the office was being expanded to occupy more. For this new ransacking, Hand and Yates were joined by Hill, by George Shaw, and also by the mystery man of Nugan Hand, perhaps its most important figure—Maurice Bernard Houghton. In fact, it was Houghton who had met Hand and Yates at the airport.

HOUGHTON: "Bernie" Houghton was so secretive about his past that he wouldn't tell his own lawyer if he had any traceable wives or children when the lawyer was trying to draw Houghton's will. A Texan, he was known as a camp follower of America's Asian wars, always as a civilian since his few years in the army air corps during World War II. He had been to Korea, and to Vietnam, and had made what seemed a lot of money, buying and selling war surplus and supplying the "recreational" needs of GIs. Though ostensibly occupied in Australia only as a honky-tonk bar impresario, Houghton's movements were facilitated whenever he needed by that country's secret security agency, and he displayed a smooth working relationship with all levels of the U.S. Government.

Admiral Yates won't talk about it, but by most accounts Houghton recruited Yates into the Nugan Hand job. And, as one of the first people Michael Hand met after he came to Australia, Houghton may well have introduced Hand to Nugan.

To the rape of the Nugan Hand files, Houghton brought not only himself, but Michael Moloney, fortyish, a Sydney lawyer who had done work for Houghton and Hand. Moloney was used to troubles with the law. A few years earlier, he had survived the threat of criminal proceedings and disbarment in a case that did leave him financially pressed, under a $430,000 civil judgment for improperly taking title deeds from a client's mother. Before that, he had also been the target of a big narcotics investigation after anonymous tipsters reported to Australian authorities that Moloney had ferried heroin in from Hong Kong; the investigation was closed with the allegations unsubstantiated.

Although at first all the Nugan Handers stonewalled authorities, eventually three Australians—Michael Moloney, George Shaw, and Stephen Hill—tried to soften criminal charges against them in Sydney by testifying in various proceedings about the sanitizing of the Nugan Hand files.

Hill, the young financial vice-president, testified that on the Tuesday and Wednesday following Frank Nugan's death, with no interference from any police agency, the files were purged by a team including him, Michael Hand, Bernie Houghton, Admiral Yates, lawyer Moloney, secretary Swan, vice-president Shaw, and Jerry Gilder. Gilder was an Australian with a background in the hard sell of shares in a mutual fund that then went bankrupt; he had been hired to staff and direct a worldwide sales force for Nugan Hand.

Shaw testified, basically corroborating Hill's story, that the ransacking team was spurred on in its work by threats from Hand, Moloney, and, by his mere presence, Houghton.

Moloney ordered the files sanitized before police arrived. By Hill's account, Moloney said, "I am fully aware of what has been going on. You all face jail terms of up to sixteen years." Gilder spoke up criticizing Moloney, but, Hill testified, Hand replied that "terrible things" would happen if Moloney's orders weren't carried out. "He said that our wives would be chopped up and posted to us in boxes. . . . Our wives would be returned to us in bits and pieces," Hill testified. Shaw remembers Hand threatening that Houghton's "connections" could take care of any necessary "arrangements" for such mayhem.

In an interview, Shaw says his instructions were coming mostly from Hand, with Admiral Yates listening on. "Under instructions from Mr. Hand," he says, "I did destroy certain records. I don't know which ones they were. A lot of sensitive documents were put through a shredding machine, similar to what your guys did in Iran before they were taken over [referring to the shredding of classified material by U.S. marines at the U.S. Embassy in Tehran in 1979]."

After the records were sorted and sanitized, Hill testified, Moloney told the group that "Normally after a situation like this there's likely to be a burglary and the records should be removed for safekeeping." Said Shaw, "It was decided that any documents that were there we ought to move to another office."

For a while, Moloney and Hand both adamantly denied taking

any files out of the office. But, faced with criminal charges, Moloney later recanted. He now readily admits in an interview, "Sure, I advised Hand to take documents out of the office. I was told there were serious deficiencies in the accounts." But, he adds, "Everything I did I talked about with Yates first."*

By various accounts, enough records to fill a small room were fed to a shredder. Others were packed in cartons, everyone helping, and carried at night down eight flights to Gilder's waiting van. Then they were driven to the back room of a butcher shop owned by Robert W. Gehring, a former U.S. Army sergeant in Vietnam who worked for Bernie Houghton's honky-tonk operation.

There the records stayed, while over the next few months Hand and Moloney fought off—sometimes physically—the timid efforts of Australian securities investigators to examine them. Hill remembered Moloney's refusal to admit two investigators from the Corporate Affairs Commission to the office to examine remaining records March 28:

"There followed a distasteful scene wherein Mr. Moloney adopted an attitude of obstruction by physically and verbally preventing them from moving about the very narrow corridor in which the records were contained," Hill testified. The two investigators finally looked at a few random records, and left without taking any, Hill says.

Meanwhile, right up to the inquest in mid-April of 1980, Nugan Hand continued to tell the world that everything was all right, continued to take in whatever deposits it could, and continued to benefit insiders by depleting whatever funds were left.

Michael Hand's testimony at the Nugan inquest was almost simultaneous with an announcement by the Nugan Hand Bank office in Hong Kong that it wasn't paying depositors anymore. The shock reverberated around the financial world. *Wall Street Journal* reporters Seth Lipsky and E. S. ("Jim") Browning in Hong Kong cabled a request for the paper's New York banking reporter, Tom Herman, to check out Nugan Hand's U.S. address.

Herman was surprised to find that Nugan Hand's Washington phone number led to the public relations firm of Cocke & Phillips International. One partner in the firm, Eugene Phillips, assured reporter Herman that he and his partner, Erle Cocke, Jr., had nothing to do with Nugan Hand, and merely allowed Admiral Yates to use

*Yates denies this and says he only carried one box of records.

their firm as his office. Though Herman had no choice but to accept the statement at the time, the evidence suggests it simply wasn't true—as was largely acknowledged, in interviews, by the firm's leading partner, *Brigadier General* Erle Cocke, Jr.

COCKE: A World War II hero, he then held various Pentagon posts throughout the 1950s and 1960s, including civilian aide to the Secretary of the Army, while also working as an executive of Delta and—simultaneously—Peruvian airlines (Washington office). Obviously able to wear many hats, Cocke was an executive director of the International Bank for Reconstruction and Development during the same period. He is a past National Commander of the American Legion. Named honorary commander of the Nationalist Chinese air force, he also received the French Legion of Honor and equivalent top medals from Spain, the Philippines, and Italy.

Treasury Department records show that General Cocke registered as the "person in charge" of Nugan Hand's Washington office. The general says he must have been registered as such by Admiral Yates, who he says never told him about it. But he agrees he's a good friend of Yates. He also agrees he met with Hand, Nugan, and Houghton in Washington and Hong Kong, that he arranged high-level meetings for Yates and Nugan in Jimmy Carter's White House (Cocke is a native Georgian who had strong ties there) to discuss Nugan Hand involvement in resettling Indo-Chinese refugees, and that he frequently talked with and even counseled at least one Nugan Hand depositor.

Wall Street Journal reporter Herman's search also took him to Nugan Hand's Hawaii-based representative, Brigadier General Edwin F. Black. Black's office told Herman he was traveling and couldn't be reached.

BLACK: A 1940 graduate of West Point, Black entered the Office of Strategic Services (OSS), which became the CIA. After holding high-level OSS posts throughout Europe during the war, he was made OSS commander in Berlin. He became chief administrative aide to (and frequent chess opponent of) Allen Dulles, Director of Central Intelligence under Presidents Eisenhower and Kennedy. Black was also wartime boss and later tennis partner of Richard Helms, who became Director of Central Intelligence after Dulles and before Colby. General Black served on the National Security Council staff under Eisenhower and later became commander of all U.S. troops in Thailand during the Vietnam War. He was named assistant chief of staff for the Pacific. He retired in 1970 to become executive vice-president of the Freedoms Foundation, headquartered in Valley Forge, Pennsylvania, a very vocal group promoting conservative political causes. He later ran some Asian operations for LTV Corporation, an important military contractor, and in 1977 became president of Nugan Hand, Inc., Hawaii, and special representative of the overall organization, making frequent trips to Asia. He said he was recruited for Nugan Hand by Admiral Yates and another admiral.

After a year or more of digging to pierce through the denials, reporters found that the resources of Nugan Hand reached still more deeply into the American intelligence community. They also included a CIA deputy director for economic research, a CIA "think tank" advisor with personal access to White House national security advisors Henry Kissinger and Zbigniew Brzezinski, the former head of flight services for the CIA's Far Eastern air transport operation, the former CIA station chief in Bangkok, two senior operations men straight out of CIA headquarters, and at least three contract agents.

Nugan Hand had enough generals, admirals, and spooks to run a small war.

What were these people doing with a mammoth drug-financing, money-laundering, tax-evading investor-fraud operation?

One man wasn't around to ask.

In June 1980, still in Australia and facing imminent prosecution by the law if not lynching by angry investors, Michael Hand was sneaked out of the country by mysterious accomplices using forged documents. A lot of people would still like to find him. But in 1987, so far as is known, none of them has.

CHAPTER THREE

The Golden Triangle

Among the international writers who flocked to Australia at the time of the Nugan Hand scandal was a Ph.D. from Yale named Alfred McCoy. By trade, McCoy is a scholar, and he got a job teaching Asian history at the University of New South Wales in Sydney. But his journalistic bent led him to take intense interest in the Nugan Hand affair, and relate it to his studies of the drug culture in Australia and Asia.

McCoy's unique perspective allowed him to see before others did that the combination in Nugan Hand of U.S. military-intelligence men and drug-related crime was no anomaly. Rather, he knew, it was part of a pattern. And only by understanding this pattern could an investigator put himself on a footing to probe the Nugan Hand mystery intelligently.

Back in 1972, McCoy (with two assistants) had written a silent bombshell of a book, *The Politics of Heroin in Southeast Asia* (Harper & Row). Although the book got a lot of attention in certain circles, it was too dense to be a bestseller. And so extreme were the book's findings that even though they weren't refuted, they weren't immediately accepted, either.

In the intervening years, however, others have followed McCoy's trail into Southeast Asia's remote "Golden Triangle" area, where Thailand, Burma, and Laos converge. What they learned only bolstered his extraordinary contentions.

These new witnesses included an intrepid British television team, and the staff of the House Select Committee on Narcotics under the direction of Washington lawyer Joseph Nellis, a veteran congressional investigator dating back to the days of the Kefauver Committee on organized crime and the dope trade in the 1950s. In addition, with the decline of American military involvement in the region, current and former U.S. drug enforcement officials, diplomats, and military personnel have talked more freely about what went on.

The gist of what McCoy reported in his *Politics of Heroin* book is now beyond dispute. Considering that, and in view of the thoroughness of his documentation (often interviews with eyewitnesses), the whole book deserves the acceptance and honor it was not originally accorded. As Nellis, the Congressional investigator, says, "I think he [McCoy] knows more about heroin production in Southeast Asia than any man living. His book is an outstanding example of intelligence in this area."

McCoy's thesis was that CIA operations against China in the early Communist years, and against Communist movements in Indochina later on, were responsible for creating the largest single source of heroin for the U.S. market. This was the famous "Golden Triangle." And according to McCoy, it flourished probably not by the original design of the CIA, but ultimately with the full knowledge and cooperation of the CIA.

At the close of World War II, he wrote, "with American consumer demand reduced to its lowest point in fifty years and the international syndicates in disarray, the U.S. Government had a unique opportunity to eliminate heroin addiction as a major American social problem. However, instead of delivering the deathblow to these criminal syndicates, the U.S. Government—through the Central Intelligence Agency and its wartime predecessor, the OSS—created a situation that made it possible for the Sicilian-American Mafia and the Corsican underworld to revive the international narcotics traffic."

The heroin market was revived first in Europe, with the help of two U.S. policy decisions. The decisions were secret at the time, but have been widely attested to since. First, American officials made a bargain with leaders of the Mafia to get criminal gangs to help in the invasion of Sicily. Mobsters were sprung from prison in exchange for their rallying the Mafia's covert army in Sicily and providing the ultimate in translator/guide services for U.S. military leaders. Lucky Luciano and Vito Genovese, maybe the two most powerful men in U.S. crime, both heavily into the dope business, were loosed on the world by such deals.

Then, in the late 1940s, the OSS/CIA became alarmed that the socialist leaders of the dock unions in southern France might side with Communist political movements. There was fear that strikes might redound against the Christian Democratic governments the United States was supporting. To forestall this threat, the United States conducted a vast covert operation to put control of the dock unions in the hands of Corsican gangsters, and take them out of the hands of the socialist unions.

The operation was funded by contributions that the State Department helped wheedle out of large American corporations, and it was aided further by the international division of the AFL–CIO. It concentrated particularly on the prime French port of Marseille. It worked. But besides chasing socialists out of power, the gangsters arranged the port's affairs for their own illicit business. Soon, the town's very name conjured up an association with heroin refining and exporting. The U.S.-installed dockworkers' monopoly in Marseilles became the heart of what was soon known in film and common cliché as "The French Connection."

During the 1950s, several things changed this European domination of the heroin trade. For one thing, occasional honest law enforcement inhibited the gangsters. For another, the Shah of Iran—for once, apparently, letting his religion overtake his greed—successfully ordered a stop to poppy-growing in what had been the region's largest producing country.

And, finally, the Cuban Revolution closed Havana as a free port of exchange between the Sicilian and U.S. Mafias. For a while, Turkey picked up the slack left by Iran. But events on the other side of Asia were already conspiring to transfer the focus of the world's heroin market away from Europe.

All this was basically documentable before McCoy came along, although few paid attention to it. What McCoy showed, as nobody else had, was that, in his words, "In the 1950s the Thai, Lao, Vietnamese and American governments made critical decisions that resulted in the expansion of Southeast Asia's opium production to feed the habits of the region's growing addict population and transform the Golden Triangle into the largest single opium-producing area in the world."

The first big decision came around 1950. At that time, the remnants of Chiang Kai-shek's crumbling western armies were chased out of China's Yunnan Province by the Communist Revolution. Thousands of these defeated soldiers from Chiang's Kuomintang, or KMT, government, melted into the jungles of neighboring Burma. Burma didn't want the KMT soldiers any more than their native country did. But when Burma threatened to chase the cornered KMT out, the U.S. Government decided the KMT were needed, to harass and possibly even reconquer China (or, as it was known then, "Red China").

So the CIA began supplying the KMT through two front companies: Civil Air Transport, headquartered in Taiwan, and Sea Supply Corporation, headquartered in Bangkok. Only a few people with top security clearance knew that both companies were covertly owned by the U.S. Government. They are important, not only for what they did in the 1950s, but also because they were precursors of organizations that touch directly on Nugan Hand in the 1970s.

After China was given up on, the focus of U.S. efforts in East Asia shifted to Indochina. Civil Air Transport was then transformed into (among several successor entities) Air America. That was the airline Michael Hand worked closely with as a CIA contract agent. Many of the CIA associates whose money first helped Hand get started in business in Australia were Air America employes.

Sea Supply Corporation, for its part, was founded and run by a lawyer and CIA operative named Paul Helliwell. During World War II, Helliwell had been chief of special intelligence in China for the OSS. Colleagues from those days told the *Wall Street Journal*'s Jim Drinkhall that Helliwell, then a colonel, regularly used to buy information with five-pound shipments of opium ("three sticky brown bars," one man said). Drinkhall also reported* being told that Helliwell ran an operation code-named "Deer Mission," in which OSS personnel secretly parachuted into Indochina to treat Ho Chi Minh for malaria.

After the heyday of Sea Supply in the 1950s, Helliwell moved to Miami and became an important figure in the Bay of Pigs invasion and the CIA's other battles against Castro. His Castle Bank both funneled money for the CIA and, privately, operated as a profitable tax-cheat business. Its unexpected demise in the mid-1970s directly coincided with the growth of Nugan Hand. Considering the gaggle of brass from the U.S. intelligence community who helped push Nugan Hand into orbit in the late 1970s, there has been understandable speculation that Nugan Hand was Castle Bank's successor. More on this later.

As Paul Helliwell's Sea Supply Corporation brought large amounts of arms and other supplies to Thailand in the 1950s, the

***Wall Street Journal*, April 18, 1980.

CIA's airline, Civil Air Transport, ferried them up to the Kuomintang army in Burma—at first by air-drop, then, later, to makeshift airstrips. With these American-supplied weapons, the KMT held off the Burmese' attempts to evict them. But their own efforts over several years to invade China were easily rebuffed, which left them frustrated.

The KMT realized, however, that the mountainous region where they had holed up was long known for its one reliable crop: opium. So they determined to make their fortune organizing the haphazard village production. With their American arms, they did this, going so far as to collect opium taxes from villagers.

The CIA's role went far beyond giving the KMT the military means to organize the heroin trade. Alfred McCoy found Burmese intelligence reports from those early days saying that the CIA planes that dropped off military and other supplies for the KMT then flew opium out to Thailand or Taiwan.

Most of the KMT's original trade, however, seems to have been carried on by mule train to the town of Chiang Mai, whose location in northwest Thailand has made it a fabled drug bazaar for years. Even today, it is accepted on the street there that the town's economy is fueled by the drug trade. Chiang Mai is to opium what Chicago is to corn and wheat, or Detroit is to cars. Chiang Mai would eventually be the location of the strangest and least innocently explainable branch of the Nugan Hand Bank.

Back in the Chiang Mai of the 1950s, McCoy explains, "a KMT colonel maintained a liaison office with the Nationalist Chinese consulate and with local Thai authorities. Posing as ordinary Chinese merchants, the colonel and his staff used raw opium to pay for the munitions, food, and clothing that arrived from Bangkok. . . . Usually the KMT dealt with the commander of the Thai police, General Phao, who shipped the opium from Chiangmai to Bangkok for both local consumption and export."

Thus General Phao and the elite from his Thai national police force provided the vital link between the landlocked KMT opium lords and the sea. But after establishing this, McCoy also establishes something else: General Phao was the CIA's man in Thailand. The overwhelming evidence comes from contemporary news reports, on-the-scene interviews, and documents from *The Pentagon Papers* (the Pentagon's secret history of the Vietnam War, much of which was published by the *New York Times*).

Phao obtained his strong position in the factionalized Thai power structure directly from CIA backing—and in particular from the lavish arms shipments that Paul Helliwell's Sea Supply Corporation sent to Phao's national police. The CIA also financed General Phao's opium purchases from the KMT. Phao and so many other players in this game were actually written up in the *New York Times* back in the 1950s that it is impossible to believe that the CIA—which, after all, secretly *owned* Sea Supply Corporation—hadn't put the picture together and didn't know what was going on.

Of course they knew. To the CIA, Phao appeared useful as a staunch anti-Communist who would employ his power to keep any Thai government from going too far left. Phao would also maintain the KMT as a well-supplied thorn in the "Red Chinese' " side.

To be sure, all this doesn't mean that U.S. policy-makers originally envisioned the final result of their script. The Washington planners may not have foreseen that the KMT would come to be virtually a country within a country in the anarchic Shan States of northern Burma, easily crossing over into the unpoliceable jungles of western Laos and northern Thailand. And Washington may not have foreseen that the efficiencies being wrought by this KMT sub-state would bring the Golden Triangle to dominate the world heroin market.

But it gradually worked out that way, under Washington's nose, and no one saw fit to stop it. Soon, just as happened in Marseilles after the gangsters took over the waterfront, refineries were springing up in the Triangle, so that pure heroin could be shipped instead of bulkier raw opium.

Readers who are too young to remember the 1950s may find it hard to understand just how shocking these revelations would have been in those times. The KMT leader, Chiang Kai-Shek, on Taiwan, had a mammoth lobbying and propaganda operation that overwhelmed the U.S. Congress and press. In a way, the United States was the victim of its own World War II propaganda. Chiang had deceived the American public into thinking he was the popular leader of a united China, when in fact he was merely preeminent among many leaders—warlords, they were sometimes called. Chiang's KMT ruled the capital of Peiping, but never, from Chiang's ascendency in 1928, a united China.

The most powerful American press voice during the Chinese Revolution and its immediate aftermath was Henry Luce, head of Time Inc. Television was in its infancy, and *Time* and *Life* magazines had no close competition. Luce, a staunch Christian moralist, and his wife, Clare Boothe Luce, were close personal friends of Chiang and

Madame Chiang. They drummed their support weekly in their magazines, and the rest of the press followed.

Chiang had another powerful cheerleader in General Claire Chennault, hero of the China theater in World War II. Chennault had organized and directed Chiang's air service since 1937. The popular Chennault and his highly visible wife Anna lobbied tirelessly for Chiang. They helped see to it that public humiliation awaited any U.S. Government figure whose support flagged. During the Truman and Eisenhower presidencies—both in the administration and in Congress—Chiang was not an ally of convenience, but a sacred cause.

Loyalty to that cause led the United States to turn its initial Korean War victory into a disaster. The North Korean army almost overran South Korea after its invasion in June 1950. But by early October, the United States (acting under the auspices of the United Nations) had cleared South Korea of northern troops, secured its independence, and moved northward to provide a more defensible border. The fighting capacity of the North Korean army had been broken.

But instead of stopping there, the U.S. commander, General Douglas MacArthur, another Chiang buddy from World War II days, insisted on taking the war to China in a coordinated effort with Chiang to help the KMT reconquer the mainland. Chiang's coordinated attacks against his mainland foes were secret from the U.S. public, but not from the Chinese, who were getting shot at. It could be seen as a turning point in U.S. history—the beginning of the anticommunist folly.

The Chinese were understandably unwilling to have hostile, constantly attacking forces on their northern as well as their southern border. Having promised all along to invade North Korea if MacArthur's forces reached the Chinese frontier, they did so. The result was a tenfold increase in U.S. casualties and the conversion of the Korean War from a win into a tie.

Yet one Washington politician after another continued to talk of restoring Chiang to power. To question Chiang was to call one's own patriotism into question—and, indeed, several State Department careers were ruined for just that reason.

Yet the result of the KMT buildup in the Golden Triangle was the mushrooming of the heroin plague in the United States. By the early 1950s, the drug problem became a nationwide concern as millions of families watched the Kefauver crime hearings. A few years later, Frank Sinatra's terrifying portrayal of a junkie in the movie version of Nelson Algren's bestselling novel, *The Man With the*

Golden Arm, made heroin addiction a stark nightmare to more millions. Soon, criminologists and police chiefs everywhere were blaming addicts, desperate for money to buy a fix, for the soaring national crime rate and the resultant spread of fear through American cities and suburbs.

Knowledge that Chiang and his KMT were constructing the world's preeminent heroin factory to support their cause would have flabbergasted almost everyone. So would the knowledge that the heads of the American Legion and the Freedoms Foundation—the very soul of American anticommunism—would help run a bank for the heroin trade (even if Generals Cocke and Black were, as they have said, unwitting of Nugan Hand's dope deals).

If such shocking news about the Kuomintang could be kept secret for twenty or thirty years, one has to wonder what might have gone on with Nugan Hand in the 1970s—or what might be going on now—that is similarly being kept secret. At any rate, the events described here all did happen. Officially, they happened only for the purpose of helping our "friends," the KMT, who never had a realistic chance of overthrowing Mao Tse-tung's new mainland government anyway.

If the petty harassment of Mao justified starting a new heroin trade, soon there was a much bigger stake. There was the Vietnam War. From 1954, with the arrival of General Edward G. Lansdale and his crack teams of CIA operatives, the United States slowly took over from France the conduct of a war against various Indochinese independence movements. The French, McCoy shows, had cooperated in the export of Golden Triangle heroin through Saigon in order to keep the cooperation of the corrupt local elite. Corsican gangsters even arrived from halfway around the world to smooth out logistics.

This intermingling of heroin traders and the government of South Vietnam only intensified under American administration, McCoy shows. He makes clear that Ngo Dinh Nhu, brother of the U.S.-selected and U.S.-installed President Ngo Dinh Diem, got rich trading dope, as did other U.S.-backed Vietnamese leaders.

The real expansion of opium production, however, was in the mountains, where the U.S. military mission had suddenly discovered some important potential allies. These were the Montagnard (or Hmong, or Meo) tribesmen, constantly lauded by U.S. Government spokesmen and the U.S. press during the Vietnam War as "heroic," "pro-Western" and "our allies." And it's true that the Montagnards fought harder and more loyally with U.S. forces than did other South Vietnamese.

But our brave new allies happened to live on prime poppy-growing land. As U.S. aid and advisors came, landing strips were built for the CIA's special short-take-off and -landing craft. The opium trade grew proportionately. By McCoy's and many other, first-hand, accounts, opium was regularly flown out on flights of the CIA's Air America (formerly Civil Air Transport). The Montagnard villages flourished, as intended.

But a lot of opium wound up as heroin on the streets of the United States. Some was sold directly to American G.I.'s in Vietnam. Addiction plagued the U.S. forces, to the point of reducing their fighting capacity, and when the men came home their addiction came with them. Some of the Air America crews made a lot of money on this trade.

Wilfred P. Deac, senior public relations man for the Drug Enforcement Administration, offers this explanation today: "Their mission was to get people to fight against the Communists, not to stop the drug traffic."

Adds DEA Far East regional director John J. O'Neill, "The kind of people they were dealing with up there, the whole economy was opium. They were dealing with the KMT and the KMT was involved in heroin. I have no doubt that Air America was used to transport opium."

Joe Nellis, of the special Congressional investigation: "The CIA did help bring some very powerful cheap heroin into Vietnam out of the Shan States, the northern states of Burma . . . for radio communications, intelligence. In return for that intelligence, the CIA winked at what went in its airplanes."

A former military intelligence noncom tells of a 1960 operation in which an airstrip was hastily built on Borneo as a transfer point for goods going into and out of Vietnam. Curious about the cargos that were being dropped off by the first planes out of Vietnam, awaiting shipment back home, he says he pried open a crate that was labeled "munitions" but was suspiciously light of weight. It was filled, he says, with parcels wrapped in manilla paper. Opening one, he says, he found small plastic bags of a white powder that he has no doubt was heroin.

The U.S. Government not only promoted this drug traffic, it intervened to make sure the traffic wouldn't be discovered. A former officer who did criminal investigations for the Pentagon in the Vietnam theater, and who now works on the staff of the inspector general for a major federal agency, vividly remembers political interference with criminal justice. "Some of the times when you'd be running a criminal investigation, say narcotics, you'd find out that Inspector

So-and-so of your national police is involved in this," the former officer says.

"You investigate it up to a point and then you can't go any further," he says. "It would go to our headquarters and then it would go to Washington and nothing would ever happen. The intelligence gleaned from these people was more important than stopping the drug traffic." At least that's what he was told.

For many, letting the drug traffic go was also more profitable than stopping it.

Another former officer from the army's Criminal Investigation Division recalls a mammoth heroin scheme he and his colleagues uncovered by accident. He says he and four others from his unit were investigating corruption in the sale of supplies to commissioned- and noncommissioned-officers' clubs. The corrupt U.S. and Vietnamese officers they caught tried to bargain away jail terms by describing the heroin traffic involving Vietnamese politicians and senior U.S. officers. The reports checked out, the investigator says.

The investigator, now a stockbroker, says that his investigation group filed reports to the Pentagon revealing that G.I. bodies being flown back to the United States were cut open, gutted, and filled with heroin. Witnesses were prepared to testify that the heroin-stuffed soldiers bore coded body numbers, allowing conspiring officers on the other end, at Norton Air Force Base in California, to remove the booty—up to fifty pounds of heroin per dead G.I.

The army acted on these reports—not by coming down on the dope traffickers, but by disbanding the investigative team and sending them to combat duty, the former investigator says. Other reports corroborate the use of G.I. bodies to ship dope back to the United States via military channels.

This was the prevailing atmosphere when Michael Jon Hand arrived in Indochina.

CHAPTER FOUR

The Education of a Banker

Michael Hand was born in the Bronx, December 8, 1941. His father, a New York civil servant, still lives in a condominium in Queens, but absolutely will not discuss his son, or anything else, with reporters. Visitors are barred from the building by locked doors and security guards. A sister, reportedly severely handicapped, is also said to live in the New York area. Hand is said to have sent home money for her care regularly over the years.

The old Bronx neighborhood is now a slum, but when Hand was young it was upper middle class, and his high school, De Witt Clinton, was considered one of the city's best. He graduated 248th in a class of 695, won a scholastic achievement award, was appointed student prefect, and was starting receiver and defensive back on the football team. He passed every class he took, and was noted for exceptional character, courtesy, cooperation, and appearance. His IQ registered an also exceptional 131.

Graduating in 1959, he stated that his ambition was to become a forest ranger. Shortly afterward, his mother died in a fall from a third-floor window; the question of accident or suicide was never resolved.*

*Thanks to an unidentified researcher for the *National Times* of Sydney, Australia, who dug all this out in 1981, making it much easier for me to verify later. The researcher also reported talking to former neighbors, who "have only fond memories of Hand, his father and his mother."

I tried to augment the researcher's findings, but was blocked by the New York

Mike Hand turned into a bearish man, with thick layers of muscle that melted largely to flab in later years. On the one hand, he developed an aggressive, macho, locker-room image that put more sensitive men off; on the other, he was known as a devout Christian Scientist and regular churchgoer, who rarely drank.

When Hand became a prominent banker in Australia, he told the world he was a graduate of Syracuse University, and mentioned to some that he had taught school in California before joining the army. The record shows instead that in 1961 he completed a one-year course at the New York State (forest) Ranger School. The school was attached to Syracuse University but hardly the equivalent of its B.A. program.

Hand's teacher, David Anderson, says Hand finished thirty-eighth in a class of forty-nine, though Anderson has a lasting impression of Hand as extremely personable. He must have been that, just to be remembered after all these years. Anderson says that Hand wrote from California in 1962 that he was managing a swim and sports school in the swank Los Angeles suburb of Palos Verdes Estates. The next year, Hand wrote back that he was taking Green Beret training at Fort Bragg, North Carolina. The record shows he enlisted in the army in May 1963.

In Vietnam, Hand won a Silver Star, a Purple Heart, and the Distinguished Service Cross, second only to the Congressional Medal of Honor as the nation's highest military award. On June 9, 1965—according to the Distinguished Service Cross citation—he almost single-handedly held off a fourteen-hour Vietcong attack on the Special Forces compound at Dong Xaoi.

According to newspaper accounts at the time, Hand braved a barrage of fire in an attempt to rescue a wounded buddy, then darted into a building and dragged to safety a wounded American captain—Hand's commanding officer—and another wounded soldier. Wounded by shrapnel himself, he still grabbed a machine gun and held the enemy off until the weapon jammed. Hit by another shrapnel blast, he was ordered to withdraw, but despite his wounds went under further fire to rescue one or two other wounded men. One account says he "acted as a live target to flush out enemy snipers."

A resumé Hand later submitted to the State Department to keep

City Department of Health, which suddenly, in 1986, perhaps because of pressure from the families of AIDS victims, banned public access to previously available death records. These records clearly seem public under the state's open information law, but there wasn't time to fight that legal battle before publication.

his passport current says he left the army in May 1966. The next entry reads: "1966–1967, worked directly for U.S. Government." Banking associates say he sometimes referred fleetingly to his undercover activities in Laos during those years, and sometimes took a perverse joy in describing the bodily mutilations the local people had liked to perform on their slain enemies.

By accounts of men who say they encountered him back then, Hand helped train the mountain people—Montagnards—and worked closely with the Air America crews that supplied them. But there are no detailed accounts of his activities. He migrated to Australia in September 1967.

About the time Nugan Hand was organized, in the early 1970s, Hand married Helen Boreland, an Australian woman nine years his senior. By all accounts, they had a close and loving relationship, though an unusual one: people remark that Helen Hand seemed more like a mother than a wife to her husband. When he finally fled in June 1980, she stayed in Australia, worked for a while in a high-priced Sydney jewelry store, then disappeared from public view. Numerous requests for an interview with her were left with acquaintances and a lawyer who had represented her, but she didn't respond.

Even more important than Hand's wife was the person he fairly adopted for a substitute father—Maurice Bernard Houghton (pronounced "*How*-ton"), the mysterious puppetmaster of Nugan Hand, who, while posing as a simple barkeep, moved intimately among diplomats, spies, and military brass in many countries. The circles Houghton traveled in included the covert action specialists who would become central figures in the foreign policy scandal that engulfed the Reagan Administration in 1987—air force generals Richard Secord and Harry C. ("Heinie") Aderholt, and former CIA officers Edwin Wilson and Thomas Clines.

Bernie Houghton had preceded Mike Hand to Vietnam. He then preceded Hand to Australia, by eight months, arriving in January 1967.

Today, Houghton is still there. Once again, he is ostensibly just a barkeeper, now with a few years of part-time banking in his past. A lot of people think Houghton is a spy, and he has been called one by the looser Australian press. Whatever his business, secrecy is a big part of it. And he is very good at secrecy.

A fleshy, gray-haired, outwardly unobtrusive man with eyeglasses, Houghton seems to pride himself on a quiet demeanor. He is missing a couple of fingers on one hand, and there is no explanation for it in general circulation. He will not talk to reporters. If one hangs out in his bar, or waits at the main entrance to his penthouse ocean-front condo, it doesn't help. Houghton has lookouts protecting him, a tightly knit circle of confidants. They observe visitors and profess ignorance of Houghton's whereabouts until the visitors go away.

Adopted sons, they seem to some. They work at one of his bars, or he sets them up in other enterprises. Often, one is staying at the condo with him. Some are ex-army men from Vietnam. Some are "boys" who appear to be in their late teens or early twenties. Houghton is not known as a womanizer.

Impressive as he is at avoiding reporters, Houghton is even more impressive in his ability to avoid police, even those who have subpoena power. During the most aggressive investigations into Nugan Hand, which lasted several years, he simply slipped out of Australia when the heat was on, and returned when the investigation was over. Amazingly, he alone among his colleagues at Nugan Hand continues to hang around Australia and has still stayed out of the criminal docks.

He did agree to one transcribed interview with the Joint Task Force on Drug Trafficking, a top-level police group that was mandated by the prime minister of Australia and the premier (like a governor) of the state of New South Wales to investigate the Nugan Hand collapse. But Houghton refused to go to the police. He insisted the cops come to him—in Acapulco, Mexico, where he was holing up on the twenty-sixth floor of the Princess Hotel. They did, in June 1981.

His vague and convoluted answers, as transcribed, reveal him as a master of conversational evasion—as other native Texans might put it, he is a virtuoso bullshitter—and one can only wonder at the extent to which he was simply pulling the cops' legs.

"I had come to Australia because in World War II I had served alongside Australian servicemen and had gained a great deal of fondness and appreciation for them," he said. He told the police that he had been "engaged in business activities in Southeast Asia, including Vietnam," for several years. But he never said what business. "In 1966 I became disenchanted with the activities in Southeast Asia and determined to return to the United States, but wanted first to stop off and see Australia since I had heard so much about it in my association with Australian military men."

He said he didn't meet Michael Hand until Hand arrived in Sydney in the fall of 1967. But Houghton said he'd "heard of his

[Hand's] reputation as early as 1964 or 1965." Houghton said, "I had heard of Mike Hand's great combat exploits and courage, which was well-known in Vietnam. In fact, the image I had of him was comparable to that of the famous Sergeant York* in American history. He conducted himself in such a manner in the war as to receive high praise and commendation, including from the President of the United States,"** Houghton said.

Houghton said he met Hand "casually and through some social acquaintance, the exact particulars of which I cannot now recall. . . . Since we both lived and worked in the Kings Cross area [of Sydney], thereafter I saw him almost daily when we would run into each other all the time."

As for himself, Houghton said he was born July 25, 1920, in Texas "and lived in various cities in the Southwest. My father was an oil driller, which meant we had to move from city to city. I graduated from all the elementary schools and high school and was going to Southern Methodist University, studying business management, when the United States went to war. [Southern Methodist says he attended during the fall semester of 1939–40, a year before the United States went to war, and that he received no degree. It says he also spent the summer of 1946 there.]

"I enlisted in the U.S. Air Force Cadet Training Program and went to many schools," Houghton told the police. "I was discharged in 1946 and went into business, restaurants, clubs, surplus war material and miscellaneous." He said he "went to Vietnam, early in the 1960s, and I went to work for a construction material expediter [apparently in Vietnam] until such time as I came to Sydney, Australia, in January 1, 1967 [*sic*]."

In 1969, a problem with Houghton's visa caused him to give a statement to Australian immigration officials. He said then that he had spent the early 1960s with two San Francisco-based companies—the East India Company and J. G. Anderson, neither of which lists a telephone there now. He said he then went to Saigon to work for a Bruce Ficke "who is now a resident of Anchorage, Alaska." There is no telephone listing for a Ficke in Anchorage now.

In another brief interview with police in 1980, Houghton told a different story. He said he went to Saigon after seeing "job offers"

*Alvin York of World War I, probably the greatest noncommissioned combat hero the United States has had.

**Like the Sergeant York comparison, the remark must be recorded as of questionable accuracy.

in U.S. newspapers. "The same day I arrived," he said, "I got a job with an individual, by that I mean he ran his own company, named Green. He was later killed with his wife in Saigon."

This is how the Australian Joint Task Force on Drug Trafficking reported the rest of that police interview: "Asked to elaborate, Houghton said Green was an American whose Christian name was William. According to Houghton, his job with Green entailed 'traveling. . . . I was in Saigon for a while and then I went to Bangkok and did the same thing there. All this time I was working for Green.' Houghton described this work as being involved in a minor way in the construction of airport and military bases. He maintained that he worked for no one else whilst in South East Asia.

"Later, when asked about Bruce Ficke—the person referred to in his 1969 reply to the Department of Immigration—Houghton said, 'I met him years ago in Alaska. I was working for a company called East India and he was a distributor for goods I was selling. That association goes back over twenty years.' "

Efforts by the author to locate the companies or people Houghton said he knew back then have failed.

Returning to his 1981 formal interview in Acapulco, Houghton gave this account of what happened after he landed in Australia in January 1967: "I went to work for Parkes Development as a real estate salesman and opened the Bourbon and Beefsteak Bar and Restaurant."

Even the date of the Bourbon and Beefsteak opening is mysterious. Houghton said it opened "November 4, 1967." The task force that interviewed him, however, determined in its final report that the restaurant actually opened in September. The date is significant, because the Bourbon and Beefsteak was designed to cater to the U.S. military.

To relieve the growing strain on the honky-tonk neighborhoods of Hong Kong and Bangkok, the U.S. Government had negotiated a deal with the Australian Government whereby Sydney would open its doors for U.S. soldiers to receive the rest and recreation periods their Vietnam War service entitled them to. According to the task force, Houghton somehow learned of Sydney's selection as an "R and R" center "prior to it becoming public knowledge." The task force said "Houghton did not explain how it was" that he found out early about the R and R deal. But before the first soldiers arrived, in October 1967, Houghton had arranged to be at the center of the action.

That's as far as the cops got regarding Houghton's history before Nugan Hand. It leaves out a lot.

Alexander Butterfield, a former Asian-intelligence officer, had some helpful advice for a reporter asking questions about Bernie Houghton. In 1973, Butterfield had attained instant celebrity by revealing to Congress and the world that Richard Nixon's Watergate conversations were secretly taped in the Oval Office. (Little if anything was made of the curious circumstance that a career intelligence operative had played such a pivotal role in the downfall of a president.)

Asked about Houghton, Butterfield quickly said to call Allan Parks, a retired air force colonel who now runs the flying service at Auburn University in Alabama. Sure enough, Parks remembered Houghton well, mostly, he said, from his days as intelligence officer at the U.S. Embassy in Bangkok during the war. Parks recalls constantly stumbling over Houghton's name in cable traffic.

Military secrecy still prevents Parks from telling all he knows, he says, but he remembers meeting Houghton—and he places Houghton in Asia well after Houghton allegedly retired to Australia to become a barkeep.

"He ferried C-47s, cargo airplanes, from Thailand," Parks says. "The man, he was running everything. Between Australia and Thailand. I met him in Bangkok in a bar. I was involved in Laos in some things I can't discuss in '70 and '71. There was traffic I read relating to that. But I can't go into it because it's all secret." It was something to do, Parks says, with "Project 404," which is still "classified." (Asked about Michael Hand, Parks has the same response: "I can't tell you. It's classified. No comment.")

But the mention of Houghton elicits reminiscences from Parks: "There's no doubt about it, he'd fly anything. The Golden Triangle, that's where he got his opium from. There was one flight, he flew in slot machines. He did some deals over in India."

Asked the name of Houghton's airline, Parks just laughs, and says, "He didn't call his planes anything. Nobody could track his airplanes. He didn't have an airline, like. The embassy was always trying to run him down. It was funny." Asked for other sources, Parks says, "Anybody who would know would give you the same answer I would."

Then he refers a reporter to General Aderholt, who he says also observed Houghton from the U.S. Embassy in Bangkok. Aderholt went on to become commanding general of the U.S. Military Assistance Command in Thailand, and, with General John K. Singlaub, ran covert air operations throughout the Vietnam-Laos-Thailand war zone. Retiring from active duty after the war, generals Aderholt and Singlaub took command of various right-wing paramilitary groups in the United States.

During the mid-1980s, when the Reagan administration was barred by Congress from supplying and directing Contra rebels trying to overthrow the Government of Nicaragua, but was determined to do so anyway, Generals Singlaub and Aderholt played important roles in keeping the Contra rebellion alive. Though they were supposedly working through private channels, their efforts were coordinated by the White House through Lieutenant Colonel Oliver North, and the source of their funds was open to question during the Contra scandal investigations of 1987.

Aderholt seems to have been in good position to know what was going on in Southeast Asia during Bernie Houghton's days there. Aderholt had combined his air force career with work on the side for little airlines and medical relief agencies overseas, creating the aura of someone involved all along in private "front" operations for the CIA or some related U.S. intelligence agency. But Aderholt's recollections of Houghton contradict with the accepted chronology of Houghton's life.

Bernie Houghton? "There was a guy named Bernie Houghton with the Nugan Hand Bank," Aderholt says. But Nugan Hand wasn't officially chartered until 1973, and really didn't begin to burgeon until 1976—well after the time Parks said Aderholt had encountered Houghton in Thailand during the Vietnam War. It was even after Aderholt had supposedly retired from the air force. But Aderholt is vague on dates.

"I had lunch with him," Aderholt recalls. Describing the lunch, he continues to set off alarm bells. Also present, he says, was an American named William Bird. Bird, the reporter knows, was the almost legendary operator of a seat-of-the-pants southeast Asian airline called Bird Air, and was involved with other concerns linked to U.S. military and secret paramilitary involvement there. Although Bird's precise relationship with the CIA has never (to the author's knowledge) been publicly documented, he is widely believed to have had such a relationship for many years.*

*Bird was always in some other country when the author tried to find him, both in the United States and in Thailand.

"Mr. Bird and I had run an airlift out of Bombay," Aderholt continues. "Houghton was with a company in Bangkok [Aderholt names a company, the Alkemal Company; it couldn't be located]. He was interested in opening a restaurant in Bangkok." Aderholt also confirms that William Young, who worked briefly for Nugan Hand in Chiang Mai, Thailand, was for many years a CIA agent (more on Young later). But Aderholt says he is unable to supply further information or leads on Bernie Houghton.

Looking into Houghton's past, all you can come up with is mystery. "He was doing something in Vietnam, but he won't say what," says Houghton's lawyer in Sydney, Michael Moloney. "Nobody really knows. He won't talk about his past."

Even for those who enjoy fairy tales, the available version of Houghton's first weekend in Australia may seem fanciful. Supposedly he was broke and on the street. The police task force report says, "Asked if he had had introductions to Sydney people on his arrival in the city, Houghton said, 'No.' "

But through a *deus ex machina* unworthy of a made-for-TV movie, the story has Houghton quickly falling in with a circle of Australia's leading businessmen. They were friends and business associates of transportation tycoon Sir Peter Abeles, who owns Australia's biggest trucking, shipping, and airline companies.

Sir Peter's shipping and trucking operations extend to the United States and throughout the world. Publishing and television tycoon Rupert Murdoch, perhaps Australia's premier international citizen, is Sir Peter's sometime bridge partner. Murdoch is also Sir Peter's 50–50 partner in ownership of Ansett Airlines, Australia's biggest.

Among the circle of business and card-playing associates of Sir Peter's, besides Rupert Murdoch, are another Knight of the Realm, Sir Paul Strasser, and John Charody, who, with Strasser, was involved in some real estate development companies and an oil company based in Sydney. Sir Paul remembers the weekend in January 1967, when "a friend, I can't remember who" brought Houghton into the coffee shop where Sir Paul was sitting.

Houghton told police that the "friend" was the manager of the not-particularly-elegant hotel Houghton had happened to check into. The hotel was in the honky-tonk King's Cross section of Sydney, a district of B-girl bars and sex shows, where Houghton would eventually become the impresario of U.S. military R and R. What landed him at the King's Cross Hotel just off the boat? And what led him to immediately seek the hotel manager's help in finding work? Unanswered questions. But it is doubtful that everyone who stumbles into the King's Cross finds himself having coffee a few hours later with a knighted multimillionaire tycoon like Sir Paul Strasser.

Sir Paul remembers* that Houghton was described as just out of Vietnam, flat broke and desperate. "Somebody who couldn't find work, he didn't have any money," Sir Paul remembers. Yet, says Sir Paul, Houghton "gave as a reference two high-ranking army people. Admiral Yates was one. Yates gave him an excellent reference." ** So Sir Paul agreed to take Houghton on as a condominium salesman for one of his development companies.

The police had asked Houghton who his references were, and he had replied, "I'm sorry, I don't remember." But Sir Paul told the police that he sent two telex cables to verify Houghton's credentials, "one to the military in Hawaii and one to Washington. . . . Both cables were sent to army departments." The replies, he said, "were in glowing terms."

Later, Sir Paul said, Houghton introduced him to both General Black and Admiral Yates. Sir Paul became convinced that Houghton had a "top connection with the U.S. administration." Sir Paul has also told Australian reporters that Houghton was recommended to him by CIA associates and a "top politician in Washington."

This was a pattern that almost everyone around Houghton noticed quickly. As Sir Paul put it, "He was connected with top army people. I have no doubt about that. He was very close to the American embassy. I was once invited by him to the American embassy and he introduced me to all the top people. When [U.S.] senators or top officials came to town they would always see him. I heard he got flights to the States on U.S. military aircraft from Richmond Air Base [in Australia]."

"All the time I asked him about Vietnam," Sir Paul recalls. "But he didn't want to talk about it. He was the best salesman I ever had in my life. I always wondered. He came in literally without a penny in his pocket. I had to give him a loan on Friday [to tide him over] till Monday morning."

Houghton's arrival in Sydney in 1967 could not have been better timed for him or the military. The Bourbon and Beefsteak was soon

*In telephone interviews with the author.

**Yates denies knowing Houghton that long ago.

overflowing with incoming shiploads of America's fighting men, and with the prostitutes they picked up in the neighborhood. Houghton soon opened two similar establishments nearby: the Texas Tavern, and Harpoon Harry's.

Because "loose lips sink ships," and because the toughest front the Pentagon had to face in the Vietnam War was in the press back home, Washington doubtless would have wanted eyes and ears on its vacationing troops. As much as their play could be controlled, Washington would have wanted to control it. And no one was better positioned to do that than Bernie Houghton.

Houghton became close friends with Lieutenant Colonel Bobby Keith Boyd, whom the U.S. Army assigned to be commanding officer of the R and R center in Sydney. Houghton told police, "We are both Texans and that automatically makes you friends."

Besides being a Texan, Boyd had been a former U.S. embassy military attaché in Latin America, among other assignments. The prime minister's police task force concluded thus about him: "It would be extremely naive to suggest that with a military career of this type . . . that Boyd was not closely allied with U.S. intelligence, if not more directly involved." In 1971 Boyd resigned from active duty—and went to work helping Houghton run his bar-restaurants. He also occupied various positions in the corporations Houghton set up as holding companies.

During R and R, Houghton received all sorts of special benefits. When the troops came to port, Sydney residents recall that Houghton was sometimes helicoptered out to the flagship to greet his prospective customers and meet their commanding officer.

And as Houghton grew bigger and more visible, so did his friendship with Michael Hand.

Despite his denials, a circumstantial case has been made by some that Bernie Houghton was wearing the cloak of patriotism as a U.S. intelligence agent. The case is furthered by his otherwise hard-to-explain relationship with the Australian Security Intelligence Organization, a government agency best known to Australians by its acronym, ASIO. While doing for Australia some of the work that the CIA does for the United States, ASIO also functions domestically, much as the FBI's counterintelligence branch does in the U.S.

ASIO's name showed up when, after the collapse of Nugan Hand, Houghton's immigration file was investigated. Curious references were found both by the police task force and by the local press, which obtained documents through devices of its own. It was learned that on October 21, 1969, ASIO had given Houghton a security clearance; this was after he applied for permanent residency status in Australia.

Then, on February 12, 1972, ASIO did Houghton a very special favor. He had been traveling abroad—to "Saigon to check on the feasibility of buying surplus war material," he later explained. But he had neglected to obtain a re-entry visa for his passport. His original Australian visa had expired November 10, 1971. In the palaver at the airport immigration desk, he gave the officers two references, who quickly saw to it that he was admitted. One was John Charody, Sir Paul's business partner.

The other was Leo Carter of ASIO—not just an ordinary ASIO agent, but the director of ASIO for the whole state of New South Wales, the largest in Australia. Why did one of the handful of top intelligence officials in Australia, one who had direct contact with U.S. intelligence agencies, personally take time out to clear a simple barkeep for admission to Australia? Carter cannot be asked; he died of a heart attack in 1980. The immigration officer who signed Houghton in died the same year.

ASIO declined to talk about it with a reporter. In a written statement to the police task force, ASIO said it couldn't explain "the apparent references to ASIO on Bernie Houghton's Department of Immigration papers . . . since he does not appear in our records. . . . It is only possible to speculate that Carter may have known Houghton privately as a restaurateur," ASIO said.

Maybe—except that when the police task force asked Houghton if he knew an Australian named Leo Carter, he replied, quite unequivocally, "No."

Not only did Houghton get admitted to Australia on Carter's word, he also received an immediate and very special "A" stamp—permission for unlimited re-entries to Australia in the future. One can imagine the embarrassment of the immigration officer who dared question Houghton as he went through the line, only to have senior government and business leaders roll out the red carpet for him on receipt of a telephone call.

Another item stands out from the police task force's report on Houghton's immigration file. There are records of Houghton leaving Australia only twice in the early years he was there. Yet if the recollections of the former U.S. military officers in Southeast Asia are correct, he must have been gone more than that. The story, relayed by Sir Paul Strasser and others, that Houghton flew in and out from a military air base on U.S. military aircraft provides one possible explanation. His apparent connection with ASIO provides another.

Nor is it likely that the regional head of ASIO, along with assorted generals, admirals, high-ranking senators and congressmen, U.S. Embassy officials, and two CIA station chiefs in Australia (Milton Corley Wonus and John Walker), all of whom socialized with Houghton, did so because of his establishments' haute cuisine and ambiance.

His Texas Tavern and Harpoon Harry's have long since folded, but around the corner from their old locations the Bourbon and Beefsteak, where all the dignitaries came to dine, still swings. Just inside the doorway to the left of the entrance are women in thick makeup, tight tops, miniskirts, and fishnet stockings. You know why they're there.

In the doorway to the right of the Bourbon and Beefsteak, through the dinner hour and late into the evening, stands a barker. Sometimes it is a man, sometimes a woman, but always the barker is advertising a sex show that occurs at the top of the stairway behind him. During the show, the barker says loudly enough for anyone entering the Bourbon and Beefsteak to hear, you can see "two young Asian girls shooting Ping-Pong balls out of their pussies."

Inside the restaurant, the lighting and furnishings are reminiscent of a steakhouse not exactly like, say, Christ Cella or Peter Luger, but more like, say, Tad's. So are the steaks—thin and greasy. No one but a sailor long marooned at sea would ever come here for the food. If there is one thing Sydney abounds with, it is truly wonderful places to eat, with seafood and fine local wine that thrill the palate and well occupy the expense account; the Bourbon and Beefsteak is not, by any stretch, one of those places.

Operating the most notable bars in King's Cross, where the biggest rush of customers in years scooped up every prostitute in sight and sought every form of vice that could be crammed into a weekend, Bernie Houghton probably needed approvals that even the U.S. and Australian Governments were unequipped to provide. Abe Saffron, the local version of the Mafia, has long run King's Cross the way that Matthew ("Matty the Horse") Iannello runs Times Square in New York.

The police task force described Saffron as "a man who by reputation has for many years dominated the King's Cross vice scene. He has been described in the Parliament of this State [New South Wales] and elsewhere as 'Mr. Sin,' and is reputedly involved in vice and other questionable activities in other states of this country. . . . His activities are carefully hidden behind complex corporate structures."

Judges and state governors have attested on the record to the foulness of Saffron's character, and to his role, in the words of the South Australia attorney general in 1978, as "one of the principal characters in organized crime in Australia." In a cover story headlined "Who Is Abe Saffron?," the *National Times,* a major Australian newsmagazine, said in 1982, "The New South Wales Licensing Courts over 30 years have heard police officers rise to their feet to argue against Saffron, his family or associates getting one more liquor license—yet he and his associates still own or control a string of licensed bars, restaurants, clubs and hotels throughout the country."

The article noted that Saffron hadn't been convicted of a crime since 1940—but then, of course, close to the same could be said until recently of Matty the Horse.

Saffron became front-page news in Australia in 1982 for two reasons. One was his meetings with high-ranking police officers caught up in a corruption scandal. But his name also kept cropping up in the Nugan Hand affair.

A royal commission assigned by Parliament to investigate crooked unions was pursuing a former Nugan Hand executive, Frank Ward. The commission turned up a memorandum written to Ward by an associate at Ward's new investment bank: "Abe Saffron phoned 8:30 A.M.—is in city—has balance sheets—wants to settle Friday. He confirmed in no uncertain terms that the fee . . . is agreed at 5 cents. I have enough regard for my knees to agree! . . . I/we should clarify today to avoid future problems—physical or financial."

Before the ink from the resultant headlines had dried, news came that the police task force investigating Nugan Hand had uncovered another memo regarding Saffron. It was clearly in Michael Hand's handwriting, and said: "$50,000 Aust in H.K. to be repaid at $5000 per month for 10 months. It is Bank T.N.? Call 322215. Abe Saffron. Referred by Bernie Houghton. regarding yesterday's discussion—ABE SAFFRON."

The phone number 322215 was Saffron's headquarters.

The memo had been produced by former Nugan Hand executive Stephen Hill, who was giving investigators selective information to try to save his skin. Hill said he had no personal knowledge of the transaction referred to in the note. (Hand and Houghton had both left the country for undisclosed locations when the investigations began.) Hill said he kept the note because "I was interested in what association Saffron had with Hand."

Asked if the note indicated that Saffron wished to transfer $50,000 in Australian money overseas—the kind of illegal deal Nugan Hand specialized in—Hill replied, "That may be the case." He said, "T.N." may have referred to Treasury note, and "H.K." to Hong Kong.

Houghton's acquaintance with Saffron should have come as a surprise to no one. It seems unlikely that Houghton could have moved so heavily into the King's Cross vice district without making his peace with Abe Saffron. The buildings where Houghton's restaurants were housed had a tangle of corporate owners, but two were connected to associates of Saffron. Furthermore, the soldiers who flocked to Houghton's drinking establishments were referred for further recreation to Saffron's nearby gambling dens. When one of these dens, the Aquatic Club, declared bankruptcy in the mid-1970s to escape paying creditors, it was kept in operation by a new team of owners, including Houghton.

Houghton admitted to the police task force that he had known Saffron for many years "as a result of visits by Saffron to the Bourbon and Beefsteak restaurant." Houghton told the cops, "I would have a social drink with him. Our interests in the restaurant [business] are mutual." But, the task force report said, "Apart from one instance, unrelated to this inquiry, Houghton said that he was unable to recall ever having had any business dealings with Saffron."

Houghton recalled luncheons at which he had introduced Frank Nugan, and "visiting military personnel," to Saffron. Whether the "visiting military personnel" knew exactly whose hand they were shaking when they met Abe Saffron isn't spelled out, but the contact alone could have been embarrassing for some, if publicized. Houghton also said that Mike Hand met Saffron "under similar circumstances," after which "they had a very casual relationship."

Saffron, however, denied to the police that he had ever met Hand, and said he met Nugan only once, socially. Commented the task force, "This claim is, of course, irreconcilable with the statements of Houghton."

The police task force showed both Houghton and Saffron the memo from Michael Hand about the $50,000. "Each denied any knowledge of it," the task force reported. Saffron denied he had ever had "any association with the Nugan Hand group of companies," and Houghton said he wasn't aware of any.

The task force concluded, "It is not clear from the note whether the money was 'loaned' to Saffron or was paid by him into Nugan Hand, but there is little doubt that Saffron was at one time involved in at least this one transaction with Nugan Hand. . . . That at least Saffron chose to lie about his association with Hand, and both Houghton and Saffron chose to lie about the transaction, only adds to suspicion that there was something either illegal or improper about it," the task force said in its final report to the prime minister and governor.

That report went on:

> "A number of observable strands existed within Nugan Hand.
>
> "First . . . there is some evidence that Hand retained with U.S. intelligence personnel ties throughout the 1970s and into the 1980s.
>
> "Second, on the evidence available there is little or no doubt that Houghton was until at least the early 1970s and perhaps is involved, in Australia and elsewhere, in some way with U.S. and Australian intelligence personnel.
>
> "Third, Houghton was and still is closely associated with two other U.S. citizens resident in Sydney. Both have military backgrounds and there is strong reason to believe that at least one of them, Bobby Keith Boyd, was in the 1960s–70s and perhaps is still connected in some way with U.S. intelligence activity. The other, Robert Wallace Gehring, if not at that time then later, became exposed to intelligence personnel through his close association with Houghton, Boyd and Hand, and his later role in the 'disappearance' of Hand from Sydney.
>
> "Fourth, Houghton and Hand were extremely close by the early 1970s and there is every indication that Hand regarded Houghton as a 'father figure.' More probable than not it was because of Houghton's U.S. armed services and intelligence connections that Hand regarded him so highly. It was frequently said that Hand's view was that 'anything is all right so long as it is done in the name of America.' "

CHAPTER FIVE

Corporate Veils

Outsiders were kept away from the secrets of Nugan Hand until the summer of 1980. That was six months after the supposed brains of the operation had, literally, been splattered all over the roof of Frank Nugan's Mercedes.

Nugan had made his bloody and widely publicized departure from corporate office in January. In April, Michael Hand had put the company under control of a bankruptcy court in order to free his own door from the line of increasingly panicky depositors, sleazy businessmen, and others Nugan Hand had dealt with who now wanted their money back. If that wasn't enough of a hint that something was terribly wrong, anyone interested had been alerted to the likelihood of scandal by Hand's testimony at the Nugan inquest later in April. Finally, at the end of June, it came out in headlines that both Hand and Houghton had vanished.

Even with all that, it wasn't until about a week later, in July, that a truly independent accountant, the newly appointed liquidator John O'Brien, was authorized by the courts to delve into Nugan Hand's books. By that time there was precious little left of them.

O'Brien's was the first of four major, official, widesweeping investigations of Nugan Hand in Australia. (There were also countless lawsuits, death inquests, criminal complaints, tax cases, and commissions looking into this-or-that-other-problem, all of which got caught up in the Nugan Hand mess, and many of which turned up valuable information. Moreover, some of the best investigating was done by the press, which for years regarded any new crumb about Nugan Hand as the day's main meal.)

About the time O'Brien, the liquidator, plunged into the case, in midsummer 1980, a second big official effort began at the New South Wales Corporate Affairs Commission—the equivalent of the Securities and Exchange Commission in the United States, but on an individual state basis. The Corporate Affairs Commission had theoretically been investigating Nugan Hand since shortly after Nugan's death, but the early attempts were amateurish and easily manipulated by Mike Hand and other insiders. By summer, the commission had geared up its staff and hired a leading outside lawyer, Geoffrey Nicholson, to head a real inquiry. In March 1983, the Corporate Affairs Commission published its report in two hefty volumes, which were particularly helpful in unraveling the complex financial dealings of Nugan Hand.

Also in March 1983, the last of a series of reports was published by a third body of inquiry, the police Joint Task Force on Drug Trafficking—"joint" in the sense that the prime minister of Australia had ordered the federal police to join forces with the New South Wales police to investigate Nugan Hand. The investigation grew out of the frustration felt by a royal commission that had been appointed to investigate drug trafficking, but that kept running into Nugan Hand and lacked authority and manpower on its own to open that huge can of worms. The Joint Task Force attacked the problem, and was particularly active in pursuing the importance of Nugan Hand's ties to Americans, both high office-holders and racketeers.

But basic questions remained unanswered, even with the publication of the mass of details in the Corporate Affairs Commission and Joint Task Force reports. Outstanding among the unsettled issues were the significance of the Pentagon and CIA links, and the question of who should be given criminal responsibility for what everyone agreed had been vast crimes.

So a new royal commission under Justice D. G. Stewart was appointed by Parliament to carry on the work. The Stewart Royal Commission's two-volume report in June 1985 was a deep disappointment and shed little new light, for reasons best described later, in chronological sequence.

The results of all four investigations—liquidator O'Brien's reports, the Corporate Affairs Commission report, the Joint Task Force reports, and the Stewart Royal Commission report—are incorporated into this book, as, of course, are the results of the myriad of other inquiries so far as they are known, and of the author's own four-year effort.

Back in April, when Hand had been forced to turn the company over in court, he had been allowed to select the accountants who would act as liquidators. They apparently didn't press him, or Houghton, or others who might have been able to supply information or return stolen money. A mass of mail was pouring in from the bank's hapless victims, and what replies the temporary liquidators managed to get off were, judging from the ones forwarded to O'Brien, unhelpfully noncommittal.

John O'Brien was a bearlike, prematurely gray accountant and professional bankruptcy liquidator. With the Australian front pages daily full of Nugan Hand scandal, including the comings and goings of U.S. spies and generals and the horror stories of victims, a judge had picked O'Brien from an independent roster of liquidators to replace the temporary liquidators chosen by Michael Hand.

From that day in July, it was clear to O'Brien that Nugan Hand must have been the product of an intelligence beyond Frank Nugan's. If nothing else, the successful damage control carried out in the six months since Nugan's death was impressive. Either Nugan had been survived by very skillful and organized co-conspirators, or, in the only alternative, the law enforcement officials of Australia and a dozen other countries were stupid and lax beyond belief.

O'Brien got more than a few jolts reading the bills that were piling up. One, for $45,684.09 of legal work, was from William Colby, former head of the CIA. The CIA was well known in Australia, where the United States kept its most important overseas electronic spy installations. The CIA had been openly accused of helping overthrow the Australian Government in 1975. Many Australians still believed that the CIA had subverted their democracy.

The cover letter for Colby's bill to Nugan Hand was addressed to Hand personally, and dated April 4, 1980, long before the bank fell under O'Brien's skeptical purview. The bill was on the stationery of the Washington office of Colby's law firm at the time, Reid & Priest (home office, 40 Wall Street, New York).

"Dear Michael," it began, "I regret to be communicating with you about the subject of our fees, but I am afraid I owe you an explanation of the attached bill. It obviously represents a summarization of the various activities that we did for Frank and separately for you over the past several months. . . .

"Obviously, we still stand ready to continue on the line Frank had intended to follow, a general consulting relationship on various matters involving United States law," Colby wrote to Hand—who had previously helped train and supply Montagnard recruits under Colby's overall supervision during the war.

"After you are able to regroup for the future in the unfortunate absence of Frank, I would hope you would find some further utility in consultation with us. If that does not work out, however, please accept my very best wishes for your success and that of the institution Frank and you started so effectively. If you do come in this area, I hope you will feel that the welcome mat is out, either professionally or personally. Sincerely, Bill."

Hand, however, apparently didn't have time to accept this offer of hospitality before he was driven underground by the several investigations and by the thousands of angry citizens of many countries who had trusted the Nugan Hand Bank. The letters they wrote asking for their money back made painful reading for O'Brien.

The assets underpinning Nugan Hand's business were supposedly lodged in accounts at major Sydney banks. But as O'Brien began unsealing these accounts, it did not take him long to discover that the purported assets—millions of dollars in highly rated commercial banking instruments—simply didn't exist. And never had. The full list of numbers wasn't in, and perhaps would never be, but the bottom line emerged to O'Brien early on.

Whatever else Nugan Hand was, it was surely a giant theft machine. Judging from the victims' letters, as O'Brien perused them, Bernie Houghton had actually gone around with a big plastic garbage bag slung over one shoulder, like some kind of reverse Santa Claus, taking bundles of cash savings from Americans serving overseas, mostly in Saudi Arabia.

The depositors were told their savings would be invested in the high-interest commercial banking instruments. But instead, the money just seemed to disappear. General Manor collected checks from his former subordinate officers at the U.S. air bases he used to command, and delivered them back Nugan Hand certificates of deposit. Those certificates were now next to worthless. Other depositors had donated their cash in various ways around the world.

Big and little victims all over Southeast Asia wrote in that they had given money to the staff at Nugan Hand, men like George Shaw. But liquidator O'Brien found no records of their accounts among the bank's files—or in some cases, he would find only a puzzling reference to the depositor in the records of some related company.

There turned out to be a dozen related companies, with strange names that neither the investors nor O'Brien had ever heard of. There were even complaints on O'Brien's desk from depositors in the United States—where Nugan Hand had no legal authority to take deposits. Letter after letter referred to the vaults of commercial banking paper that was supposed to stand behind the deposits. But O' Brien knew the paper wasn't there.

Who else knew? That was the question that bothered O'Brien, and would plague every other investigator assigned to the case. How much did the executives working for Nugan Hand know about the fraud they were perpetrating?

It was possible, of course, that people were duped into working for Nugan Hand. It was possible that they solicited deposits in the genuine belief that the money would be prudently invested. It was possible that they really believed the depositors would reap the high interest promised. That was exactly what the American military officers who worked for Nugan Hand later argued: that they had been duped just like the depositors.

But O'Brien's efforts at intellectual charity toward such fellows kept running into obstacles. Once inside the bank, how dumb would you have to be to stay duped? Could that level of stupidity be ascribed to high officials who only recently were responsible for supervising *billions* of dollars in U.S. taxpayer funds—hundreds of thousands of troops and whole fleets of aircraft and aircraft carriers, who specialized in, of all things, "intelligence"?

True, Colby was just a lawyer for Nugan Hand. Lawyers had somehow managed to establish years ago that they had not only the right but the ethical responsibility to maneuver with all the vigor and genius at their command on behalf of even the most palpably sinister of clients. Indeed, legal "ethics," as they are called, are said to require that lawyers be discharged of all responsibility for the injustices that may result from the successful practice of their craft. So Colby, by such measure, might stand not only discharged but a hero for his efforts on behalf of the bank.

But for nearly three years, Admiral Yates, no lawyer, had been *president* of the Nugan Hand Bank, the entity that took in most of the money. How much brainpower, how much clarity of observation, should one attribute to an admiral? To the former chief of staff for plans and policy of the entire U.S. Pacific Command, largest in the U.S. military? To a man who, as commander of the aircraft carrier *John F. Kennedy,* had been entrusted with nuclear weapons?

Now suppose, on the other hand, that the brass wasn't innocent at all. Suppose they had been in on the plot. Did this mean that the U.S. Government had employed, and promoted to the highest offices, a bunch of thieves who were now living high and mighty off the riches of defrauded investors?

Or was it more likely that they *weren't*, at least most of them, thieves—that there was some political motive behind their work?

O'Brien resolved to try to talk to spy chief Colby, Admiral Yates, General Manor, General Black, and all the other Yanks. But, at least for now, they were far away, on U.S. soil. They were protected from him. And if they did agree to sit down with him there, they would face no compulsion to tell him the truth (unless, of course, he could get the cooperation of the U.S. Government). The return addresses of the potential witnesses against them, the depositors, were spread all the way from Kuala Lumpur to Udhailiyah (wherever *that* was).

For the meantime, O'Brien set about to deal with the complainants who were right there in Australia.

A few weeks after John O'Brien was handed the Nugan Hand mess, he received a letter from Dr. John K. Ogden. Ogden was a disabled, sixty-year-old former gynecologist from Toowoomba, a town of eighty thousand souls about six hundred miles north of Sydney. "I understand from the papers that you have taken over the onerous task of winding up the affairs of the Nugan Hand Bank," Dr. Ogden's letter began. It then noted that Dr. Ogden had already submitted his and his wife's claim to the temporary liquidators; the amount—$689,000.

"As you might imagine, I am desperately worried as this was my retirement and security for my wife in old age," Dr. Ogden wrote. "Sixty years of age is too old to start again! I trusted Nugan as my solicitor and banker, and the agreement was that my funds and capital gains would be available when I wanted them. If the bank cannot cover all of this amount, one has to raise the question, Was it not insured? And if not, is not the Reserve Bank [of Australia] and the auditors to some degree culpable for allowing this sort of situation to occur?"

O'Brien knew the money wasn't insured, that the Reserve Bank would be embarrassed, and that the auditors might go to jail. But he also knew that none of the above would get John and Barbara Ogden their $689,000 back. In many ways, the Ogden's letter was typical of the sackfuls the mailman dumped on O'Brien's desk. But in size, and poignancy, their case stood out.

The Ogdens, who say they were "completely wiped out by this affair," met Frank Nugan on the advice of their banker in Sydney. "I was incapacitated with cervical spondylitis [inflammation of the vertebrae]. The insurance company wasn't paying and I needed a lawyer," Dr. Ogden recalls.* Nugan was a lawyer, and the banker recommended him as someone who could help the Ogdens with their insurance problem. He did. Then, says Dr. Ogden, "the relationship developed into advisor and finally banker. When my neck got better, we came back to Toowoomba to resume practice and used to fly down to Sydney and stay with the Nugans, and he always seemed a devoted family man and absolutely straight."

Nugan, in fact, *was* a family man, having in 1970 married Charlotte Lee Sofge Nugan of Nashville, Tennessee—a symmetry, since his partner, American Michael Hand, had married an Australian. Unlike the childless Hands, though, the Nugans had two children and seemed, at least, devoted to them.

Nugan billed himself not only as a lawyer and banker, but most of all as a tax specialist. He told the Ogdens he could help them save on their tax bill by making more careful investments—such as in Nugan Hand. "He said he could get a better return for the money," Dr. Ogden says. "Frank told us that the bank *never* lent money and that it was absolutely secure and that the Reserve Bank audited their books every two weeks." Besides, at that point the Ogdens were putting in only their cash savings. They still had substantial life insurance investments to fall back on.

Then tragedy struck. In 1978 the Ogdens' twenty-three-year-old daughter was killed in an automobile accident, and less than a year later their twenty-nine-year-old son died in a hang glider accident in Spain. Frank Nugan reacted with a characteristic show of concern. He had Nugan Hand's office in Hamburg, Germany, fly the Ogdens' son's body home, and he personally handled the other arrangements the Ogdens were too grief-stricken to deal with.

Then he suggested the Ogdens were so grief-stricken they should turn everything over to him. Mike Hand then gave the Ogdens the same pitch. "They could manage our affairs much better than we could ourselves," Dr. Ogden says they told him. "We were so upset that we gave Frank Nugan power of attorney. We thought we were

*The Ogden quotes in this book are intermingled from their correspondence with the two liquidators, which is on public record in Sydney, and interviews conducted by the author.

incompetent to look after our own affairs. . . . We never doubted his integrity. He was after all a Master of Law and we thought we knew him."

So, Dr. Ogden says, "I was persuaded and encouraged to sell all of my real estate and cash insurance policies. . . . All the money was put into the Nugan Hand Bank."

Did Nugan and Hand know that they were ripping the bereaved couple off? Did either of them somehow believe his own lie because the other one, and all their staff, were telling it, too? To the Ogdens, such questions are immaterial. When Frank Nugan died, Dr. Ogden raced to Mike Hand to inquire about his money. He says he "received powerful reassurance that all was well," after which "Hand pushed off to Hong Kong for a few days. I feel that if you can find Hand and Bernie Houghton, you will find a lot of money," he says.

Trying to recoup, Dr. Ogden went to the New South Wales state Law Society, the equivalent of a bar association in the United States, and applied for relief from its client protection fund. But the society rejected him, he says, "because Nugan acted as both a lawyer and a banker and it would depend on which hat he was wearing"; apparently the society decided that when Dr. Ogden's lawyer counseled him on matters other than the insurance claim, the lawyer was moonlighting as a banker, and so he was no longer the responsibility of the law society.

Then, to add insult to injury, the Australian Taxation Office decided that several of Nugan's plans to minimize his clients' taxes were illegal. The office began auditing Dr. Ogden and other Nugan Hand victims, looking to collect money the victims no longer had, to cover back taxes on income they had already been robbed of.

"Certainly we were incredibly naive and stupid to put so much trust in one person," Dr. Ogden says. Then he volunteers, "The impeccable front of the bank was immeasurably helped by having the likes of U.S. admirals and generals actively working in the bank and on the board of directors." In a letter about this, he adds a P.S.: "Don't you think the remaining directors should be brought to trial and Mike Hand located?"

Frank Nugan.

There is as much mystery in his origins as in his death. His parents are widely known as Spanish immigrants who settled in Australia in 1938. Yet the January 29, 1943, birth record of Frank Nugan in Sydney shows that his father, then thirty-seven, had been born in Brackwale, Germany, and his mother, then thirty-two, had been born in Schwedt, Germany. It shows they were married in Jerusalem, Palestine, December 30, 1938—the same year that recent oral and published accounts have had them settling in Australia.

A call to the father, Alf Nugan, produces flustered, sputtering denials of the recorded evidence. He hangs up. Called a second time, Nugan again denies what is on the records, but on continued questioning concedes that he was, indeed, born in Germany.

"I was a Spanish citizen," he insists. "I left Germany as a baby. I left to find a better life." He says his mother brought him to Spain and that he married his wife in Madrid in 1930. He says they left because of the Spanish Civil War, and became Australian citizens in 1945. He says neither he nor his wife was either Jewish or Nazi. He refuses to say more and hangs up again.

They settled in Griffith, a town nine hundred miles west of Sydney. Griffith is associated in the average Australian's mind with two activities: the farming of fruits and vegetables, and the open, criminal farming of marijuana. All of Griffith's crops, legal and illegal, are raised for both domestic and export markets. In about 1941, Alf Nugan began what became one of the largest fruit and vegetable operations in the area. It is called the Nugan Group, which led to some confusion in the public's mind when Nugan Hand was started in the 1970s.

By the time of Nugan Hand, the Nugan Group fruit and vegetable business had gone public—its shares were traded on the open market. The company was run by Kenneth Nugan, Frank's older brother by two years. One of the Nugan Group's major customers, according to Ken Nugan, was the United States Government. Among other things, he says, the Nugans supplied fresh veggies to the big U.S. Navy base at Subic Bay in the Philippines. This relationship, Ken Nugan says, predated his brother's relationship with Michael Hand.

Just as Miami is known not only for its sunshine but also for its drugs, most Australians associate the town of Griffith with more than just fruit and vegetables. As a center for marijuana and the mob, Griffith has long been a national scandal.

In the mid-1970s a furniture dealer and family man, Donald Mackay, decided to speak up and organize to stop the drug traffic. He circulated a petition demanding that the New South Wales state parliament take action. So enthusiastic was the response that Mackay decided to run for public office on the issue. On July 15, 1977, Donald Mackay disappeared.

The disappearance of Mackay was roundly denounced in Parliament. An investigative authority known as the Woodward Royal Commission (after the judge who headed it) was formed. In 1979, amidst much publicity, it reported, "A secret criminal society named L'Honorata Societa, which is comprised of persons of Calabrian descent, exists within Australia. A 'cell' of this society existed and probably still does in the town of Griffith." Visiting Italian officials testified before the commission that marijuana grown in Griffith was processed by a Mafia drug network and showed up in Europe and North America.

The Woodward Royal Commission declared that Robert Trimbole of Griffith was head of the Calabrian Mafia there, and was involved in the marijuana trafficking. So, it said, was a prominent grape-growing and wine-producing family, the Sergis, which it also included in the Mafia. Big headlines told of the 1976 wedding of a Sergi daughter, where, in a scene reminiscent of the opening scenes of *The Godfather, Part Two,* the twelve hundred guests brought cash gifts, which were banked by the father of the bride, with the groom's blessing.

John Hatton, an independent member of the New South Wales Parliament, whose district covers Griffith, says flat out,* "The Mafia killed Mackay. I don't like to use that term because I don't generally think that organized crime is ethnic, but in Griffith's case I think it's appropriate. Donald Mackay stumbled onto a very valuable field and he persisted in making a stink about it. They brought in somebody from the outside to kill him, figuring that if they knocked off somebody with that high a profile nobody else would want to get involved in it. I think they realize now they made a big mistake. The investigation into it, the interest in it, is still going on."

Among other things, investigators turned up Nugan Group checks for thousands of dollars made out to members of the Trimbole and Sergi families. Ken Nugan argued that these checks did not indicate payments to the Trimboles or Sergis. He said the payee names on these checks were just phony "code names" used to cover the conversion of corporate funds to cash for legitimate reasons, though he didn't say what the legitimate reasons for this internal money-laundering might have been.

It seemed a strange practice to some—and an even stranger coincidence on the choice of names.

Investigators found other suspicious links between Robert Trim-

*In an interview with the author, elaborating on charges he has made in public.

bole and the family of Sydney organized-crime boss Abe Saffron—Bernie Houghton's effective landlord. After Frank Nugan died, the newspapers were able to show business connections between Sergi and Houghton, and between Sergi and the U.S. Army men and Australian businessmen around Houghton.

The bad reputation of Griffith dogged both Nugan brothers in their businesses. At one point the publicity proved so hot that the Nugan Group actually flew a planeload of reporters to Griffith to try to restore some respect. The reporters were shown carrots and onions being crated, and grapefruit being squeezed by juicing machines. Then they heard Ken Nugan declare that he had never dealt with the Trimboles or Sergis. On the other hand, he said, he *had* known and respected Donald Mackay.

Frank Nugan got a law degree from Sydney University in 1963, then set out for North America, where he pursued two highly unusual postgraduate degrees in law. His only real achievement during his American stay, though, was constructing, with some artifice, the résumé that was to lure many clients when he returned down under.

Nugan later claimed he achieved a reputation as an international tax expert—the result, he said, of his studies at the University of California, Berkeley, for a master of laws degree. Master of laws is a degree most lawyers don't think worth the trouble of obtaining, but which Nugan won in 1965. A veteran professor at the Berkeley law school, Richard Jennings, recalls Nugan as "a kind of wild fellow" who "dropped into Berkeley with an XKE, kind of a playboy type." He remembers Nugan spending time with glider airplanes, and laughs at the idea that Nugan was a tax expert. "He never even studied taxes when he was here," Jennings says.

Next, Nugan went to Toronto, where he studied for the even more arcane degree of doctor of laws (he never got it). To help pay the Jaguar's gas bills and other expenses, he worked for a corporations task force performing an overhaul of Canadian corporate law. Nugan later claimed—and it was widely believed in Australia—that he had a big hand in rewriting the Canadian legal code. In fact, the task force's report names three authors and twenty-four valuable assistants, none of whom was Frank Nugan.

Philip Anisman, a professor of law at Osgood Hall Law School of York University in Toronto, remembers that in 1967 Nugan got a clerical and research job with the task force. But Anisman says Nugan never had a hand in the task force's recommendations. Anisman says Nugan was "kind of wild, loquacious, fun." But on the main expertise Nugan claimed to bring back from North America, Anisman says, "I never heard anything about any work he did on tax."

Recollections of when Nugan returned to Australia vary—from late 1967, about when Hand arrived, to early 1969. And just how did Nugan—the playboy heir to a modest food-processing fortune with strange beginnings, even stranger criminal associations, and built in part on U.S. military contracts—happen to meet Hand, just coming off active duty as a U.S. intelligence operative in Southeast Asia? Nobody seems to remember that, either. Asked under oath at the inquest, Hand declared that he didn't remember how he met Nugan—highly unlikely, considering that for better or worse they became the most important person in each other's lives.*

*The Stewart Royal Commission report offers its own typically unreliable account of the meeting. At two different places, the report says they met in 1968, while Hand was working as a security guard at a mining company (Meekatharra Minerals) Nugan had invested in. Elsewhere in the report, however, Stewart acknowledges (as corporate records attest) that Meekatharra wasn't formed until 1970, making this sequence of events impossible. (In addition, other corporate records to be cited here later, which the Stewart Commission may not have been aware of, show that Nugan and Hand had a business relationship before Meekatharra started.) There are no other accounts of Hand's working as a security guard. At yet another point, the Stewart report says Hand met Nugan while Hand was selling real estate—without bothering to note that this completely contradicts information elsewhere in the same report.

CHAPTER SIX

Sleight of Hand

Where did the Nugan Hand Bank get its money?

After Nugan and Hand became famous as big-spending bankers in the late 1970s, a legend arose that they spent the years around 1970 building independent reputations in the financial community as astute speculators. That was when they were said to have accumulated the capital that would launch the Nugan Hand Bank. But the legend doesn't match the facts.

After arriving in Australia, Hand went to work selling development lots along the Australian coast five hundred miles north of Sydney. His prey was mostly his former fellow spooks and war heroes. He made many trips back to the war zone to see these men. But not many actually bought.

Over several years only a few dozen men are on record as having paid cash for the lots, and they paid only in the low- to mid-four figures. This would have provided a total gross under $200,000, leaving Hand with a commission share that wouldn't even have met his living and travel expenses. And there's still more mystery.

His employer in the real estate sales was a company backed by, of all people, Pat Boone, the blond, goody two-white-buckskin-shoes Christian revivalist singer with the toothpaste-ad smile. The money to develop real estate on Boone's good name was put up by someone who seemed almost equally out of place on the outback, D. K. Ludwig, the reclusive multibillionaire shipping magnate then reputed to be one of the two or three richest men alive, and certainly one of the two or three hardest to get to talk to.

Ludwig's operations in Australia were managed by a lawyer named Fred Millar. Millar was and is senior executive and general counsel for the shipping empire of Sir Peter Abeles—Rupert Murdoch's longtime business partner, and the knight whose small circle of friends also picked Bernie Houghton up off the street when he arrived in Australia and put *him* to work selling real estate.

Thus both Hand and Houghton, on arriving from overseas, quickly landed real estate sales jobs tied to the same multimillionaire crowd that was politically supportive of U.S. hard-line foreign policy.

There is, of course, nothing to prove that this wasn't just a coincidence. Fred Millar insists* he didn't know who Michael Hand was back in the 1960s, before the newspapers became full of Hand. Even after Hand was a celebrity, Millar says, he never met the man. All Millar says he remembers of the whole real estate deal is that Ludwig advanced money to "some American" whose name he doesn't remember, the company went bust, and Ludwig had to take over.

Paul Stocker, now an Everett, Washington, lawyer, was running the operation, originally known as Ocean Shores. Stocker says he went to Australia with his family in 1964, and bought some property. In need of financing and a promotional vehicle, he says, he contacted Boone through an old law school classmate Boone was associated with.

Boone was enthusiastic enough to fly to Australia, and, according to Stocker, was "quite a success" in attracting buyers. (Boone failed to respond to messages left with his agent and manager.) But Stocker says not enough money came in to repay Ludwig, who he says took over the development from him in 1970. Servicemen who bought properties say the names of both Boone and Ludwig were used heavily in the promotions.

Stocker says Michael Hand came aboard through a buddy, Kermit L. ("Bud") King, a former CIA pilot in Southeast Asia, who had come to Australia after his war duty and got a job selling lots for the Boone operation. Lots initially went for $2,500, and salesmen got a 25 percent commission, Stocker says.

Brochures poeticized Ocean Shores the way brochures poeticize vacant lots everywhere: "Landscaping of the 3,200 acres has pre-

*Interview with the author.

served the natural beauty of the site, which has miles of white sandy beaches and rolling green hills threaded by the North Arm of the Brunswick river. . . ." Also as usual, the poetry was accompanied by prophecy: "7,500 fully improved homesites with underground power and water, modern motel facilities and an adjacent airport. . . . Over $2 million will be spent on clubhouse facilities which will include . . . an international class 18-hole golf course . . . a yacht club-marina complex" and "a permanent art and cultural center."

The Ocean Shores development company was reorganized in 1968 into Wendell West, whose corporation filings in Australia that year show an interesting board of directors: besides Stocker and four Washington State businessmen, the registered directors included Charles Eugene ("Pat") Boone of Beverly Hills, California, and one Pat Swan of Sydney, Australia.

Swan soon became, if she wasn't already, the private secretary and administrative assistant of Frank Nugan; she was eventually committed for trial (indicted) for helping rape and destroy Nugan Hand's files in the days after his death.* (As of March 1987, Australian authorities still hadn't set a trial date.)

Records, however, show that in 1969, Hand formed a company called Australian and Pacific Holdings Ltd, which announced that it would develop an island off Australia's renowned barrier reef. Hand did this with two other men: an otherwise unidentified fellow named Clive Wilfred Lucas (now also unfindable) and John J. Foley, a lawyer from little Griffith, the family home of Frank Nugan.

Why a lawyer from, of all places, Griffith? A reporter from the local Griffith newspaper said Foley had claimed credit for first bringing Nugan and Hand together. Foley denies that now,** and insists he was never in the same room with both Nugan and Hand. He says he doesn't remember how he met either of them—though he acknowledges he knew both. Lucas, he says, was a friend of Hand's whom he met only once or twice.

According to Foley, Australian and Pacific "was only a small shell, it didn't own anything. He [Hand] had only just come from Vietnam. . . . Nothing ever happened. I'm not too sure who suggested it. It was just an idea, really."

*I tried to ask Swan how this happened, but ever since the Nugan Hand scandal she has made herself just as hard to interview as D. K. Ludwig.

**Interview with the author.

Records show that in August 1969 the idea—Australian and Pacific—held its first board meeting. The directors present were Hand, Lucas, and Foley. The minutes show that the company's accountants expressed alarm at the directors' plan to sell stock in the company to the public. The directors agreed that for now they would sell stock to "only close and intimate friends." Hand said he had "many friends in Asia who were with the U.S. Armed Forces there, or in the civil service in Hong Kong or Vietnam" who would gladly invest "in excess of $100,000," the minutes say.

But minutes of the next meeting, January 10, 1970, show that Hand and Lucas had gone to Asia and raised only $16,000. Minutes show that six days later, another directors' meeting was held, at which time it was decided what to do with the money that the new stockholders had put up. "It was resolved," the minutes say, "to lend $16,000 to Mr. F. J. Nugan for a six-month period at 10 percent interest."

And thus we have the first definitive evidence that the Green Beret–CIA operative from the Bronx, and the U.S. Navy carrot-packer-cum-self-proclaimed-tax-expert from Griffith, Australia, had joined league.

When Nugan returned from Canada with his puffed-up account of his exploits and accomplishments there, he went to work for a Sydney law firm, representing a brokerage house and other corporate clients. The law firm was where, in 1969, his friend Paul Lincoln Smith met him. Smith, an older and palpably well-heeled lawyer, recalls, "He didn't have much money then. [Smith doesn't mention the Jaguar.] But he was bright, hard-working. I invited him out to dinner. I took him fishing a lot."

Early in 1970, Nugan and a man named Donald O'Callaghan formed a company called Meekatharra Minerals. They boasted big nickel deposits in Queensland. "Everybody was forming mining companies in those days," says Smith.

Smith asserts, and Australian opinion generally seems to agree, that through a bonanza in mining shares Nugan struck his fortune. There is precious little evidence for this, however.

The highly volatile shares of Meekatharra did rise quickly from ten cents a share to six dollars a share. But they fell just as quickly when the promised nickel deposits proved to be about as slow to develop as the Ocean Shores arts and cultural center had been.

O'Callaghan says the notion that his partner Nugan made a bundle off Meekatharra is "total bullshit." He points out that as a co-promoter, Nugan was forbidden by corporate rules from unloading most of his start-up shares on the open market during the quick price-rise. O'Callaghan says Nugan's profits from Meekatharra "would have been minimal, in the forty-to-fifty-thousand-dollar range."

Meanwhile, the affairs of Meekatharra and Michael Hand's Australian and Pacific Holdings intertwined. On February 3, 1970, according to the company minutes, Australian and Pacific "was offered and accepted" fifteen thousand shares of Meekatharra, apparently as collateral for the $16,000 loan to Nugan. Then, on April 14, "a further $3,500 was lent to Mr. F. J. Nugan for a period of six months at an interest rate of 10 percent," the minutes say.

Then, in May 1970, a list of Australian and Pacific's shareholders was filed with the government. The list was to become famous when reporters discovered it in the aftermath of the Nugan Hand collapse, for of the thirty-seven listed shareholders, four had the address "c/o Air America, A.P.O. San Francisco." Air America had by 1980 been exposed as a CIA front.

Another of the Australian and Pacific shareholders had the address "c/o Continental Air Service," whose relationship to the CIA had also been exposed. Five more shareholders were reachable through the U.S. Agency for International Development, also A.P.O. San Francisco; AID was a known funnel for CIA funds. Several shareholders were listed at Michael Hand's own Australian post office box, and many others were listed under post office box numbers or strange business names in Vietnam or Laos.

Was this evidence of a U.S. Government plot?—or was Michael Hand just exploiting his former colleagues in the U.S. service? Despite all the fuss made over the list, it does not provide much evidence of government connivance. In all, the persons named were shown owning 29,200 shares, apparently representing an investment of an equal number of dollars, not a munificent sum.

Over the summer of 1970, Foley and the mysterious Lucas resigned as directors of Australian and Pacific. O'Callaghan and a Sydney lawyer, John Jeweller, were appointed in their place.

The minutes of September 22, 1970, say, "It was noted that Mr. F. J. Nugan had not repaid the first loan of $16,000 and that repayment of the second loan of $3,500 was due to be paid on 17 October 1970. The secretary was authorized to effect immediate repayment."

There is no evidence repayment was made, however, and during 1971 Australian and Pacific made $8,500 in new loans to Nugan.

About all the money taken in by the company was accounted for by the loans to Nugan. Any development costs at the barrier reef were certainly minimal. The company's expenses totaled zero in 1970, $200 in 1971, $1,071 in 1972, and $381.11 in 1973, the only years for which figures are available.

What was Hand really doing with his time all this while? A colleague from CIA airline days, Douglas Sapper—who became close to Hand again in the late 1970s—remembers that in the 1969–73 period, "Michael showed up in Laos a lot. I saw him in Phnom Penh [Cambodia] from time to time." (Laos and Cambodia, of course, were not favored vacation spots on most itineraries in those war-torn years.)

Houghton also made some trips to Southeast Asia in the early 1970s, immigration records show. He told police he went to explore the possibility of starting a business with Hand in Vietnam, buying surplus U.S. war materiel for resale, though he said the deal never came off.

Sapper recalls Hand introducing him to Houghton in 1969. Sapper says he was working for a photo agency based in Saigon during this period, helping supply U.S. television with pictures. Since Sapper had just previously been working for the CIA, could the photo agency have been another CIA operation, using U.S. taxpayer money to propagandize the U.S. taxpayers? "No comment," Sapper says.

Sapper says that he, like Hand, knew Bill Colby. But he adds that "it was very difficult to live at a certain level in Saigon there and not meet certain people at cocktail parties."

Evidence just doesn't bear out the myth that Hand or Nugan raked in millions from mining or real estate in the early 1970s. They did try to make a second round of profits from the U.S. servicemen who had invested in the Ocean Shores/Wendell West scheme. Nugan and Hand, using a Panama City-based front company they controlled, wrote the servicemen offering to buy back the plots at cut-rate prices. About two dozen men, now back in the United States and eager to get rid of their annual Australian real estate tax bill, agreed.

There is no recorded explanation of how Hand and Nugan got rights to the plots from D. K. Ludwig, the billionaire, whose company held mortgages signed by the servicemen. But with Ludwig either agreeing to it or ignorant of it, they resold some of the lots to

Australians for about $7,000 each—several times what they were paying the servicemen. Not all the lots were sold, however. Years later, some were still listed as meager assets in the portfolio of a Nugan Hand affiliate company when Nugan Hand collapsed in bankruptcy.

Examining all the recorded land sales records, it appears that Nugan and Hand might have pulled in $100,000, maybe even a bit more, over what they had to lay out to buy the properties. That's not much for two years' work by two men. Nor does it count any overhead of the sales operation—let alone trips to Panama.

And what of the supposed mining bonanza? O'Callaghan says he fired Nugan from any connection with Meekatharra Minerals in 1973. He says he "severed relations both socially and in business," because Nugan "adopted an attitude toward life that I would not have wanted a director of Meekatharra to have. Totally abhorrent." O'Callaghan declines to be more specific about this, but does say that Nugan had owed him a hefty sum for a long time, and didn't pay.

He also says that under their agreement Nugan upon his departure had to turn over 490,000 shares of Meekatharra—most of what he had—to the company at five cents a share. "He could not deal with them without my signature," O'Callaghan says. "He was a great story-teller. He was always talking millions." But O'Callaghan estimates that Nugan had perhaps $20,000 to $30,000 to his name, the family vegetable business aside, when he left Meekatharra.

Thus known events do not bear out the notion that big killings in real estate and mining stocks provided the $1 million in capital—let alone evidenced the genius—that supposedly went into Nugan Hand. Frank Nugan and Michael Hand were pulling in the kind of money that buys Chevrolets, maybe Buicks, but not the kind that buys XKEs, and certainly not the kind of money that capitalizes multinational banks. Yet by early 1975, while the land-sale operation was still winding down, Nugan Hand was already well underway.

Paul Stocker, the Washington lawyer who failed developing Ocean Shores, says he was later amazed to hear that Hand was running a bank. "That was like hearing that my brother had become a ballet dancer. It didn't make sense. He had no education in banking," Stocker says.

Before leaving the subject of northern Australian real estate, there are two mysterious events to note. Perhaps they were portentous, perhaps just coincidence. But among the two or three dozen lots Hand and Nugan sold were eight that happened to go to men employed by the Australian customs service. Two of the conveyances to customs men were dated June 19, 1974, well after Nugan Hand was functioning. The other six were dated six days later, on June 25. On seven of the transactions, the same attorney represented the customs men; on the eighth no attorney is listed.

Considering that one of the renowned charms of Nugan Hand was always its ability to move great sums of money illegally under the noses of the customs service, it has struck any number of investigators that these transactions might have served as payoffs.

Nevertheless, the customs men have demonstrated to the satisfaction of the law that they paid $7,000 each, the going price for the lots. They have insisted that there was nothing unusual or untoward about any of the transactions. No one has been able to demonstrate otherwise. The lawyer on the seven transactions failed to return numerous telephone messages.

There is also the matter of Bud King, the CIA pilot who went to Australia after his war duty. King sold lots for Boone and Ludwig. He lived in what was by all accounts a very nice house, in the remote area where the land was located. There was an airstrip. King's job sometimes involved flying customers or interested businesspersons in to look at the place. Hand spent a lot of time at King's house. Other visitors sometimes stayed there.

King had a Thai housekeeper whom he had brought with him from Asia and allegedly mistreated. The housekeeper got into an automobile accident in about 1973, and George Shaw, already working with Nugan and Hand, sent the housekeeper to a Sydney solicitor, Ivan Judd, who could sue for injury compensation.

After the case was resolved, Judd placed a confidential telephone call (at least it was confidential until the Nugan Hand case blew up) to Australian narcotics investigator Russ Kenny. Judd told Kenny that according to the housekeeper, King regularly flew in planeloads of narcotics from Asia to the secluded airstrip. Hand, according to the housekeeper, was part of the operation.

Nothing seems to have been done with this allegation at the time, except for the filling out of the first of many dope-smuggling complaints involving Nugan Hand principals.

There is a certain perverse irony in the idea that Pat Boone, however unwittingly, may, like the national commander of the American Legion and the executive director of the Freedoms Foundation, have been part of a major heroin racket. But when the allegation was finally looked into by several authorities in the 1980s, it couldn't be confirmed, and so had to be discounted.

Judd confirms that he filed the report, but won't say any more. The Thai housekeeper is long gone.

And so is Bud King. Shortly after Judd filed his report, the CIA aviation whiz somehow managed to fall to his death from the tenth-floor window of his fashionable Sydney apartment building. Case, to this date, unsolved.

On June 25, 1973, in Sydney, Australia, there was incorporated the firm of Nugan Hand Needham Ltd. Its office was a suite at 55 Macquarie Street, the same posh downtown office tower Nugan Hand would occupy several floors of when it filed bankruptcy seven years later. An early brochure employed all the euphemism, hyperbole, and mystery that would continue to enshroud the bank as it grew:

> "This Company's purpose is to act as a trusted Investment House prepared to make all of its services and facilities available to all persons and enterprises, large or small," the brochure said.
>
> "Australia is a land of great natural wealth. It's wealth is to be measured in terms of proven natural resources; industrial and primary development already undertaken or underway and an increasingly educated trained and prosperous population.
>
> "Australia's wealth lies mainly in its depth of vigorous and able people and their growing and effective business enterprises.
>
> "Services and facilities will be available for corporate financial advice and assistance, investment management, economic and security analysis and advice, money market operations, advice and facilities for international commercial activities and any specialised services sought by a client designed to meet special needs."
>
> *Special needs?*
>
> "There are specialised services required from time to time by clients of investment houses that, if not previously catered for, are often not available to clients of investment houses in this country.
>
> "This Company is prepared to consider any such special request on the basis of a full and proper exercise of the judgment of our Board of Directors and staff. We shall give any such special request proper study, consideration and the application of the best judgment our Board and staff can apply to the matter as skilled and prudent men of affairs."

And that's as detailed as it went.

The Needham of Nugan Hand Needham was John Charles Needham, a Sydney solicitor (lawyer) who quit the bank after about a year. Needham moved to Queensland (in northeastern Australia), began horse farming, and acquired—apparently from Nugan and Hand—what purported to be a rubber company and a real estate company.

He reappeared in spectacular fashion after the bankruptcy, however, when it turned out that million-dollar "assets" claimed by Nugan Hand were in fact IOUs (of a variety known in Australia as "bills of exchange") issued by the rubber and real estate companies while they were under Needham's control. The rubber and real estate companies refused to honor the IOUs, which proved basically worthless.

Needham steadfastly refused to make himself available for interviews for this book. He told the Stewart Royal Commission (it said) that the IOUs had been issued in exchange for loans from a Nugan Hand affiliate. But he also said that he had sold the rubber and real estate companies by 1979.

Who then became responsible for repayment of the IOUs? The Stewart commission either didn't ask Needham, or didn't record his answer. The commission did say Needham had stopped practicing law in 1979, and that he had served as a director and meeting chairman for the Nugan Group fruit company during its time of trouble in 1977.

In the late 1970s, Nugan Hand pledged the IOUs issued by the rubber and real estate companies for substantial credit with a large Hong Kong bank, which eventually went to court claiming it had been swindled. But no one was ever able to tie Needham to Nugan Hand's fraudulent use of the IOUs his companies had issued, and he was never criminally charged. Long efforts in court by the liquidator John O'Brien and the Hong Kong bank to get cash for the IOUs proved fruitless. All the bank could get were some stock shares in the questionable rubber and real estate companies.

The five original stock shares in Nugan Hand Needham Ltd. were recorded as having been distributed to Frank Nugan, Mike Hand, John Needham, the accountant Brian Calder, and Pat Swan—certainly by then Nugan's secretary and administrative assistant. Needham's resignation was recorded June 28, 1974, and Calder's November 25, 1974. There is no record of what capital Needham or Calder may have contributed or withdrawn.

Nugan and Hand later told the public that the bank was started with $1 million paid-in capital, contributed $500,000 by each of them, with the stock divided between them 50–50. Testifying at the inquest, though, Hand told a different story. Nugan had put up the whole original $1 million from his mining stock profits, Hand said, and had awarded Hand 50 percent of the stock—or maybe only 49 percent—for the time and effort Hand would put in. But, if you believe him, there weren't any formal records of their arrangement.

By the late 1970s, Frank Nugan was calling himself, in the words of his brother Ken, "one of the wealthiest men in Sydney. He made his money out of the mining boom." Frank's wealthy lawyer friend, Paul Lincoln Smith, says, "I never did any business with Frank. We didn't need each other. He was rich and I was rich. People who have money don't often do business with each other. We're looking for people with propositions. He was very excited about Nugan Hand."

At a meeting of Nugan Hand's executive staff in October 1979, Bernie Houghton gave a speech recalling the start of the bank. There were nearly two dozen people present, including Admiral Yates, General Manor, just-retired CIA deputy director for economics Walter McDonald, and still White House and Pentagon advisor Guy Pauker. To everyone's later embarrassment, Houghton's speech, like others at the gathering, was recorded.

Said Houghton, "My approach is, people will always say Nugan Hand is a Vietnam bank and you go through a variety of things like this and I say, 'No.' The genesis of it was a movement of bonds, or trying to be helpful, for people out of Southeast Asia during the Vietnam War, so that they needed to buy property and they needed to buy gold and they needed to put their money on deposit and they couldn't have it up in Thailand or Laos or Cambodia or Vietnam, so one thing led to another and the company determined that it needed to have a bank, and then not one bank but two, three and four, and one thing led to another."

What exactly did he mean? Especially interesting is the use of the word "company." If that word refers to Nugan Hand itself, the word is used strangely, because Nugan Hand from the beginning *was* a bank; the original brochure says, on its cover, "Nugan Hand Needham Limited/Australia/Investment Bankers," and nothing more. On the other hand, as almost every reader of spy literature knows now, people working for the CIA often refer to it as "the Company."

Among those who have wondered exactly what Houghton meant were investigators from the Commonwealth/New South Wales Joint Task Force on Drug Trafficking. They, alone, are on record as having asked him, in their interview in Acapulco, June 9, 1981.

Houghton—whose obvious goal throughout the interview was

damage control—told the investigators: "Before the formation of the bank, Mike Hand was selling gold and real estate in Vietnam, I should say to people, expatriates, who were in Vietnam or Thailand. Apparently at that time the need for such a merchant bank became apparent to Mike Hand and Frank Nugan."

Further trying to explain the 1979 remarks, Houghton added that "although the transcript is ambiguous, this is in effect what I was trying to say. Also, I was attempting to convey that the word 'Nugan Hand,' although sounding like a Vietnamese name, was not a Vietnamese name or bank. The bank was not set up specifically for the purpose of dealing with the people in Vietnam, Thailand and Laos and it was not my intention to say that at that meeting. However, there is no question that those were also opportunities that would be available to the bank."

Few records have been found relating to the bank's activities during its first eighteen months. It solicited depositors and tax clients (who were usually told to become depositors). The office was still being used to sell development lots.

Expansion began in mid-1974. As Needham and Calder left the firm, some important people joined. A hard-sell mutual fund, the Dollar Fund of Australia, had stopped redeeming its shares in July 1974, and within a few months some of its sales force had taken jobs with Nugan Hand. They would provide the key sales personnel in Nugan Hand's own overseas expansion.

On August 2, 1974, Hand, Nugan, and a man named Douglas Philpotts legally incorporated Nugan Hand, Inc., in Honolulu, Hawaii—apparently the first overseas branch. Philpotts was (or quickly became) vice-president of Hawaiian Trust Company, a major Honolulu bank. By the end of the year, Nugan Hand, Inc. had a substantial account in Hawaiian Trust Company.

Records obtained by Australian investigators after Nugan Hand's collapse showed that in October and November 1974, loans were made from the account—$23,500 to Nugan, $30,000 to a George Ibrahim Chakiro, $25,450 to a Robert W. Lowry of whom no more is known, and $9,600 to a Kiowa Bearsford, another unidentified character. The loans were at rates of 5 to 5¾ percent interest. Where the money came from to fund the account has never been learned. Philpotts has rebuffed every effort to talk to him about it, saying client affairs are confidential.

In January 1975, there were two critical moves. Clive Collings, known as "Les," one of the big performers from Dollar Fund of Australia, went to Hong Kong to open the second Nugan Hand branch out of Australia. And Michael Hand left, to go fight "Communism" in Africa. He pictured himself as restless, wanting to leave his desk and neckties behind for new challenges in exotic places.

To friends, he complained that the Labor Party government of then Australian Prime Minister Gough Whitlam was stifling for business and freedom in general. It was part of a worldwide leftist tide that Mike Hand sincerely believed had to be stopped. Hand talked of places where combat, which he so dearly loved to reminisce about, was still going on against movements he called Communist.

No one who knew Mike Hand was left to doubt his opinions of Communism. But from remarks made by Houghton, and from the prior activities of Hand himself, we can conclude that Hand contemplated the money to be made from such combat as well. To many people, and there is every reason to believe Hand was one of them, the freedom to gather money as they choose is what anticommunism is all about.

During his testimony at the inquest, Hand insisted that when he left in 1975, he had thought he was permanently severing all relationships with Nugan Hand. "I wrote him [Nugan] a resignation on each and every company that I was a director of, and signing over all my powers, etc., to him," Hand testified. "Frank Nugan . . . made an agreement with me when we had separated company that he was going to pay me out for my time and effort, what he could afford over a period of years, when we had separated company on January 10, 1975." Hand said he turned back all his stock.

Interestingly, there are no documents to corroborate Hand's story. No documents remain of any legal separation of Hand from his partnership with Nugan, or from the bank, which continued to call itself Nugan Hand Ltd. Hand did indeed take off for fifteen months, and certainly visited some exotic places. But he returned to Australia during that time, and was in regular touch with the office.

It was an eventful period, politically. There is much evidence that throughout it, Hand continued to work for the bank. There is also enough evidence to have set some people wondering as to whether, in addition, he might have been working for another, higher authority.

Before turning for a while to political concerns, it is worth addressing again the question: Where did the Nugan Hand Bank get its money? The drive to provide an answer, spurred in part by Nugan's and Hand's early claims that they had $1 million or $2 million behind them, has helped perpetuate the myth about mining and real estate profits, and has even spawned speculation that the CIA might have bankrolled them.

In truth, there is no reason to believe they needed much of an initial bankroll. They created some paperwork to make it appear they were injecting capital, but this was clearly a sham. Nugan wrote a check to the company, and then, to cover it, purported to borrow back the money. The result was a simple check kite.

As the Stewart Royal Commission correctly notes, "Mr. Nugan had less than $20,000 in his bank account at the time when he purported to write a check for $980,000. . . . Nugan Hand Ltd. had only $80 in its account when a check was drawn on that company in the same amount. . . . Throughout the life of the company the only money ever in fact paid for shares out of funds belonging to either Mr. Nugan or Mr. Hand and actually received by the company remained at $105."

The question of how Nugan Hand got its money, meaning its seed capital, fades before the real question of how Nugan Hand got its money *after* it started. And the answer is that no investment profits, or CIA subsidies, were required.

The money came mostly in two ways: from high fees charged for performing illegal (or at least very shady) services, and from the fraudulent procurement and subsequent misappropriation of investments from the public.

CHAPTER SEVEN

Terrorists and Patriots

The United States Central Intelligence Agency's main work, as President Truman envisioned it when he set it up, is keeping the president accurately informed about the world forces he must deal with. Yet the CIA seems perennially distracted from this mission by its embroilment in covert operations.

This obsession with political activism tends to dam up the best channels of information, and bias the remaining ones. Worse still, operations seem to be self-perpetuating. Instead of achieving their objectives, they wind up causing so much inadvertent damage to American interests that new operations are constantly being dreamed up to try to straighten out the results of the old ones.

Of examples, 1975 offered more than its share. President Gerald Ford, with his relative lack of experience in foreign dealings, was mesmerized (as was most of the press and public) by the supposed expertise of that most unshrinking of all violets in the field of foreign intervention, Secretary of State Henry Kissinger.

Both the Director of Central Intelligence, William Colby, and the deputy director of the CIA's covert action division, Theodore G. Shackley, were men after Kissinger's own heart. Neither of these top spooks—both of whom were about to become involved in the Nugan Hand scandal—had, in his career, shown any reluctance to shed American or foreign blood in covert military operations as a means to carrying out their assignments.

The most prominent of these assignments had been gory and

monumental failures. The first was to replace Fidel Castro with a friendly and popular government in Cuba. (This was Shackley's job during the 1960s, running an anti-Castro terror program called JM/WAVE.) The second assignment was to ensure that the Communist government of North Vietnam did not spread its influence over South Vietnam and the rest of Indochina. (This was first Colby's, then Shackley's task, as CIA station chiefs in Saigon.)

The results of Colby's and Shackley's terrorist tactics in accomplishing these missions speak for themselves. Castro and Ho Chi Minh were not thwarted. Instead, they were handed victories over a foreign invader, the United States, that solidified popular support for their otherwise vulnerable socialist governments.

Beyond creating political enemies abroad, the CIA's Cuban and Indo-chinese operations were distinguished by the seemingly endless number of thugs and dope dealers on whom they bestowed the legitimacy of U.S. Government service. The Vietnam War dope connection has already been discussed in these pages.

In south Florida, by the 1970s, police could scarcely arrest a dope dealer or illegal weapons trafficker without encountering the claim, often true, that the suspect had CIA connections. Perhaps the largest narcotics investigation of the decade, the World Finance Corporation case, involving scores of federal and state agents, had to be scrapped after a year because the CIA complained to the Justice Department that a dozen top criminals were "of interest" to it.*

All this accomplished by 1975, more work lay ahead. There are two well-known missions that the Kissinger-Colby-Shackley team undertook that year: first, making sure that friendly governments stayed in power over the long term in Iran and Afghanistan, and second, making sure that a Soviet-allied government did not come to power in Angola when Angola achieved independence from Portugal.

Obviously, the "success" of these missions fairly rivaled that of the Cuban and Vietnamese campaigns. In both the Iran and Angola disasters, Nugan Hand played a demonstrable, though relatively minor, role, according to the findings of the Commonwealth/New South Wales Joint Task Force on Drug Trafficking.

*Assertions made in this section are all documented at length in *Endless Enemies.* I regret any annoyance created by these references to a prior book. They are here not for self-promotion, but to assure the reader that certain strong statements made here as background to the Nugan Hand affair are not being made without proper documentation. It seems silly to repeat tangential details in this text that are available elsewhere, but the reader should be assured that they exist.

It's also been discussed that there may have been a third operation that year, and that Nugan Hand may have played a role in that, though it's never been demonstrated. This third operation would be the overthrow of the Labor government in Australia, which fell to a highly unusual legal coup in November 1975.

Speculation about U.S. and Nugan Hand roles in the Australian coup have been fueled by the known attempts of both the United States and Nugan Hand to interfere in Australian politics during the 1970s, and by the fact that Shackley, the covert operations chief and later a Nugan Hand character, struck out vigorously against the Labor government a mere three days before it fell.

Nugan Hand's known role in U.S. intelligence activities in 1975–76 was played out through the star-crossed marriage of a career CIA officer named Edwin Wilson and a special U.S. intelligence unit known as Naval Task Force 157.

The one best metaphor for the distance U.S. foreign policy has strayed from its constitutional purposes in the latter half of the twentieth century is that the profession founded by Nathan Hale has produced an Edwin Wilson. When a federal judge finally put Wilson away in 1983, probably his only regret was that he had but one life sentence to give for such betrayal.

Wilson joined the CIA in the 1950s, and over the years established a reputation as a tough, fearless, independent field operative. Those were qualities that earned him respect and loyalty among other operatives. No one knew him really well, but in the clandestine services that was merely one more virtue. A veteran of CIA covert activity around the world, he was certainly the kind to appeal to his superior, Ted Shackley, whose closeness and loyalty to Wilson helped prove Shackley's undoing.

In 1971, Wilson "retired," in official parlance, from the CIA. Coincidentally, the official account goes, he went to work that same year as a civilian employee of Naval Task Force 157. Throughout his service with 157, however, he continued to converse regularly about matters of business not only with Shackley but with two active-duty CIA field officers, Patry E. Loomis and William Weisenburger.

These CIA contacts have prompted speculation—so far, it's only that—that Wilson was planted by the CIA as a mole inside Task Force 157, a rival U.S. intelligence agency. (Such interagency spying wouldn't be unprecedented; from 1970 to 1972, navy Yeoman Charles Radford was planted as a mole on the clerical staff of the National Security Council, and secretly delivered more than five thousand of Henry Kissinger's staff papers on peace talks and other matters secretly to Admiral Thomas Moorer, chairman of the Joint Chiefs of Staff.)*

The independent existence of a unit like Naval Task Force 157 is in itself a testament to the CIA's misuse. The reason the task force was created was that the CIA's involvement with covert operations had handcuffed the agency in doing its original and necessary work—gathering and transmitting intelligence.

Instead of fulfilling its intended and proper mission, the CIA spent its time organizing and maintaining full-scale armies fighting wars in various parts of Africa, Asia, and Latin America; promoting economic havoc here and there in all three regions; attempting to bring down foreign governments (those of Guatemala, Nicaragua, Chile, Zaire, Zambia, South and North Vietnam, Iran, Afghanistan, Albania, Cambodia, Laos, Brazil, Guyana, the Dominican Republic, Angola, Cuba, Lebanon, Indonesia, and China, to name a few publicly documented cases) and often succeeding; bringing about the death of any number of foreign heads of state (Lumumba, Diem, possibly Allende) and hundreds of thousands of other foreign political figures (the deaths in Indonesia alone might justify that number); reporting on the domestic political activities of U.S. citizens; and carrying out other assorted adventures. With all that activity, the CIA has understandably become not much more clandestine than any other branch of government, maybe less so.

In need of the kind of low-profile, workaday spies that the CIA was supposed to provide, the government was obliged to set up a supersecret task force under the Office of Naval Intelligence. Starting slowly in the mid-1960s and named after something so arbitrary as the room number of someone's office, Task Force 157 quietly gathered information about maritime affairs all over the world. It paid particular attention to the activities of the Soviet Navy and the movement of nuclear cargoes, but also kept tabs on cargo movements in general.

Partly because it was small and self-contained, the task force developed such a secure system of coded communications that Kissinger himself came to prefer it to standard embassy transmittals when he wanted to send messages to the White House while visiting foreign dignitaries. The 157 communications system was used for arranging his secret mission to China before President Nixon reopened relations with the Chinese.

To facilitate 157's work, the navy allowed the men and women

*See Seymour M. Hersh, *The Price of Power.*

who did the spying to set up business fronts on their own and to recruit foreign nationals as agents. Says one former 157 operative,* "My job was to find out what the Soviet Navy was doing here, here, and here [pointing to locations on a make-believe map]. I had a great deal of leeway in how to go about it. If I wanted to set up a shipping company, I became president of a shipping company." Beginning with about thirty naval officers and seventy civilian spies, its payroll grew to include more than eight hundred human sources of intelligence.

There is no record of 157's ever engaging in any covert operations to change the events it reported on. Admiral Thomas H. Moore, then chief of naval operations, says that during the Vietnam War the task force penetrated the North Vietnamese transport industry and provided precise shipping schedules that helped plan the mining of Haiphong harbor. But 157 didn't get involved in the mining; it merely produced an accurate schedule of ship traffic.

Indeed, from all one can learn about it, Naval Task Force 157 seems to have been the very model of the kind of intelligence agency the United States needs—until CIA cowboy Ed Wilson got into it.

Exactly what Wilson's circumstances were before he joined the task force, and exactly what job he had there afterwards, aren't clear. For obvious reasons, the officials who ran 157 have tried to minimize his role, to say he was just one agent in the field and had no influence in central planning or operations.

That explanation is suspect, however. Unlike other 157 agents who were scattered to port towns on all the seven seas, Wilson's field office was in downtown Washington. Rather than found a little dockside expediting company in Copenhagan or someplace, as other agents did, Wilson founded a roster of shipping companies and international consulting firms.

His associates in these firms included some big names, like Robert Keith Gray, President Eisenhower's appointments secretary and now an influential Republican Party figure who served in 1981 as co-chair of the Reagan inaugural committee.** The clients of Wilson's front companies included such firms as Control Data Corporation.

Some say Wilson was used by 157 as a specialist in procuring

*One of many the author interviewed, who agreed to the interviews on condition their names not be disclosed.

**Gray told *Inquiry* magazine in November 1981 that he didn't know his name appeared on the board of directors of a Wilson company. But Wilson's biographer, Peter Maas *(Manhunt,)* established close personal and professional links between the two.

fancy spy gear (unusual boats, or electronic equipment, for example) for its worldwide needs. Others say his specialty was setting up corporate covers for others to use. Witnesses say he showed up only occasionally at 157 headquarters. It is hard to believe, however, that his bosses at 157 weren't aware—as so many others in Washington were—that Wilson, who was paid less than $35,000 a year for his spy work, lived as a multimillionaire on a fabulous estate he had recently acquired in Virginia.

On this estate, valued at $4 million, he regularly entertained senators (Hubert Humphrey, Strom Thurmond, John Stennis) and numerous Congressmen, generals, admirals, political officials, and senior intelligence officers (such as Ted Shackley). It soon became public record that Wilson was selling his services for high fees to companies or foreign governments that wanted help obtaining U.S. Government contracts or weapons.

The denouement occurred in February 1976. Admiral Bobby Ray Inman, recently returned to Washington to run the Office of Naval Intelligence, recalls he was lunching with a staff member of the late Arkansas Senator John McClellan's appropriations committee. Unexpectedly, another member of Senator McClellan's staff arrived with Ed Wilson.

According to Inman, Wilson promptly announced that he could influence appropriations bills for the navy if more business went to his companies. Then, Inman says, Wilson added, "By the way, I work for you," and explained that he ran fronts for Task Force 157.

Inman says he was "absolutely astounded" when he learned that Task Force 157 operatives could run their own businesses on the side, and a week later arranged another meeting with Wilson. He says Wilson urged him to set up an independent intelligence program for Wilson to run, and then invited Admiral and Mrs. Inman to a Sunday lunch at his estate. Inman says he phoned 157 immediately and ordered that Wilson's contract not be renewed when it came up that spring.

When the task force's own budget came up for renewal in 1977, Inman simply scrapped the operation. He says the reason was that overall budget cuts forced him to use the naval officers employed by 157 in other jobs. Wilson, who was already under investigation by the Justice Department, couldn't have been out of Inman's mind, however.*

*The shutdown of 157 provoked such bitterness among former civilian members of the task force that many sued the government claiming that their job rights

Inman went on to become deputy director of the CIA. He resigned soon after President Reagan took office in 1981 (some say so he would be a better candidate for CIA director in a future Democratic administration). He took a job running a computer consortium headed by Control Data Corporation.

Three former 157 operatives, including Thomas ("Smoke") Duval, who helped organize the task force and run it, left government service to take jobs with Wilson himself.

Wilson kept running the maritime and consulting companies that he had created as fronts for Naval Intelligence. These companies, originally U.S. Government creations, continued to be regarded as such by outsiders even after Task Force 157 had secretly gone out of business.

Wilson continued to swap information regularly with Shackley. He hired some CIA personnel. Though most were formally retired, two CIA men—Pat Loomis and Bill Weisenburger—moonlighted for him while still officially on active duty. Among other things, they tipped him off to the equipment needs of foreign governments, so Wilson could steer his corporate clients toward the contracts to supply the equipment.

Wilson's associates later claimed they thought he was still working for the agency. Whether this is because he had created a clever ruse, or because the associates needed an alibi for their own illegal behavior, or because he really *was* still working for the agency (or maybe some faction within the agency), is nothing you'd want to bet the ranch on.

But in September 1976, one former CIA analyst who had gone to work for Wilson, Kevin Mulcahy, developed serious qualms about what Wilson was doing. Mulcahy called headquarters and asked if Wilson's operation really was agency-approved.*

What finally drove Mulcahy to question Wilson's bona fides was seeing Wilson export high explosives and other dangerous weapons to Libya. Using a company Mulcahy was titular president of, Wilson

---

had been violated. In order to preserve the secrecy of 157, the navy refused for a while to acknowledge that its civilian members had ever been employed there, causing them problems in claiming government pension and pay rights and in getting new jobs.

*Mulcahy's story was revealed in a stunning series of articles by Seymour Hersh in the *New York Times,* June 14–21, 1981. Even before Hersh's stories ran, the *Boston Globe* team of Stephen Kurkjian and Ben Bradlee had exposed the gist of what Wilson was doing. I talked to Mulcahy many times after those articles appeared, confirming them and additional information.

had provided Libyan President Muammar Qaddafi with heat-seeking ground-to-air missiles of a type that could shoot an airliner out of the sky, and training programs covering "espionage, sabotage and general psychological warfare."

Mulcahy also learned that Wilson was carrying out assassinations in his spare time, mostly for Qaddafi, but also out of pique. For example, Wilson bombed a car owned by a Paris merchant who Wilson believed had gypped him on an order of wool uniforms six or seven years earlier—when Wilson would have been a full-time CIA officer. Mulcahy later said the merchant's wife had been killed in the bombing (Hersh's report says severely injured); the merchant escaped.

Having decided to check on Wilson, however, Mulcahy evidently picked the wrong CIA officer to call: Ted Shackley. Shortly after Mulcahy had gone to work for Wilson, Wilson had brought him with great show to Shackley's house. There, Mulcahy said, they discussed Wilson's forthcoming meeting with Qaddafi in Libya, and Wilson's efforts to get a U.S. Government export license for some high-grade communications gear Wilson wanted to sell abroad. Mulcahy figured that with Shackley's senior position in the agency and his obvious familiarity with Wilson, he would be the right person to go to.

Instead, Shackley's noncommittal response over the phone was so alarming to Mulcahy that he reported it to the FBI and to an old friend who still worked in the CIA. Immediately after placing these three "confidential" calls to government officers, he said, Wilson fired a message from overseas telling him to "shut up" and "knock it off." Mulcahy went into hiding under an assumed identity.

Wilson's friend Shackley hadn't even reported Mulcahy's call at the CIA.*

*In several places in this passage I have stuck very close to the language of Hersh's articles simply because that language apparently passed the scrutiny of all involved.

In preparing this material, and other material in this book about Shackley, I tried relentlessly to talk to him about all of it. My calls to him were returned at times by a Barbara Rosotti (spelling phonetic) and at times by a Ken Webster, each of whom insinuated without quite saying so that she or he was Shackley's lawyer. They insisted that their relationship with Shackley could be disclosed only under an agreement that it would not be reported. Each offered to supply me with the "facts" only if I would accept these "facts" completely off the record, without letting the reader know anything about the source of them. Never having taken any other information under such a stricture, I declined. But I offered literally dozens of times to discuss everything either with Shackley himself or with any authorized spokesman; I was denied access to anyone who would so identify himself.

After the Justice Department finally began investigating Wilson, it gathered more material, showing that Wilson and another former CIA officer, Frank Terpil, for very large fees had also supplied Qaddafi with a laboratory that turned out sophisticated assassination gear, and bombs disguised as household trinkets using plastic explosive that could slip through airport metal detectors. Wilson and Terpil were hiring anti-Castro Cubans from Shackley's old JM/WAVE program to assassinate Qaddafi's political opponents abroad.

Then came still more material, showing that Patry Loomis and other Wilson agents were hiring U.S. Green Berets for Qaddafi. Some U.S. Army men were literally lured away from the doorway of Fort Bragg, their North Carolina training post. The GIs were given every reason to believe that the operation summoning them was being carried out with the full backing of the CIA—and they made the transition, just as Mike Hand had gone from the Green Berets to the CIA a decade earlier.

Wilson supplied planes, men, and weapons for Qaddafi's military forays against neighboring Chad and Sudan. Wilson's recruits staffed and trained Qaddafi's air force, and maintained the equipment. Wilson personally is said to have cleared at least $15 million from all this, investing heavily in real estate in the United States and England.

In 1982, Paul Cyr, a former Energy Department official, told a federal court in Washington that he attended several meetings in the late 1970s between Wilson and Shackley. These meetings, he said, left him with the same impression Mulcahy got watching Wilson and Shackley together: that even after Admiral Inman had separated Wilson from the navy, Wilson was operating with the CIA's okay.*

These conversations with Rosotti and Webster were followed by a letter to me from a Washington lawyer, J. Patrick Hickey, who referred to Shackley as "our client." Hickey's letter showed a familiarity with at least parts of my conversations with Rosotti and Webster. The letter said that the "Australian-New South Wales Joint Task Force" had "informed us" that Shackley wasn't suspected by the task force of having violated any laws. The letter accused me of having "despite several requests . . . failed to provide us with the substance of other comments you may be including with regard to Mr. Shackley and have thereby deprived him of the opportunity to correct possible inaccuracies."

I immediately wrote to Mr. Hickey objecting to his mischaracterization of my conversations with Rosotti and Webster, and offering again to talk to Shackley or an identifiable, authorized spokesman. I got no reply. After that, substantial material about Shackley derived from the work of the Commonwealth/New South Wales Joint Task Force on Drug Trafficking and other material appeared under my byline in the *Wall Street Journal,* and to my knowledge nothing further was heard from Hickey, Shackley, or the others.

*Cyr made these statements as he was about to be sentenced for the crime of taking between $3,000 and $6,000 in bribes from Wilson for introducing some

Whether or not people were correct in the implications they drew from the Wilson-Shackley connection, it is a sad commentary on what our irrational, undiscerning war against a vague "Communist" menace has done to American values. People everywhere accept it as perfectly plausible that the United States Government is routinely engaged in secret, highly illegal, absolutely stomach-turning activities, with profits to be pocketed privately along the way. Unauthorized crimes have become hard to distinguish from the authorized ones. You can no longer tell the crooks from the patriots.

For many years after Wilson's transgressions came to the government's attention, no action was taken. Whether this inaction was due to Cold War politics, ineptitude, or some other reason can only be wondered at. Meanwhile, Wilson continued to operate.

His deals proved especially ironic under the Reagan administration. It served the administration's propagandistic purpose to hold up the bloodthirsty Qaddafi as the leading example of Soviet-orchestrated world terrorism. According to Reagan White House pronouncements in 1981, Qaddafi's violence was made possible by the help of Russians, East Germans, North Koreans, and Cubans.

But all the time the administration was delivering that line, it had evidence that Qaddafi's violence—from his repeated invasions of neighboring Chad to his assassination attempts against political enemies in the United States and elsewhere—was instead made possible by the men of the United States Central Intelligence Agency.

It should come as no surprise that slime like Edwin Wilson and Bernie Houghton should, at some point along the line, have met and found a common bond. Though Houghton has denied it, there is evidence that the bond was made while Wilson was still officially in U.S. Government service—and that through it, Houghton helped involve Nugan Hand in U.S. covert activity in southern Africa and Iran.

Energy Department colleagues—procurement officers—to representatives of Wilson's client Control Data Corporation, which wanted to sell computers to the government; the company wasn't charged with any crime. Judge John H. Pratt evidently accepted Cyr's word about the Shackley connection and its implication of CIA approval for Wilson's operations, because the judge dealt Cyr a particularly lenient probationary sentence.

Wilson met Cyr through the friendship of their children, and, Mulcahy said, "Paul [Cyr] got Ed some contracts." According to Mulcahy, Wilson not only bribed his way into the Energy Department via Cyr, but also sent a paid mole into Army Materiel Command meetings to "find out what kind of stuff the army would be buying."

Later, after Wilson was off the payroll but while he continued to deal with active CIA officers, there were undenied meetings between Wilson, some other officially retired CIA men, and Bernie Houghton, acting for Nugan Hand. The result of these meetings was some strange movements of money around Europe and the Middle East.

Michael Hand's first reported destination when he left Australia in January 1975 was South Africa. To understand what he did, it is necessary to understand, at least briefly, the situation. The bottom half of the African continent in 1975 was teeming with what the U.S. foreign policy establishment contended was the continuing worldwide war over Communism.

Hand quickly journeyed to Rhodesia, where he helped defend the

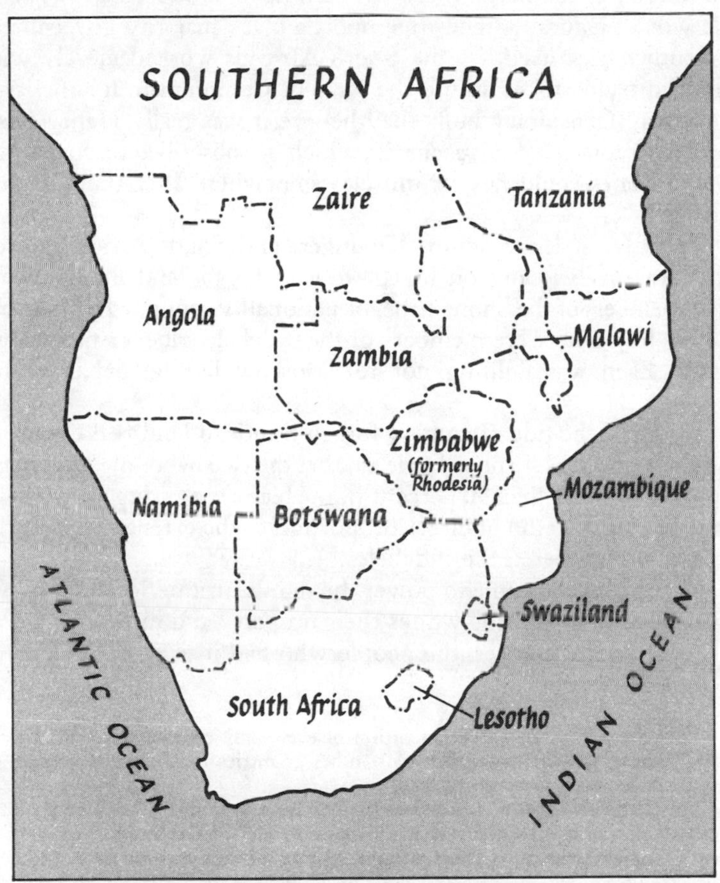

government of Ian Smith, a white man "elected" to his job by a "democracy" in which only the 250,000 whites in the country could vote. Smith's opposition came from two "terrorist" groups who didn't think much of a democracy that excluded the country's six million blacks.

To raise aid from abroad, Smith and his colleagues advertised fiction that the two "terrorist" leaders, Robert Mugabe and Joshua Nkomo, were Soviet agents—split perhaps by a few arcane ideological differences, but both Kremlin-controlled Marxist-Leninists at heart.

Like Smith, the South African Government was also vitally concerned with keeping the black majority out of power in Rhodesia—and the rest of southern Africa. Governments produced by majority rule would, naturally, tend to support a black majority government in South Africa itself. So the South Africans worked closely with Smith in trying to substitute the issue of Communism for the issue of racism. (Conspiracy buffs may believe it was really Henry Kissinger who conceived this scenario, which he subscribed to, so that the United States could flex its muscles somewhere after the Vietnam disaster.)

Publicly, at least, Smith, Kissinger, and South Africa ignored what was really going on in Rhodesia. Mugabe and his followers were members of the Shona tribe, or nationality group, while Nkomo and his followers were members of the Ndebele tribe, or nationality group. Each was fighting not for Moscow but on behalf of his people.

By 1980, the tide of combat forced Smith to hold real elections, and the world was surprised to learn that the two bands of "terrorists" represented more than 90 percent of the black vote. Mugabe won the election over Nkomo in direct proportion to the extent to which the Shonas outnumbered the Ndebeles.

When Mugabe came to power, he didn't turn to Soviet Communism. Instead, he left the whites their property and turned for aid to the most logical sources, the people who had it to give: the United States and Britain.*

*Mugabe did announce the intention of eventually creating the kind of one-party "African socialist" state that most other countries in Africa had created on independence and that many still had.

This "African socialist" system has severely hurt economic development on the continent, but hasn't posed any security threat to the United States. Not only do many of our best friends on the continent operate through the one-party "African socialist" system, but in Zaire and possibly elsewhere the CIA helped install the system! And Mugabe, preoccupied with achieving racial and tribal peace at home

Ironically, it was largely Britishers and Americans who had aided Smith. Some of the aid the Smith regime had received in its fight against Mugabe and Nkomo was given for mercenary reasons, some for ideological. Probably most of the aid, from people like Michael Hand, was motivated by a little of both. But despite the wishfulness of some in Washington, none of the aid to the Smith war machine was ever shown to have come from the U.S. Government.

In Rhodesia, the U.S. Government appeared to have followed, however minimally, the two basic rules for winning friends abroad: we had a strong economy that a foreign country would want to trade with and emulate, and we made sure that the people who came to power there had never been shot at with an American gun.

To the west of Rhodesia (now Zimbabwe), however, the second of these rules was forgotten. In Angola, forces were at work quite similar to those in Rhodesia. Two nationalist groups were fighting a tiny, white-minority government.

There were differences, however. First, whereas the white Smith government in Rhodesia was in outlaw rebellion against its own British colonial roots, the minority government in Angola was still that of the colonial Portuguese. The Portuguese were America's NATO allies. And so, in the case of Angola, the U.S. shunned even the polite cover of official netrality and openly supplied weapons for the suppression of Angolan independence, thus making ourselves the enemy of the Angolan nation.

Further complicating things was the legacy of our earlier interventions in the land just north of Angola, the vast country of Zaire. Through a series of American-run coups, the United States had installed a dictatorial and hugely corrupt one-party government in Zaire, with a nationally controlled, socialist-type economy. The dictator we installed, Mobutu Sese Seko, had a cousin*who aspired to rule Angola, and for many years the U.S. had financed this cousin in the training of an army.

When the Angolan independence movement gained the upper hand in the spring of 1975 (largely with the help of a coup in mother Portugal), the U.S. was stuck with the cousin. It was a classic example of how old covert actions beget new ones.

To excuse its support, first of the Portuguese, then of Mobutu's

---

and good relations with the rich Western countries, put all plans for this system on long-term hold anyway.

*Relationships in African extended families are hard to correlate with Western usage. "Cousin" conveys the idea.

cousin, the U.S. did just what Smith and the South Africans had done in Rhodesia: we created a mythology in which the two tribally based independence organizations were called Communist. On the other hand, the army supported by the socialist dictator Mobutu represented, we said, democracy and free enterprise. These were the players:

MPLA (Popular Movement for the Liberation of Angola), made up mostly of Mbundi tribe members;

UNITA (National Union for the Total Independence of Angola), made up entirely of Ovimbundu tribe members;

Holden Roberto (Mobutu's cousin).

To keep the supposedly Communist MPLA and UNITA out of power, the U.S. launched a direct, U.S.-run military operation in support of Roberto. It was intended to be covert, but by year's end it was all over the newspapers (thanks again to Seymour Hersh and the *New York Times*). Our intervention was described by Kissinger as a response to Soviet and Cuban intervention, but in fact it *preceded* (and could logically be seen as provoking) Soviet and Cuban intervention.*

When Roberto's army crumbled, the CIA began recruiting U.S. and European mercenaries and sending them into Angola to fight. Still, by independence day in November 1975, it was obvious that our force didn't stand a chance against the much bigger Mbundi population of Angola, the MPLA. The other main force, the Ovimbundu—UNITA—sought to wrest power for itself, which was nothing new since the two tribes had fought for centuries over the best farmland. But the MPLA group dominated the capital city, and Mao Tse-tung, an early backer of UNITA, was fading.

Seeing its dream of ruling Angola shattering, UNITA, whose members populated the outlying southern and eastern reaches of the country, struck a desperate bargain with South Africa.

Just as in Rhodesia, the South Africans wanted to prevent a truly representative government in Angola, which might support majority rule for South Africa as well. South African whites figured they could protect themselves by putting a dependent Ovimbundu (UNITA) government in Angola.

Shortly before independence, the South African army began to drive from the south to try to take the capital of Luanda, and put a compromised Ovimbundu (UNITA) government in power. Rather than cave in before an armed invasion from South Africa, the preemi-

*Detailed documentation of these events is given in *Endless Enemies*.

nent Mbundi (MPLA) accepted an offer of Cuban troops to offset the South African troops on the other side. This guaranteed that the Mbundi (MPLA) would accede to power—as an election probably would have established anyway.

So the Mbundi (MPLA) became the government. The Ovimbundu (UNITA) were reduced to an armed guerrilla movement in the outlying regions, lumbered with a humiliating tie to South Africa. And the United States, throwing worse policy after bad, lavished more weapons and mercenaries on the hopeless and discredited third faction in Zaire. We even covertly cooperated with the white South African Government to do so.

Despite this aid, our side was wiped out in early 1976, leaving behind only some U.S. and European mercenaries in Angolan prisons and cemeteries. South African blacks, who would one day run their country, had been given sobering evidence that the United States of America, which should have been their friend, wasn't.*

The Mbundi government in Angola maintained a primary alliance with the Soviet Union, as its only lifeline in a sea of American and white South African hostility. But it was practical enough to maintain commercial ties to U.S. companies, and sell the U.S. Angola's main product, oil—a blessing during the 1979 oil crisis. By the mid-1980s, the Soviets had proven themselves such ill-humored and ill-equipped friends that a U.S.-Angolan deal to the benefit of both countries was still a possibility, even under Mbundi rule.

At any rate, that was the situation into which Nugan Hand inserted itself in 1975: the United States and South Africa were allying to intervene militarily against an Angolan tribe, the Mbundi, that was destined to win control of that country. While the Mbundi represented no security problem whatsoever to the United States, they most certainly did represent a problem to continued racist minority rule in South Africa.

*Trapped by their own predictions about the dire consequences of an MPLA victory, the U.S. foreign policy-makers decided to join league with South Africa in support of the UNITA rebels. This in turn required them to write UNITA's "Communist" origins out of history and to let UNITA wear the mantle of democracy and free enterprise that Mobutu's cousin was no longer able to shoulder. All this has been accomplished under the Reagan administration with a facility Stalin would have marveled at.

CHAPTER EIGHT

Into Africa

Michael Hand laid the groundwork for arms deals before he even left Sydney for South Africa. Or so says Wilhelmus Hans, a fifty-year-old Dutchman who had been hired by Nugan Hand about six months before Hand took off in January 1975.

Hans talked to two investigative bodies the Australian Government assigned to investigate Nugan Hand—the Joint Task Force on Drug Trafficking, and the Corporate Affairs Commission. Both bodies, in their reports, specifically noted that based on much corroborating evidence, they tended to believe Hans, and to disbelieve the former Nugan Hand employes who denied the arms involvement he described. According to Hans, both he and Frank Nugan had been instructed by Hand to check out sources for military weapons.

The Corporate Affairs Commission found a handwritten note from Hand to Nugan, dated January 12, 1975, located in a file entitled "South Africa." According to the commission's 1983 report, "Mr. Hand was concerned that a project in which he was involved was against United States law, and requested that his name be removed from the records of Nugan Hand in Hawaii so that he would not have to include bank account details in United States taxation returns." It was and is illegal for U.S. citizens, no matter where they live, to help arm the white South African Government.

After Hand reached South Africa, he phoned back to Nugan to discuss arms deals. The evidence is in handwritten notes of Nugan's, found in undestroyed files after his death, some of which were apparently taken during a phone call from Hand. The notes read:

Military Weapons Rhodesia
Pay in Gold
Recoilless Rifles
Mortars 60/80 ml
M79 Grenade launches [*sic:* "launchers"?]
Quad 50 Calibre machine guns

It would be significant, of course, if it were shown that the United States Government cooperated with South Africa in the war against majority rule in Rhodesia (now Zimbabwe). The timing of the action, however, exactly coincides with the CIA's raising of arms and men on the black market for the intervention in Angola.

Another set of Nugan's handwritten notes in the "South Africa" file had, on one side, apparent jottings of a telephone talk with Hand, and on the other, some instructions to Les Collings, the head of the new Hong Kong office, for carrying out Hand's proposals. The notes detail Hand's ability to obtain Rhodesian ivory. The front contains such phrases as "Ex factory . . . ship self . . . expecting phone call . . . in Les Collings . . . referred by Hand . . . can send for inspection . . . to be sold in two lots 8,000 kilos each mixed . . . Estimates $22/$23 Rhodesian/$40 US approx per kilo."

The back says:

"Les [underlined]
(1) HK [Hong Kong] importer of hand guns or sporting fire arms Singapore
(2) NHHK [Nugan Hand Hong Kong] Ltd. purchases hand guns direct from US for re export SE Asia
(3) Charter planes capable of flying one ton or less to S.A. [South Africa] 100 lbs
Initial under 100
3 brand names
Smith & Wesson   Colt   Ruger
All models .357 magnum   .44 magnum
In 4 and 6 inch barrels   50/50
Some ammunition for each [indecipherable word]
1,000 rounds per gun

The re-exporting from the United States to Singapore to South Africa in small lots via chartered planes would lead anyone to suspect that something illegal was being attempted. But the notes in the file were far from conclusive, and the U.S. Government basically wasn't helping. (O'Brien, the Corporate Affairs Commission, and the Joint Task Force all complained of across-the-board stonewalling by American authorities.)

In their attempts to follow this up, Australian investigators questioned their star Nugan Hand witness, George Shaw, who recalled dealings with a Sydney outfit called the Loy Arms Corporation. Shaw hadn't been involved in the details. But Loy's proprietor, Kevin Joseph Loy, acknowledged he had been approached by Wilhelmus Hans on behalf of Nugan Hand. In fact, a search of Loy's records produced copies of a weapons import permit from South Africa, dated September 18, 1975, another import permit from Singapore dated November 4, and an Australian export permit dated November 10—all involving weapons, but the lists not identical.

Loy insisted that although Hans had discussed all sorts of new weapons, Nugan Hand placed an order for the export to Singapore of only ten used pistols. His records did include a copy of a letter he sent to Nugan Hand November 14, 1975, referring to Smith & Wesson and Colt revolvers. It said, "On information available we would hope to supply approximately 20,000 weapons per year of the two above mentioned brands." Loy said the order had never been placed.

Soon after the Corporate Affairs Commission visited him, the commission's report says, Loy closed his long-standing arms business and became unfindable.

The trail then led to Wilhelmus Hans, who reported that Hand had telephoned and telexed long lists of weapons and desired small aircraft, from both South Africa and Rhodesia. As a result, Hans told investigators, "I wrote to every gun manufacturer in the world asking for brochures and price lists." Hans said he forwarded the information he received to an eager Hand, whose need for weapons was "as many as possible as soon as possible." He remembered that Hand had said Loy, in particular, couldn't supply enough of the right kind of weapons.

Hans told the investigators that on orders from Nugan, he traveled to Africa to meet Hand, who was in Rhodesia with his wife. The mission, as Nugan had described it, was "to assist persons to transfer funds elsewhere through a corporate structure which was not to be entitled Nugan Hand." But Hand instead had talked of setting up a Nugan Hand branch in South Africa, Hans said. He also told Hans of the market for helicopters and guns.

Most interesting, both the Joint Task Force and Stewart Royal Commission (accepting task force data) report that Hans went to Angola and Mozambique on his trip. Both countries—under Portuguese rule and later under their own independent governments—were *extremely* hard to get visas to. (The author of this book was repeatedly denied visas, first as a student/tourist, later as a journalist.) For the Portuguese colonial rulers to have granted Hans entry would be evidence of some sort of special consideration, not necessarily but possibly government sponsorship.

Hans recalled that Hand told him "it was his intention to sell . . . weapons to whites in South Africa and Rhodesia who were concerned at the possibility of civil commotion and that there was a ready market." The Corporate Affairs Commission's report doesn't distinguish between, on the one hand, the suggestion that Hand was catering to the home protection needs of nervous civilians, and, on the other hand, his desire for 60/80 ml mortars, M-79 grenade launchers, recoilless rifles, and .50-calibre machine guns. It does say that Hand discussed with Hans "the establishment of a helicopter squadron in Rhodesia." The Joint Task Force on Drug Trafficking reported that Hand went so far as to set up a company known as Murdoch Lewis Proprietary Ltd. to receive arms in Pretoria.

At bottom, however, Hans denied knowing of any completed weapons deals, and said he dropped out of that end of the business because of squeamishness. Further dealings on weapons, he said, were handled by Frank Ward and George Shaw—both of whom have acknowledged being aware of weapons negotiations by Nugan Hand, but both of whom have denied knowing the result.

Ward did acknowledge to investigators that he had obtained government clearance for the shipment of thousands of rounds of army surplus ammunition to South Africa, but said he "was unable to recall" if the deal went through. Reported the task force, "Ward is simply not telling the truth, or at least the whole truth"; it noted that in 1983 Ward was again under investigation by Australian authorities over arms dealings.*

The scene then shifted to Washington, where task force investigators found some old associates of Edwin Wilson. They did so with the aid of U.S. Justice Department lawyer Lawrence Barcella,

*The investigation resulted in two criminal tax charges against Ward, which, in February 1987, still had not been tried. Most of the findings of the investigation as related to Ward are still classified secret, according to my Australian researcher, Andrew Keenan of the *Sydney Morning Herald.*

who was prosecuting Wilson. For years, until the Stewart Royal Commission got a few other favors, the interviews Barcella arranged stood as the one recorded instance of cooperation between the U.S. and Australian governments in the Nugan Hand investigation.

One star witness against Wilson whom the Justice Department produced was identified in the task force's report only as "J," apparently because Wilson hadn't been tried when the report came out in March 1983, and "J," the witness, feared for his life. But Australian journalist Marian Wilkinson tracked down "J" and identified him as Douglas Schlachter. For years, Schlachter's lawyer said he and his client wouldn't comment on the identification, and that Schlachter was afraid because two other expected witnesses against Wilson had already died mysteriously. Finally, in 1987, Schlachter, living under another name, agreed to meet with a reporter and confirm his story.

Schlachter entered the Wilson mess innocently enough, while repairing engines at his brother's Texaco station in Bailey's Crossroads, Virginia, in 1969; it happened to be Wilson's favorite. Friends say Wilson took a liking to the young man, they became hunting pals, and finally in 1974 Wilson hired Schlachter to work in World Marine, Inc., a Task Force 157 undercover operation Wilson had set up in Washington.

Kevin Mulcahy, the former CIA analyst who served as president of one of Wilson's companies and later blew the whistle on him, said Wilson treated Schlachter "like the son he never had."* Wilson's two real sons "weren't like Doug, who could hunt and shoot," Mulcahy said. He said Wilson gave Schlachter a horse farm, and trusted him with business matters. He said Schlachter had even been seen with members of a Libyan hit team in Europe. "Schlachter was privy to everything Wilson was doing. He'd be a tremendous witness."

The Justice Department thought the same thing, and while waiting to use Schlachter in the Wilson prosecutions introduced him to the Australian Task Force on Drug Trafficking, which was looking into the Nugan Hand affair.

*The information in this paragraph came from an interview Mulcahy gave to agents of the Bureau of Alcohol, Tobacco and Firearms. The information is consistent with what Mulcahy said in interviews with me, but couldn't be confirmed because I obtained the ATF report after Mulcahy's mysterious death in October 1982, outside a Virginia motel room he had rented by the month. His was one of the two mysterious deaths that frightened Schlachter, according to Schlachter's lawyer.

"J"—Schlachter—told the task force investigators that in 1975 or early 1976—while Wilson was clearly still on the U.S. Government payroll with wide discretion to spy as he saw fit—two CIA men based in Indonesia visited the World Marine headquarters in Washington. Schlachter identified the CIA men as James Hawes and Robert Moore, and the task force—through means it never spelled out—confirmed their connection to U.S. intelligence in Indonesia.

The rest of the story was recounted in detail in the task force's official ultimate report to the prime minister of Australia and premier of New South Wales. "Hawes told Wilson that there would be some Australians visiting Washington," the report says. It says Hawes told Wilson the Australians were coming to discuss an African arms deal 'that had to be put together,' " and that "there was also some discussion about Agency [CIA] operations in Indonesia and the name Nugan Hand was mentioned in a general way." Soon afterwards, possibly on their same visit to Washington, Hawes and Moore returned to the World Marine office with Bernie Houghton and two Australians whom Schlachter couldn't name but who he understood represented Nugan Hand.

The official task force report continues:

"There was a number of meetings between Wilson, Houghton and the others over a relatively short period of time. Subsequently, under the cover of Task Force 157, Wilson placed an order for something like '10 million rounds of ammunition, 3,000 weapons including machine guns, M-1s, carbines and others.' The shipment is believed to have left the U.S. from Boston. The End Users' Certificate indicated that World Marine was the U.S. purchasing agent while the middle company or buyer's agent was an Australian company but not Nugan Hand. The name given as the buyer was Portuguese, and was a name that had been used previously and possibly after by World Marine in other unrelated covert operations. 'J' [Schlachter] said that the shipment never formally entered Portugal, but was re-directed to Africa, possibly South Africa, where someone was waiting to receive it. 'J' believes that the weapons were then moved up the African continent and were eventually delivered to U.S. intelligence-supported forces in Angola.

"World Marine paperwork for the transaction was completed and payment for the shipment is believed to have come out of Hong Kong and to have been paid into a Swiss bank," the task force report continues. Throughout the time frame given, the CIA was recruiting men and weapons for its Angolan war, always through private channels. Much of the money was actually being spent on the private market by Holden Roberto, an ersatz Angolan actually from Zaire, who was Zairian dictator Mobutu's cousin, and who was in turn spending money the CIA was giving him for this purpose.

One real disappointment in the Stewart Royal Commission report was its failure to deal substantially with the task force's findings about arms deals. The Stewart commission mentioned the task force findings only obliquely by way of introducing a statement it said James Hawes had made to the Australian Government in response to the task force report. The statement denies that Hawes knew or ever met Houghton, or dealt with Nugan Hand.

The statement doesn't mention Hawes's suggested relationship with the CIA. It tacitly confirms his relationship with Wilson, but says Wilson "never once made any mention of the Nugan Hand Bank or any person who has subsequently been identified or connected with it." The commission apparently never questioned Hawes—for example, about Moore, Schlachter, and Wilson.

The Stewart commission also reported that Houghton had denied meeting Wilson until 1979, and had said the names of Hawes and Moore "meant nothing to him."

Almost incredibly, in reporting "allegations . . . that 'Nugan Hand executives' were involved in weapons shipments to American aided forces in Africa," the Stewart commission listed the source for these "allegations" not as the Joint Task Force, but as *Penthouse* magazine, May 1984!

Ironically, the *Penthouse* article had been excerpted from a book chapter, and both *Penthouse* and the book publisher later conceded that without their knowledge the author had lifted her information, at times almost word for word, straight from the *Wall Street Journal*, which published the first detailed American accounts of the Nugan Hand investigations. Thus the Stewart commission bypassed the task force's formal finding, and the report of the more respected *Wall Street Journal*, and pinned the "allegation" on *Penthouse*, making it much easier to dismiss.*

Without further discussion of specifics, the commission report merely says, "None of these allegations [from *Penthouse* regarding Africa and from other publications regarding other places] fell within

*Both *Penthouse* and the book publisher, Doubleday & Company, issued gracious apologies and published acknowledgments.

the terms of reference [the commission's authority]." Evidently, this meant that the allegations, even if true, still wouldn't involve violation of Australian law, and therefore needn't be looked into. But the commission went on, "However, in the course of examining the material before it, the commission has found that there is not the slightest evidence to support them." The commission didn't mention "J," or Schlachter.*

For his part, Schlachter** differs from the task force report only in that he says the ammunition and the machine guns were shipped separately, and that he was aware of at least three shipments in all, each sent as the task force describes. He says Hawes and Moore were working under cover as telephone systems installers in Indonesia, and regularly visited Wilson at the office of his Navy Task Force 157 front.

Schlachter recalls in vivid detail chauffeuring Hawes, sometimes with Wilson, to CIA headquarters in Langley, Virginia, sometimes accompanying them inside to an office, but then leaving them off and picking them up later in the day. He says Nugan Hand came up frequently between Wilson and Hawes as a financing facility.

The U.S. armed support for the Zairian-backed minority faction in Angola didn't collapse until late February 1976, with the rout of some U.S. mercenaries. The mercenaries had been recruited via local American newspaper publicity by a man named David Floyd Bufkin. Although the CIA "had never signed a piece of paper with him" (according to John Stockwell, the CIA officer who ran the Angolan mission†), Bufkin was transported and instructed by CIA officers who knew everything he was doing, he stayed in CIA safe houses, and was paid by Roberto with CIA money. This kind of practical,

*The commission at times came dangerously close to sophistry to explain away its disinclination to pursue leads. For example, the notes found in Nugan Hand files about an ivory-for-arms trade were summed up as an "allegation . . . that Mr. Hand corresponded with Mr. Nugan from South Africa about arms sales to be paid for with Rhodesian ivory." Without adding any new information, the commission reported, "The only connection between 'ivory' and 'arms sales' arises from Mr. Hans' interview with the Joint Task Force and from the fact that notes on both subjects were made, apparently by Mr. Nugan, on the same sheet of paper. The Commission has not located any correspondence between Mr. Nugan and Mr. Hand in relation to such matters. Accordingly the Commission finds that the allegation is without substance."

**Interviews with the author, February 1987.

†In interviews; Stockwell has provided the best history of the whole Angolan episode in his book, *In Search of Enemies* (1984).

unofficial arrangement illustrates the kind of relationship the CIA has with many cooperating private citizens and may have had with Nugan Hand.

The Joint Task Force report on Nugan Hand continues:

> Whilst there is no known available documentation to support the claims of "J" [Schlachter], there are certainly strong grounds for accepting his claims that a transaction took place. First, the whole of "J" 's circumstances in relation to U.S. enforcement and Justice Department authorities . . . make it highly unlikely that he would lie. [Schlachter had a plea bargain under which he had served about a year in prison, and been released to live with an assumed identity under the government's witness protection program; his only obligation was to testify truthfully, and by lying he could land himself back in the pen.]
>
> At any rate [the task force report continues], there is no known reason for him to lie. Second, there is no reason to believe that "J" knew of the 1975 arms allegations respecting Nugan Hand prior to his interview with the Task Force. Third, the time frame of the incident described by "J" fits neatly with Nugan Hand's known attempts . . . to purchase weapons for that general geographical area. Fourth, the type of weapons nominated by "J" are basically similar to those being sought by Nugan Hand in Australia and elsewhere at that time. Fifth, a connection between "J" and Hawes and Hawes and Wilson has been established, as has a connection between Hawes and Indonesia. Sixth, a CIA or other U.S. intelligence connection between Wilson and Indonesia, and Hawes and Moore has also been established. Seventh, Hand was, during 1975 and until March 1976 waiting in Africa to receive any weapons that could be supplied. "J" said that there was someone waiting there to receive the weapons. Eighth, on five occasions during 1975 and one in January 1976 Houghton departed Australia. On five of those occasions he visited the U.S.
>
> Accepting the probability that the transaction described by "J" was carried out, it remains to be determined on whose behalf. Was it an official U.S. intelligence operation carried out by either the CIA or ONI [Office of Naval Intelligence], or both? Or was it the activity of private entrepreneurs using an available official cover for an operation which was not opposed to prevailing U.S. policy? No assistance was forthcoming from U.S. intelligence or related authorities which might have helped resolve this question. . . . But still there must be an attempt made to resolve the matter.
>
> There is no doubt that Wilson was still officially with Task Force 157 at the time of the arms deal. Certainly "J" [Schlachter]

believes it to have been an officially sanctioned operation, but there are obvious gaps in "J's" knowledge of Wilson's intelligence activity. There is also the strong risk that "J's" perception of the situation was an illusion deliberately created by Wilson to give the impression of an officially sanctioned operation. . . . It is clear that Wilson did act as an individual entrepreneur on other non-Nugan Hand matters whilst in the employ of ONI and when not in the employ of any U.S. intelligence organization purported to be so. Nugan Hand itself, acting for Hand, went about the attempted purchase of weapons in a fashion which displayed little professionalism and a deal of amateurism.

The task force then sets about to give its official conclusions:

In short, it is the view of the Task Force on the available information that in all probability the efforts of Michael Hand to supply weapons to some non government force in Africa—likely Rhodesia or Angola—were successful and that they were provided in the manner outlined by "J." It is likely that the forces to which the weapons were supplid were the same forces to which the U.S. government of the day was offering and providing covert military support.

The final judgment rendered by the task force on the weapons matter must be examined in its wording, for it shows some naivete for how the CIA has actually conducted covert operations over the years. The task force report says, "All things taken into account, the operation is considered likely to have been carried out as a result of private entrepreneurial activity as opposed to one officially sanctioned and executed by U.S. intelligence authorities, specifically Task Force 157."

For those, both Australian and American, who haven't paid much attention over the years to the CIA style, perhaps the main problem in understanding Nugan Hand has been this seeming analytical choice between "private entrepreneurial activity" on the one hand and "officially sanctioned" activity on the other. In fact, the two have never been so clearly distinguished. In phrasing the choice, one may inadvertently rule out what is really the most likely explanation.

Of the many former CIA men who have left the agency and written candidly about their experiences, Victor Marchetti is probably the most relied-on for the versatility of his knowledge of the agency. His accuracy and veracity haven't been challenged. Unlike the other best-known CIA renegade, Philip Agee, Marchetti has clearly spoken out from a desire to help, not hurt, the country.

Marchetti has explained that there are basically three kinds of purportedly private organizations that the CIA relies on in its work. One kind is known as a CIA proprietary—a concern that has been designed to provide some service wanted by the CIA, and is secretly wholly owned by the CIA itself while disguised to appear in public to be a private business. Obviously the CIA hires and could fire the heads of such businesses.

Yet Marchetti's book *The CIA and the Cult of Intelligence,* written jointly with former Foreign Service officer John Marks, says, "For all practical purposes, the proprietors conduct their own financial affairs with a minimum of oversight from CIA headquarters. Only when a proprietary is in need of funds for, say, expansion of its fleet of planes, does it request agency money. Otherwise, it is free to use its profits in any way it sees fit. In this atmosphere, the proprietaries tend to take on lives of their own, and several have grown too big and too independent to be either controlled from or dissolved by headquarters."*

Paul Helliwell's old Sea Supply Corporation was such a company. (It was the outfit designed to supply U.S. "allies" in Southeast Asia, whose guns-for-heroin trade was described in Chapter 3.) Other proprietaries numbered a whole gaggle of CIA-owned airlines, including some in the United States whose growth into the domestic freight market threatened the existence of some free-market competitors.**

A second kind of operation, Marchetti has said, is a "front," an organization whose purported business is a sham, kept in place to provide a cover for other activities. Like the little cargo-expediting companies set up by members of Naval Task Force 157, it offers a place for agents to get mail or phone calls, and provides an answer to otherwise embarrassing questions like, "What are you doing here?" Fronts are less tightly controlled than proprietaries, but can do plenty of damage, as revealed by the activities of the fronts set up by Edwin Wilson for Task Force 157.

*Asked for comment, a CIA spokesman called the Marchetti remarks "way off base," and said, "Any activity with a financial basis is of the nature that CIA would try and keep a hand on it." She said any financial organization is kept close track of. In early 1987, as it is daily revealed that tens of millions of dollars is missing and unaccounted for from accounts created for no other purpose than the direct funding of covert action, and there is evidence that the true figure could be in the hundreds of millions of dollars, such contentions seem ludicrous.

**That situation was exposed by reporter Jerry Landauer in the *Wall Street Journal,* February 16, 1979.

But, as Marchetti explained on Australian radio October 25, 1980, in the wake of the Nugan Hand scandal, "There's a third kind of organization which is really an independent organization, but it is closely allied to the CIA, not only in ideology but because many of the people who work for it are ex-CIA people. They have mutual goals [with the CIA] in some instances, or at least their goals run parallel in some instances. On the other hand, they operate independently.

"This is like Interarms Company," Marchetti said, citing what is probably the world's largest private arms dealer. Interarms operates mostly overseas, but is run by an American, Samuel Cummings—a career CIA officer whom the CIA set up in private business, whereupon he severed his official ties with the U.S. Government. Since then, Cummings has amassed a fortune buying up arms from some governments or private groups and selling them to others around the globe, apparently always in line with the CIA's wishes. Explained Marchetti about Interarms, "Of course it's an independent organization but it's run by a former CIA man, Cummings, and he does favors, or he used to do favors, for the agency and vice versa.

"Nugan Hand, from what I know about it, seems to fall into this latter category," Marchetti said. "It doesn't seem to be a proprietary in the full sense of the word, that is, owned and controlled by the agency, nor does it seem to be a simple front organization. It seems to be more of an independent organization with former CIA people connected with it, and they're in business to make money, but because of their close personal relationship with the agency they will do favors for the agency.

"This," Marchetti said, "would include providing cover in some instances for operators, it would include laundering of money, it would include cutouts for any sort of highly clandestine activity the agency is involved in but does not want to be any way directly connected with. When these organizations cooperate with the agency, the agency uses its influence, both directly within the government and indirectly through other proprietaries and through other friendly organizations within the establishment, to throw business the company's way because they want the company to flower and succeed because it provides good cover for them."

Richard Bissell, who ran the CIA's clandestine services section when Marchetti, Shackley, and Colby all worked there, once said, "It is possible and desirable, although difficult and time-consuming, to build overseas an apparatus of unofficial cover. This would require the use or creation of private organizations, many of the personnel of which would be non-U.S. nationals, with freer entry into the local society and less implication for the official U.S. posture."*

Asked about that on the same Australian radio program, Marchetti replied, "Bissell was making a point that proprietaries were a very dangerous instrument, they're hard to control, they're easy to be exposed. He was advocating the use of private institutions, and he meant not only independent little operations that would get started up and grow into something big, but also banks and other business corporations that had offices overseas, and working through them, putting people into them, and putting . . . people from other countries in as cutouts and agents for the CIA."

Thus it is possible—in fact customary—for a business to be both private, for-profit, and yet also have a close, mutually beneficial relationship with the CIA. The men running such a business are employed exactly as if it were a private concern—which it is. But they may have been steered to their jobs by the CIA, and they never forget the need to exchange favors.

CIA men on covert missions do not identify themselves as such. They know to be aloof even to each other, except as there is a need to know. Those exposed to the culture of spying learn how to interpret the word of members of the spying community, whether active or retired. They know, as any Mafia member does, that the business of the organization cannot always be identified by an official seal. But it can be recognized nonetheless.

It is in this sense that one must judge what Nugan Hand was, and what moral responsibility the United States Government has for what Nugan Hand did.

Victor Marchetti: "If Nugan Hand is what it seems to be, this is just one of the kinds of organizations that Bissell would advocate as being used to facilitate operations overseas. He probably would prefer to be working through First National City Bank, or Chase Manhattan, or something like that, because there it's almost impossible to penetrate the cover. But Nugan Hand, here you have all these CIA people associated with it. You know, it's like they say, if it looks like a duck, and walks like a duck and quacks like a duck, pretty soon you can come to only one conclusion: it is a duck."

*At a discussion on Intelligence and Foreign Policy, January 8, 1968, according to official minutes reprinted in Marchetti's and Marks's book.

Schlachter also told the task force agents that Houghton had involved Nugan Hand to handle "funds" and "payouts" in a U.S. military deal with Iran. "About the same time as the [African] weapons deal," the official task force report continues, attributing this to "J," "the U.S. Navy through Edwin Wilson at Task Force 157, arranged the supply of a spy vessel to Iran. James Hawes [the CIA man], who was still operating out of Indonesia, was also involved. While 'J' did not profess to know the details of the transaction, he said that Wilson had used Task Force 157 proprietary companies to arrange the sale and that the vessel went first to England, before being sailed down the west coast of Africa, around the Cape of Good Hope up to Bondeshipure, Iran, where it was turned over to the Iranian Navy. According to 'J,' at some point in the operation there was a mix up and Wilson flew to Iran to correct it." Schlachter told the investigators that he didn't understand the details of Nugan Hand's role.

The report continues, "Some support for the allegation of 'J' can be seen in Wilson's January, 1976, three-day visit to Australia." Having checked immigration records, the task force learned that Wilson "arrived at Sydney from Indonesia and declared to immigration authorities his intention of staying at the Lakeside Hotel, Canberra. Perhaps coincidence, perhaps not," the report notes, "but Canberra is the center for U.S. political and intelligence authorities in this country. When Wilson departed Australia he traveled to Iran." That was January 31, 1976. He had come into the country January 28.

The investigators report that "further support" for Schlachter's story came from a man whose identity was withheld, who visited Wilson in Virginia during August and September of 1976, and said Wilson left the United States four times in that period. Once, the task force's source said, Wilson "indicated . . . that he was 'going from Switzerland to Iran to sort out some trouble.' "

Next, the task force found an Australian businessman—whose name was also withheld—who told them that on March 8, 1975, he had traveled with Bernie Houghton from Sydney to Iran, returning March 16, 1975. Immigration records confirmed the dates. Furthermore, the businessman said that he and Houghton had been accompanied on this trip by an active U.S. Air Force colonel—name also withheld.

Sure enough, immigration records showed that the colonel had arrived in Sydney from the United States aboard a commercial airliner on March 3, 1975, and left Australia for Iran March 8. The colonel had made one previous visit to Australia, in March

1974, arriving and leaving at the U.S. military air base in Australia.

The local businessman "satisfied the task force" (it said) that he had been going to Iran on business anyway, and that Houghton, learning of this, "volunteered that a close friend of his," the air force colonel, "was well-connected in that country and might well be able to assist." The businessman said Houghton and the colonel, who was expecting to retire in a few years, were looking to make money from a commercial venture, although the businessman said he "didn't properly understand" the details.

"There is every reason to accept that 'J' related events as he understood them to have occurred," the task force reported to the prime minister and premier. "This being so, the probability is that the U.S. Naval intelligence community was involved in the sale of a spy ship to Iran in or around 1975. Bearing in mind 'J's' allegation that Nugan Hand, which term includes Houghton, was involved, it seems a strange coincidence that Houghton's only known trip to Iran occurred within the rather narrow time frame of the spy ship incident. Further, that at such time Houghton should have been accompanied by a senior serving member of the U.S. Armed Services who, according to [the businessman], was well connected in Iran." Thus, the task force suggested, the trip and the spy ship sale were no coincidence at all, but interrelated.

"It is recognized," the report went on, "that Wilson's known visits to Iran do not on the surface coincide with the travel of Houghton, but the reality is that the Task Force does not know how long it took to effect this transaction. Perhaps more than a year was involved. [Or perhaps, one could suggest, more than one ship was involved.] Houghton could have been involved in preliminary negotiations and Wilson in attending to final arrangements. There is no way of knowing how many times Wilson went to Iran in the relevant time frame, or indeed if there was any necessity for him to go there prior to January, 1976. Similarly, Houghton could have travelled to Iran from countries other than Australia, so there is no way of knowing for certain how frequently he visited Iran. Finally, the possibility that Houghton's visit was in no way connected with the spy vessel is not dismissed. However, in the end the allegation contains insufficient detail so far as the involvement of Nugan Hand/Houghton is concerned and insufficient is known of the transaction itself to enable the Task Force to form a view one way or the other respecting that involvement. But as opposed to the [African] arms deal, there seems little likelihood that the spy ship incident could have been carried out as part of private entrepreneurial activity and perhaps this is, on one view, the greatest difference between the two incidents."

The Pentagon's reply to all this is simple and straightforward: "Any sort of a sale of that sort would have been under the auspices of the Naval Intelligence Command, and, of course, their activities are classified," a spokesman says. And he won't comment further.

The Stewart Royal Commission's follow-up was just as uninformative: "Major transactions involving spy ships, aircraft, howitzers, patrol boats and various other military equipment have been suggested. As mentioned, none of these allegations fell within the terms of reference. However in the course of examining the material before it, the Commission has found that there is not the slightest evidence to support them."

And that, apparently, was enough about that.

Iran was to pop up again in the Australian investigation, as evidence surfaced that Michael Hand and others at Nugan Hand had been negotiating to move hundreds of millions of dollars of the Shah's fortune among various embarrassed banks at the time of the Shah's fall from power.

Neither the task force nor the Corporate Affairs Commission saw fit, however, to address what may have been a more pressing question, at least in the minds of most Australians. That was whether the CIA, through Nugan Hand or any other device, intervened in the internal politics of Australia, even to the point of overthrowing the Labor government there in November, 1975.

That both the CIA and Nugan Hand acted to sway Australian politics can be demonstrated. That the efforts were coordinated, or that either the United States or Nugan Hand actually helped overthrow the government, remains a matter of rumor, circumstance, and speculation.

CHAPTER NINE

The Spooking of Australia

In almost the exact center of the vast Australian landmass, far from the population concentrations on the east and west coasts, near the town of Alice Springs, is an American base. Some say it is the most important foreign outpost we have. It is certainly among the most secret.

You would need impressive security clearances to get near it and scientific degrees to understand it. Supplies and personnel are ferried in and out by U.S. military aircraft. It represents a taxpayer investment probably measured in the billions of dollars.

At the base, known as Pine Gap, American personnel read and relay back to the United States data from spy satellites stationed over the Soviet Union, China, and Europe. Through Pine Gap and two related bases in Australia, the United States picks up coded messages from Soviet missile launchings, and intercepts radar, radio, and microwave communications. Greeks have accused the Americans at Pine Gap of listening in on their telephone calls in Greece.

If an arms control agreement is to be reached, the base at Pine Gap, or one just like it, will be indispensable.

Information flows the other way through Pine Gap, too. With its Buck Rogers-style communications gear, the base relays orders from the Pentagon to our nuclear submarine fleet as it moves about, silently threatening to level the Soviet Union whenever it is thought the Soviet fleet is doing the same to the United States.

But as the CIA presence in Australia grew, so did the temptation to manipulate events, even in such a friendly country. In ways, what happened in Australia shows how the productive and the counterproductive sides of the CIA work everywhere. The vital operations at Pine Gap have been threatened by the political resentment of Australians, who, inevitably, learned their democracy was being manipulated.

Australians were suspicious from the founding of the huge Pine Gap base in 1968. They were told the base was part of the United States's space study program, a plausible enough explanation with the lunar landing scheduled for 1969. The sales pitch presented Pine Gap as a means by which Australian scientists might share in the knowledge brought home from galactic frontiers. But the pitch smelled fishy to many people, one of whom, in 1972, was elected prime minister of Australia.

His name was Gough Whitlam, and three years into his prime ministership he was suddenly ejected from office and replaced by the opposition without an election. This was done through an unprecedented, but constitutionally provided-for, maneuver. It would not be going too far to call it a constitutional coup d'etat, and it followed by three days a similarly unusual action by the CIA to halt some things Whitlam was doing.

Whitlam's Labor Party had long doubted the wisdom and morality of America's interventionist foreign policy, not only in Vietnam—the focal point of world attention at the moment—but also in Indonesia (an Australian neighbor the United States had unsuccessfully invaded in 1958 and helped change the government of in 1965) and throughout Asia. In these matters, Whitlam actually stood closer to the United States than many of his Labor colleagues, who, in fact, had criticized his seeming approval of the takeover by Indonesia, with U.S. support, of nearby Timor.

Whitlam was, however, in tune with other Laborites on many issues, including a belief that the Australian people had a right to know if the base operating at Pine Gap would make Australian territory a target in a nuclear war.

Whitlam made the CIA nervous, to say the least. Just as nervous was the Australian Security Intelligence Organization, or ASIO, which had close associations with the CIA. ASIO's franchise to operate domestically as a security organization, which the CIA isn't supposed to do in the United States, gives ASIO more influence in domestic politics than the CIA has.*

*ASIO has a franchise different from the CIA's. It is less concerned with the foreign intelligence and secret operations the CIA handles, and is more concerned

The CIA, with its own political agenda, was all too ready to encourage and assist ASIO's tendency to oppose Labor, and to support the opposition coalition, which was made up of the Liberal Party, which most Americans would think of as conservative, and the Country Party, which is considered farthest to the right.

A CIA document from all the way back in 1949, obtained by Australia's *National Times,* concerns "communist influence in Australia," and says that the "U.S. Naval attaché in Melbourne has reported that the Labor Government is under communist domination, with two Cabinet members probable communists and the Speaker of the House a communist sympathizer." With some reason, the *National Times* calls this claim "wild."

Over the years, CIA and ASIO men have forged links that bypassed the Labor Party, even when it was in power. In 1969, when the CIA's guru emeritus Allen Dulles was in the hospital, the director general of ASIO, C. Charles Spry, wrote him a gushing letter. After reporting his severe distress at having missed "the honour" of a meeting with Dulles on his last trip to the States, Spry says:

> I shall never cease to be grateful to you for the initiation and development of relations between your Service and mine. I consider, without any reservations, that this was the turning point which has enabled ASIO to reach the level of sophistication which it now enjoys. Jim Angleton [then head of counterintelligence for the CIA] and others have continued to assist us. I always consider you as the No. 1 Honorary Australian in our Organization, and Jim No. 2.

Agents from sister branches of Australian intelligence that operate overseas worked with the CIA in Vietnam, Indonesia, China, and Timor, and according to some Australian press reports helped the CIA shuffle governments in Cambodia and Chile as well. A secret report prepared by a senior civil servant at the direction of the Aus-

---

with the counterintelligence function that in the United States is performed by the FBI. As a result, ASIO operates openly within Australia, as the CIA is not supposed to do in the United States (though the CIA has sometimes been caught at it).

The assignment of the FBI rather than the CIA to domestic counterintelligence in the United States is important. Because the FBI is basically concerned with the impartial enforcement of laws, it is a much less politically oriented organization than the CIA or ASIO. If law enforcement is in some ways inclined toward the "tough" attitudes generally associated with the Republican Party, it is also very conscious that it directly benefits from the more open-purse attitudes of the Democrats—including not only social programs that tend to soothe law enforcement's underclass clentele, but also programs that directly funnel money to cops, such as the Law Enforcement Assistance Administration (which the Republicans killed).

tralian Parliament in 1979, also obtained by the *National Times,* says, "Our intelligence partners, notably the U.S., are not very active in the South Pacific and look to Australia and New Zealand in this region."

Meanwhile, the CIA developed close links to the Liberal-Country coalition, and by some knowledgeable accounts funneled cash to it. Through the CIA's long-standing secret cooperation agreement with the AFL-CIO, it had a part in bringing potential union leaders to the United States, training them, and later orchestrating their rise to power. Possibly most insidious, the CIA and ASIO swapped derogatory information they collected on Labor and other politicians in Australia. ASIO, at least, leaked the information to selected political opponents who could make the best use of it.*

So close was the CIA-ASIO connection that some operatives went into undercover work of the most literal kind. John Walker, a career cold warrior who had been entrusted with running the vital CIA station in Israel, was CIA station chief in Canberra during the Whitlam years, from 1972 to 1975, though he was replaced just before Whitlam was removed. During his time in Australia, he and his wife of thirty years got to know Colin Brown, the deputy director of ASIO, and his wife, so well that Mrs. Walker left him for Brown, who divorced his wife and married her.

The original Mrs. Brown later complained** that she knew of her husband's affair early on and wanted to put a stop to it by telling the CIA man, Walker. But she said, "I was told that if I did, it would destroy ASIO's relationship with the CIA." She claimed her thirty-four-year marriage was broken up "in the name of the ASIO/CIA cause."

Walker says† his marriage broke up because of the long hours he was forced to devote to his job. Walker also recalls spending long hours at Bernie Houghton's Bourbon and Beefsteak, insisting, without the trace of a smile, that it was "a good place to eat." Walker, back

*This material summarizes an impressive array of documents uncovered and published over the past five years by the *National Times,* a mainstream weekly published by John Fairfax & Sons, one of Australia's three big publishing empires. Most of the documents are from secret official reports prepared for the Australian Government. Another source for a discussion of CIA-ASIO relations is the booklet *The CIA's Australian Connection* by Denis Freney, a reporter for the openly Communist Australian paper, *Tribune;* but while Freney has compiled a lot of good information, he tends to mix it at will with speculation and with occasional wrong historical facts, and his work needs to be read discerningly.

**In a letter published in the *National Times.*

†Interview with the author.

home now, says Houghton still stops by Walker's New York apartment on trips to the United States and has remained good friends with Walker and his daughter.

The CIA's involvement in Australian politics, which had long been rumored in Australia, became official record in the United States in a startling spy case—the case of Christopher Boyce and Andrew Daulton Lee. Boyce and Lee are now best known as the Falcon and the Snowman, after the title of Robert Lindsey's wonderful book about them and the movie based on it. Childhood friends in southern California, they became a two-man Soviet spy network in the mid-1970s.

Lee was addicted to heroin and other drugs. He needed money, and was mentally deteriorating. But there was no such desperate explanation for the treason of the clean-cut Boyce, an FBI agent's son who began a career with TRW Corporation, a communications company doing contract work for U.S. intelligence.*

So why did Boyce slip documents to Lee for sale to the Soviet embassy in Mexico on Lee's drug runs? The only available explanation is Boyce's own: his alarm, disillusionment, and disgust at what he learned the CIA was doing. And much of this involved Australia—for it was Boyce's job to sit in the communications room of TRW in Redondo Beach, California, and monitor the traffic coming in from Pine Gap.

At their spy trial in 1977, Boyce told of a conversation he had with his old buddy Lee just before they formed their arrangement. They had been criticizing the CIA, among other things blaming it for overthrowing a democracy and installing a dictatorship in Chile in 1973. Relating that to his own drug problems, Lee lashed out at the U.S. Government.

And Boyce responded: "If you think that's bad, you should hear what the Central Intelligence Agency is doing to the Australians." Then, said Boyce from the witness stand, "He asked me what, and I told him that—"

At this point, on a motion from the government, the judge refused to allow the details onto the record. The government tried to keep the Australian secrets as secret as possible throughout the

*Characteristically of such arrangements, TRW says it won't comment on whether it works for the CIA, but if it doesn't, then it's hard to understand what the Russians were paying Boyce for, or why he went to jail.

Boyce-Lee prosecution. But much of the story did get told, partly through the probing of author Lindsey (who is also the *New York Times* bureau chief in Los Angeles).

Among the things Boyce discovered was that Australian labor unions were infiltrated by U.S. agents. The American operatives manipulated the unions on CIA orders to prevent strikes the CIA objected to. Boyce also learned that the United States wasn't disclosing all its Pine Gap activities to the Australians as called for in the treaty that permitted the base.

In fact, he learned, the Australians were being deceived about a whole satellite system that could overhear telephone conversations and other communications in Europe and dump them down to Pine Gap for relay to Washington. All of this soured Boyce on his job and his loyalty to the United States.

In his book, journalist Lindsey even conjectured that information about all this, sold by Boyce and Lee to the Soviet Union in Mexico City, may have been relayed by the Russians to the Labor Party in Australia, and that this information may have touched off the dispute about the CIA that immediately preceded the constitutional coup in Canberra in 1975.

From the Labor Party's electoral victory in 1972, the CIA's allies in Australia were in high dudgeon, and not entirely without reason. Whitlam was no enthusiast for spook work. He quietly closed an Australian electronic spy post that had been operating in Singapore.

By March, 1973, the Laborites had become worried that ASIO was a renegade agency, not informing the elected government of its activities. Attorney General Lionel Murphy led a team of deputies on a surprise raid of the ASIO office to investigate. It was as if the U.S. attorney general and senior FBI staff one day invaded the office of the CIA boss to examine the files and see what the agency was really up to.

Thoughts turned to the critical Pine Gap post near Alice Springs. Whitlam never breathed a word about closing it, and apparently wanted only to restore the Australian government's authority as guaranteed by treaty. But that was no solace to Shackley. Frank Snepp, the operative who helped close CIA's station in Saigon in 1975, then wrote a book about it, has said that his boss, Shackley, was "paranoid" about the Laborites, and ordered the flow of information to them held to a minimum. Ray Cline, the CIA's former deputy director, has recalled "a period of turbulence to do with Alice Springs."*

Shackley's boss, Colby, in his memoirs *Honorable Men,* listed "a left-wing and possibly antagonistic government in Australia" as among the "crises" of his tenure as director of Central Intelligence—right up with the Soviet threat to intervene in the 1973 Israeli-Egyptian war. The CIA seemed to react almost as if our Australian ally had actually fallen to communists.

James Angleton, the CIA's longtime chief of counterintelligence who was pushed into early retirement in 1975 because of his paranoia about security, was quite spooked by Whitlam. It was Angleton whom ASIO Director General C. Charles Spry had labeled "the No. 2 Honorary Australian in our Organization" because of his assistance in running it.

"He [Whitlam] was elected by Australians for better or worse," Angleton said in a 1977 interview with Australian radio and television. "In my own view for worse, but it did not affect our relationship until his Attorney General Murphy barged in and tried to destroy the delicate mechanism of internal security which had been built on patiently since the end of World War II. . . . Some of the major secrets that deal with the world I was once in were given to the Australian security services. . . .

"When we saw this Whitlam government come into power and this attorney general moving in, barging in, we were deeply concerned as to the sanctity of the information which could compromise sources and methods and would compromise human life," Angleton said. "This was one of the most extraordinary acts that one has ever seen. It was not done in a friendly manner. . . . It was a raid."

At this point, the interviewer protested, "It was done by the elected attorney general of the country . . . senior people."

Replied Angleton, "I'm not disputing the fact that he was elected. I'm only speaking to the outrageous lack of confidence inherent in his act. When we and others in the Western world had entrusted the highest secrets of counterintelligence to the Australian services and we saw the sanctity of that information being jeopardized by a bull in a china shop who would not understand that the compromise of information, or its exposure, would result in a destruction of life, sources, and methods, and this does violence to the confidentiality that must exist on the counterintelligence level between services of sovereign countries. How could we stand aside without having a

*Both men were originally quoted in interviews with the *National Times,* and have confirmed the quotes.

crisis, in terms of our responsibilities as to whether we would maintain relationships with the Australian intelligence services?"

The interviewer again noted that Whitlam and Murphy were the men the Australian people had chosen to run their government. But Angleton just complained of "the jewels of counterintelligence being placed in jeopardy by a party that has extensive historical contacts in Eastern Europe, that was seeking a new way for Australia, seeking a matter of compromise, seeking roads to Peking when China used to be one of the major bases of the illegal NKVD [the NKVD is a Soviet security agency; Angleton didn't mention that President Nixon also sought 'roads to Peking']."

Still, Angleton said, "we did not break off the relationship" with the Australian intelligence agencies. "And I believe our judgment was justified," Angleton continued, as after the 1975 removal "the Australian people simply did not put him back into office."

Angleton was asked repeatedly on the program whether the CIA intervened to dump Whitlam. Each time, he replied at length, seemingly in the negative, but each time his answer was cryptically couched in phrases to the effect that the CIA wouldn't undertake such work without the knowledge of the heads of the Australian intelligence services. Despite the interviewer's efforts to eliminate the equivocation, Angleton never denied that the CIA might have engineered the anti-Whitlam coup *with* the knowledge of its Australian counterparts.

At one point the interviewer said, "The picture you've just painted is one of a crisis. Was it serious enough, if the situation was as you described it, to warrant the removal of Gough Whitlam?"

Replied Angleton, "Of course not, absolutely not. It would simply be inconceivable to meddle in the internal affairs of Australia. I could not go to a man such as Sir Charles Spry, Brigadier Spry [former head of ASIO], and deal with him in good faith and be party to any kind of activity without his knowledge."

Pressed further, he said, "I will put it this way very bluntly. No one in the agency would ever believe that I would subscribe to any activity that was not coordinated with the chief of the Australian internal security."

Ray Cline, the CIA's former deputy director, in an interview with William Pinwill of the *National Times,* went even further about just what might have happened. "The CIA would go so far as to provide information to people who would bring it to the surface in Australia. . . . Say they stumbled onto a Whitlam error which they were willing to pump into the system so it might be to his damage. . . . If we provided a particular piece of information to the Australian intelligence services, they would make use of it."

To anyone familiar with the political events in Australia in 1975, it would not be hard to guess what particular pieces of information Cline might have been talking about.*

Twice during 1975 the Whitlam government was embarrassed by sensational scandals broken open by mysterious leaks to the press. Each time, a cabinet minister was forced to resign. One of these ministers was the head of the treasury, Jim Cairns, who had particularly angered Washington by his public denunciation of American bombing in Vietnam two years earlier.

Cairns and some other Whitlam underlings had in some off moment agreed to a harebrained scheme to repatriate petrodollars from the Arabs. To help finance the Australian budget, they decided to borrow $4 billion in Arab cash, and allowed some indiscreet middlemen to go out in search of the loan.

At some point Cairns signed an authorization letter, including the offer of a commission on the deal, to a businessman friend of his named George Harris, who Cairns thought had a connection to a deep-pocketed Arab. The letter wound up in print, and Cairns explained that he was unaware of the commission provision and wouldn't have agreed to it had he known about it.

But then a British businessman announced he had a telex in which Cairns had agreed to give a commission on the deal to his stepson. The press staged a bidding war for the telex, the most surprising aspect of which was that Rupert Murdoch lost out to a competitor for a reported $7,000.

The telex was later exposed as a fake, and the British businessman admitted as much, but it was too late. The press had uncovered some other government deal on which the stepson had turned a dollar, and Cairns was out in July 1975.

Then in October, a Middle Eastern hustler with a long history of shady associations publicly claimed that he, too, was a broker for the sought-after $4 billion. His tales of dealing with Australian cabinet officers sent Rex Connor, the energy minister, packing.

Connor's crime was stupidity, not theft, but the whole "loans

*Cline verified the quotes in a telephone interview, but told my researcher Vicki Contavespi that he had really meant to refer to information against the common interest of the U.S. and Australia, such as a critical attack by the Chinese. "There was no, repeat no, CIA campaign to damage Whitlam within his own country," he told her, though he acknowledged open criticism of Whitlam's policies throughout the CIA and State Department.

affair," as it became known, was seized by the opposition Liberal Party as an excuse to hold up passage of the budget in Parliament, to try to force an election while Whitlam was weak. As embarrassing details dribbled out, Whitlam backpedaled and his popular support faded.

While all this covered the front pages, a far more important struggle was being acted out, partly in private. It focused on Richard Stallings, a career CIA officer who had run the Pine Gap installation from its inception until—according to the best accounts one can find of a highly secret business—1969. He spent some time in the United States recuperating from injuries suffered in a bad car crash, then returned to Australia in another CIA capacity.

Stallings had been operating all along under cover of a Defense Department job. Whitlam was outraged in 1975 to discover his true identity and publicly accused the Australian military-intelligence apparatus of having deceived him and his civilian government about Stallings and the nature of Pine Gap.

Though Americans might think it makes little difference which branch of the government Stalling's checks came from, CIA is a dirty word in much of the world, including, apparently, Australia. Whitlam's complaint struck a responsive chord in the public.

Stallings, who can't be located now, was himself "very upset" over the CIA's activities in Australia, according to Victor Marchetti, the former CIA officer, whose accounts have been consistently reliable. Marchetti says he was a close friend of Stallings.

Marchetti says Stallings complained that his work at Pine Gap was being jeopardized because the CIA station in Canberra was infiltrating labor unions and funnelling money to the Liberal and Country parties. "He was working on what I considered to be a very legitimate project," Marchetti says. "He was very annoyed at what the station chief was doing, getting involved in covert activities. . . . There were rumors going around that the station chief was involved in local politics, which he knew to be true."

Stallings's case wasn't helped any by the discovery that he was renting his house from a friend who was none other than Doug Anthony, the head of the right-wing Country Party. Anthony had been a guest of Stallings's in the house, and Marchetti says Stallings was considering going to work for Anthony after his retirement from the CIA.

In late October 1975, Whitlam further upset the intelligence community by sacking the head of the overseas intelligence agency, whom he accused of deceiving him about its work in East Timor, where the military dictators in Indonesia were trying to put down an independence movement. The United States was backing the military dictators (having helped put them in power in the first place).

Whitlam then asked his foreign affairs department for a list of all CIA officials who had served in Australia. Dissatisfied with the list he received—Stalling's name, for example, wasn't on it—he probed further. This turned up Stallings's identity, and also stirred a defense chief to let his pals in Washington know that the prime minister was probing into sensitive areas.

Knowing of Stallings's relationship with Anthony, Whitlam said in a speech at Alice Springs November 2 that the CIA was helping the Country Party; he didn't disclose Stallings's name. Two days later Anthony offered his reply in Parliament, which introduced Stallings's identity to the record.

Anthony said he hadn't known that his friend Stallings was connected to the CIA, adding, "I imagine it is not the sort of thing the CIA would go around telling people."

The chronology of the next critical days before the downfall of Whitlam November 11 can best be relayed in the actual protest note the CIA issued. It was delivered to the Washington representative of ASIO by Deputy Director for Operations Theodore Shackley—Bernie Houghton and Mike Hand's eventual business associate.

Shackley's biting and threatening message, delivered November 8, 1975—three days before the constitutional coup—was quickly cabled back to the director general of ASIO in Canberra. In fact, Shackley expressly asked that the message be relayed at once to "DG"—the director general.

Exactly who was behind Shackley's move can only be speculated on. The looser Australian press has reported without documentation that Shackley made his strike on personal orders from Secretary of State Henry Kissinger. The tone and style do match Kissinger's, and the sentiments were no doubt present in whatever passes for Kissinger's heart. But in the absence of an American investigation in public, with the ability to compel sworn testimony and the production of documents, one can only assume that Shackley would not have taken so drastic a step without at least consulting higher authority.

The message follows (the Australian press obtained and published copies a few years ago. The authenticity of the message was confirmed in Parliament and not denied by the U.S. Published versions have varied minutely—a word or punctuation difference here or there, never affecting meaning—and what follows is a consensus):

On 2 November the PM of Australia [*Prime Minister Whitlam*] made a statement at Alice Springs to the effect that the CIA had been funding [*Doug*] Anthony's National Country Party in Australia.

On 4 November the U.S. Embassy in Australia approached the Australian Government at the highest level and categorically denied that CIA had given money to the National Country Party or its leader nor any other U.S. Government agency had given or passed funds to any organization or candidate for political office in Australia and to this effect was delivered to Roland at DFA [*Department of Foreign Affairs*] Canberra on 5 November.

On 6 November Asst. Sec. Edwards of U.S. State Department visiting DCM [*Deputy Chief of Mission, number two to the ambassador*] at Australian Embassy in Washington and passed the same message that the CIA had not funded an Australian political party. [*The State Department said in 1987 that it never had an assistant secretary named "Edwards."*]

It was requested that this message be sent to Canberra. At this stage CIA was dealing only with the Stallings incident and was adopting a no comment attitude in the hope that the matter would be given little or no publicity. Stallings is a retired CIA employe.

On 6 November the prime minister publicly repeated the allegation that he knew of two instances in which CIA money had been used to influence domestic Australian politics.

Simultaneously press coverage in Australia was such that a number of CIA members serving in Australia have been identified—Walker under State Department cover and Fitzwater and Bonin under Defense cover. Now that these four persons have been publicized it is not possible for CIA to continue to deal with the matter on a no comment basis.

They have now had to confer with the cover agencies which have been saying that the persons concerned are in fact what they say they are, e.g., Defense Department saying that Stallings is a retired Defense Department employe.

On 7 November, fifteen newspaper or wire service reps called the Pentagon seeking information on the allegations made in Australia. CIA is perplexed at this point as to what all this means.

Does this signify some change in our bilateral intelligence security related fields?

CIA cannot see how this dialogue with continued reference to CIA can do other than blow the lid off those installations where the persons concerned have been working and which are vital to both our services and countries, particularly the installation at Alice Springs.

On 7 November at a press conference, Colby was asked whether the allegations made in Australia were true. He categorically denied them.

Congressman Otis Pike, chairman of the Congressional committee enquiring into the CIA, has begun to make enquiries on this issue and has asked whether CIA has been funding Australian political parties. This has been denied by the CIA rep in Canberra in putting the CIA position to relevant persons there.

However CIA feels it necessary to speak also directly to ASIO because of the complexity of the problem.

Has ASIO HQ been contacted or involved?

CIA can understand a statement made in political debate but constant further unravelling worries them. Is there a change in the Prime Minister's attitude in Australian policy in this field?

This message should be regarded as an official demarche on a service to service link. It is a frank explanation of a problem seeking counsel on that problem. CIA feels that everything possible has been done on a diplomatic basis and now on an intelligence liaison link. They feel that if this problem cannot be solved they do not see how our mutually beneficial relationships are going to continue.

The CIA feels grave concern as to where this type of public discussion may lead. The DG [*Director General*] should be assured that CIA does not lightly adopt this attitude.

Your urgent advice would be appreciated as to the reply which should be made to CIA. Ambassador is fully informed of this message.

All year long, the CIA had been assessing Whitlam's popularity—which in itself is among the things the CIA is supposed to be doing all over the world. But the secret assessments the CIA came up with in its daily newsletter for the president and other top officials certainly show an atmosphere in which the CIA might have wanted to act. Copies of the relevant newsletters were obtained by Jack Anderson's reporter Dale Van Atta and published in Australia's *National Times.*

During the year, as the Whitlam scandals mounted, the CIA noted Whitlam's falling popularity and noted that "an early national election—a distinct possibility—would almost certainly result in a sweeping victory for the Liberal-Country opposition." Then came the opposition's decision to block the passage of the budget in order to force an election.

But on November 8—the very day Shackley called in the ASIO representative to convey his protest—the CIA reported to President Ford, "The determination of the Australian opposition to force a general election is weakening. Prime Minister Whitlam has managed to raise real alarm about the dire consequences of government bankruptcy, which he claims will result from the opposition's blocking of government appropriations.

"Disenchanted Australians are swinging, at least temporarily, in support of Whitlam's Labor Party. They agree with the Prime Minister and blame the Liberal-Country coalition for the mess. . . . Several Liberal senators . . . are threatening to break ranks . . . [and] are talking of replacing opposition leader [Malcolm] Fraser." The CIA said Fraser's "ability to force an election has clearly been weakened."

An important date was coming up. The treaty creating Pine Gap was signed December 9, 1966, and provided that after an initial nine years, either party could terminate the agreement on one year's notice. Whitlam to this day has never indicated other than support for the existance of the base, but he was questioning the way it was being run and on December 9, 1975, he would be empowered to act.

Adding to the urgency, Anthony had challenged Whitlam in Parliament to supply proof that his friend Stallings was a spook. Whitlam promised to supply it when Parliament re-opened November 11. Thanks to John Kerr, he never got the chance.

Kerr had been appointed—by Whitlam, of all people—to the largely ceremonial post of governor-general in February 1974. The governor-general was a throwback to the old days of the British viceroy, an official representative of the queen. Through him, Australia, which is entirely self-governing, continues tied to the British Crown so it can enjoy the benefits of such things as knighthoods and royal commissions.

Kerr had been a lawyer, judge, and finally chief justice of the New South Wales Supreme Court, most important in the land. His closest political connections were through his industrialist friends to the Liberal Party, which appointed him to his chief justiceship. But he was a consummate diplomat, avoided partisan wrangling, and kept himself ideologically and socially open to the spectrum of Australian politics, including Whitlam.

Whitlam apparently appointed Kerr as a gesture to those who were suspicious of his own ideological associations. He also used the governor-general's post for ceremonial diplomacy abroad, a function for which Kerr seemed well-suited.

There is no indication he gave a second thought to one of the governor-general's powers: to appoint and dismiss the prime minister. Like the Crown's power in England, it consisted of nothing more than a formal, pompous ratification of decisions actually made by a democratically selected Parliament. Nothing more, that is, until 1975.

Besides his Australian political connections, John Kerr also had long-standing ties to the CIA—a fact Gough Whitlam either was unaware of or ignored when appointing him.

As early as 1944 Kerr had been sent by the Australian Government to Washington to work with the OSS, which in 1947 became the CIA. In the 1950s he became a member of an elite, invitation-only group called the Australian Association for Cultural Freedom, which in 1967 was exposed in Congress as being founded, funded, and generally run by the CIA. The group, like similar CIA-backed groups in other countries, held seminars and get-togethers on the general theme of anti-communism, and brought together promising young figures from various countries.

In the 1960s Kerr helped organize and run (as founding president) the Law Association for Asia and the Western Pacific. He traveled to the United States to arrange financing for this body from a tax-free group known as the Asia Foundation; that, too, was exposed in Congress as a CIA-established conduit for money and influence. In fact, Victor Marchetti, the retired CIA officer, says in his book with former Foreign Service Officer John Marks,* that the Asia Foundation "often served as a cover for clandestine operations,"

*Marchetti and Marks, *The CIA and the Cult of Intelligence.*

though "its main purpose was to promote the spread of ideas which were anti-communist and pro-American."

The CIA paid for Kerr's travel, built his prestige, and even published his writings, through a subsidized magazine. According to Kerr's biographer, Richard Hall,* at least one Australian colleague became nervous when the U.S. Congress exposed some of Kerr's sponsoring organizations as CIA fronts, but Kerr "brushed his worries aside." Kerr continued to go to the CIA for money.

There is, of course, no more evidence than the circumstances listed here that the CIA had anything to do with Kerr's decision on November 11, 1975, to remove Gough Whitlam as prime minister of Australia. But remove Whitlam he did, and appoint Liberal Party leader Malcolm Fraser to form a caretaker government pending elections by the end of the year. Kerr says he acted because of the budget crisis. He says he is "pretty sure" he was unaware of the CIA's concern, and at any rate it "absolutely" didn't affect his decision.**

Whitlam isn't shedding any light on the matter, insisting that he is saving his theories of what happened for his own memoirs.† He did later reveal in Parliament what it was he was going to say about the Stallings affair on November 11 if he hadn't been dismissed first. His message was short. It noted that Country Party leader Anthony was the one who first identified Stallings in public as a CIA man, but confirmed the information from official records. It disclosed no other names.

One Labor Party official who will speak up is Mike Costello, who held the job of "principal private secretary," a sort of chief aide and official spokesman, to Bill Hayden, the Labor Party opposition leader during Fraser's prime ministership. Asked if he thinks the United States had a role in dumping Whitlam, Costello replies, "I don't have any doubt about that. Fraser could not have held the line [on the budget] for another day or two."

Former CIA analyst Kevin Mulcahy, who blew the whistle on Edwin Wilson, said shortly before his death that he had been told of CIA complicity in the events of 1975, and that the effort was spearheaded by a CIA man named "Corley." It was later learned that the CIA man who replaced John Walker as station chief that year was

*Richard Hall, *The Real John Kerr: His Brilliant Career* (Sydney and London, 1978).

**Interview with the author.

†In a brief phone conversation I had with him, Whitlam angrily accused me of using unfair tactics in calling him during the lunch hour when his secretary was out, because otherwise, he said, he would not have returned my call.

Milton Corley Wonus, called Corley, and another devotee of the Bourbon and Beefsteak and Bernie Houghton.

A CIA spokesman says Wonus "will not be available for comment."

As for Nugan Hand, Michael Hand and Frank Nugan were no friends of the Whitlam government, and were mightily pleased at its downfall. Soon afterward—and after the collapse of the CIA's war in Angola in February 1976—Hand was headed back to Australia from Africa. At some point in his fifteen-month absence, he took time to make at least one trip to Panama, where one of his and Nugan's land companies had been based.

There he opened the third international office (after Australia and Hong Kong, and not counting whatever he did in Africa) of the Nugan Hand Bank.

CHAPTER TEN

The Un-Bank

The Nugan Hand Bank never did any banking. It never hired any bankers—until in its death throes it brought Donald Beazley in from the United States. And he stopped banking as soon as he got to Sydney.

Nugan Hand hired people with contacts. And it hired aggressive professional salesmen—some of whom paid little heed to the worth of the product they were selling.

Les Collings was a Britisher who came to Australia in 1960 at the age of twenty-three with a grammar school education and career experience as a deck apprentice on an oil tanker.* He took up selling real estate and eventually moved into mutual fund shares. Mutual fund salesmen sometimes begin to think of themselves as being entitled to 8 percent of the life savings of anyone they meet. That is the commission they often take off the top. Then they turn over the remaining 92 percent of the savings to a fund manager at no risk to themselves, and move on to the next prospect. So did Les Collings make his living.

In July 1974, the fund Collings was working for—Dollar Fund of Australia—did the one thing that every investor is told his mutual fund will never, ever, do: it stopped redeeming its shares. What happened to the unlucky investors? "They would probably still be

*That's the version he gave me. The Stewart Royal Commission described him as a deck *officer.*

holding the securities," Collings says. In other words, the money those people worked for and saved, perhaps over the course of a lifetime, is gone forever.

But, as would happen later with Nugan Hand, Collings doesn't like to talk so much about the investors. "That firm had an elite group of salesmen," he says of the Dollar Fund. There is wonder in his eyes as he speaks of this hustler's pantheon, and it becomes clear who are the true objects of his sympathy. "Peter Dunn and [Jerry] Gilder were with that firm. [Frank] Ward was the administrator. There were eighteen guys around the world and we were just suddenly told by cable that we had to pay our own way home."

As one might expect, they somehow made it. One Dollar Fund salesman, Wilhelmus Hans, got a job with Nugan Hand, selling silver bullion investments (and, eventually, scouting out arms suppliers for Michael Hand's clients in Africa, whoever they were). When Collings had foraged his way back to Sydney, he ran into Hans, who said, "I think I can get you a job selling bullion."

Dunn and Ward went to work at Nugan Hand for a year or so, and Gilder for the duration. A Dollar Fund veteran named Karl Schuller also joined. In one of the many ironies of the Nugan Hand story, the liquidator John O'Brien back in 1974 was called in to wrap up the affairs of the Dollar Fund, and for the first time heard mention of the company that would become his biggest case. Questioning Schuller about the Dollar Fund, O'Brien was told that Schuller was working for a company called Nugan Hand "and making lots of money on the gold and silver market."

Apparently Nugan Hand decided to specialize in commodities at first. Advertising for salesmen, the company hired a Lebanese immigrant, George Shaw, who had been running a coin dealership. His commodity specialty was silver. Shaw brought in a friend, Andrew Lowe, who ran an illegal gambling den in Sydney's Chinatown. Lowe's commodity specialty was number four grade (pure) heroin. He imported as much as sixty pounds of it at a time, until he was caught and sent to prison for it in 1978.

Shaw and Lowe, respectively, brought in banking customers from the large Lebanese and Chinese communities in Sydney. Many of these customers were involved in the dope trade, and wanted to get money across international boundaries without attracting the attention of authorities. Other customers, for reasons of their own, such as tax evasion, also sought ease and secrecy in international currency shipment.

"The whole purpose," Shaw told the Stewart Royal Commission, "was to attract people with 'black money' and to assure them that their anonymity would be preserved."

Nugan Hand began a mutual fund called Ingold. As Collings remembers it, it was "80 percent bullion—gold, silver, platinum—and 20 percent money market." Schuller went to Germany seeking investors, and Nugan Hand eventually took over a small bank there, though Schuller dropped out of the company. Shaw went to Lebanon and tried to open a Nugan Hand branch, but found the civil war had ruined the business climate and came back to Sydney.

In the move that was to have the biggest impact, Collings was sent to Hong Kong. Before Hand left for Africa, he went to Hong Kong to help Collings legally establish companies there to represent the Ingold fund.

"They gave me $2,000 and an air ticket," Collings recalls over drinks in a Hong Kong bar. "I arrived here with a suitcase and I got the firm established. I was trying to get people to invest in Australia. A mutual fund with silver bullion seemed to me like a very worthwhile investment."

But after a few months, he says, Nugan notified him that the bullion idea wasn't working out. "Nugan told me he had set up an investment bank in Panama called Nugan Hand, Inc. They were selling 10 or 12 percent certificates of deposit." Collings was instructed to offer Ingold investors their cash back, but to try to talk them into converting their investments into Nugan Hand certificates of deposit instead. Most, he says, converted. "I'm a damned good salesman," he explains.

From the beginning, Nugan Hand offered essentially four services, which changed only in size and detail as the bank grew. It offered a way to move money overseas flouting Australia's and other countries' laws; it offered tax avoidance schemes based on Nugan's supposed expertise (though these schemes now seem to have been patently fraudulent); it offered extraordinarily high interest and yet great safety for savings; and it offered international trade connections.

Because the United States has such a long, strong tradition of free trade and free commerce, it is sometimes difficult for Americans to understand the currency flow restrictions most countries have. But these are the laws Nugan Hand most flagrantly violated.

America, the land of opportunity, has always attracted capital from abroad. So it has been in our interest to allow capital to flow freely. Of course, it could also be argued that our lack of restraint on capital is one important reason people want to invest it in the United

States. At any rate, other countries have built all sorts of regulatory barriers to keep their citizens from exporting capital. It is thought that these laws foster development at home.

One might assume that Australia, with its American-sized territory populated by only about fifteen million people, would offer such enormous development opportunities that it would attract capital the way the United States has. But for whatever reason, the Australian Government saw fit to join the majority of countries that have erected barriers to the free flow of money.

No matter how much money you have in Australia, the Banking Act says that if you leave you can't take more than $250 with you, unless you can persuade the Reserve Bank to give you special permission because you are going to do something good for Australia.

If, for example, you want to start a trading company and need to pay a staff stationed abroad, you may be able to persuade the Reserve Bank to allow you to do that on the ground that you will be helping Australian exports. But you will still be limited to, say, $4,000 per employe for the first two months and $1,500 a month thereafter, and will have to show air tickets or other evidence as proof of what you are doing.

Nor can you invest money abroad without such permission. You can pay properly incurred debts abroad; for example, if you are an Australian book publisher and contract to publish a book by a foreign author, you may send the author his royalties. (Of course, if you are a book publisher, you will probably find some other excuse *not* to send the author his royalties.) If you are a non-resident who comes to work a while in Australia and then wants to go home, you will be allowed to take back only as much money as you brought in.

As John Booth, a senior finance officer of the Australian Treasury Department explains it, "We do not wish Australian currency to be an international currency. Australia is a capital-importing country. We need capital here."

Although in 1981 the Reserve Bank loosened its guidelines about giving permission for overseas investment (because of an especially favorable balance of trade), during the Nugan Hand years those guidelines were stringent. And then, as now, you can be sure of one thing: before the Reserve Bank will approve your sending or taking that first dime abroad, it will demand proof that you have paid taxes on it and all other income it can trace to you.

A lot of Australians wanted to be able to put their money wherever they desired, without approval from anyone. So did a lot of

Malaysians, Thais, Indonesians, Filipinos, Hong Kong residents, and others burdened with similar currency restrictions. For them, there was Nugan Hand.

Donald J. Daisley owned an engineering company in Sydney, but he did some business overseas and parked the profits in Hong Kong, where the taxes were lower and the regulations less stringent than if he had brought the money home to Australia. Through an encounter with George Shaw in mid-1975, Daisley met Frank Nugan, and talked about his financial situation.

Before long, Daisley was putting some of his Hong Kong savings on account with the Nugan Hand Bank in Hong Kong. And at just about the same time, he took out a $15,000 loan from a Sydney company named Yorkville Nominees, which had been founded by Frank Nugan many years earlier to handle some of the land sales that he and Hand carried on in their salad days.

Thus Donald Daisley put some money into one Nugan Hand entity, and took some money out of another Nugan Hand entity. If you wanted to subject this money to the Australian income tax, you could say that Daisley was repatriating to Australia some of his overseas profits. If you *didn't* want to subject it to the income tax, you could say the two transactions were a coincidence. It was $15,000, it was called a loan, and who would holler about it?

That's the way Nugan Hand worked—on a simple level.

Then, in 1976, Daisley spotted his dream house in the posh Hunter's Hill area of Sydney. The price was $260,000. It was a good buy, later valued at over $1 million. But Daisley's bank would cough up only $160,000 of financing. He had plenty of money in low-taxed Hong Kong. But how was he to get that money back to Australia to buy the house without paying Australian taxes on it?

This was Frank Nugan's genius. At just about this time, Nugan was oiling up his relationship with the injured, disaster-stricken doctor, John K. Ogden. Nugan, who had settled Ogden's insurance case, was trying to persuade the physician that through his tax expertise, allegedly acquired at the University of California, Nugan could handle the Ogden family's finances better than the Ogdens themselves.

Now, Nugan showed Ogden just what he meant. Nugan would arrange for Ogden to buy a house—the one Daisley wanted—for $260,000. Then Nugan would arrange for Ogden to sell the house to Daisley for $160,000, creating a $100,000 loss. The loss would be reported to Australian tax authorities for a considerable savings on the Ogdens' annual tax bill. But, then, nothing would really be lost, because the $100,000 would magically reappear in an account with

Ogden's name on it in Hong Kong, where it would earn more interest anyway. The money would come from Daisley's account in Hong Kong.

And that wasn't the end of the supposed benefits. Under Australian law, Ogden wasn't entitled to invest in Nugan Hand's higher-interest overseas bank. But since the money to open the account would already be in Hong Kong, the device of the house would solve both problems. It would produce a tax loss, and a high-interest Nugan Hand Bank account at the same time. And, Nugan assured Ogden, lying through his teeth, it was all perfectly legal.*

Still, a corporate veil was created. Yorkville Nominees, as agent for Ogden, bought the house high, and turned around and sold it low to Yorkville Nominees as agent for Daisley, who was handed the title. Meanwhile, Wilkinson Holdings, a company Daisley formed in Hong Kong, generously donated $100,000 to an account with Ogden's name on it at the Nugan Hand Bank in Hong Kong—all by coincidence, of course. (Daisley declines to discuss it.)

By the time the liquidator, John O'Brien, took over Yorkville Nominees' books along with Nugan Hand's, they showed scores of client accounts through which millions of dollars disappeared in one country to magically reappear in another. Because these transactions were so informal and so secret, and the records ill-kept or destroyed, O'Brien found it impossible to estimate either the assets or the liabilities of Yorkville Nominees.

Australian tax authorities investigated many of the cases. The outcome of any civil tax claims isn't public information, and no criminal charges are known to have been filed.

At times, Nugan Hand didn't bother with such complicated book-work. Cash was physically, illegally, carried across boundaries in pockets and suitcases. George Shaw did it, according to fellow insiders. (Shaw himself stopped talking to the author before the question came up.) No doubt others did, too.

*Nugan assured many people that what they were doing was all perfectly legal when it wasn't legal at all. I've talked to a lot of those people and believe that often Nugan was just creating a mutually convenient story so that the new and unpracticed criminal would have a rationalization to use in fighting off pangs of conscience. It also gave them something to tell the tax collector if eyebrows were ever raised. If they were caught, the phony story would never work to relieve the clients of the civil responsibility to pay their taxes. But it might keep them out of jail by calling their criminal intent into question.

In at least a few cases, though, I think the people really believed it. After talking to the Ogdens, I tend to give them the benefit of the doubt. I think they were genuinely taken in.

But in mid-1976, a real pro came onto the payroll: a mysterious and secret Britisher named Ron Pulger-Frame. Pulger-Frame had worked for Deak & Company, probably the best-known U.S. international currency and coin exchanger until its bankruptcy filing in December 1984.

For years, it was whispered that Deak had a close working relationship with the Central Intelligence Agency. Certainly the CIA would have been derelict not to try to keep tabs on Deak. And there would have been a lot for Deak to gain by trading off with the world's biggest spy agency, because much of the company's business involved speculation about the relative future value of the world's currencies.

Pulger-Frame talks only sparsely about his work for Deak and Nugan Hand. "I was a courier," he says. "I carried things."

Money?

"Of course."

Large amounts?

"Fifty, a hundred thousand dollars."

Neil Evans, whom Nugan Hand had hired to run its branch in the drug capital of Chiang Mai, Thailand, said that while with Nugan Hand, Pulger-Frame would carry a pencil behind one ear, or make some other sign under a pre-arrangement with customs personnel of various countries who would then let pass what Pulger-Frame wanted passed. Asked about this by a reporter,* Pulger-Frame indignantly denied ever crossing frontiers with cash. "I'm not that dumb," he said.

But the Stewart Royal Commission learned of an interview Pulger-Frame gave to the official bankruptcy receiver's office in Hong Kong in 1981, during which he declared, "Deak's had a system which was devised by me to circumvent Australian exchange regulations." When the commission pressed him about what he meant, Pulger-Frame explained the rather ingenious system:

He opened a foreign exchange account in Australia, telling banking authorities that Deak wanted to import Australian cash from Asia, sell it in Australia at profitable exchange rates, and export the proceeds—all perfectly legal, if registered. He would then carry suitcases of Australian currency into Australia from Hong Kong, notifying banking authorities of his arrival.

Once in the country, however, on his way to the bank where he had the account, he would rendezvous with Australians who wanted to illegally export money. He would add their saved-up cash to his imported bundle. He would then turn the combined amount over the

*The author.

bank, which would credit the entire sum as imported cash. It could then be put in international exchange accounts, where it could all be exported if desired. (Pulger-Frame told the Stewart commission that he really didn't devise this system, he just implemented it.)

The Hong Kong liquidator who took testimony from Pulger-Frame in the Nugan Hand case also recalls* his boast that while with Deak he played a role in the delivery of Lockheed Corporation cash to Japanese public officials, in a well-known bribery case that helped bring down a Japanese government. There have long been suspicions that such bribes to foreign leaders by American firms, especially defense contractors, are really payments from the U.S. Government in disguise.

"He [Pulger-Frame] took the view that the movement of money was every man's right," says the liquidator. "He said there was one time customs in Japan opened his suitcase and it was full of money. And the man [customs official] said, 'Hmmm, money,' and closed it up again."

Les Collings, the Nugan Hand representative in Hong Kong, says Pulger-Frame dealt directly with the Sydney office, not with him. Collings says the mysterious courier "used to bring in depositors" from Indonesia and other places.

John Owen, the Nugan Hand Bangkok representative, calls Pulger-Frame "a bag man," and recalls running into him in Sydney once "on one of his clandestine sort of deals." Owen says he asked Pulger-Frame about rumors then circulating that the Nugan family might be connected to narcotics trafficking. He says Pulger-Frame told him, "They are all involved in drugs. Nugan fruit group and Nugan Hand," whereupon Owen says he backed off.

Pulger-Frame testified before the Corporate Affairs Commission that he catered to clients mostly in Melbourne who presumably didn't trust the mails. Sometimes, though, even in Sydney there were clients who "wished to remain anonymous," and so used him as an intermediary, he said. According to his testimony, he merely carried cash to the Nugan Hand office in Sydney, then went back to Hong Kong with empty pockets so as not to violate the currency laws. (Apparently he never told the Corporate Affairs Commission that at Deak he had specialized in violating such laws.) Back in Hong Kong, Pulger-Frame said, he would report the transaction, and an international certificate of deposit would be issued to the client by the Nugan Hand Bank.

*Interview with the author, on the condition he would be identified only as official receiver, and not by name.

For this seemingly modest service, Pulger-Frame testified that he extracted the impressive fee of 4 percent of the money he carried. He said he had received 5 percent from Deak. Why he was able to demand such high fees if all he did was carry money across town from one office to another can only be speculated on—especially since Nugan Hand regularly used an armored car service in Sydney to perform that task.

The guard service was K & R Cash Transit, whose main business was providing payrolls for Sydney companies that paid their workers in cash (a much more common practice there than in the United States). Interviewed in his home, Eric Francis Lambkin, who ran K & R, recalls regular trips for Nugan Hand throughout 1977 and 1978, the same period Pulger-Frame was working for the firm. Lambkin would come to the Nugan Hand office, pick up a bundle of cash, and write a check to Nugan Hand (or Yorkville, or whoever) for however much money he was collecting in cash.

"They'd call in the morning and ask us to pick up about noon," he says. "Maybe once a month, maybe twice a week. Very spasmodic." The largest single sum he recalls picking up at Nugan Hand was $350,000, the smallest, $12,000. "When you think about it, it's a bloody good way to wash money," he admits.

Lambkin ought to know about money laundering. He spent eighteen months in prison for it after K & R was liquidated in bankruptcy in 1979. Nugan Hand's name wasn't sullied in that affair.

To get the clients it wanted, Nugan Hand needed public trust. And to get that trust, it needed two things: it needed reputable banking and other official references. And it needed a certified public accountant to sign off that its books were true. It got both.

"If there was one thing that was most responsible for the rapid growth of the bank," says Les Collings, "it was the quality of banking references they got." In Sydney, Nugan persuaded officers at two of the biggest banks in Australia, the kind everybody goes to, with branches all over town, to write testimonial letters and even answer telephone inquiries from potential Nugan Hand clients. The men who signed the letters aren't answering inquiries about the bank anymore, at least not for an American reporter.

The first big endorser for Nugan Hand was Ron McKinnon, head of the New South Wales branch of the Australia and New Zealand Banking Group Ltd., popularly known as the ANZ Bank. McKinnon is now dead. The Joint Task Force on Drugs worked for a while on the theory that McKinnon had somehow been bribed by Nugan, but never came up with usable evidence.

J. K. Nicholson, however, lives. And as late as July 1979, six months before the bank collapsed, Nicholson—senior manager of ANZ's international division—supplied Nugan a copy of the report that ANZ was putting out on Nugan Hand.

Under the heading "Ability and Integrity of Management," the ANZ report said, "Directors have proven, in their dealings with the Bank [ANZ], capable and reliable and unlikely to commit the company beyond its means." Under the heading "Remarks on Financial Position," it said, "On information available to us, financial position is considered sound." Under "Conduct of Account," it said, "Good—arrangements have been observed at all times." There was not the least hint of anything derogatory.

Nicholson attached the disclaimer that, "As is our standard practice the report is supplied without responsibility on the part of the bank [meaning ANZ Bank] or writer." But ANZ apparently made the report available for those who inquired about Nugan Hand; certainly Nugan Hand made it available to its clients, along with Nicholson's cover letter on ANZ stationery. (Nicholson, still an officer at ANZ, did not respond to telephone messages.)

With only the same kind of perfunctory disclaimer, the Bank of New South Wales, whose letterhead boasts "First Bank in Australia," also backed up Nugan Hand. Ronald J. Regan, who signed himself "assistant representative" of the Bank of New South Wales, prepared a form report saying that Nugan Hand's account at his bank "opened 1973 and operates with substantial turnover. Directors are considered capable and reliable and we consider they would not enter into any commitment they could not expect to fulfill," the report added.

Possibly the most important banking reference Nugan Hand picked up was that of Wing-On Bank, a major institution in Hong Kong controlled by the wealthy Kwok family, which also owns department stores and other enterprises. Besides kind words in response to inquiries, Wing-On offered a prestigious depository into which Nugan Hand customers could send their investment money, and out of which the investment could presumably be retrieved (through checks Nugan Hand wrote on its account there).

But Wing-On did something much more important even than that. Wing-On actually guaranteed, with its own money, deposits that Nugan Hand took in from certain elite customers—like other banks. Thus, with the help of Wing-On, Nugan Hand acquired prestigious investors, like the Chase Manhattan Bank, the Fidelity Bank of Philadelphia (the third and forty-fifth largest banks in the

United States, respectively), the Bank of Nova Scotia, and a dozen other banking behemoths from Europe and North America.

In each case, the major bank would deposit hundreds of thousands of dollars—in Chase Manhattan's case, once $1 million—with Nugan Hand, which offered a high Australian interest rate for a short period of time. The banks were induced to do this because Wing-On Bank, a substantial entity, guaranteed repayment of the money and the interest.

For its guarantee, Wing-On charged a slight fee, which Nugan Hand was more than happy to pay. And Wing-On took care to guarantee its own stake, by requiring Nugan Hand to open an escrow-like account at ANZ Bank in Sydney, containing enough high-grade money market securities to satisfy the debt that Wing-On was guaranteeing. ANZ certified the contents of the escrow account, from which Wing-On could draw if it was ever called upon to bail out Nugan Hand.

In themselves, these deals lost money for Nugan Hand. The money-market securities required to fill the escrow account at ANZ normally paid Nugan Hand less in interest than Nugan Hand was offering to get the deposits. Yet Nugan Hand sought out big, prestigious depositors who required the Wing-On guarantee, because they created still more prestigious references. Potential clients from the general public could then be told that big banks like Chase Manhattan were depositing, which would quell their own doubts about the stability of Nugan Hand.

In Fidelity Bank's case, for example, Les Collings arranged for deposits by getting to know Fidelity's Hong Kong representative. Later, Nugan traveled to the United States and visited senior executives in Fidelity's home office. According to David Carpenter, Fidelity's vice-president in charge of Asia and Latin America, Nugan impressed the bankers as "smart" and "personable."

As for references, Carpenter says, "If anybody called us, our standard reference is that we have had a relationship that has been conducted X period of time and it's been satisfactory." But Nugan got Fidelity to go still farther. On June 30, 1978, William F. Morgan, an assistant vice-president at Fidelity, wrote a glowing "Dear Frank" letter to Nugan, signed "Bill," which Nugan made no effort to hide from those he wanted to impress.

The letter was in response to one Nugan had written to Fidelity, explaining the scandal that was enveloping the family fruit and vegetable business. Wrote Morgan, on Fidelity letterhead, "We had read several newspaper reports on the matter, but knowing you and

Nugan Hand Limited, did not feel it necessary to ask you to defend yourself to us. . . . I should like to wish you and your family well as this situation resolves itself. You and Nugan Hand Ltd. will undoubtedly come out of this period stronger and better for it. With warm personal regards . . ."

Irving Trust Company, seventeenth largest bank in the United States, is where Nugan Hand did its own banking in the U.S., shuffling money in and out of a New York account. An Irving Trust spokesman says his bank was introduced to Nugan Hand through Wing-On, which has a correspondent banking relationship with Irving. The spokesman says that unnamed "sources and references indicated the quality of the organization met our standards."

Irving says there is no record of whether or not Irving provided references to prospective Nugan Hand clients, and won't comment on the other business they did. But Nugan Hand staffers were advised that they could refer a potential client to David Fung, an Irving vice-president, and presumably they did so without ill result. (Fung says he did a lot of correspondence banking with Nugan Hand, which he says was a "sister bank" of Irving, but that he didn't refer any customers.)

When John O'Brien, the liquidator, went for information, he reports, "The Irving Trust guy in Hong Kong was the most nervous person I ever saw in my life. He says he knows nothing about it. He had computer printouts of the monthly balances but no details of transactions. The balances are nominal, the low six figures, but he acknowledged there was a lot more going in and out."

Albert Kwok, Wing-On Bank's chief manager, refuses to say who introduced Nugan Hand to its critical connection at Wing-On. But there is one person he says absolutely *wasn't* involved: Andrew Lowe.

Lowe, it may be recalled, was a major international heroin trafficker who was hired by Nugan Hand to bring in clients from the Chinese and drug communities in Sydney, where he was well-connected with people who wanted to move money secretly. Strange as it may seem, Lowe had a brother, Stephen, who was married to the daughter of Alwyn Kwok, patriarch of the whole Kwok family. Alwyn ran the department stores and sat on the board of directors of Wing-On, the family bank. A coincidence? Absolutely, says Albert Kwok. He says Nugan Hand came to him on the recommendation of "a respectable, responsible financial institution in Australia." He just won't name it.

You get a very different story, however, from Les Collings,

Nugan Hand's Hong Kong manager. Collings explains the Wing-On relationship very simply: "*I* established the relationship with the Wing-On Bank," he says. "I was walking down Des Voeux Road [a main drag in the Hong Kong business district] and I saw this bank. I thought, 'I'll see if they'll invest.' "

At the time, Collings was still selling shares in Ingold, the metals fund. He says Wing-On turned down his efforts to get it to invest. (The idea of a bank investing in a precious metals mutual fund seems strange to begin with.) But, Collings, says, he struck up an acquaintanceship with Albert Kwok—even arranged for Frank Nugan to give legal advice when Kwok was sued for fraud—and later, when Collings was selling certificates of deposit, the acquaintanceship paid off.

At first, the certificates Collings was selling were issued by the Nugan Hand company in Panama. By the end of 1976 or early 1977, however, Nugan and Hand had moved their offshore haven to the Cayman Islands, where they set up a company called Swiss Pacific Asia Ltd.

A lot of banks, even some legitimate ones, open subsidiary companies in places like Panama or the Caymans, because the governments of those countries don't pay much attention to what goes on. The "office" is often just a manila file of legal documents in the office of some lawyer, who also serves as a mail-forwarding service; real business is conducted from New York, Paris, or—in Nugan Hand's case—Sydney and Hong Kong.

You'd think investors would know that banks located in such offshore havens aren't subject to normal scrutiny. But a lot of them apparently don't think about that—or else a lack of scrutiny is the very thing they're looking for, because they are trying to avoid paying taxes in the country where they live, or to evade some other law.

The reason Nugan and Hand picked the name "Swiss Pacific Asia" should be obvious. It certainly was obvious to the Government of Switzerland, which protested to Hong Kong authorities in 1977 and forced a change. Inclusion of the word "Swiss" encouraged investors to overlook the Cayman Island address and falsely assume that the bank was connected to Switzerland, which cares very much about how its banks do business, and therefore has developed a great reputation for safety.

So, on Switzerland's protest, the name was changed to the Nugan Hand Bank. And somewhere along the line, Les Collings says, he persuaded Albert Kwok to put in Wing-On's money—and name.

By March 1977, Nugan Hand had picked up another impressive reference: the United States Government. The U.S. consular offices in Sydney and Hong Kong cabled reports on Nugan Hand to the Commerce Department, and the reports fairly glowed. How often the Commerce Department or the embassies gave the reports out in response to public inquiries isn't known, but Nugan Hand got hold of copies of the reports. And for potential customers, the clearly labeled words of the U.S. Government made impressive reading.

The data in the reports conforms to false figures handed out by Nugan Hand itself. The Australian report, dated March 1977, says Nugan Hand, Sydney, was established in 1970 and had eighty employees. The Hong Kong report, dated April 1977, says the office there—identified as Swiss Pacific Asia Ltd.—was established in 1972, and had fifty employes.

Both reports, prepared by the State Department for the Commerce Department, list the reputation of the company as "good." Both list the ANZ Bank as a banking reference, and the Hong Kong report also lists Wing-On and the Hong Kong office of Banque Nationale de Paris (a major French bank whose name hasn't turned up elsewhere in Nugan Hand literature).

The report from the U.S. Embassy in Australia says Nugan Hand "acts as a holding company, investment banker and banking service company, providing services as money market operation, financial advice and assistance, economic analysis and information, investment and portfolio management, credit services, custodian and nominee facilities." At January 31, 1976, it says, Nugan Hand had $22.7 million in assets and $1.1 million in working capital.

All this sounds as if it were pulled off one of the fancy advertising brochures Hand and Nugan were distributing. The report repeats the fiction that "Financing for operations is from money market borrowing."

The State Department apparently had talked to ANZ Bank and the Bank of New South Wales, because the U.S. Government report is worded so similarly to the two bank reports. "Banker [unidentified] states directors are considered capable and reliable, unlikely to enter into commitments they could not fulfill," the U.S. Government report assures its readers. "Firm's above balance sheet indicates a good financial position," the State Department adds. "No adverse information is known about Nugan Hand's operations and banker considers directors are reliable."

The report notes that Nugan Hand had incorporated itself in Hawaii, and even asserts that Nugan Hand, Inc. of Hawaii "owns Nugan Hand (Hong Kong) Ltd. and Nugan Hand Bank & Trust Co." It is, of course, illegal for a company operating from the United States to sell banking securities or even call itself a bank without U.S.

banking regulation, which Nugan Hand decidedly was not getting. But apparently the FBI, which is in charge of enforcing this regulation, was not among those receiving the State Department report.

The Hong Kong report says Nugan Hand's (Swiss Pacific's) U.S. representative "is Rear Admiral Earl P. Yates, USN (Retired), who would be the appropriate person to contact for U.S. individuals wishing to do business with subject firm.

The report also lists Yates as a "trade reference" for Swiss Pacific, and gives his address in Virginia Beach, Virginia. And it says Swiss Pacific was capitalized with $10 million Hong Kong, the equivalent of about $2 million U.S. or Australian. By all available evidence, of course, this capitalization appears to have been a complete hoax.

Yates was brought on board by Bernie Houghton. Although Houghton had no official capacity with Nugan Hand at the time, he acted as an unofficial third partner. Yates has given Australian investigators* different versions of when he met Houghton, according to their reports. The Joint Task Force says, and at one point the Stewart Royal Commission says, that Yates told them that he met Houghton in 1972 or 1973 through a Colonel William Prim, who was serving on Yates's staff at the U.S. Pacific headquarters in Hawaii. According to this version, Prim had recommended that Yates look up Houghton, an old Vietnam buddy of Prim's, on a trip to Australia.**

This account accords with the one Houghton gave. But it quite contradicts the recollection of the prominent businessman Sir Paul Strasser. Strasser has told official investigators and reporters alike that a glowing reference from Yates led him to hire Houghton as a real estate salesman in 1967.

Strasser's account accords with the one the Stewart commission says Yates gave while testifying in Sydney in 1984. There, the commission reported, Yates said he "met Mr. Houghton during the late 1960s when he (Admiral Yates) was in Sydney overseeing the details of the establishment of rest and recreation leave pursuant to which scheme American servicemen serving in Vietnam would come to Sydney as part of such leave. Subsequently Mr. Houghton introduced him to Messrs. Nugan and Hand."

Taking what is consistent in Yates's contradictory accounts, Yates got the standard invitation to the Bourbon and Beefsteak from Houghton, and they struck up a social friendship. When Yates re-

*He declined numerous attempts by the author to interview him.

**The air force located Prim (who gives his formal name as "Billy") and agreed to forward a letter to him from the author, asking for comment. He did not reply.

turned to Australia with his boss, Admiral Noel Arthur Meredyth Gayler, Commander-in-Chief of the U.S. Pacific Command, Houghton threw a party for their entourage, and, in the words of the Stewart Royal Commission, "introduced Admirals Yates and Gayler to several political and financial figures in the Sydney area."

Yates told investigators the friendship with Houghton lasted after he left the navy in 1974 and went to work with a U.S. engineering company. Then, early in 1977, Houghton invited him to come to Sydney, meet Nugan and Hand, and join their organization as its U.S. representative.

We are told the initial impressions were splendid. "I thought Frank Nugan was very, very honest and straightforward, and a Christian gentleman," Yates said in an interview with U.S. journalist Jonathan Marshall* on September 29, 1980, long after the bank had stopped paying depositors and been exposed as a sham.

Yates said he and his new associates even went to church together. "I never knew him [Nugan] to do anything illegal or dishonest," Yates told Marshall. "Michael Hand [who by the time Yates was speaking had fled Australia and vanished] also was highly decorated. . . . I never heard him swear. He was a very religious and dedicated Christian."

Yates's employment agreement called for him to receive $50,000 a year in salary, and another $50,000 in expenses. He told the Stewart Royal Commission that he never received the salary, and that his real interest was an agreement that he would receive a 20 percent equity share in the enterprise, equal to that of Nugan and Hand, after the bank had achieved "a measure of success." (The commission doesn't explain who would have held the other 40 percent of the shares.)

Yates also told Australian investigators that although he was given the title of president, he "was not given any authority to commit the bank nor direct any of its operations outside the U.S." Yet he was soon representing the bank in public, and also in private business deals in Asia and Europe. A 1977 feature in the business section of Hong Kong's respected *South China Morning Post* featured Yates's picture, and said:

> Hong Kong will rival London and New York as a financial center in a few years and will require the presence of more institutions for the large international financial arrangements that will undoubtedly be made here. This is the prediction of the visiting

*Then with *Inquiry* magazine, now editorial page editor of the *Oakland* (California) *Tribune.*

president of Nugan Hand Bank, Admiral Earl Yates, who is in Hongkong to lay the groundwork for the bank's activities here. The bank has a representative office and a deposit-taking company in Hongkong.

There followed a long exposition of Yates's opinions on various banking and trade matters, with plenty of puffery about Nugan Hand's special ability to serve almost every kind of customer.

Yates was joined by Brigadier General Edwin Black "early" in 1977—that's as specific as Black could be about the date. A former OSS man during and after World War II, former Green Beret commander, former commander of the covert Vietnam War support programs run out of Thailand, former executive director of the Freedoms Foundation at Valley Forge, Black said Yates recruited him to the job. Nugan and Hand were flown to Hawaii by Yates to meet him, Black said, after which Black became president of Nugan Hand Hawaii.

As such, he carried on yet another important relationship, with the Hawaiian Trust Company, a large legitimate bank, and its vice-president, Douglas Philpotts. Philpotts will say nothing about the relationship. But millions of dollars flowed through Nugan Hand's account at Hawaiian Trust on its way to or from Europe, Latin America (particularly Panama), and Asia.

What was the money used for? We can only guess. For example, Panama was and is a big center for drugs. It also was, for those years, the main base for U.S. covert military operations in Central and northern South America. General Black insisted in interviews until his death in 1984 that he himself didn't know what the money he shipped around was being used for; he said he was just following orders he got from Frank Nugan and Mike Hand.

No amount of financial treachery by Hand, Nugan, Houghton, or any of the talented staff they employed would have succeeded without the signature of a trusted accountant. The role was filled, first, by George Brincat of Sydney, and, later, by the Price Waterhouse & Company office in the Bahamas (which covered the Cayman Islands).

Price Waterhouse, one of the "Big Eight" international accounting firms, is rather larger and better known than Brincat. But its professional employes are, like George Brincat, certified public accountants. (In Australia, they're called chartered accountants).

A CPA is much more than a bookkeeper. A CPA does not just organize numbers. He does whatever investigations he considers appropriate under standard professional guidelines in order to give his certification—his assurance to the public—that the numbers "fairly reflect" the status of the business.

In certifying the books of a manufacturing company, for example, a CPA may actually go into the warehouse (or send someone) and open up some boxes to see whether they contain as many widgets as the company management says they contain. The CPA for a bank may check the vaults and see if the money is really there. He's not expected to count every dime, or widget, which would take forever, but to test according to standards the profession has set for itself—such as by sending mailings to a sampling of alleged depositors to see if they agree with the bank's records of their accounts.

A CPA license requires a vigorous examination, overseen by state agencies, and continuing professional education. Because finance is so complicated, the public has come to regard the signature of a certified public accountant as something it can bank on.

Brincat, of the firm of Heuschkel & Pollard (later Pollard & Brincat), became Nugan Hand's accountant in 1974, before its big growth. He was only twenty-three years old. The Corporate Affairs Commission concluded, "The more dominant character of Mr. F. J. Nugan and the comparative inexperience of Mr. Brincat, whilst perhaps rendering the behavior of Mr. Brincat more understandable, do not in the estimation of the delegates [commission members] in any way combine to excuse the active role played by Mr. Brincat in the financial deceptions . . .

"Whilst it is accepted that by January, 1979, he had become uneasy at the contents of the accounts of Nugan Hand Ltd., and in the underlying transactions concealed by those accounts, his uneasiness could have been equally attributable to his own position as to the behavior of Mr. F. J. Nugan," the commission said. In other words, he may have been less worried over the welfare of the depositors than over his prospect of going to jail.

Brincat's very first "audited" statement for Nugan Hand, covering the year ended June 30, 1974, accepted Nugan's and Hand's word that they had invested $1 million in capital in the company. A company's capital acts as a base, to assure clients that temporary operating losses won't leave the company short of funds to pay its debts. But the financial records Brincat relied on to show the $1 million paid-in capital in fact establish nothing of the sort. As noted earlier, they were merely the result of the kiting of checks among accounts with under $20,000 in them—which would have been evident from the very records Brincat cited.

The Corporate Affairs Commission found that Brincat had "knowingly engaged in the preparation of false accounts for Nugan Hand Ltd." from that day forward. So did the Stewart Royal Commission. In fact, in his testimony before the Stewart commission, Brincat tacitly admitted it, though he argued that he always thought Nugan was so rich he could, if needed, pay from his own pocket the money Brincat knew the company didn't have.

There is no way to say just why Brincat falsely certified these statements. Nugan is dead, Hand is gone, and Houghton, Yates, and the others are not being held accountable for what Nugan Hand did while they were associated with it. Brincat won't talk to journalists, and the only Australian officials he admitted anything to, the Stewart commission, had too little curiosity to ask the right questions.

The Nugan Hand Bank was incorporated in the Cayman Islands July 6, 1976, and got its license to operate there on August 26, 1976. The legal papers were arranged by the Cayman lawyer for the Bank of Nova Scotia (Canada), a bank Nugan Hand had courted in Hong Kong. Nugan Hand's mail-drop office in the Caymans was in the Bank of Nova Scotia building there.

How the association with Price Waterhouse came about isn't known. But the Bahamas branch of the big international auditing concern proved ready to sign the books Nugan concocted, just as Brincat had done.

Nugan and Hand shuffled some checks back and forth among the accounts of the Nugan Hand offices in Hong Kong and Panama, and on this basis asserted that the Cayman-based Nugan Hand Bank had received $1 million in fresh capital. This made $2 million in all that they had supposedly invested in the various Nugan Hand entities, but neither the Corporate Affairs Commission nor the Stewart commission could find evidence that any real money was injected at all. (The Stewart commission put the total at $105.)

Financial swindlers do this kind of thing all the time in order to make a worthless enterprise look like it's worth investing in. The difference in this case is that Price Waterhouse certified the financial statements.

Price Waterhouse's New York headquarters says the Bahamas branch is an independent entity, and not a responsibility of the main organization. Investors, however, might be forgiven for not knowing that.

In 1977 and 1978, some combination of Nugan, Brincat, Steve Hill (the in-house financial officer), and Admiral Yates flew to the

Caribbean and delivered Nugan Hand's books to Price Waterhouse. Notwithstanding the fact that the books contained bald lies and gross deceptions, Price Waterhouse attested to them. Occasionally the firm would ask for some sort of certification from bank officials that this or that security actually existed.

But then the formal financial statements would be drawn up. Price Waterhouse would sign. At least in 1977, maybe in 1978, Admiral Yates signed. And Nugan Hand's team of salesmen would go to work using these assurances to bilk the governments and citizens of many countries—including the citizens of the United States.

Eventually, in 1979, new management was imposed on the Nugan Hand account at Price Waterhouse in the Bahamas. The resultant investigation may have been what triggered the collapse of Nugan Hand.

In 1976 and early 1977, just as Nugan Hand was expanding into a global organization and hooking up with Price Waterhouse in the Bahamas, two other banks were collapsing. Both were based in the Bahamas, and both had ties to the Central Intelligence Agency. According to reports in the *Wall Street Journal* and elsewhere, both had for many years been used by the CIA to pay anti-Castro Cuban agents and others. At least one of them, Mercantile Bank and Trust Company, annually had its phony books certified by the Price Waterhouse Bahamas office.

Mercantile and the other failed institution, Castle Bank & Trust (Bahamas) Ltd., shared some common officers and directors. Their affairs were intertwined. Each owned a large block of stock in the other, and each deposited substantial funds with the other. The central mover behind both banks was a man we encountered back in Chapter 3—Paul Helliwell, the former OSS chief in China during World War II, who then operated (for the CIA) the Sea Supply Corporation, which traded guns for drugs in Thailand.

As the U.S. Army openly took over the fighting in Southeast Asia, Helliwell went to Miami and became paymaster for the Bay of Pigs operation and the subsequent anti-Castro terror campaign. He organized and ran Castle Bank. Jim Drinkhall reported in the *Wall Street Journal** that a former federal official familiar with Castle said the bank "was one of the CIA's finance channels for operations against Cuba."

The same official said Helliwell was "deeply involved" in terror

*April 16, 1980.

operations run out of the Bahamas against the Cuban government. (Throughout the 1960s, Cuban exiles on the CIA payroll repeatedly invaded Cuba to blow up commercial installations, sabotage agriculture and the sugar harvest, sink ships, and try to murder Fidel Castro.)*

Helliwell's Florida law firm represented Castle in various dealings. The *Journal* reported that a former law partner of Helliwell's said it was common knowledge at the firm "that Castle was a CIA account." Former law partners would not return calls made by the author of this book, though other lawyers involved in litigation over both Castle and Mercantile said they were told by numerous sources that there was CIA involvement in both banks.

Like Nugan Hand later, both Castle and Mercantile ran afoul of their illegal doings on matters apparently unrelated to intelligence. Castle was believed by the U.S. Internal Revenue Service to have opened its doors to people trying to cheat on their U.S. taxes, just as Nugan Hand later opened its doors to people trying to cheat on their Australian taxes.

In 1973, the IRS—then unaware of the CIA connection—launched a big investigation of Castle. The IRS hired a woman of great charm to lure a Castle executive to dinner one evening, while an IRS informant entered her apartment and stole the banker's briefcase. The briefcase yielded a revenuer's bonanza, including a client list of 308 names. Of course, there was nothing necessarily illegal about having an account at Castle. But among those who suddenly drew IRS attention because their names were on the list were a host of celebrities and some organized crime characters.

Suddenly, the IRS and Justice Department called off the prosecutions, saying that the surreptitiously obtained client list couldn't be used in evidence. This sounded suspicious to some people. Other evidence was available—including the same client list obtained legally in other court proceedings. Drinkhall and the *Journal*'s editors were persuaded that the CIA connection was probably the real reason the investigation was ended. One "government official close to the investigation" was quoted as saying, "The CIA convinced Justice that exposure of Castle and, of necessity, other Helliwell dealings, would compromise very sensitive and very significant intelligence operations. It's as simple as that."

The *Journal* even identified a CIA lawyer, John J. Greaney, as

*Details in *Endless Enemies.*

being responsible for closing the investigation. Greaney wouldn't comment one way or the other.

One client company of Castle Bank was tied by the *Journal* to the laundering of $5 million for the CIA's use between 1970 and 1976. The client company was run by Wallace Groves, who had served two years in prison for one of the biggest stock frauds of the era, and then had gone into Caribbean casino operations with crime syndicate leader Meyer Lansky.

The CIA knew all this when it hired Groves "as an adviser and possible officer for one of [the CIA's] Project entities," as a CIA document puts it. Groves's general counsel in the operation was a Helliwell law partner, who has declined to discuss it. (What a shame that crooks like Groves, when they go to work for the CIA, never manage to do to the Kremlin what they did to the U.S. public!)

Mercantile folded after hapless depositors discovered in 1976 that most of its assets were worthless. According to the lawsuit the creditors filed, of $25.1 million in assets that Price Waterhouse certified to, $20.7 million didn't exist. The real money had been disseminated in the form of "loans" to unidentified figures. The "loans" weren't repaid.

Not only were Mercantile's cooked books signed by Price Waterhouse, but a Price Waterhouse partner, on retirement, later went to work for Mercantile. The *Wall Street Journal* reported he continued to do work for the accounting firm, while it continued to certify the books of his new employer, Mercantile.

The *Journal*, without being contradicted by any of the participants, reported that "the same group of directors and shareholders operated three other Caribbean banks, which the CIA reportedly used to launder money. A CIA spokesman says his agency never comments on such allegations."

Was Nugan Hand expanded under an arrangement with the CIA to replace the failing Caribbean front banks? We can only speculate. What can be asserted is that if Nugan Hand *was* operating with CIA participation, and if it collapsed because its operators were engaged in fraud, there certainly was copious precedent for it.

CHAPTER ELEVEN

Laughing at the Law

Nugan Hand told the world it made money in two ways: first, by arbitraging the customers' deposits on the commercial money market (paying the customers one interest rate to get their money, then obtaining a slightly higher rate by investing the money in corporate debt notes) and second, by collecting commissions for facilitating international trade deals.

Yet records indicate that the interest rates Nugan Hand earned on the money market were consistently much *lower* than the rates it paid to depositors. For the most part, Nugan Hand offered certificates of deposit (fixed-term, lump-sum deposits) paying 10 to 15 percent interest, then turned around and invested in similar CDs issued by legitimate Australian banks and paying 9 or 10 percent.

This is not a surefire way to make money. It is, rather, a surefire way to *lose* money. And the Hong Kong liquidator's office calculated that from 1976 to its demise, Nugan Hand *lost* $7.9 million trading securities. The much-ballyhooed international trade business also was deeply in the red.

But these banking operations were really just a polite front for the actual business of Nugan Hand. The kind of deal the company thrived on was the kind offered to L. P. Barnes and Arnold Waters, commercial farmers from near Wudinna in the state of South Australia (details as gathered by John O'Brien, the Sydney liquidator).

Each year from 1976 through 1979 (possibly except 1977), the two farmers gave Nugan Hand (via its Yorkville Nominees affiliate) an amount of money they wanted sheltered from Australian income tax. And each year, Nugan Hand would keep 22 percent of the money and return the rest along with Frank Nugan's legal opinion that the farmers did not have to declare it as income.

The legal smokescreen for the tax exemption was a phony sharecropper arrangement. Nugan, as a lawyer, formed corporations for the farmers, and had Yorkville make contracts with the corporations to engage in a joint farming venture. The money the farmers turned over to Yorkville was recorded not as deposits, but as profits to Yorkville from the farming venture. Thus it was alleged to be tax-deductible to the farmers as a business cost. The money that then flowed back to the farmers was recorded not as income, but as a loan, from the Nugan Hand International Holdings affiliate—and thus it, too, was tax-free.

Nugan provided his clients with documents releasing them from any obligation to pay back their loans. And he also put on a show of keeping things straight inside Nugan Hand, by making book entries balancing the accounts between Yorkville and Nugan Hand International Holdings.

The amounts of money thus "sheltered" by the two farmers rose from $110,000 in 1976 to $675,000 in 1979, according to O'Brien's figures. After the records washed up in bankruptcy court in 1980, the deal was challenged by Australian tax authorities. Not only that, but O'Brien set about to try to collect on the "loans" on behalf of Nugan Hand's gypped depositors. (The outcome of the tax case is private; O'Brien says most of his cases were thrown out of court, but a few are still in contention. Barnes says he has forgotten how his tax case came out except that he wasn't fined. Waters couldn't be reached.)

The arrangement with the two farmers wasn't unique. In fact, it was prototypical. Nugan claimed he made $100,000 a year for the bank just in tax advice fees. But from the evidence, he was charging fees not for advice, but rather for laundering. And the "fees" usually came out to exactly 22 percent of the money being laundered, and appear to have amounted to far more than $100,000 a year.

The owner of a furniture company washed money through Nugan Hand the same way the farmers did. O'Brien found outstanding loans to the furniture dealer from Nugan Hand of $322,847—78 percent of the total originally washed, or, in other words, the original amount less Nugan Hand's 22 percent laundering fee. The dealer claimed that he had been given a satisfaction-of-debt release in September 1977, asserting that the loans were permanently taken care of.

Steve Hill, the internal accountant, testified as to just how the deal worked: "The procedure was to issue a loan agreement and a deed of release simultaneously," he said. But neither O'Brien nor the tax collectors accepted that procedure as legal, and the furniture dealer wound up in the same pickle the farmers did.

So did a businessman for whom Nugan arranged the purchase of a commodities contract in Sydney—followed by the immediate sale of a similar contract in Hong Kong. The sale was made through a front company Nugan Hand set up there for just such contracts. Until the bank collapsed and the government caught on, the businessmen thought they were cleverly exporting cash to Hong Kong around exchange control laws.

Any number of Australian pharmacists were lured into letting Nugan Hand set up phony import firms in Hong Kong and elsewhere. Pharmacuticals being imported from Europe or the United States, instead of being shipped directly to the purchaser in Australia, would be shipped to the phony import firm. That firm would jack up the price to double or triple the true cost, then sell it to the Australian pharmacist who secretly owned the phony import firm. The result: the pharmacist was able to write off as a tax deduction a large amount of money that not only was still his, but which he had successfully moved offshore past duped Australian customs inspectors.

If the pharmacist didn't want his money overseas, Nugan Hand could easily repatriate it for him, merely by adjusting its own books to keep accounts straight between its offices in Sydney and Hong Kong (or Singapore, Bangkok, Manila, or wherever else someone might want to do business). For one pharmacist, Peter Harding, Yorkville Nominees imported the drugs right into Sydney, marking them up for resale to Harding and putting the tax-deductible "markup" in his Nugan Hand account—less Nugan Hand's fee, of course.*

When Dr. Bronte Norman Douglas, a Sydney pathologist, needed a Sequential Multiple Analyser with Computer machine (known in the trade as a "SMAC") for his office, he found Nugan Hand most useful. Dr. Douglas arranged financing independently, and had a friend in the United States buy the machine for $239,086.-75, including delivery to Australia. But the machine was billed in the name of Nugan Hand Trade Finance Ltd., Hong Kong. Nugan Hand Trade Finance then sent its own bill to Dr. Douglas for $317,000—one-third more than the actual cost of the machine.

*Detailed in the report of the Corporate Affairs Commission.

From the $317,000, Nugan Hand deducted the cost of the machine and the money transfers, and its commission (apparently about 22 percent again, based on the difference between $317,000 and the real price of $239,086.75), then put the rest of the money—about $56,000—in a corporate front account it set up for Dr. Douglas in Hong Kong.

So Dr. Douglas wound up with a tax deduction on the inflated price of $317,000, and had an offshore nest egg in Hong Kong to boot. The transfer of this nest egg out of Australia had even been approved by the Australian Reserve Bank—though the approval was granted only because the bank had been lied to about what was happening. Records show that the paperwork for the transaction was handled by Les Collings under detailed instructions forwarded to him by Michael Hand in Sydney.

Dr. Douglas also had a standing arrangement with Yorkville Nominees to provide "administrative services" for a fee of 5 percent of his laboratory's gross billings. This amounted to more than $100,000 a year. Although Dr. Douglas doubtless did get some advice from his friends at Nugan Hand—and it turned out to be pretty bad advice—the Corporate Affairs Commission concluded that "the underlying purpose behind the Administrative Services Agreement was to gain a substantial tax deduction."

Dr. Douglas deducted his payments to Yorkville as a business expense, then got a loan back from Yorkville for about 78 percent of the amount he sent in. With the loan, of course, came a document forgiving repayment. And Yorkville eventually wrote the money off on its own books as a bad debt.*

For clients who lacked some ready-made excuse like SMAC machines or pharmaceutical imports to cheat on their taxes, Nugan Hand in 1978 created a phony franchise scheme called Distravite Proprietary Ltd. Distravite supposedly sold franchises to Nugan Hand clients to distribute brand-name vitamins, fruit juices, or other products in a certain region.

The price of a franchise was whatever amount the client wanted to shelter from taxes in a given year. Some goods were actually distributed through a supermarket chain whose owners were big clients of Nugan Hand. But it didn't appear that a sincere effort was ever made to profit through the sale of health products.

Something else was happening: when a "franchisee" bought his "franchise," Distravite transferred the money to Nugan Hand, under

*Detailed in the Corporate Affairs Commission report.

some excuse, such as a loan repayment. Nugan Hand then transferred the money to Yorkville Nominees—which was constantly shuttling money back and forth with Nugan Hand under so many business arrangements they could never be sorted out.

Yorkville would then keep the standard 22 percent and return the remaining 78 percent to the "franchisee." To shield this last transaction from the tax collector, Yorkville would book the payment as a purchase of capital stock in the client's franchise business. But the "stock purchase" had no more effect than the "loans" Nugan Hand gave in other deals. The loans weren't repaid and no equity was transferred. Paying Nugan Hand 22 percent was simply cheaper than paying the tax collector as much as 50 percent.

The difference between legitimate tax avoidance and laundering was well put by one of the liquidators assigned to Nugan Hand in Hong Kong: "A tax-avoidance scheme is one where you're able to tell everyone what happened and it still works." When the tax collectors found out what really happened at Nugan Hand, it *didn't* work—as Frank Nugan must have known it wouldn't all along.

Whether the customers knew the score—or the admirals, generals, spies, and sales staff—is something one can only speculate about. Certainly the customers and staff were told by Frank Nugan and Michael Hand that the tax deals, and even the shipment of money overseas without government permission, were perfectly legal—even though they were blatant frauds.

George Shaw insists, "We never thought about it when we were doing it. We never said, 'Now I'm going to break the law.' If Frank Nugan had come to us and said, 'Look, we're going to break the law, we probably won't get caught but there's a chance we will,' I wouldn't be in this."

Exactly how some of the international money-shuffling took place was painstakingly worked out by the Corporate Affairs Commission. From the commission's work, it seems clear that the big international banks in Hong Kong that deposited funds in Nugan Hand were in fact providing an excellent facility for an illegal scheme.

For example, on July 15, 1976, the Overseas Trust Bank of Hong Kong, after listening to Les Collings's sales pitch, bought an 8½ percent certificate of deposit for $650,000* from Nugan Hand Ltd.

*Actually $648,403.30, an odd figure because it is the converted equivalent of HK$4 million.

in Australia. Principal and interest on the CD were fully guaranteed by the Wing-On Bank under its standing arrangement with Nugan Hand.

The certificate was due to be paid in Hong Kong on February 10, 1977. And, in one sense, OTB got its money as promised. But in another sense, it got someone else's money—because the payment wasn't made from Nugan Hand Australia, which got the original deposit; the payment to OTB came from Nugan Hand's overseas operations, whose only funds were the non-guaranteed deposits coming in from smaller depositors.

This switch of obligations was hidden on the company books by the same system Frank Nugan and Mike Hand had been using to hide other shady deals. Generally, cash assets that came in to Nugan Hand—like the deposit of the Overseas Trust Bank, or the cash from the many tax-avoidance deals—would be spent as needed, or embezzled. The cash would be replaced on the books by IOUs from the affiliate companies Nugan would incorporate, like Yorkville Nominees, whose accounts outsiders would never think to examine.

Periodically, the mounting IOUs from related companies grew to be an embarrassment on Nugan Hand's balance sheet. Holding too many of them as assets might—with reason—make Nugan Hand look as if it didn't have real resources to pay the depositors back. So a way was found to reduce these internal IOUs.

One such reduction occurred on February 10, 1977, the day the Overseas Trust Bank was due to collect its CD—$700,000, including interest. On that day, Nugan Hand gave Yorkville back a $700,000 IOU that Yorkville had written, in exchange for which Yorkville simply agreed to assume the responsibility to pay the Overseas Trust Bank on its CD.

The accounts *appeared* to even out. Nugan Hand's balance sheet was changed by the elimination of a $700,000 asset (the IOU from Yorkville), and the compensating elimination of a $700,000 debt (the debt to the OTB). But the reality was drastically altered, because the asset had been phony, and the debt had been real. The Corporate Affairs Commission said that the acceptance of the Nugan Hand bookkeeping devices by George Brincat, the young auditor, was "not merely careless, it was dishonest."

Concluded the Corporate Affairs Commission, "The debt [to OTB] incurred by Yorkville Nominees was probably paid by Nugan Hand Bank [based overseas]. Nugan Hand Bank . . . probably had no net earnings available to it from which to meet the debt and simply met it by dipping into depositors' funds."

The $700,000 CD of the Overseas Trust Bank was merely one item, used here for illustration. Similar shuffling was done with the money of other banks, and even of the individual investors in Hong Kong. Nugan Hand applied for, and got, permission from the Reserve Bank of Australia to bring deposit money in for money market operations, and then to send it out again. Nugan Hand Ltd. in Sydney even paid the withholding tax due on the interest that was supposedly being shipped back to Hong Kong.

But this was all just another ruse. The money never left Australia. The money being paid out abroad was coming in from new depositors, and from other illegal transactions. Nugan Hand had obviously devised a brilliant stratagem for looting the proceeds of an international bank operating offshore, beyond the purview of Australian or American banking authorities.

The president of the Nugan Hand Bank when the OTB deposit was paid, and when other such frauds were occurring, was Admiral Earl Yates, U.S.N. (ret.). Among the bank's depositors were citizens of the United States.

Nugan Hand's Hong Kong office went after deposits with gusto, methodically working down lists of expatriate residents, offering high-interest Australian CDs, with no exchange control problems. So persuasive was the pitch that accountant Tony Robertson, who is now an official Hong Kong government liquidator working on the Nugan Hand case, says, "I almost put money into it myself. Somebody else in this [the liquidator's] office *did.*"

The main object, Robertson says, "was to get money offshore in Hong Kong dollars so there would be no tax. If the money stays here, tax is withheld." What deterred Robertson, however, was that "they said they couldn't produce a balance sheet because of the secrecy laws in Cayman." That, he says, "struck me as rather odd, so I didn't do it." (This was apparently before Price Waterhouse signed a purported "audit" of the bank at the end of 1977.)

There were other warning signs. One American banker who was approached about putting in his personal money remembers, "Collings was a nice enough chap, but he was unable to explain how the company in Sydney made their profits." Still, the banker was intrigued enough to contact both Hand and Nugan personally. But, he says, they, too, failed to satisfy him. "The most disturbing thing to a banker was that they always left it for a dealer to explain how it was that they made their profits. They could not sit down and tell you." So the banker decided to leave his money where it was.

And a good thing, too, because, as it turned out, individuals were treated very differently from banking institutions. When the big banks like Overseas Trust Bank and Fidelity Bank agreed to deposit money with Nugan Hand, their deposits were guaranteed by Wing-On Bank.

In the case of the individual depositors, however, Wing-On wasn't involved. The individual depositors' money went into the Nugan Hand Bank, which was headquartered first in Panama, then in the Cayman Islands. The Nugan Hand Bank's money was tossed about among various accounts—and often just spent. Instead of being guarded by ANZ Bank, the individual depositors' money was overseen by nobody more reliable than Frank Nugan, Michael Hand, Admiral Yates, and the rest of the military-intelligence group that was coming on board.

This distinction, important as it was, was concealed from the depositors. "In my instance," says the liquidator Tony Robertson, "there was no mention of the Nugan Hand Bank until I saw the actual blue form I was to sign. If I hadn't read it, I would have thought the money was going into Nugan Hand Hong Kong, which [deposits] were all guaranteed."

Nugan Hand's deception was helped along by the depositors' own desire for secrecy. For many of them, the whole idea was to evade government regulation. Thus the very element that created risk also created protection.

On the back of each certificate of deposit, for example, was this message: "If to further assure banking secrecy and confidentiality the depositor wishes to observe special instructions as to correspondence, delivery of certificates of deposit to a custodian . . . or any other special services, kindly advise the bank of these special requirements by mail."

Secrecy was a byword at Nugan Hand. There were all kinds of affiliate companies through which money was moved in and out of the bank. Nugan's Yorkville Nominees was the biggest, but he and the other Nugan Hand executives developed a web of fronts. Steve Hill alone was an officer or director of: Hidex Proprietary Ltd., Frapat Proprietary Ltd., Illarangi Investments Proprietary Ltd., Leasefast Proprietary Ltd., NHN Nominees Proprietary Ltd., Nugan Hand International Holdings Proprietary Ltd., Nugan Hand Ltd., Queen of Diamonds Proprietary Ltd., S. L. Notwist Proprietary Ltd., and Nugan Hand (Trade Services) Proprietary Ltd. These companies constantly lent to and borrowed from each other to create a bewildering chain of debt.

In addition, elaborate codes were worked out, growing ever more complex as the Nugan Hand organization itself grew. This, for reasons one might guess at, was Michael Hand's department. He was rabid about adherence to the codes. Each employee was given a number, and was to refer to others in the organization only by number when using international communications. Nugan was 536, Hand 537, Houghton 538, Pat Swan (Nugan's executive assistant) 531, Admiral Yates 533, Collings 534, Shaw 541, Hill 535, General Black 532, and so on.

Then came the code for currencies. Woe to the company if the Reserve Bank ever found out that Nugan Hand was running roughshod over exchange controls—or if the central banks found out in any of the growing list of countries where Nugan Hand operated. "We dealt in money, so that's what we'd want to hide," explains Wilf Gregory, who ran the Manila branch with General Manor.

So Hand ordered that in all communications, currencies were to be referred to by a coded commodity. U.S. dollars were "grains," Dutch guilder were "wheat," Swiss francs were "oats," Australian dollars were "soybeans," Hong Kong dollars were "cookers," and Thai baht were "washers." There were code words for dozens of international currencies—even Portuguese escudos ("berries"). When Hand fled Australia, an even more complex code of symbols was found taped to his dresser; the cryptologist who can decipher it has not yet been found.

The names of money-laundering clients—the so-called back-to-back deals where a customer's money would be "lent" back to him supposedly tax-free for a 22 percent fee—were kept strictly confidential. Steve Hill testified that the clients "would have to have been approached by or introduced to one of the employes of Nugan Hand Ltd. or its associated companies and then in turn introduced to Frank Nugan."

Only on rare occasions would another executive or employe become involved. . . . By far the majority of clients would know only two people within the group of companies, Frank Nugan and the person who introduced them to the company. There was great importance placed on segregating knowledge of a client's affairs."

Records were kept cryptically. Australian clients in the Sydney office sometimes appeared as no more than mere jottings on scraps of paper in Nugan's pocket. Although the bank was headquartered legally in the Cayman Islands, most of its money came and went through the Hong Kong office. Its records were kept in a new office in Singapore, supervised by Michael Hand—who began spending much more time in Singapore and Hong Kong than in Sydney. A local accountant Hand had met and trusted, Tan Choon Seng, was given substantial record-keeping authority in Singapore. (He has ducked all attempts at interviews.)

Michael Moloney, Hand's and Houghton's Australian lawyer, describes the confusion that this system quite intentionally produced. "You could never balance the books," he says. "You can't tell what the deficiency is now, because most of the books are back-to-back deals. You can't tell what's a deposit and what's not, what's a real loan and what's not. They kept a million dollars in the safe," and there was no accounting for that money at all, Moloney says. Liquidator John O'Brien basically agrees.

Mortgage loans were given to one party, paid back by another. Who was lending or paying what to whom? You can't tell from the records, O'Brien says.

Former mutual fund salesmen like Les Collings were accustomed to not asking too many questions. "Our position was to get the money so they could use it to make more money," he says. "I was never in charge of investing the money. . . . I placed money wherever I was told to place it. And then the money market took over." He remembers that "all these banks asked why we wanted the money and what we were going to do with it. It was all sent to Australia."

Both Collings and his colleague at Nugan Hand in Hong Kong, John McArthur, say that for a brief period in 1975–1976, the system seemed logical. Interest rates were so much higher in Australia than in Hong Kong that it really did seem feasible for Nugan Hand to have paid premium rates in Asia and still made money—that is, if you just didn't ask how the bank got around exchange controls. But after that brief period, when interest rates again equalized, even Collings and McArthur admit that the bank's story seemed suspicious.

Says McArthur, "I asked Hand and Hill when Australian notes went below world rates, it seemed strange that we could continue to pay out more money than we were able to get in interest. The answer was that we could do better with a larger book, that it was worthwhile to bring in marginal funds to keep the book big and that there was a large pool of low-interest deposits, a lot of which was Frank Nugan's own money. It was supposed to be a highly organized, very efficient banking operation. That's where the admirals and generals came in. You thought that if somebody like the admiral was involved, he surely had checked it out.

"The truth of the matter," McArthur says now, "is that at the core of the operation were a small group of people who were misappropriating funds."

Contrary to any normal banking practice, salesmen were paid not just salaries ($250 a week, Hill testified), but also commissions on the money they brought in. A list circulated in May 1977 told how the commissions were awarded. Commissions ranged from 1 percent for deposits of six months to 7 percent for deposits over ten years.

For the money-losing institutional accounts such as those of Chase Manhattan or Overseas Trust banks, the commission scale ranged from only ¼ of 1 percent to a high of 2 percent—drastically less than for the individual, unsecured, accounts. This distinction should have been a tip-off to anyone who saw it. If *all* of Nugan Hand's money was to be invested in the same high-level banking instruments, why would there be such a difference in the value of deposits between those to be overseen by an outside authority and those to be overseen only by the executives of Nugan Hand? The obvious conclusion was that the individual accounts were being played with, even looted.

Yet the salesmen told customers that all investments were equal, as secure as the highest-class banking instruments. The Nugan Hand literature said so.

Says John McArthur, "I think now it was all bullshit."

Says the Hong Kong liquidator, "What they were, were salesmen. They got themselves lots and lots of money. What they didn't do was invest any of it."

If the commission incentives weren't enough, there was also the prod. Jerry Gilder, the former Dollar Fund of Australia sales manager, became the Sydney-based ringmaster for the team of salesmen. Gilder gave his typical pep talk in a March 21, 1977, letter to John Owen, who had just opened the Nugan Hand office in Bangkok.

"Well, John, it really is happening," Gilder wrote. "You are in Bangkok, you are talking to locals and you have now [had] a number of productive interviews. All things considered, I think that is pretty good in the time, and I am quite certain if you keep up your rate of interviews that all-important first sale will soon appear. [It was very much against Thai law for Nugan Hand, a foreign bank, to export capital by taking deposits in Bangkok. That is why the word "deposit" was habitually avoided. But there was no mistaking Owen's mission.] It is essential simply to keep up numbers of interviews," Gilder wrote, "and to continue to discuss the Group's services with everybody and anybody and making no attempt to be selective. In this way you will quickly get a feel for where your time is best spent and what constitutes a good prospect as opposed to a poor prospect.

"The interesting thing is that you are having as expected no difficulty getting appointments," Gilder wrote. "That really is 90 percent of the battle because after a while, once your skills sharpen, any person that you sit down with will be vulnerable to your sales expertise and will be very likely to buy from you sooner or later. In other businesses, such as life insurance, it is a battle even to get an appointment, so you can see the advantage that you have in this regard. Be particularly careful to leave the door open as a result of every interview, as you may well find yourself going back to these prospects at a later point.

"I am interested to note your own observation that you are not closing hard enough," Gilder continued. "You may recall that before you left . . . I predicted this would be the area with which you would have the most difficulty. It will not be too long before necessity forces you to be a little less British and a little more Jewish and to [come to] the realization that it is only on a rare occasion that a person asks you to buy something. Almost invariably he has to be coaxed into it, and 'forced' to take the first step."

Then Gilder told Owen how to apply this "force": "Standard practice is to have an application form beside you while you are talking, and then instead of asking the man to give us a deposit, simply ask him a less direct question, which is far more easily answered, such as, 'When we correspond with you, where would you prefer we direct our mail?' Then write in the response he gives, under 'Correspondence' on the application form. Or, 'What period of deposit seems most appropriate for you?', and then write in beside 'Type of Account', I.C.D. [International Certificate of Deposit] 10 years, etc. Or, 'What is the currency of money you have available for investment?', and write in his response beside 'Currency of Account.'

"In other words, you do not confront the prospect head-on with a demand for a deposit, but rather sneak in through the back door," Gilder wrote. "You then proceed to complete the form to the point where you finally ask him for his signature, and then close again with another question, such as, 'Do you have a checkbook for your Hong Kong Account which we can use to finalize this deposit, or would you prefer to give written instructions to your bank to transfer funds to us?' These 'closes', by the way, are purely off the top of my head and are without any real thought or practice. . . .

"It is a shame that there is a back-wash from Mutual Funds and previous sales organizations," Gilder lamented. "However, such organizations have no connections whatever with Banking. Banking is an altogether different business and involves ultraconservative usage of funds for the achievement of earnings as opposed to property and share mutual funds, which primarily sought capital gains with their attendant risks.

"As I indicated to you on the telephone, I should be up there within the month and look forward to going out on some calls with you. . . . In the mean time . . . just keep moving. Soon enough sales will come, and you will find out what I already know—that John Owen is going to be extremely successful in Bangkok."

For all its secrecy and deviousness, Nugan Hand was becoming a high-profile organization by 1977. The client list grew to include prominent people—the host of a popular Sydney radio show, the owner of an Australian major league football club, and some star players. Nugan Hand backed a booster organization for the team. Dennis Pittard, a well-known retired football hero, was hired onto the staff.

Still, a lot of clients seemed to be hiding something. A frequent guest on the radio show and several members of the football team all got into legal trouble over their involvement in heroin deals. (One star of the team is now serving a twenty-year sentence in a Bangkok prison after being arrested with seventeen *pounds* of the drug—which he argued had been planted on him.) A prominent society doctor who used Nugan Hand (and eventually lost a lot of money in it) had a reputation as an illegal abortionist (though he was acquitted the only time he was ever charged and tried).

Nugan Hand served as financial intermediary on the business deals of a Sydney insurance company and its president. In 1979, the company went into bankruptcy and the president fled the country, more than $1 million missing from the company's funds. Bankruptcy officials now say they think Nugan Hand moved the money overseas, but they can't prove it.

Football team booster organizations, known as "leagues clubs," are popular in Australia, and Nugan Hand went after their bank deposits, often successfully. The "leagues club" clubhouses do a big business in booze and, frequently, slot machines, which they are legally able to offer for use by members. "Leagues club" deposits were mostly of the guaranteed type, like those of the big banks.

Because of the high interest Nugan Hand paid to get the accounts, they were—like the accounts of the big banks—surefire money-losers, acquired for prestige. Any questioning staff members were told that once the bank obtained enough large, well-known customers, it wouldn't need to pay so much interest to get deposits.

A "strictly confidential" operating manual for the Nugan Hand staff included a list of "people in banks who are friendly to us," who are "ready, willing and able to give references as required." These included not only Albert Kwok at Wing-On and Ron McKinnon, the senior manager of the huge ANZ Bank, but also several other ANZ Bank officers and David Fung, an assistant vice-president of Irving Trust.

Nugan Hand was written up regularly in newspapers and magazines. Reputable international publications like *Asiaweek* seemed willing to print almost any nonsense Nugan or Hand told their reporters. The news was widely published, without any verification, that Nugan Hand now had a gross annual turnover of more than $1 billion. Nugan's international legal training and Hand's war record (the Green Beret, not the CIA part) were displayed and exaggerated, and their early accomplishments in real estate were grossly puffed up.

In June 1978, *Rydge's,* a kind of Australian *Forbes,* gave Nugan Hand a real testimonial. "It is the concept of low-key conservative operations, and a commitment to permanence that has guided the group through to its present day growth," *Rydge's* said. Almost all the publicity was in a tone indicating that Nugan Hand wasn't seeking out publicity, but was a quiet, conservative organization that was being discovered and talked about by people in the know.

Nugan Hand also became involved in Australian politics. There was a mixture of commercial and ideological motives for this. As they did with the big banks and the football leagues clubs, Nugan and Hand persuaded some city councils in New South Wales to deposit the tax money they were holding. These accounts were worth as much as $5 million each.

The accounts were all guaranteed, backed up by high-grade securities. Therefore, they were money-losers for Nugan Hand, though this fact was never admitted at the time. The city council accounts helped Nugan Hand acquire prestige, and thereby bring in more business.

There can be no doubt, however, that all financial considerations aside, both Frank Nugan and Mike Hand were ideologically driven to promote antisocialist and anticommunist political causes. Their fund-raising parties and financial contributions were modestly successful toward that end. While they made connections with the more right-wing parties, their biggest inroads were with the right-wing faction of the Labor Party.

As in the United States during the Vietnam era, the biggest ideological gap was probably not between the two parties, but within the more liberal party. The Lyndon Johnson wing of the Democratic

Party in the United States probably was closer ideologically to the Republicanism of Richard Nixon, Nelson Rockefeller, and Gerald Ford than it was to the Democratic wing led by Eugene McCarthy and George McGovern. So it often goes in Australia.

By associating with the more hard-hat attitudes of the right wing of Labor, Nugan and Hand may have done more to help their cause than they could by sticking to the more right-wing parties. Certainly it is a standard ploy of the CIA to work less with the most openly anticommunist parties than with the anticommunist wing of the party on the borderline.

Of course, there is also the point that many of the city councils dominated by right-wing Labor were associated with the corruption Nugan Hand fed on. The council in blue-collar Leichhardt, for example, invested millions in Nugan Hand. An important official there was later caught up in a big financial scandal and a heroin ring involving other Nugan Hand clients.

Nugan Hand also did business with Liberals, such as the deputy party leader in New South Wales, Bruce McDonald. Frank Nugan contributed to his campaigns, and Nugan Hand was involved in a deal for McDonald's business.

Yolanda Lee, mayor of the white-collar suburb of Ku-Ring-Gai, and her husband, lawyer Alex Lee, both became close to Nugan Hand. Ku-Ring-Gai put taxpayer money in the bank.

Another important political inroad was with Leon Carter, the town clerk (or chief administrator) for Lane Cove and later Sydney itself. Carter is a member of the prestigious Order of the British Empire, which ranks just below knighthood. Although elected on a "civic reform" ticket, he regularly welcomed Frank Nugan to his Sydney town office and lunched with him, according to liquidator John O'Brien.

Back in 1976, according to O'Brien, Nugan Hand (through a separately formed holding company) paid Carter $225,000, about twice the market price, for a piece of land he owned. Meanwhile, Nugan Hand got the cash accounts of both the Lane Cove and Sydney councils when Carter was clerk. An internal Nugan Hand memo O'Brien obtained credits Carter with getting Nugan Hand the Lane Cove account, which it estimates at "$20mil per week."

The 1976 land sale was accompanied by a flurry of loans and counterloans, involving Carter, Yorkville, and an outside bank, and left Carter with continuing financial ties to Nugan Hand.

Another political figure who used Nugan Hand—it's never been learned exactly how—was Neil Scrimgeour, a resident of Osbourne

Park, Western Australia, whose connections go beyond Australian politics. Dr. Scrimgeour, a surgeon by trade, ran an organization called the Australian Association for Freedom.

The name is much like that of the global circuit of local organizations that were funded by the CIA over many years. But Dr. Scrimgeour says he'd "rather not comment" about whether his group has a CIA connection, or why his and the organization's names were listed as "sundry debtors" in the books of a Nugan Hand affiliate.

Another interesting thing about Dr. Scrimgeour: he was a good friend and traveling companion of General Edwin Black. "His views were very right-wing and anticommunist, which I was very sympathetic to," General Black said. "He's got very extreme views that Western Australia ought to go it alone. I'm all for him."

This is a reference to a movement, which Scrimgeour was part of, for Western Australia to secede and become a separate country. He was even a candidate for Parliament on a secessionist ticket. Black and Scrimgeour were often seen together at the preliminary hearings that resulted in criminal charges against Frank and Ken Nugan for their manipulation of the family fruit business.

CHAPTER TWELVE

The Asia Branches

Nugan Hand's Hong Kong office grew to comprise at least a dozen full-time professionals plus support staff. Collings, the top dog when Hand wasn't in town, acquired a $20,000 Chinese junk and a $125,000 yacht, as well as a company junk used to entertain prospective clients. Former colleagues estimate he drew down $250,000 a year.

In selling the junk—named the *Dolphin*—as one of the few assets around, the Hong Kong liquidators say they discovered that the boat had previously been used to carry money out of Vietnam for South Vietnamese politicians before the fall of Saigon. But they say they couldn't find out who owned it then.

Douglas Sapper, Hand's old Green Beret buddy who kept running into Hand in Southeast Asia in the 1970s, became a sort of casual aide to Nugan Hand in Hong Kong. Sapper, who doesn't want to talk about whether he worked for the CIA, says he spent some of the intervening years working with an airline supplying the U.S.-supported side in Cambodia until it fell to Pol Pot in 1975. Then, he says, he helped the Drug Enforcement Administration check out aircraft for drugs.

Something—he doesn't say what—brought Sapper into the northern hills of Burma, the Shan States, where he says he got to know most of the local leaders. The Shan States were, and may still be, the world's leading source of opium and heroin. A sort of perpetual civil war waxes and wanes there among several drug-funded armies, including the old Kuomintang army of China.

Sapper even spent some time in a Nepalese jail in 1978—the result, he says, of a dispute over customs duties on five thousand wristwatches he happened to have with him. Back in Hong Kong, Sapper worked out with Hand in a gym every morning when Hand was in town ("sometimes twice a day," he says). They would also cruise on the yacht Hand had bought with depositors' money.

Into the bank's Hong Kong executive suite, Sapper brought an acquaintance, John McArthur, still an honorary captain in the British Army—the rank he held when he left active service in 1947. He went into the shipping business, wound up in Australia running a unit for the American Machine and Foundry Company there, then began investing in real estate, mining, and construction. He also held several posts in the Liberal Party.

Sapper brought McArthur into Nugan Hand in 1977, supposedly working on international trade deals, although McArthur in an interview can't cite any successful ones. Nor, by his account, did he lure any depositors. He says he spent much of his time in the People's Republic of China, "mainly negotiating on behalf of European and U.S. clients interested in supplying plant, equipment, and technology for major projects." None came about. McArthur won't identify any clients.

He does say that arms were among the commodities he unsuccessfully tried to trade on behalf of Nugan Hand. Probed for examples, he mentions negotiations contemplating the sale of bayonets to a Britisher who ran a whorehouse in Bangkok.* McArthur also says, "If anybody had come into Nugan Hand Trade Asia and said, 'I want twenty widowmakers'—F-15s or F-16s—we'd have said you could have them."

At one point, McArthur recalls, there was a lot of talk about a big shipment of gold belonging to Philippine President Ferdinand Marcos and his wife Imelda, from the Philippines into Hong Kong. "A woman set it up, a middle-aged woman, of Chinese origin, from Thailand," McArthur says. "But nothing happened. People went to the airport, but the plane never came." Still, rumors about movements of money for Marcos, the Shah of Iran, and others persisted within the Nugan Hand organization.

Jill Lovatt now asserts that she was "only a secretary" in the Hong Kong office. Promotional literature the bank issued in the 1970s called her a "Monetary Specialist with a strong background

*Lloyd Thomas, of whom more later.

gained from working with a Hong Kong finance house, a major tobacco company, a Commonwealth Trade Commission and a firm of solicitors in Hong Kong." By general account, she seems to have been the equivalent of office manager, handling the bustle of paperwork—and also moving great sums of money.

"Sometimes telexes would come up from Sydney to pay So-and-so," she says. "Les Collings would say, 'Please make out a check to So-and-so, they'll be coming by to pick it up.' Sometimes we were advised by [Michael] Hand that money would be arriving in Irving Trust [the New York account], be on the lookout, make out a certificate [of deposit] when it arrived, $10,000, $100,000, or whatever. There would be telexes coming in two, three times a week, saying money was going on deposit. You were used to money going from A to B to C and back again. So there was nothing terribly unique in money going around the world all the time."

Prosaic as it was to Jill Lovatt, the Hong Kong liquidator* was intrigued by the way money always seemed to be changing hands, with no real indication of source or destination. "There were lots of instances that A makes a deposit and B gets the check, all out of the same client account. Many checks were coming in in Sydney and going out here," the liquidator says.

Since the accounts were all identified by coded numbers, they have proven impossible to trace except when a client has come forward, or a participant (like George Shaw) has agreed to cooperate with authorities. In short, almost any imaginable kind of transaction could easily have been hidden.

In Singapore, Michael Hand opened a branch office in 1977 with Graham R. Steer, an Australian who studied at the University of California (Davis) and the University of Florida. He eventually worked as a management consultant in Malaysia and Singapore, and then with Nugan Hand.

Pitches were made to people working for foreign firms there. Two Chinese, who lost $100,000 each, wrote to John O'Brien, the Sydney liquidator, that they had turned their money over to Hand, Steer, and Tan Choon Seng, the accountant Hand hired and apparently trusted implicitly to run the office when he and Steer were away.

*The liquidator's office is a permanent government agency in Hong Kong; in the United States and Australia, courts appoint independent professional liquidators one case at a time. Two senior officials of the Hong Kong Liquidator's office were interviewed on condition that individual names wouldn't be disclosed.

A third depositor, also Chinese, described himself as chief engineer for the Shell Refining Company in Negri Sembilan, Malaysia. He wrote O'Brien that he began investing in 1979 and turned over a final $10,000 to Steer's secretary as late as March 29, 1980, after the bank was as good as dead. He says he got a letter from Steer dated March 29, promising to pay 18.5 percent interest, but not enclosing a new certificate of deposit because, Steer wrote, "we are presently awaiting details from the bank regarding your account number." He got neither the certificate nor the money back.

One common tactic the Singapore office used was promising to arrange Australian citizenship for Chinese families who wanted to emigrate there, according to John McArthur in Hong Kong and press reports. This played on a wave of racial laws that discriminated against the Chinese residents of Malaysia.

Press reports also said that Frank Nugan and Admiral Yates campaigned for the business of a Malaysian government agency that dealt with small rubber-growers, and claimed to control half the rubber production in Malaysia, the world's rubber leader. Admiral Yates was reported to have squired the agency's executive director, Dr. Mohammed Nor Abdullah, on a trip to the United States; but Dr. Nor, it was reported, ended the relationship when he arrived home.

The Stewart Royal Commission reported that a Malaysian government official had complained of Nugan Hand falsely claiming to act for the government on rubber sales. According to McArthur, in Hong Kong, Nugan Hand's attempt to take over the business "fell apart" because the Malaysian politician they were relying on "lost power or got arrested."

Michael Hand used the Singapore office to funnel Nugan Hand money and legal help to a company, called Medevac Shipping Proprietary Ltd., that announced plans to build a hospital ship. The company was run by an American who, according to the official Hong Kong liquidator, previously occupied himself running gold bullion out of Vietnam (where he was known as "Mr. Gold") and running a floating casino off the coast of Panama.

The Hong Kong liquidator also says the planned "hospital" ship seemed especially adaptable to military intelligence-gathering, and it was written up as such in the local press. It was to cost $5 million to $6 million and would be capable of landing directly on shore.

According to the Hong Kong liquidator, Medevac spent $300,000 on plans and design, but the ship was never built.*

*I was unable to locate the operator of Medevac, Arthur Morse, whose real name, the Hong Kong liquidator says, is Morselino.

Eventually independent offices were opened in Kuala Lumpur, Malaysia; Santiago, Chile; Buenos Aires, Argentina; Frankfurt and Hamburg, West Germany; London, England; and San Francisco. No major business has been reported to have occurred at any of those offices.

A branch in Taipeh, Taiwan, was more significant, not only because it garnered deposits but because of who was chosen to head it: Dale C. Holmgren, who fits the picture of a CIA careerist. A former U.S. Army officer stationed in Taiwan, he wound up manager of flight services there for Civil Air Transport, later Air America, the CIA's covertly owned airline throughout our long covert and overt wars against China and Indochina. The airline's job, according to *The Pentagon Papers* (the secret 1968 Pentagon war history later leaked to the *New York Times*), was to provide "air logistical support under commercial cover to most CIA and other U.S. Government agencies."

After helping run the CIA airline, Holmgren went into what Nugan Hand called "trading, manufacturing and investment counseling." But even then, Admiral Yates described him* as working with the U.S. military on Taiwan to develop "within the social structure of the Chinese in Taipei a close relationship with the U.S. military forces and the business and government community." Admiral Yates also said that Holmgren had worked for Nugan Hand without pay, at least for a while, because he had independent income.

Holmgren told Australian investigators, the Stewart Royal Commission said, that "he was not aware of any deposits being taken in or paid out in Taiwan." Numerous Nugan Hand documents contradict that declaration, however, as the Stewart commission also said.

One memo from Holmgren to McArthur, dated November 23, 1979, says his deposit-taking business "as the record shows has been increasing quite rapidly." The memo also says the work is done gingerly because it is illegal. "We must advise the client that we actually are only doing a service to them and the business will actually be processed through Hong Kong and Singapore," Holmgren wrote.

The liquidator in Hong Kong says Holmgren brought in deposits from Taiwan. Holmgren himself didn't return telephone messages from a reporter.

Wilfred Gregory, a Britisher, fiftyish, was picked to be the first Nugan Hand representative in the Philippines. For a year or two he

*Remarks made at Nugan Hand's 1979 conference in Sydney, which will be described later.

commuted from Hong Kong, staying in the Philippines no more than sixty days at a time (the maximum allowed by a provision of Philippine law for certain foreign businessmen). In May 1978, Admiral Yates came to Manila ("for several days of business meetings," the press release said) and announced plans to open a permanent office.

Philippine records show the office was opened in July 1978, though Gregory says it was April 1979, before he began full-time occupancy of it—a swank, richly paneled corner suite with heavy wooden furniture and a glorious view of Manila harbor. A few months later, General Manor joined him.

Gregory declines to talk about his past, or how he was introduced to Nugan Hand, saying just that he was involved in "estate planning." The bank's literature describes him as having "a strong financial and engineering background," saying he "held several important positions in Hawker Siddeley Aircraft . . . including coordination of production at all United Kingdom factories," before moving to Perth, Australia, in 1966, where he "established his own financial and management business with offices in Australia and Kuala Lumpur."

Gregory takes but few words to define his political outlook: he calls Philippine dictator Ferdinand Marcos "the best thing that ever happened to the Philippines since it was discovered by the Spanish." He adds (in a 1982 interview) that "the Marcoses are bringing simple things to the people that you and I take for granted."

Gregory identified with the regime, and wanted Nugan Hand to work with it. "You know, I have pretty good contacts here—otherwise I would have been thrown out," he says. The public relations man he hired was well-connected enough to eventually become the newscaster on a government television station. Gregory frequently got stories about Nugan Hand into the controlled press, sometimes with himself pictured alongside some high Philippine government official.

He befriended Marcos's brother-in-law, Ludwig Rocka, whose wife, Elizabeth Marcos, was the appointed governor of a large province. Rocka even moved into the Nugan Hand office with Gregory to conduct his own business.

Records show that the Rockas deposited $3.5 million in Nugan Hand; the records were slipped to Mike Hand by personal courier from Gregory on March 17, 1980, in connection with a trip by Rocka to Sydney to retrieve the money before the impending collapse of the bank.

It's been widely rumored that President and Mrs. Marcos, and others in the family, used Nugan Hand to ship out of the Philippines some of the gold and cash they were stealing from the country's economy. But the Rocka records, which surfaced in connection with his visit to Sydney, are the only ones to have turned up. Gregory absolutely denies knowing about such deposits, and Elizabeth Marcos went to almost bizarre lengths to avoid an interview.* Australian authorities apparently never tried to talk to her.

The records show the Rockas withdrew $1.3 million of their deposit, but odds are they got the other $2.2 million out, too, because the relationship remained friendly enough that Rocka continued to share office space with Gregory until Rocka died in 1982.

Gregory also befriended Marcos's old friend Robert Benedicto, whom Marcos appointed to run the Philippine sugar industry, the biggest industry on the islands. Late in 1979, Benedicto attended Gregory's wedding to a prominent Filipino businesswoman. It was widely believed at Nugan Hand that the Marcoses themselves were at Gregory's wedding, but Gregory denies that-"though a lot of their close relativies were there," he says.

As with several Nugan Hand offices, the one in Manila was in a building, the Ramon Magsaysay Centre, that was popularly associated with the U.S. Government. The adjacent suite was occupied by the U.S. Agency for International Development (AID) mission, and other nearby offices included the Drug Enforcement Administration.

Gregory even thinks he has identified the CIA station chief in Manila, working under cover in another U.S. agency in the building. After a visit to the office by Walter McDonald, the CIA's chief economics and energy expert, who went to work for Nugan Hand right after his announced retirement from government, Gregory says another American in the building recognized McDonald as an old CIA colleague.

The visit by McDonald was good for still more big newspaper publicity. Pictures in the Manila press showed him alongside Nugan, Gregory, and the Philippine trade minister. McDonald was identified correctly—though hardly completely—as a former U.S. Energy Department official. The report told of a "two-hour" meeting with the trade minister, and said Nugan Hand was engaged in joint ventures with Filipino businessmen involving waste oil recycling, waste water management, knitted garments, light engineering, electronics, cos-

*At the time of my interview with Gregory, I was unaware of the Rocka records and so didn't ask about them. I got contradictory information about Ms. Marcos's whereabouts, calling her office many times and visiting her home, as she apparently moved about to avoid me.

metics, furniture, and hardware. The idea was to "bring foreign capital into the country."

Apparently none of the joint-venture talk was true. It could have been a cover story, it could have been a dream.

Part of the fairy tale of justice told by the Marcos government was that foreign banking was tightly regulated. Gregory says his office was "set up under a special presidential decree, a stipulation. Deposit-taking and other cash banking wasn't permitted, he says. "We . . . were not allowed to earn income in this country. This office was financed by the bank from outside sources," he insists.

At first, Gregory denies that cash ever changed hands in the office. He notes it was only four blocks from the Central Bank, which forbade such things. Then, he admits, "there was one guy, a big fat Australian," who drew cash.

Then, he admits, there were more: "I used to get involved only with Australians who were stranded here. They used to have deposits in Australia and come up here and need money. After we verified that they really had an account, we used to keep a little cash in the office here. There was one guy who had his wallet stolen."

On further probing, however, it turns out there was much more activity—and it's hard to believe that all of it took place while Marcos's brother-in-law and General Manor were out to lunch. Gregory reveals that telexes would come in from other Nugan Hand offices ordering payments to be made to this or that person who "could walk in here and show his passport and say, 'I'm here to pick something up.' Money came in from other places and was used to settle accounts."

While admitting these pay-outs, Gregory at first denies up and down that his office also took deposits. "The law here doesn't permit you to do that," he notes.

Nevertheless, according to the Hong Kong liquidator, many people were foolish enough to deposit money at the Philippine branch of Nugan Hand, and two of them lost over $1 million each when the bank went under. Another man, Bong H. Kay, lost $40,437.91, according to the statement he submitted to liquidator John O'Brien in Sydney. A receipt for a final investment of $12,000 by Kay is dated August 31, 1979, on the letterhead of the Asian Development Bank in Manila where he apparently worked. It is signed on behalf of the Nugan Hand Bank by "P. W. Gregory, regional representative for the Philippines."

Confronted with this, Gregory replies, "All those things were confidential. I don't know who made sworn testimony about this, but I think it's in very poor taste to reveal confidential information." Apparently he believes that victims like Kay should have just swallowed their losses in order to protect the reputations of men like Gregory.

According to depositor Kay's Sydney accountant, "Representatives of the Nugan Hand group in the Philippines assured him that the certificates of deposit were guaranteed by a counter deposit with the Bank of New South Wales, or other similar institutions." In other words, the depositors were told they were getting the same protection Chase Manhattan got; but they weren't.

Gregory himself is indignant, though not for the same reason Kay is. "Nugan Hand ruined a lot of good people," he says—"the people like me, who were representatives in countries overseas. Admittedly, you have people like Bernie Houghton, who were naughty boys. But Singapore, Hong Kong, Malaysian offices—they're good people who set up offices in Asia and were let down." Gregory complains that the bank still owes him $30,000 in back salary and expenses.

Ronald L. Donegan, a retired coconut farmer from Papua New Guinea, had settled in the Philippines and made the mistake of doing business with Nugan Hand. "In common with many others, I invested my life savings in this organization and am appalled at the present situation," he wrote liquidator O'Brien in August 1980. Donegan lost $166,782.

But it wasn't coconut money. Donegan turns out to be one of four partners, or former partners, in something called the Kangaroo Travel Club, which has a storefront opening onto a busy street in the honky-tonk Ermita section of Manila. The store front seems at first to be a travel office. The real attraction, however, seems to be upstairs at the well-appointed bar, where each of the white, male customers seems to be having a good time in conversation with not one but several scantily clad Filipino girls.

At one end of the room is a hotel desk, with a clerk, a rack of boxes, and keys. The Kangaroo Club looks like a bright, cheerful, first-class whorehouse. And all four of its partners lost large deposits with Nugan Hand. One, Stanley Whitelock, a retired aircraft engineer from Sydney, says the club also owns four "hotels" just outside Clark Air Force Base, the big U.S. installation that General Manor commanded. What goes on at the hotels? Well, says Whitelock, "We have to put a delicate approach in our advertising." But he adds, "We know what the fellows want."

Whitelock is very open about why he and his colleagues invested with Nugan Hand. They wanted to move money out of the Philippines in apparent violation of the exchange control laws—ironic, in light of Frank Nugan's publicized assurances to the Philippine trade minister that he would "continue to bring foreign capital into the country."

Two other Australian expatriates in the Philippines, both named Oslington, lost at least $285,500 that bankruptcy-claim records indicate they gave to George Shaw. Shaw made many trips to the Philippines to canvass for clients—which got on the nerves of Wilf Gregory, who complains that Shaw took too many chances.

"George is a very foolish man," Gregory says. "Taking money home in his pockets. In his luggage. If he had been caught at the airport this office would have been closed." But the bank seemed to be operating under Marcos's protection, and Gregory from time to time almost admits as much. Shaw himself, asked if the bank had a special relationship with the Marcos government that allowed it to conduct its illegal business, tells a reporter, "It would be very dangerous to print that. Gregory is still there."

One fellow at Nugan Hand's Manila office was certainly known to the Marcoses. He was three-star General LeRoy J. Manor, who had just spent seven months across a table from Marcos negotiating a new ten-year lease on the U.S. bases he had commanded at Clark and Subic Bay. In October 1979, at a gathering of Nugan Hand executives and sales staff in Sydney that was tape recorded, General Manor gave the following account of how he came to join the bank.

Back in 1977, he said, "I was still on active duty sitting in my office in Hawaii when my good friend Buddy Yates stopped in to have a visit with me. . . . I've always had a very high regard for Buddy. I saw him operate in the military, and if you think he's a go-er now you should have seen him then. Very highly respected in the military, obviously. He told me about the firm he was with, Nugan Hand, which was the first time I'd ever heard of Nugan Hand, and he said that he thought that there would be a place for me in Nugan Hand upon my retirement. I said, 'Buddy, I don't know anything about banking. I've dedicated my whole life to the military.' . . . He said, 'You can learn, can't you? . . .

"So this was a great opportunity," Manor told the group. But on his retirement from active duty in July 1978, "there was another job that had to be done that I felt that I ought to accept, and that was the negotiations in the Philippines. I was asked by my government to head the . . . negotiations for the bases. This delayed my accepting this offer. . . . However, it wasn't all lost, because during my stay in Manila, working on the negotiations, I made many more contacts, and I think that this is probably of special importance."

He went on to say that the lease agreement he had negotiated provided $500 million in aid. In addition to $250 million in military hardware—the very thing the impoverished Filipino people needed—there would be $250 million in "security assistance funds," which could "allow the Philippines Government to divert some of the funds . . . from military support to some projects that will probably have a bearing—very definitely will have a bearing—on the economy of the Philippines." He mentioned power plants, or a port facility.

Thus he noted with pride that some little part of the $500 million in U.S. aid might, indirectly, reach the Philippine economy, where it could benefit people and companies. Maybe it would even help Nugan Hand. And he went on to ask, "Now how can I contribute? . . . Under the tutorship of Buddy Yates, Wilf Gregory, and I'm sure many others, I hope that I will learn to be productive. . . . I feel very humble standing before you today, because I have been tremendously impressed with the knowledge, the professionalism, and the mission orientation that I see here in this organization. . . . As the newest member of your firm, it's a tremendous opportunity for me to be here."

Manor spoke of how much he and his wife liked living in the Philippines, and how valuable his contacts were there—all indicating that he intended to serve Nugan Hand from Manila. But Gregory insists that Manor was in Manila only temporarily, and was being groomed for a Nugan Hand management post in the United States as the bank expanded.

Gregory also says Manor kept dual offices for a few months, both at Nugan Hand and at the U.S. Embassy a few blocks away. Manor denies that, and says he didn't join Nugan Hand until he thought his government work was concluded.

Of all the people in Nugan Hand, Manor is the hardest to classify. If you had to be either a crook or a fool, it's hard to imagine what Manor was doing there. His case cries out for some other explanation.

His military career was more than merely distinguished. He was a fighter pilot hero of two wars—World War II (Europe) and Vietnam. He spanned the eras of pistons and jets. The list of medals he's won as listed on his official air force biography (coming from Korea, Vietnam, and the Philippines as well as from the United States) is so long that if he wore them all he probably couldn't stand upright.

His best-known mission, however, while honorable, was an embarrassing failure. Having been promoted to general and made commander of the U.S. Air Force special operations force in February 1970, he spent August to November of that year organizing and leading a daring commando raid to capture U.S. prisoners of war behind enemy lines in North Vietnam. At great risk, Manor and the task force reached the Son Tay prisoner of war camp. But they found nobody home.

The raiders all managed to return safely, conceding that the camp had been empty for from three weeks to three months. Exactly what went wrong has never been established. Manor was quoted in the *New York Times* as calling the raid "a complete success with the exception that no prisoners were rescued."

He went on to become commander of the Philippine air bases and eventually chief of staff of the entire Pacific Command. In that role, he coordinated air force, navy, army, and marine corps operations throughout 100 million square miles from the west coast of the Americas to the east coast of Africa, and from the Arctic to the Antarctic. That was his last job before his 1978 retirement, and his call back to negotiate the Philippine base leases and perform other work the air force says is so secret it can't be talked about.

In December 1979, records show, an application was filed with the Philippine Government to change Manor's status from that of a foreign government official to that of an executive of a foreign multinational with a salary of no less than $12,000 a year. A month later, a red Ferrari arrived for him from Hong Kong and was exempted from customs duties.

That same month, General Manor pitched Nugan Hand investments during a speech at the officers' club at Hickam Air Force Base, according to Colonel H. Kirby Smith, chief judge of the U.S. Air Force Seventh Judiciary Circuit at Clark Air Force Base. On January 22, 1980, five days before Frank Nugan was shot, Colonel Smith says* General Manor instructed him how to deposit money in Nugan Hand by wire, which he did—$20,000—two days later. General Manor says he "wasn't soliciting, I was merely answering questions."

The next month Manor presented Smith with Nugan Hand certificate of deposit number 11531, promising 15.125 percent interest—without telling Smith of Nugan's death, which he says he didn't learn

*In his claim filed with liquidator O'Brien and in correspondence with the author.

of until the bank collapsed in April. According to his claim, this was "somewhat of a shock! Twenty thousand dollars is a lot to a military man and his wife!"

Colonel Jimmy Maturo, who has since retired, was stationed in Hawaii when he deposited $27,000 after hearing about the bank from his old boss, General Manor, they agree. Colonel Maturo deposited the last $16,000 on March 12, 1980, long after Nugan Hand insiders had rifled the files and were preparing for its demise.

"There are plenty of others around town," Colonel Maturo tells a reporter. "If you can put it to these rats, more power to you." The reporter brings up Manor's name, and Colonel Maturo will say only, "I know Manor." Then, repeating himself for emphasis, he asserts, "If you can put it on these bastards, more power to you."

Two months after Colonel Maturo unknowingly bid permanent good-bye to his last deposit—and a month after Nugan Hand entered formal liquidation proceedings—General Manor was assigned by the chairman of the Joint Chiefs of Staff to head the Pentagon's investigation into the failed attempt to rescue fifty Americans, mostly diplomats, being held hostage in Iran.

The attempt had been aborted April 26, 1980, after three of eight helicopters failed mechanically en route to the staging area in Iran. A fourth helicopter and an Air Force C-130 cargo plane crashed into each other at the staging area. Ironically, General Manor was chosen to head the inquiry, apparently because of his own previous experience leading a failed rescue mission.

The investigation completed, General Manor was chosen to be executive director of the Retired Officers Association, headquarters in Alexandria, Virginia. His biography, as issued by that organization, omits reference to his banking career. It doesn't even mention Nugan Hand. The general then undertook to start a scholarship fund for the seventeen children of the eight American servicemen killed in the Iranian raid.*

*The fund, the Arthur D. "Bull" Simons Scholarship Fund, is under management of Communities Foundation of Texas, Inc., Dallas.

CHAPTER THIRTEEN

The U.S. Branches

General Edwin Black had the most thorough intelligence background of all the flag officers in Nugan Hand. He was a graduate of West Point and the National War College. In 1962, he paused to get a master's degree in international relations from George Washington University.

Black was an OSS veteran. He was Allen Dulles's right-hand man, and Richard Helms's boss. (Both went on to become CIA directors.) He played tennis and chess with them.

After the war he got involved in assignments like "military assistant to the deputy for psychological policy," and the military staff of the National Security Council under President Eisenhower. He was military advisor on Philippine base negotiations in 1956, twenty-two years before General Manor conducted his own round.

Going back to the field, Black was active in the U.S. Government's anti-China undercover operations in Thailand and elsewhere in Southeast Asia. When his friend, the American "businessman" and eccentric Third World operator Jim Thompson (widely assumed to be working with the CIA), mysteriously disappeared in Malaya's jungly Cameron Highlands in 1967, causing an international furor, Black was sent to lead the search. (He came up empty-handed.)

A specialist in "special forces"-type operations, General Black commanded all army troops in Vietnam in the early stages of U.S. involvement there. When the war became big and official, he took command of all U.S. forces in Thailand. Later, he was made an assistant division commander in Vietnam itself. He was made assistant army chief of staff for the Pacific Command, then left the army in 1970 (he said because he failed to get his promotion to major general in the prescribed time).

He ran the conservative and militantly anticommunist Freedoms Foundation for a while, then took no doubt more lucrative jobs with CIA-military contractors. Eventually, he settled in Hawaii for semi-retirement under the palms.

One day, he said,* he was approached by two admirals—Buddy Yates and Lloyd R. ("Joe") Vasey, whom Yates had replaced as chief of planning for the Pacific Command. Vasey, the son of a naval officer, was an Annapolis graduate and spent most of his early career in submarine work. But 1965 found him deputy director for operations at the National Military Command Center in Washington, and the next year he became secretary to the Joint Chiefs of Staff, work for which he was awarded the Legion of Merit.

Although Vasey officially retired in 1971, he stayed on for an extra year in his Pacific Command planning job at the navy's request. For that, he was recognized with another Legion of Merit award that says, in part, "During this turbulent period of withdrawal from the Republic of Vietnam and major forces adjustments, [Admiral Vasey] personally developed major plans and policy concepts which, when implemented, have substantially improved the progress of Vietnamization and the posture of friendly governments in Southeast Asia, and strengthened the position and influence of the United States throughout the Pacific, Indian Ocean and Asia areas."

In 1977, when Black says Vasey and Yates approached him, Vasey was running something called the Pacific Forum. It was a Honolulu-based organization promoting scholarly and cultural understanding among the Pacific countries by bringing leading citizens together. There are a lot of such organizations, some of them fronting for the CIA, probably many more of them not.

We have Vasey's word that he isn't, and never was, involved in the intelligence business—though it's hard to believe anyone who was secretary to the Joint Chiefs and head of planning for the Pacific Command was a total stranger to it. Told that the Australian Labor Party suspected U.S. agencies of having overthrown the Gough

*Black died in 1985. He was interviewed by the author in Honolulu in June 1982.

Whitlam government, Vasey replied, face totally straight, "Whitlam is a friend of mine, or he was. I *wondered* why he hadn't been in touch with me."

Vasey says Yates, his successor on the planning job, had come to him for advice on who might represent Nugan Hand in Hawaii. Vasey says he naturally thought of General Black—who had already met Yates while both worked for the Pacific Command in Honolulu. Vasey says he also gave Yates another name, that of Peter Wilcox, a British-born U.S. citizen who operates internationally out of Honolulu.

Were Wilcox's credibility more fully supported, he would rate much more space in these pages, for he later made some bold allegations about Nugan Hand, the CIA, and drugs. Wilcox, who calls himself an international investor and contractor, claims a strange and unverifiable past with British intelligence. Admiral Vasey told Admiral Yates that Wilcox was reputable and capable. General Black and the Australian police have said they were impressed by him.

On a visit to Australia in November 1977, months after he had been approached by Admiral Yates, Wilcox called a prominent member of Parliament who had been cited in newspaper reports as a leading critic of the Nugan fruit company. The story Wilcox told was so startling that the member of Parliament notified the Australian Narcotics Bureau, whose agents promptly "debriefed" Wilcox in his Melbourne hotel room.*

Wilcox told the narcs that he knew Vasey as the former head of a U.S. military intelligence agency where Bernie Houghton had also worked. He said Houghton was "still affiliated with the CIA."

After Vasey had told him about the possible job opportunity with Nugan Hand, Wilcox told the police, he telephoned Yates. Without their even meeting, he said, Admiral Yates arranged for him to get acquainted with the other Nugan Hand officials on his next trip to Australia and Southeast Asia.

He described a visit he made to Les Collings in Hong Kong, who he said told him the business of Nugan Hand involved "shifting bundles of money." He said Collings told him about the world-famous courier Ron Pulger-Frame, and reported the opening of a new branch in Chiang Mai, the Thai drug center.

*A copy of the "debrief" report eventually made the rounds of Australian journalists, was publicized, and has been obtained by the author.

Then, Wilcox said, he stopped in Singapore and visited Mike and Helen Hand in their "luxury $1 million penthouse, which apparently they leased from an Indonesian general who had been depositing money with the bank for placement." Hand told him the bank handled "black money"—then was interrupted by a phone call from Frank Nugan, Wilcox said, during which they discussed the news that $200,000 had arrived in a safety deposit box in Sydney.

Next stop, Sydney. Wilcox said he was told that Nugan had just left. But he reported meeting Houghton, whom he said he had met some years earlier while Houghton was with Vasey's military intelligence unit. Then it was back to Hawaii, where he finally met Nugan.

Nugan, he says, was drunk, and insulted Wilcox and Wilcox's wife during a long afternoon in a hotel lobby. He quoted Nugan as saying of Nugan Hand, "We put people away. . . . We do the bastards over, anybody that gets in our way we can take care of. . . . I want you for deep cover to infiltrate the other side."

Then, Wilcox said, he learned of the drug connections being made in the Australian press, and he resolved to call the chief parliamentary critic of the Nugan brothers the next time he was in Australia. This led him to the narcotics bureau. In their report, the cops wrote that Wilcox appeared "quite reasonable" and "truthful."

Wilcox certainly knew enough about the people he said he'd met to show he had, in fact, met them. And he made his statements before Colby, McDonald, and the other well-known CIA types were ever linked to Nugan Hand. When Wilcox met the cops, the newspapers were still taking pains to point out that Nugan Hand wasn't involved in the drug and financial controversy over the fruit company. The CIA connection that later dominated the headlines wasn't even being mentioned. Nor was Nugan's drunkenness a public legend at the time.

But there has been no corroboration of what Wilcox told the police about his own and others' intelligence backgrounds. Although he talked with at least one Australian reporter at first, he has lately ducked interviews. Admiral Vasey has recently downplayed their relationship, saying he met Wilcox sitting next to him on an airplane, was impressed by his knowledgeable talk of international finance, and so recommended him to Yates. Years later, General Black continued to speak highly of Wilcox, calling him "a super entrepreneur and organizer," but said Wilcox "didn't think they were giving him enough money" and so refused a job with Nugan Hand.

All this can be taken for what it's worth, which may be nothing.

By the time Wilcox met the police, General Black had long since been given the Hawaii job. Nugan, Hand, and Houghton all came to Hawaii to welcome him aboard, and, he said, Vasey and Yates were there to make the introductions. What a collection: two admirals, a general, an ex-(?)-CIA man, an Australian banker who was imbibing at least a fifth of Johnnie Walker Black Label every day, and the man who seemed able to orchestrate all of them—a quiet saloon-keeper with a strange life-long proclivity for military-intelligence intrigues and a reputation for liking nubile boys.

Black died in 1985. But in June 1982, he recalled the story to a reporter over lunch at his private club. He said that he had some doubts about taking the job because of the drug rumors. "I didn't want to have anything to do with any drugs," he said. But he traveled around with the friend he says he much admired, Dr. Neil Scrimgeour, the "right-wing" (General Black's term) Western Australian separatist whose "Association for Freedom" organization was listed as owing money to a Nugan Hand affiliate.

Black and Scrimgeour sat in on preliminary hearings in the criminal case against the Nugan brothers in the fruit company controversy. Black said he saw the favorable reference letter that the international vice-president of Fidelity Bank in Philadelphia had written Nugan about the trouble. And Black proclaimed himself "personally satisfied" that the drug rumors were false.

As president of Nugan Hand Hawaii, he drew $1,500 a month unaccountable expenses, wrote checks on the company account for other expenses, and traveled around a lot, particularly to Thailand. But it's hard to see what, if anything, he did to further Nugan Hand as a commercial banking establishment.

"Nugan Hand was going to have an office here. Money was left in escrow," Black explained. But the plan was changed "because Frank figured he couldn't get around U.S. laws."

Certainly one would have to "get around U.S. laws" to take bank deposits on American soil without subjecting oneself to regulation by the American banking system. It would seem to be plain illegal. And Black insisted, "I never took deposits."

But a 1978 letter he wrote Frank Nugan, quoted by the Stewart Royal Commission, says he was trying to. And in the 1982 interview, he said, "They were hoping I would get $1 million or $2 million in deposits. I never was able to get a deposit. Most of my friends were too smart to go putting their money out of the country for higher interest. I never really tried too hard."

Admiral Vasey, however, said General Black tried hard on him.

Michael Hand in his office, with silver ingots, 1974 (© John Fairfax & Sons Limited. Photo: Lee/SMH 1974)

Frank Nugan (© John Fairfax & Sons Limited)

Frank Nugan *(right)*, Michael Hand *(center)* at work (© John Fairfax & Sons Limited)

William Colby (AP/Wide World Photos)

Facing page: The exhumation of Frank Nugan's body (© John Fairfax & Sons Limited. Photo: Nigel McNeil/SMH 1981)

Admiral Earl Yates as a Navy Captain in 1964 (UPI/Bettman Newsphotos)

Rafael ("Chi-Chi") Quintero *(right)* in a Mexican jail (AP/Wide World Photos)

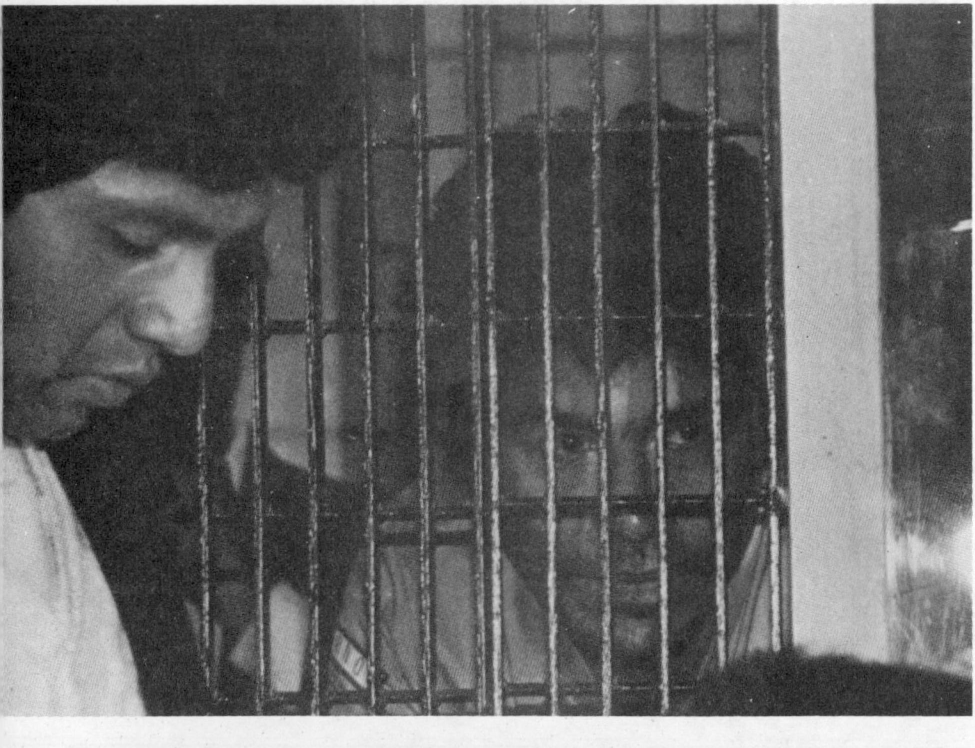

General Erle Cocke, seeking election as a national commander of the American Legion in 1949 (AP/Wide World Photos)

Gough Whitlam, then Prime Minister of Australia, in 1975 (UPI/Bettman Newsphotos)

The Sultan of Brunei (AP/Wide World Photos)

Facing page: Edwin Wilson *(center)* being led from the federal courthouse in Alexandria, Virginia, in 1982 (UPI/Bettman Newsphotos)

General LeRoy Manor being decorated by President Richard Nixon in 1970 (AP/Wide World Photos)

PARKING
OADING
ZONE

General Richard V. Secord testifying before Congress in 1987
(AP/Wide World Photos)

He said Yates made the first pitch, and encouraged him to bring in his friends. "But it was my basic instinct, and my wife's, not to send money out of the country. Black urged me to see [Douglas] Philpotts [the Hawaiian Trust Company banker] to get the real facts," Vasey said. But that wasn't good enough to overcome his and his wife's "basic instinct."*

If Black wasn't trying "hard" to take deposits, what did he think he was doing for the bank? "I was told I would be an ambassador of good will, arrange meetings with high-level people when called on," he says. "I introduced them to some important people. I traveled around Asia. None of these things materialized, unfortunately." One business idea he helped promote, he says, was an electron machine to enhance the power of seeds. "But the Philippine Government never jumped on it the way I thought they would and the company folded."

Douglas Philpotts, vice-president and treasurer of Hawaiian Trust Company, is listed along with Frank Nugan and Michael Hand as constituting the three-man board of directors of Nugan Hand, Inc. when it was incorporated in Hawaii in 1974. At least through 1977, Nugan Hand continued to list Hawaiian Trust's address as its own in filings to state regulators. Philpotts continued to handle Nugan Hand's high-six-figure account at Hawaiian Trust until Nugan Hand's demise.

General Black: "I was never consulted by Philpotts in any of these transactions, and there was no reason I ever should have been. He [Philpotts] was a banker taking orders from a bank."

And that is exactly what Philpotts told to a representative of the Australian liquidator who went to Hawaii trying to track $700,000

*When the *Wall Street Journal* ran a series of three page-one articles about Nugan Hand, including some of the above quotes, Black became furious and fired off a letter saying he had believed his entire conversation with the reporter, the author, was off the record.

I stand by all this material as accurate and the quoted material as verbatim. Black didn't say anything about the conversation's being off the record until midway through the lunch, and I had been taking notes the whole time. While I tried to keep him talking, I replied to his "off-the-record" requests several times by saying that I considered anything he said reportable, and I never told him anything to the contrary.

Black's letter-to-the-editor was followed by another, from Vasey, with a copy to Black, stating in full: "Regarding the [articles], I would like to clarify for the record that Gen. Edwin F. Black USA (ret.) did not try to get me to invest in Nugan Hand, or anything else for that matter." This completely contradicts what Vasey told me to my face, and that is the statement I give credence to. Black never denied he had tried to solicit depositors.

that had been shipped through the Nugan Hand account there. According to the affidavit of the liquidator's man, Philpotts said he prepared the balance sheet of Nugan Hand Hawaii as Nugan instructed him, "notwithstanding that certain of the monies apparently had been paid to other recipients" than shown in the balance sheet. Philpotts then told the liquidator's man to talk to Black, who was no more helpful.

Philpotts declined to answer questions for a reporter. He says Hawaiian Trust was merely acting as agent for Nugan Hand. "All our business is confidential," he said. "We wouldn't be in business if we revealed confidences. I don't see any reason why we should talk."

On May 14, 1979, Admiral Yates filed a legally required form with the U.S. secretary of the treasury in Washington ("Attn: Office of International Banking and Portfolio Investment"), registering Nugan Hand International, Inc., of 1629 K Street, N.W., Washington, as the American representative office of the Nugan Hand Bank and several other Nugan Hand affiliates. The office, he submitted, was engaged in "liaison and international trade related advisory services" and "public relations."

In the space for "name of person or persons in charge of the representative office," Yates listed two names: his own, and that of Brigadier General Erle Cocke. Cocke was a Dawson, Georgia, boy, whose acquaintanceship with residents of the Georgia-dominated Jimmy Carter White House was being exploited for all it was worth in those years. Cocke's consulting business was called Cocke & Phillips International, and it had the same address as Nugan Hand International. In fact, Nugan Hand's office was *in* Cocke's office.

Besides his Georgia connections, Cocke had a name of his own that he could exploit. His entry in *Who's Who in America* includes the following passage: "Entered U.S. Army as lt. Inf. [lieutendant, infantry], 1941; wounded 3 times; prisoner of war 3 times (actually 'executed' by German firing squad and delivered the coup de grace but survived, 1945); disch. as major, Inf., 1946; brig. gen. N.G. [National Guard]." There follows a list of citations eight tiny-type lines long, from the Silver Star to the Chamber of Commerce award as outstanding young man of the year, 1949.

Cocke had gone on to hold various posts at the Defense Department, was an executive at Delta Airlines, and for a while served as national commander of the American Legion.

General Cocke says he never knew that his good friend Admiral Yates had registered him with the Treasury Department as the "person in charge" of Nugan Hand's office. He says he thought Nugan Hand was just renting space from him, though he agrees they shared a phone number, address, and receptionist.

Yates told the Stewart Royal Commission that Cocke was a consultant to Nugan Hand, attended an International Monetary Fund meeting as its representative, and let Bernie Houghton use his office on business related to American clients whose money was taken in Saudi Arabia.

The commission found a letter Yates wrote to Hand saying that Cocke was to be paid $2,000 a month, though both Yates and Cocke said payments were never actually made. The commission reported as a finding of fact that Cocke "agreed to work as a consultant for Nugan Hand (while retaining his own consultancy practice) and assisted Admiral Yates in the formation of Nugan Hand (International) Inc."

Cocke acknowledges he visited Nugan Hand's office in Hong Kong, and that he welcomed Messrs. Nugan, Hand, and Houghton in Washington. He acknowledges he arranged White House meetings for Admiral Yates and Frank Nugan to advance their plans to move Indo-Chinese refugees to a Caribbean island, and to salvage U.S. military equipment. But General Cocke denies that he ever did any work for the Nugan Hand deposit-taking enterprise.

Enter Moosavi Nejad, 52, an Iranian lawyer, who says otherwise. Nejad, his wife, and their four young children sought refuge in the United States from Khomeini justice in 1979. In the Cocke-Nugan Hand suite, he gave $30,000 to Nugan Hand representative George Farris, a Green Beret veteran whom Hand had befriended in Asia. According to Farris's army records, he also served as a "Military Intelligence Coordinator."

Using his best English, Nejad wrote liquidator O'Brien that the $30,000 he gave operative Farris represented "only a saving made almost within the last 25 years in order to live." In other words, this was his life savings, carpet-bagged across the sea to the land of freedom and opportunity in hopes of parlaying it into a productive career. He had enrolled in Georgetown University for a doctorate in political science, Khomeini having rendered his law degree useless at home. Unfortunately for Nejad, George Farris enrolled at Georgetown Law School that same fall of 1979, after he returned home from Asia.

According to Farris's testimony in a deposition in federal court, Washington, after Nejad sued him, Farris had been assigned by his friends Hand and Admiral Yates to hunt up banking clients in Hong

Kong. When he announced he was returning to the United States for law school, they suggested he work in the Washington office of Nugan Hand, he testified.

Farris met Nejad at a cocktail party at Georgetown, and mentioned that Nugan Hand could pay 14 percent interest on his nest egg instead of the 11 percent Nejad was making at a local bank. Farris testified that the Iranian was afraid of keeping his money in the U.S. because of the strained relations between the two countries. After considering the deal for a few weeks, Nejad decided to go ahead. On Farris's instructions, he turned over a check for $30,000, which Farris forwarded to the Nugan Hand Bank account at Irving Trust in New York City.

General Cocke flatly denies Nejad's assertions that the general reassured him time and again about the safety of the deposit, though the general agrees they met in the K Street office and talked often. Nejad says Cocke told him, "Your money is in good hands. This bank is all right. Don't worry. I have even deposited there. I have been to Hong Kong [to see the bank]."

While denying the sales pitch, Cocke does agree that he told Nejad early on that he had $30,000 of his own money invested in Nugan Hand—more than Nejad. And he agrees that after the bank's collapse, he gave Nejad the name of a Hong Kong lawyer to represent him in the bankruptcy, and that the lawyer was Nugan Hand's former in-house counsel, Elizabeth Thomson (who declines to talk to a reporter).

General Cocke says he lost the money he had invested in Nugan Hand. Nejad says General Cocke told him the deposit was retrieved after the collapse, and that Nejad could get his money, too, if he went to Hong Kong and hired Ms. Thomson. "He said, 'If you want to keep your money from going away, hire this lady.' " Nejad hired American counsel instead.

Farris talked up Nugan Hand to many potential depositors, he testified in the lawsuit Nejad filed. But he carefully denied pushing the certificates of deposit in the United States, which probably would have been illegal.

Instead, he explained his job this way: "In that it was the basic goal of the bank to do business and to make a profit, the task fell upon me to advise people on the proper way to make a certificate of deposit if they desired to do so." Again, he emphasized, this was not the same as selling them, though not everyone might find the distinction worth making. "There were times when advice was given on how a client could go about getting a certificate of deposit," he testified. "I would suppose that I gave information sixteen to twenty times in that capacity" in the fall of 1979. But he said he couldn't remember how often his advice had resulted in someone's decision to invest in a CD.

Farris said—and U.S. District Judge Thomas P. Jackson agreed—that he didn't know a fraud was being perpetrated, and that he wasn't a decision-maker at Nugan Hand. "My superiors weren't in the habit of consulting or confiding in me as to what they were doing," he testified. And Farris showed that after he found out Nugan Hand had failed in April 1980, he voluntarily telephoned Nejad and had the Iranian stop payment on a $10,000 check Nejad had sent off to increase his investment.

Without evidence that Farris knew about Nugan Hand's insolvent condition when he took Nejad's deposit, Judge Jackson threw out Nejad's lawsuit. Not only that, he granted a $3,000 judgment to Farris on a counterclaim that Nejad was slandering him by telling people he had stolen the money. Nejad was still officially appealing the matter in 1987, though he was unfindable around Washington.

Several years earlier, he had complained that he couldn't find a steady job. Sometimes he performed Islamic weddings, but otherwise lived off the $400 a month his son brought home working as a counterman at Gino's. "I have spent my last pennies," Nejad said.

General Cocke admits he "made a terrible mistake to have rented them [Nugan Hand] space." But he says he is still friendly with Farris—and with Admiral Yates, who he says "was just as much a victim as everybody else."

Farris, reached in 1982, said he had lost money in the collapse along with the many friends and relatives he had advised to invest in Nugan Hand. He said he wouldn't name them, or the large companies he said he dealt with on behalf of Nugan Hand, because he owed them all confidentiality.

"I think a lot of the clients who lost a lot of money aren't going to file," he declared. "I don't think there's going to be a nickel paid on the dollar." He was probably right on both counts.

Meanwhile, Farris had parted company with Georgetown Law School for reasons neither would disclose. But Farris was busy—"doing some consulting," he said. He wouldn't say on what. But the consultee was at Fort Bragg, North Carolina, the U.S. Army Special Forces headquarters. Farris was reached through the Fort switchboard.

There is no question that Nugan Hand bilked American citizens living on American soil.

Ruth Thierbach and Jeanne Dodds of 1912 Filbert Street, San Francisco, deposited $5,000 in October 1979, simply sending a check on their San Francisco bank account to Nugan Hand Bank in Singapore. The next month they deposited $5,000 more by telegraphic transfer to Irving Trust in New York—all according to the claim they filed with liquidator O'Brien, which, they say, hasn't gotten them a dime back.

According to his claim, Walter G. Wiedmont, 323 North Central Avenue, Ramsey, New Jersey, deposited $100,000 in the name of himself, and Jodi and Alene Wiedmont, his daughters. The money was given to Bernie Houghton.

Houghton collected $15,000 from Joe S. Rodgers, in the city of Channelview, in Houghton's native Texas. Rodgers's claim doesn't say how Houghton got the money from him. His mother, still in Texas, says Rodgers now works for the U.S. Embassy in Moscow.

There were many others across America. None of them has been paid.

According to several accounts, Michael Hand was an avid Christian Scientist. He was also a health fetishist, built like a wrestler, and didn't hide his strength. He worked out daily in a gym, popped vitamins, and ate health food. People noticed that he made them walk ahead of him, not behind. He sometimes frisked people before he allowed them into his office.

George Shaw: "Hand is an extremely cautious guy. The epitome of disguise. Hand could be involved in anything and nobody would ever know about it. But this is not to say anything bad about him."

The Hong Kong liquidator says Hand "was secretive to a ridiculous extent." And as for his knowledge of corporate finance, the liquidator says, "He got that knowledge somewhere else than was on his résumé. There are gaps in Hand's career." The liquidator says he is persuaded that the CIA connection was more than Hand admitted—that it went beyond wartime experiences in the hills of Laos.

Wilf Gregory in Manila says he always thought Hand was "quite probably" still with the CIA—which Gregory says was just fine with him.

Michael Moloney, Hand's and Houghton's lawyer in Sydney, says, "They all the time were talking about closeness to the governments of Southeast Asia, and knew what the military were doing. When I went to Hawaii, I was taken out to Pearl Harbor, or wherever, and was introduced to the admiral in charge of the Pacific Fleet. He was sitting there with a big map behind him showing where all the nuclear submarines are,* with electric lights flashing. We were taken aboard a nuclear submarine."

Les Collings, in Hong Kong: "He [Hand] used to be good at sort of hinting CIA. 'When I was in Laos' [he would say], 'When I was in Cambodia . . .' But he wouldn't discuss details. I've always had the idea that once in the CIA, always in it. I used to kid Mike about it, and he used to say, 'Oh, no, no more. That was it.' But it wouldn't have bothered me. As far as I am concerned, that's not illegality. It's propriety."

*For the record, this interpretation of the map is of uncertain accuracy, but the description speaks for itself as to the impression that was made on Moloney and a lot of other people.

CHAPTER FOURTEEN

Banking in Opiumland

When the Commonwealth of Australia/State of New South Wales Joint Task Force on Drug Trafficking issued its report on Nugan Hand in March 1983, it deleted certain passages from the version that was made public. The task force said the passages were deleted because "release of material is contrary to public interest," either because "of likely interference with ongoing and/or future official inquiries" or because "disclosure is likely to identify informants or other confidential sources of information."

A few such deletions—a name, a word, or even a few sentences—are scattered throughout the report. Then the reader comes to Chapter 34, nine legal-sized pages of text and a tenth page of footnotes. The entire chapter is marked "(DELETION)." Not one of what must have been thousands of words of text, not one of what must have been at least a dozen footnotes, was permitted to appear. Nor has it been released in all the time since then.

The title of the chapter is, "Nugan Hand in Thailand."

The heroin-fueled political corruption of Thailand long predated the arrival of Nugan Hand, to be sure. United States military and intelligence agencies were involved in the drug trade, at least purportedly for political purposes, back in the 1950s and 1960s.

And just as surely, there were reasons unrelated to drugs why Nugan Hand might have wanted to open a Bangkok branch in February 1977. Bangkok was a burgeoning commercial center hamstrung by severe currency exchange laws. It was made to order for a money-laundering tax scam.

But Bangkok was only one of the branches Nugan Hand opened in Thailand that February. The other was in Chiang Mai. Chiang Mai is the colorful market center for the hill people of northwest Thailand. Like few other cities on earth, Chiang Mai is known for one thing. Like Newcastle is known for coal, or Cognac for brandy, Chiang Mai is known for dope.

It is the last outpost of civilization before one enters the law-unto-itself opium-growing world of the Golden Triangle. John McArthur says he once visited Nugan Hand's Chiang Mai office and was taken into the countryside to see some tungsten mines. "As soon as we got out of Chiang Mai they opened up the glove box and took out the guns," he says.

If it seems strange for a legitimate merchant bank to open an office in Chiang Mai, consider this: The Nugan Hand office there was lodged on the same floor, in what appears to be the same office suite, as the United States Drug Enforcement Administration office in Chiang Mai. The offices share a common entrance, and an internal connecting door between work areas. The DEA receptionist answered Nugan Hand's phone and took messages when the bank's representatives were out.

The DEA has provided no explanation for how this came about. Its spokesmen in Washington have professed ignorance of the situation, and its agents in the field have been prevented by their superiors from discussing it with reporters.

The DEA has a history of working with the CIA here and abroad; with drug money corrupting the politics of many countries, the two agencies' affairs are often intertwined. Was that the case with the Nugan Hand office in Chiang Mai?

It was, according to Neil Evans, a young Australian, whom Nugan Hand hired to be its chief representative in town. At least one client or targeted client of Nugan Hand in Chiang Mai reports that a DEA agent visited her, and spoke favorably of Evans. After work, DEA agents played cards with him.

In recent years, Neil Evans has made daring statements to the Joint Task Force on Drug Trafficking, to Australian television, to the CBS Evening News in the United States—and for a while to anyone who would listen. He has said that Nugan Hand was an intermediary between the CIA and various drug rings. And he has said that Michael Hand sent him to Chiang Mai for the purpose of moving dope money.

Evans has said he was present when Hand and Ron Pulger-Frame—the former Deak & Company courier who went to work at Nugan Hand—discussed the shipment of CIA money to the Middle East, Saudi Arabia, and Panama. Evans has said Nugan Hand moved $50 to $60 million at a time for the CIA, and also that Nugan Hand was involved in Third World arms deals.

For his television interviews, Evans has come up with lots of details. He has also been paid—reportedly $10,000 from the Australia's Channel Nine, which sold its footage to CBS here.* The payment alone casts some doubt on Evans's veracity.

Beyond that, much of what Evans says isn't subject to verification. Much else that he says concerns transactions in Sydney and elsewhere that involve intelligence, and even if they occurred, Evans would not likely have been privy to them. Worse still, his stories have been contradictory. Both the Joint Task Force and Stewart Royal Commission rejected his testimony for some of these reasons.

In a signed but not sworn statement to the Joint Task Force, Evans said he had met Frank Nugan and Mike Hand back in 1974 while he was working as a tax consultant. He said he had heard of their ability to reduce taxes and get money out of Australia through legal loopholes. They kept in touch, he said, and Hand approached him in 1976 about going to Chiang Mai to "seek out deposit moneys from people that were involved primarily in the drug trafficking trade." Hand knew about these people, Evans said, "through his associations during the Vietnamese War . . . through his association with the CIA." Hand "felt he could use his influence and his connections with the CIA to attract the business," Evans said.

He said Mike Hand told him that their conversation about this was to be private from other officials of Nugan Hand, and that Evans should just apply to Jerry Gilder for a sales job—which he did. Evans didn't mention these secret instructions from Hand when he was interviewed by Australian journalists; he told them that he wrote to Gilder after seeing an ad for salesmen in a newspaper in December 1976.**

But much that Evans has said is provably true, and at least one colleague, John Owen, confirms that Mike Hand, not Jerry Gilder,

*Channel Nine says it "will neither confirm nor deny" the report, which came from excellent sources. CBS aired the interview on its prime news show without notice to the viewer that Evans had been paid to give it. But at least CBS pursued the story.

**By the time the author got to Australia, Evans had delisted his phone number and was lying low. I never found him.

hand-picked Evans for the Chiang Mai job. The people Evans has described dealing with in Chiang Mai, in all his interviews, exist. They agree they dealt with him. Of course, they deny that they are dope kingpins as he alleges, but it is not likely they would admit to that if it was true.

Most significant, Nugan Hand certainly employed Evans, and it assigned him to be the lone representative in a post everyone knew was extremely sensitive. It trusted him there. In fact, Nugan Hand was very high on Evans.

On February 10, 1977, Jerry Gilder sent a memo to Mike Hand announcing that the two new Thai representatives were on their way. "Both guys expect to meet you in Hong Kong for a brief orientation period, take a look at the office and receive from you specific instructions that are required relating to conduct of business in the appropriate manner," Gilder wrote.

The memo described Neil Evans as if Hand didn't know him. It said Evans was "a gunslinger, he is 39 and married with one boy aged 2½ years. Sales have always been his life and he has sold a wide range of products including encyclopedias, accounting systems and real estate. He appears to always have been a good earner, fluctuating between the $20,000 and $40,000 region. He could be described positively as . . . friendly, likeable, gregarious"—and, Gilder added, for what it was worth, "honest." As Gilder saw it, "Neil is willing to go anywhere he can make lots of money and will proceed on the basis of leaving his family somewhere safe and coming back to see them from time to time."

The other new man was John Owen. He had been a career officer in the British Navy, then went to work in the defense industry for a radar manufacturer. Eventually, he landed in Australia, where he took other jobs with cement and real estate companies.

There can be no assurance about secret arrangements made in advance—such as Neil Evans described to the police—or what phony documents might have been created for deception. But an application letter in Owen's handwriting was found in Nugan Hand's files, and it supports Owen's own story that he replied to one of the bank's newspaper advertisements for salesmen.

Owen laughs about it now in a Bangkok bar. "There were big ads in the paper," he says, asking, " 'Are you a $60,000-a-year man?' And I said, of course I was. I came up [to Bangkok] with $5,000 and a 'See how you do.' "

Owen admits he occasionally tried to lure deposits, but he denies he ever successfully reeled one in. Deposit-taking, after all, could get Owen hauled off his barstool and taken to the hoosegow. As his former Nugan Hand colleague John McArthur has remarked, "It was very risky. In Thailand they put you in jail for twenty years and then have a trial."

Owen says the deposits were sucked up by Les Collings, who, he says, "used to come in from Hong Kong. Collings got quite a few depositors. I saw Collings literally browbeat this fellow, a Thai, into giving him $300,000. He talked to him for about four hours until the guy was literally a nervous wreck."

The really big clients, Owen says, were in the $500,000 to $750,000 range—businessmen involved in "trading, banking, hotels." He speaks of one such man who withdrew his Thai deposit in Hong Kong, but then, "against my better advice he put some money in in Sydney, and he lost it."

Like Wilf Gregory and others, Owen says his main work was fostering trade deals. He denies that he knew about any kind of drug connection or that he was involved in any intelligence work.

Now for the evidence. Owen's correspondence file at Nugan Hand,* much of it in his own distinctive handwriting, shows that he did take deposits. It shows that he was very worried about dope-connected people being associated with the bank—but felt unable to do anything to stop it because Mike Hand wanted the connection.

The correspondence file also shows that periodically, former naval officer Owen sent back long reports, almost tiresome in their detail, about troop movements and other military and political activities, mostly in Cambodia (which he referred to as Kampuchea), but also in Laos, Vietnam, and Thailand. The reports appear totally unconnected to any banking or business activity, and bear notations they were to be shown to Michael Hand.

John Owen remembers visiting Neil Evans in Chiang Mai, and "sitting in his funny little apartment at the Rincome Hotel," a main hangout for foreigners. And he remembers Evans running around "saying he had great overseas loans."

According to what Owen and many small businessmen in Chiang Mai say, Evans was operating the equivalent of an advance-fee loan scheme, long popular among American confidence men. The scheme

*The file was somehow not destroyed in the ransacking of the files. But I obtained it after my interview with Owen in Bangkok, and so couldn't confront him with it.

involves telling businessmen that you have a source of loan money for them, showing them all kinds of phony documentation, and saying that you can arrange the loans if the businessmen pay brokerage fees in advance. The fees are collected, and the loans never materialize.

"I don't blame him, really," Owen says. "It was the only way he could get along."

The people at Nugan Hand, however, aimed to do more than just get along, and that's all Evans was able to do with his advance fees. From interviews with the swindled businessmen, it appears that the fees Evans obtained from them averaged only $1,000 to $5,000. Apparently the total never approached even $100,000. Evans was clearly into something bigger—at least if you consider the amazing array of U.S. intelligence veterans he hooked up with almost overnight.

For his chief aides-de-camp, in and out of the office, there suddenly appeared two Thais: Otto Suripol, who during the Vietnam War had been an interpreter for the U.S. Government at Nam Pong Air Base, and Suthin Sansiribhan, who had worked for Air America, the CIA airline. In the known interviews he gave, Evans wasn't ever asked how he found these two.

Suripol couldn't be located. Sansiribhan, living in a nice new house about an hour's drive from Chiang Mai, says he was brought in by Suripol. He proudly displays letters of high praise from Air America officials—in other words CIA men—for his work as loadmaster on planes shuttling between Udorn Air Force Base, Thailand, and Vientiane, Laos. Sansiribhan's ultimate boss back then, and Suripol's, was the commanding general of the U.S. bases in Thailand, Edwin Black.

Suripol and Sansiribhan weren't the only ones to find their way back to familiar company via Nugan Hand. Into the perceived Nugan Hand coterie, formally or informally, Evans quickly brought William and O. Gordon Young. The Youngs are sons of American missionaries in Thailand, and have served off and on as paid CIA officers in various capacities since the 1950s.

Billy Young says he "left my father's farm north of Chiang Mai" on the occasion of a coup in Laos in 1960, and went to work with the U.S. AID mission in Laos. His assigned job, he says, was helping "refugees and people about to be refugees. But, in fact, I wound up as a paramilitary officer working with the tribal people, rebels. Arming and training hill people to defend themselves," he says. "I left the service [the CIA] in 1966. I joined them again briefly in 1967. I've been here"—in Chiang Mai—"privately since then."

But for all his "privateness," Billy Young is no simple farmer. "I provide help to the MIA-POW [missing-in-action, prisoners-of-war] program, the group calling themselves Project Freedom," he says. Project Freedom operates in the belief that U.S. servicemen are still being held prisoner in the jungles of Indo-China, and that paramilitary operations are necessary to get them out.

Project Freedom gets a lot of support and direction from *Soldier of Fortune* magazine, which has half a dozen or more hairy-chested six-footers occupying a penthouse suite in Bangkok at any given time, running daring missions to do reconnaissance along the Laotian border, and at times surreptitiously crossing the border illegally.

Could *Soldier of Fortune* have a CIA connection, asks a reporter who has often wondered about that. "I've often wondered about that myself," says Young. "It's a perfectly obvious place."

The reporter brings up the tendency of *Soldier of Fortune* people to get involved with automatic rifles on U.S. soil, where it is illegal for civilians to have them. "I love weapons," Young says. "I would have twenty to thirty guns around the house. During the '73 riots [sometimes violent student-led demonstrations in Thailand] I was determined that if they came in after me I would take a lot of them along with me."

In 1977, Young occupied an apartment next door to Evans's at the Rincome Hotel. "He seemed like the ordinary nice guy," Young says of his neighbor. Young says he really never understood much about Nugan Hand's business, though he does nothing to dispel all the talk of drug deals. "They were setting up some kind of agricultural extension program," Young says of Nugan Hand. "They would lay out money in return for indigenous produce. I don't know what kind of produce." (No one so familiar with Chiang Mai could be ignorant about the paramount local produce.)

Young says he got involved with Nugan Hand "because somebody recommended to my brother [O. Gordon Young] that he get in touch with them. He was looking for work at that point." Billy Young says his brother Gordon was first in the family to join the CIA, back in 1954, and worked with the U.S. operations mission in Bangkok during the 1960s.

Gordon Young, though, asserts he left the CIA in 1960. He says the Nugan Hand involvement developed this way: Back in 1977, "somebody told me I should make every effort to go over there and meet Michael Hand, meet them [the bank executives]. There was one or two letters exchanged." Who was the "somebody" who told him to do this? "Some friend of mine from somewhere—could have been somebody back here [in the United States]," Gordon Young says. No names come to mind, he asserts.

So he talked to Mike Hand. And next thing, Gordon Young says, he was "sitting around the Rincome Hotel" with Neil Evans, talking about "selling certificates." Ultimately, he says, "no suitable post was found," and he returned to the United States. In 1982, Gordon Young was a security official at a nuclear power plant operated by Pacific Gas & Electric Company in California. The security office wouldn't precisely define his role, but the plant had been under attack by antinuclear demonstrators. It says he still works there.

A former CIA official familiar with the Bangkok station confirms that the Youngs spent a lot of time in CIA work. He says he twice fired them, only to go to another post in the Southeast Asia region and find them still on the payroll.

There is general agreement that the Chiang Mai office of Nugan Hand was going to have something to do with agriculture. Les Collings insists it was just going to try to finance local tobacco growing, for export to the United States. Evans, too, says there was a deal to raise and export a crop that was going to be called tobacco. But he says it was really going to be marijuana.

Evans says that in his seven months in Chiang Mai he corralled $2.6 million in deposits, from six big drug dealers. Owen and Collings both scoff at that.

There is also disagreement over why Evans left that fall. He says it was because a Thai general, a client, warned him that the government was going to have to crack down on the illegal money-moving. Collings, on the other hand, says he fired Evans because he *wasn't* bringing in deposits. Owen—who spent the most time with him—says Evans left because he contracted a severe case of hepatitis. (And Billy Young also says Evans suffered some bad health problems just before he left, although, as with most things about Nugan Hand, Young says he doesn't remember the details.)

If the Nugan Hand bosses weren't pleased with Evans's work, it certainly didn't show in the performance report Jerry Gilder wrote May 17, 1977, after visiting him three months into his tour. "Neil is doing a fine job," Gilder said. "He is one of about a dozen European [white] businessmen in the area and it is a remarkable effort that he has been accepted in the way that he has by the locals."

Gilder fairly gushed about his subject. "Neil has made a point of socialising practically every night," he wrote, "and has accepted every invitation to dinner at the homes of local people. He is not pushing for business in the normal sense but is quietly baiting the traps, demonstrating knowledge and patience and forever looking for opportunities to be of service in any way. . . . Neil's area is poised for a boom and prospects for significant business appear encouraging."

There are no written records to support Evans's claim of big depositors—any more than there are clear records of any other Nugan Hand accounts, except as supplied by depositors filing claims. The purported depositors Evans named are all in business in Chiang Mai. They are all in a position to have the kind of money Evans describes. They all say they knew him and talked business with him. And they all deny they deposited money with him—which is understandable, since any Thai who *admitted* depositing money with him would be applying for long-term prison housing.

The people in question include some pretty impressive figures. One is General Sanga Kittikachorn, whose warning, Evans said, made him get out. General Kittikachorn is one of the most powerful figures in the Thai military, which has ruled the country since a coup in 1976. He is a former member of the Thai National Assembly. And he is also the brother of former civilian Prime Minister Thanom Kittikachorn, whose Vietnam War-era government worked closely with the U.S. military under General Black. In fact, a Thai colonel who was on Black's staff back then had been a leader in the 1976 military coup.

Both Kittikachorn brothers, Thomas and Sanga, met daily with CIA leaders at times. General Kittikachorn says the CIA and Thai General Staff "work very closely with each other. I think you know about the function of the CIA. We were very close to the American Government."

The general—who owns the Chiang Mai Hills Hotel, and whose family owns many businesses there and in Bangkok—says he met Evans "many times." Evans, he says, "came to the hotel and said he wanted to know me. He introduced himself as dealing with the money business."

Owen remembers a meeting with Evans, Collings, and General Kittikachorn at the Thai Military Bank branch in Chiang Mai. He says the general was being advanced some money for the hotel.

The manager of the Thai Military Bank in Chiang Mai, Khun Sunet Kamnuan, concedes he referred Evans to people he thought were likely prospects for Evans's business. And he concedes that several of the prospects he recommended did pay fees to Evans, without ever getting the promised loans. The manager of another bank in town tells pretty much the same story.

General Kittikachorn agrees that somehow Evans "got in with" the Thai Military Bank. He says he introduced Evans to his own friends and "other people here" because Evans was trying to lend money. He won't say who these friends and other people were. Faced with Evans's testimony that Kittikachorn deposited $500,000 with Nugan Hand to get it overseas, Kittikachorn says, "That is a very funny story. I'm not so crazy to believe people like them."

He acknowledges that the Nugan Hand team tried to sell him and others on high-interest deposits and offshore money transfers. He acknowledges that he went to the bank's office in Bangkok, as Evans said, and even that he brought "a friend" there. But he denies making deposits or knowing anyone who did.

"Most people want to borrow money, not put money into the bank," General Kittikachorn says. Why three Nugan Hand staffers would have been present at the Thai Military Bank when Kittikachorn was receiving money—unless he was withdrawing the money from a Nugan Hand account or somehow using Nugan Hand facilities—is unexplained. Moreover, several people—including Owen, who later had breakfast with him—say General Kittikachorn seemed particularly distressed when Evans left town. "Sanga was upset Evans left," Owen says.

Another Chiang Mai resident Evans identified as a Nugan Hand depositor is the woman who owns the building where Nugan Hand and the DEA had offices. (The DEA is still there.) The landlady and her husband also own mines around Chiang Mai, and, moreover, have a franchise to sell dynamite—reputedly an exclusive franchise for Thailand and certain other places in Southeast Asia. Evans has said she gave him $750,000 in Chiang Mai, and that her husband deposited even larger amounts, but dealt exclusively with Mike Hand in Bangkok.

She flatly denies this, and says she rented Evans space because "he dressed very well and showed off that he had a lot of money. Even the American DEA came in and talked to me about Evans." But she says that all along "I suspected that they were crooks. They said they had a lot of money, but instead they borrowed money."

Khun Lertsak Vatchapapreecha, a big dealer in farm equipment and other merchandise in Chiang Mai, denies Evans's story that he made a $600,000 deposit. But Lertsak, as he is called, says he did get to know Evans on the advice of the Thai Military Bank. He says they became friends. He says he fended off Evans's sales attempts.

"High interest, I think he did discuss this," Lertsak says. "But I wasn't interested. If I want to move money around I don't need any help. I have a lot of friends in Hong Kong."

Asked about Evans's testimony that he made an appointment for Lertsak to meet the Nugan Hand executives in Bangkok, Lertsak says he just doesn't remember whether the meeting took place or not.

The DEA declined to disclose the whereabouts of its agents in Chiang Mai at the time. But Evans correctly supplied their names.

The Stewart Royal Commission report says, "The commission finds there is no evidence to support the allegation that the office in Chiang Mai was established to attract deposits from drug producers of the so-called 'Golden Triangle.' " But, typically, the report presents no independent evidence. It just juxtaposes the lone assertion of the unreliable Evans against self-serving anti-drug statements from Collings, Gilder, and another Nugan Hand officer, Peter Dunn.

Though the commission quotes Owen in contradicting what Evans said about big deposits, it doesn't quote Owen on the purpose of Evans's mission to Chiang Mai. In an interview, Owen is very frank on the point. "There was nothing there but drug money," he says. "I'm quite sure that's what he was there for. Mike Hand sent him."

What begs proof is not the proposition that Nugan Hand went to Chiang Mai because of the drug business. What begs proof is the proposition that it might have gone there for any *other* reason, and the proof is lacking.

CHAPTER FIFTEEN

Officers and Gentlemen

A month after arriving in Bangkok, on March 30, 1977, John Owen sent Jerry Gilder a list of twenty expatriate executives he said were considering a deposit with Nugan Hand. The list ranged from managing director of a TRW, Inc., subsidiary to the commercial attaché of the Israeli Embassy in Bangkok.

Owen's whole correspondence file—which was somehow rescued by fate from the shredder—makes interesting reading. He was enthusiastic about working with General Black, but alarmed that Black's lack of financial wile might cause trouble.

"He certainly knows a lot of people who are important in this country, both in political and business circles," Owen said in a letter. But Owen reported that Black had caused general embarrassment—"a horrified silence"—when he talked openly at a dinner in Thailand about Nugan Hand as a deposit-taking institution. Someone had to publicly point out for the record that "he could not take deposits here because it was illegal," Owen reported. Gilder, in reply, passed it off as a joke.

Despite the illegality, Owen seems to have been consumed with attracting deposits, as he told Gilder about this or that prospect in his letters. "This man *rang us* and asked *specifically* about deposits," he enthused, underlining as he went. Other prospects, he said, urged Nugan Hand "to set up a central finance and trade reinvoicing system for the whole of Southeast Asia including Australia and New Zealand." (Reinvoicing, as explained earlier in the case of the Australian pharmacists, is a method of creating phony tax deductions and currency transfers by importing goods through a front company in another country, which jacks up the price before the goods are brought into your own country.)

"We have a number of small deposits starting to flow in now," Owen wrote on November 4, noting that a depositor code-named "our cerebral friend" had just handed over $12,000. That account was to grow considerably before the "cerebral friend" suffered a financial lobotomy when the bank folded.

But Owen's first successes at attracting deposits were overshadowed by his unique achievement in October 1977: he produced the one big, proven trade bonanza in Nugan Hand history. Owen brokered the sale of a Thai cement plant by Kaiser Cement & Gypsum Company, Oakland, California, to some local Thai shareholders. Kaiser received $650,000, and paid Nugan Hand a 10 percent commission—$65,000—for, as Owen wrote Gilder, "arranging, cajoling and generally jumping up and down trying to keep the thing more or less on the rails."

This commission might be expected to please a merchant bank. But Owen reports he was shocked by the exuberant reaction he got from his bosses when he led his biweekly letter home with news of the commission.

"Absolutely stunned you didn't phone or telex me," Gilder cabled back. Owen says when he appeared for a meeting of staff, he was surprised by everyone's continued admiration over the deal (and a second one he says he completed, but for which there doesn't seem to be any verification). "We all went to Gilder's house," Owen recalls in an interview, "and [the accountant Stephen] Hill said, 'Thank Christ you brought in that money.' I found out I had the only profitable office. I couldn't understand how they could keep opening up new offices and Nugan and Hand kept jetting around the world."

In January 1978, Nugan Hand held the first gathering of its recently expanded staff. The Dusit Thani Hotel in Bangkok was the chosen venue for the three-day affair. John Owen was trusted to make the arrangements, from the hotel rooms and official photographer to a concluding golf outing at the Rose Garden course outside Bangkok. "We would have to be able to hire clubs at the course, and naturally we will all need the assistance of some pretty girls to help us around it," Gilder wrote, adding the warning, "I couldn't stand it if we ran into problems in any of these major areas."

Admiral Yates and his wife were on the guest list. So was General

Black. So, by several accounts, was John Charody, the business associate of Australian magnate Sir Paul Strasser. Charody was described as a consultant to Nugan Hand, and was assigned code number 519 in the company's list of reference codes for use in telex and other communications.

Mike Hand impressed the conference by announcing that Sir Robert Askin, the premier (equivalent to governor) of the state of New South Wales, who was due to leave office soon, might be joining Nugan Hand as chairman. Charody reportedly said the same thing. Askin was in a social circle with Charody's friends, but there isn't any other evidence linking him with Nugan Hand.

Probably the most striking development at the conference, however, was the introduction of another man who was supposed to become a new staffer: Robert ("Red") Jantzen. Officially, Jantzen had been the first secretary of the U.S. Embassy in Bangkok. The Nugan Hand staff was aware, however, of what was supposed to be a secret: Jantzen's real job had nothing to do with being secretary of anything. He had been CIA chief of station for Thailand, the culmination of a long CIA career, though he had recently declared his retirement from government.

Jantzen is reported living near Orlando now. There is a Robert Jantzen in the Orlando area, but with an unlisted telephone number, and he couldn't be reached. But Collings's memories of the Bangkok conference include "a friend of Ed Black, . . . a former CIA guy in Thailand," who "was going to help the firm develop contacts."* Owen remembers Jantzen by name, and describes him and Black as "two CIA guys."

Daniel Arnold, a successor CIA station chief in Bangkok, says Jantzen got involved because he had been a friend of Black and Yates. Arnold remembers Jantzen dropping by his place in Bangkok for a visit during the January 1978 meetings to discuss the Nugan Hand job.

"From what he told me, which was really all I knew, it would involve going to your friends or acquaintances and getting them to invest money, with visions of sugarplums," Arnold says. "He's a very

*Collings says he thinks the man was Edwin Wilson, the CIA outlaw who sold arms to Libya and who had frequent associations with Nugan Hand executives. John McArthur also has said Wilson was at the Bangkok conference. Neither mentioned Jantzen. But from the physical and other descriptions given (such as red hair), it seems clear that Jantzen and not Wilson was the person in question. Neil Evans has said he saw Wilson in Thailand in May 1977, on some sort of arms deal, but there has been no corroboration of this.

decent man. My advice was not to get involved." (Arnold announced his own retirement from the CIA soon afterward, and went to work as a lobbyist for the Government of Thailand in Washington.)

Though Arnold didn't mention anything about drugs, Jantzen must have heard troubling reports. Frank Nugan wrote Jantzen a memo trying to explain the drug rumors innocently. Still, Jantzen used CIA contacts to reach out to Harvey Bates, head of the Australian Federal Narcotics Bureau, to ask if Nugan Hand was under a drug investigation. Bates's reply, if any, has never become public.

But twelve days after Jantzen's indirect query, Frank Nugan visited Bates to protest that narcotics officers were embarrassing his bank. Soon afterwards, Bates's brother and second-in-command at the narcotics bureau, Brian Bates, who also attended the meeting with Nugan, wrote a "SECRET" memo to his commander in charge of the investigation.

Headed "Nugan/Hand," the memo said, "I desire that this Bureau should not for the time being engage in any active external inquiries into this matter. . . . Will you please therefore ensure that, until further notice from me, no active external inquiries are embarked upon in relation to this matter. . . ."

Several investigators who had been working on numerous leads became extremely upset. After Nugan Hand collapsed and many of its illegal activities were exposed, their inquiries were proven justified. They got hold of Brian Bates's memo, and accused the bureau of corruption—accusations that were repeated in Parliament.

The Stewart Royal Commission heard testimony from Harvey Bates that the Nugan Hand probe was called off mainly because Bates, in the commission's words, was "not convinced the Bureau had anybody capable of interpreting a merchant banker's books." Though this is hardly something an investigative agency would be proud of, the commission said it didn't find any evidence of corruption.

For whatever reason, Red Jantzen chose not to stick around Nugan Hand. Some who attended the Bangkok conference believed he had already joined the group, and he certainly seems to have been introduced there as such. But he apparently never transacted business for the operation.

Owen continued to try new trade deals. He arranged for Nugan Hand to handle payments on the export of fish from Thailand to the United States by an Australian-based company. He worked with General Black, who "brought in top people . . . brought American business people here" to put up an ethanol plant, and to start production of energized seeds. "But the deals never came to anything," Owen complains.

The home office's enthusiasm for trade commissions faded. A typed note in Owen's correspondence file, probably from Gilder or Mike Hand, shows that the emphasis was on illegal deposit-taking. "John not closing," the note said. "Potential clients escaping. Probably overemphasising trade." When Owen requested a promotion and pay raise, Gilder wrote back that Hand and Collings had rejected the request, until Owen brought in $500,000 in deposits on his own—"not as a result of introductions effected through General Black or Mr. Robert Jansen [*sic*]."

"We should be getting substantial deposits very soon," Owen wrote him. Bird dogs were employed to lure expatriate depositors. One was Lloyd Thomas, the owner of the Takara 2 Massage Parlor and Hairdressing Salon in Bangkok—and the man John McArthur says was trying to buy a load of bayonets through Nugan Hand.

Interviewed in his well-appointed waiting room among the scantily clad "hairdressers," Thomas boasts of knowing the CIA personnel at the U.S. Embassy, and offers several names to prove his point. (The names couldn't be verified anyway.) Asked if he got commissions for lining up customers for Nugan Hand, he says, "That might be true and it might not be true. I won't say." Internal Nugan Hand correspondence, however, says Thomas "worked" for the bank at least to the fall of 1979.

By the end of 1978, Owen had received his promotion. A note from Gilder to Hand said Owen "feels confident of producing $1 million for the year and anticipates additional good volume if current border wars persist."

Border wars made for turmoil, and turmoil made for a better business in sneaky money. Even the trade deals that continued in favor tended to be military-related. In one letter, Owen reported that "a large military sales contract" had been promised in connection with the Kaiser cement deal. An arms deal for 40-mm anti-aircraft guns was talked about for a while, but fell through.

Months were spent on a contract to establish an aircraft maintenance and repair center in Bangkok, to replace one that had been created and run by now-departed American G.I.s. Nugan Hand was trying to win the contract for UTA Industries, a big French firm represented by a captain in the U.S. Naval Reserve, who Owen described as "a longstanding client" of Collings. The aircraft maintenance deal was lost in infighting among Thai officials, and the navy captain, reached at his home in Connecticut, ducked efforts to question him.

One prominent figure in that deal, and other Nugan Hand activity, was former Laotian Prince Panya Souvanna Phouma, son of Prince Souvanna Phouma, for whom the United States ran a covert (and later not-so-covert) war in Laos in the very early 1960s. Prince Panya had recently fled the communist conquest of his country, and according to a John Owen letter, he "swam to freedom across [the] Mekong River in his socks." Prince Panya, Owen wrote, "has [the] reputation of being a playboy, but would appear to be a strong negotiator. [He is] fluent in six languages and has strong connections in Thailand."

Extensive Nugan Hand files indicate that the bank helped establish Panya in a strange little airline called "Sky of Siam," ostensibly used for seeding clouds to promote rainfall (a pet project of the Thai king), as well as hauling passengers and freight. Owen's correspondence says he helped arrange bank financing for Sky of Siam, and got the aircraft for Prince Panya through the U.S. Navy captain he was dealing with. A letter from Owen to Gilder dated June 4, 1979, says the navy captain was billing the U.S. Government for his expenses, leaving the implication he was on government assignment at the time.

Panya—who probably has been a major target of American affections, financial and otherwise, over the years—was a principal or front in many deals. A memo from Gilder to Owen June 21, 1979, says, "We put a proposal to Prince Panya in Singapore [Michael Hand's post] concerning Indonesia's military requirements, and I think this appealed to him. I have no doubt that he and Joel [Joel Boscher, a business associate of Panya's], between them could produce millions in volume for us."

The next day, Owen wrote back that Panya also was trying to get a contract to install a new water system for Pattaya City, Thailand, and wanted Nugan Hand to arrange financing. "With fees and l'argent sous la table perhaps we could get somewhere on this," Owen reported.

L'argent sous la table—money under the table—bribes—was apparently a specialty of Nugan Hand.

Surviving files indicate that Nugan Hand became involved in a deal to find safe overseas havens for massive amounts of graft stolen by officials at the highest level of the Thai military government. The files don't reveal how the deal wound up.

But Owen wrote a letter to Gilder about it July 3, 1979, apologizing for writing on "yellow paper as I cannot keep copies." The deal "may require some of our heavier members to come to Thailand," the letter said.

Owen talked about an intermediary, whom he referred to as "the lady with the rubber," and "our lady." He explained that the money to be moved was obtained from $400 million in loans to the Thai Government, raised on Japanese financial markets. The interest rate for the Japanese was 8 percent, Owen explained, but an extra 0.75 percent interest was tacked on to the promissory notes the Bank of Thailand issued for the loan. That was the graft—the money the officials would keep for themselves.

"The Government officials involved have discounted [cashed in] their notes at local banks here and now want their money out," Owen wrote. "Our Lady has come to me to ask that we, NH [Nugan Hand], do this for them. It has to be *discreetly* done and quite frankly I do not believe that the Chinese dealers, et. al., are quite the people to handle this . . . I really believe it should be a Deak's job," Owen said, in reference to Deak & Company, Ron Pulger-Frame's old employer.

"The people involved here are the government and should this get out, we would have another government," Owen stressed.

Asking the Sydney office "to fix this for us when I blow the whistle," Owen wrote that "the funds would be put away for at least two years, possibly more, and could be considerably more than the amount indicated.

"Following successful completion of this transaction we would be asked to act in a fiduciary capacity to raise another $400 million interest rates, etc., to be used in a similar manner. The time over which these funds are to be raised is within a matter of months. It must be done before there is any chance of a change in government."

Owen cautioned that he couldn't report the progress of the venture by telex " 'cause my telex is not discreet enough. If we are to use the telex then everything should be done in code and a one-time code at that. Use of words like 'latex' or 'transistors', etc. [from Mike Hand's currencies code] have been compromised long ago. Basically, we should alert Deak's or whoever and then give instructions to them verbally here in Thailand."

Owen went on to describe technical details of the next loan as would be required to allow for the padded interest rate containing the graft money. No written reply could be found among the fragmentary and badly shuffled records that survived the ransacking after

Nugan's death. Gilder wouldn't talk to reporters, and the Stewart Royal Commission made no reference to the situation.

On January 19, 1979, Owen submitted to Gilder a single-spaced, typewritten report of three legal-sized pages. It began, "This is an evaluation of the Vietnamese capture of Cambodia as asked for by Graham Steer in Sydney last week." There is no further explanation for why former career naval officer Owen began writing a series of long, detailed reports that read like CIA or National Security Council briefing papers.

Steer, the California- and Florida-educated management consultant, had been working out of the Singapore office under Michael Hand. Hand's primary residence was Singapore by then.

Owen's first report, January 19, contains news that Vietnamese forces in Cambodia "would seem" to "have been operating under instructions from Hanoi not to close within a certain range of the Thai border," so that "people in Thailand do not seem to be particularly worried about any immediate threat." How Owen would learn this sitting in his rented banking office in Bangkok, several hundred miles from the affected areas, isn't mentioned. But in his report, he elaborated on several reasons for the rapid collapse of Cambodian resistance.

A fair example of the text: "The Vietnamese having broken through the main Cambodian forces on the Vietnamese/Cambodian border then split up into a number of armoured thrusts which used well paved highways to approach their main objectives of the major towns. In using the highways, they by-passed many pockets of resistance leaving those to be mopped up later. It would appear that the towns were taken by determined thrusts into their centers to capture command posts, thus depriving Cambodian forces means of communication."

Owen said a guerrilla-type campaign planned by Pol Pot opposition forces had been forestalled by the Vietnamese blitzkrieg. He reported that "consensus of opinion [he did not say among whom] is that the Vietnamese army will probably be tied up in putting down sporadic guerrilla actions over the next 18 months to two years." He included detailed forecasts of probable relations between Vietnam and various of its neighbors, and predicted continued military skirmishing that was "unlikely" to "spill over into Thailand."

He predicted a diplomatic thrust by Vietnam "to improve her image" with noncommunist Southeast Asian countries. He recommended "forming some sort of military alliance" among those countries "whilst at the same time seeking to improve farm incomes and standards of living in those areas directly facing the Communist threat."

The next month came another missive of almost equal length, again detailing the tactics of both sides in the Cambodian fighting, and cataloging Vietnam's increasing diplomatic problems with other Third World countries as a result of the invasion.

There followed other reports of up to four legal-sized pages, in single-spaced typewriting, containing much the kind of thing a military strategist might hope to find out before entering war. They were sent to Gilder, but with directions for passing on to Mike Hand.

"Vietnam has 19 divisions in Cambodia, just about the whole of its front line army," he wrote. "This army is being supplied by air since it does not have full control of the highways. It is reported to have run short of fuel for its armoured divisions and its mobility is therefore severely curtailed. Vietnam would appear to control fully only the cities, which have no populations, and it is not in a position to bring people back to the cities since it does not have the wherewithal to feed them. In addition, in Kampuchea, there appears to be few indigenous Kampucheans remaining who can administer the country. . . ."

Possible Soviet and Chinese responses—military, political, and logistical—were assessed. So were the prospects of a Soviet-American confrontation in the region. In all cases, Owen's emphasis was on the fighting capacity available at the scene, and that was described in detail.

"Vietnam may in the long run have aims on turning Thailand into a communist state but it is [in] no position at this point in time to put this aim into effect by military means," he summed up. He recommended that the Thai government start social programs to cure the economic inequities he said were causing "significant discontent in the countryside."

About the time Owen was writing all this, it has since been disclosed, the United States was cooperating with China in aiding the Pol Pot resistance in Cambodia.

What Owen's reports have to do with Nugan Hand's banking or trade interests is hard to fathom. In fact, many of his recommendations, in the sudden public spirit of curtailing violence, operate against the pro-violence undercurrent elsewhere in company literature. Elsewhere, Nugan Hand correspondence suggests that turmoil is good because it fosters the shady transactions that Nugan Hand profited from.

As with other foreign businesses operating in Thailand, Nugan Hand needed the patronage of a native Thai to hold the title of "chairman." The Thai who worked with Owen in this capacity from the beginning was a shipping and finance magnate named Suvit Djevaikyl, who boasts of many connections with members of the Thai government, including the finance minister. Djevaikyl says a friend in the shipping business had introduced him to Les Collings in Hong Kong, after which Frank Nugan and Michael Hand went to Bangkok to sign him on as part of the business.

And Djevaikyl brought home some bacon. "My friends had a lot of money that they deposited with them [Nugan Hand] in Hong Kong," he says. "I cannot give you their names because it is illegal to have money outside." He stresses that his friends got the privileged, Wing-On Bank-guaranteed accounts, so didn't lose their money.

Owen says Djevaikyl was particularly interested in brokering military sales to the Thai government from foreign sources, but that Nugan Hand couldn't match the prices available in Western Europe. In mid-1979, there was a falling out. Djevaikyl threatened to sever his relationship with Nugan Hand and boot Owen out of the country. Hand transferred Owen to Singapore, and replaced him in Bangkok with George Galicek, a defector from Czechoslovakia who had been representing Nugan Hand in Chile.

Galicek, an economist for the Czech Ministry of Foreign Trade, had defected after being posted to Chile from 1966 to 1970. He had been working on a deal with Owen and Djevaikyl to sell Thai rice to Chile, so the principals all knew each other.

Nugan Hand collapsed shortly after Galicek got to Bangkok. But from what Djevaikyl says,* he had determined to break his connection anyway. He says that during 1979, Hand proposed that Djevaikyl and his family buy a bank in Florida. (At this time, Nugan Hand was looking to take over a Florida bank, but in someone else's name.)

Apparently as a result of his efforts to check out the bank offer, Djevaikyl says, "Some of my police friends told me he [Hand] was from the CIA." Djevaikyl says he also learned from his "police friends" that "these people Ed Black [and] Red Jantzen were with the CIA. A friend of the American ambassador also told me, but that was after Frank Nugan died.

"If I know all these people were CIA, I would never let them put my name on their company," Djevaikyl asserts indignantly. "Sup-

*Interview with the author.

pose you're a businessman and somebody come to see you and you find out they are CIA, you would not like that. People might get the wrong idea and think I am CIA. And there are many killings. Some of these people die."

The CIA rumors weren't the only ones surrounding the bank. By much evidence, the Nugan Hand staff was very conscious of the narrow line the company was walking with its drug connections. A letter from Gilder to Owen November 14, 1977, expresses concern about the Chiang Mai situation, and about Otto Suripol, the former U.S. air base interpreter from Vietnam War days. Since Neil Evans had taken his hepatitis-wracked body back to Australia, Suripol had been left alone representing Nugan Hand in Chiang Mai.

Gilder thought Suripol was "not up to Group Representative standard." In the November 14 letter, Gilder asked Owen to supervise Suripol carefully, because "with the maliciousness and scurrilous remarks that have been made against the Nugan Fruit Group in Australia, Chiang Mai is a situation I am sure you will appreciate which we must be right on top of all the way [*sic*]." Gilder was obviously talking about illegal drug trafficking.

In a February 21, 1978, letter, Owen wrote Gilder about "one disturbing thing to me which I think you should know about." The disturbing thing was that Otto Suripol in Chiang Mai had told people that he was under instructions from Gilder "to go to the people he thought had 'hot' money from the 'trade' to see if we could look after it for them."

A year later, Owen wrote again, expressing his concern, and that of a depositor, about the presence on the Nugan Hand staff of one Ernest Wong. Wong was from a Chiang Kai-shek–associated family that had settled on Taiwan.

"Ernest has been recruited by Les and Mike to work on deals out of China," Owen wrote. Then he added, "Wong has a long and close relationship with Kuomintang Army remnants in the North of Thailand and is or was President of a Shan [States of Burma] Association in Bangkok. Their involvement with the drug trade [as already discussed earlier in this book] is a known fact as it was this way that they were able to raise money to buy arms. I am *not* suggesting that Wong was involved in any way, but you have to be very careful in this part of the world not to be implicated by association in any way."

But having said all that, Owen immediately cautioned Gilder not "to do anything about it nor repeat it to Les [Collings] or Mike [Hand]. I don't believe that anything I or you may say could make any difference." The clear implication of this remark is that Hand wouldn't have cared—or might even have intended the drug connection.

Soon, one of Ernest Wong's northern Burmese neighbors—a man born Chiang Chi-Fu, but known in his trade as "Khun Sa"—was being exposed in the newspapers, and on television, and in the U.S. Congress, as the biggest heroin dealer in the world. Khun Sa's men had fought against the Chinese Kuomintang, and won control of most of the Golden Triangle's crop.

The ensuing truce between the two sides was still fraught with skirmishes. Like the Kuomintang (KMT), which continued to insist that it would one day re-take China, Khun Sa also claimed to be dope-peddling for a noble cause—in his case, the independence of his people in the Shan States of Burma from the Burmese majority.*

Nugan Hand's Ernest Wong seemed able to straddle the Shan-KMT wars, ingratiating himself with both sides. He was also reputed to have worked for British and German banks, and to have government connections in China. "Wong said he was tied to the KMT, and he was promoting for the Shan States," Owen told a reporter in 1982, shaking his head in amazement. "That's Khun Sa's army!"

*Andrew Lowe, the Australian dopelord who was on Nugan Hand's staff in Sydney until he was sent to jail for heroin violations, put Khun Sa in Australian headlines by alleging that among his chores for Nugan Hand was arranging a meeting between Khun Sa and Michael Hand in Sydney to discuss a heroin deal. The police were unable to find any corroboration for Lowe's story and discounted it.

CHAPTER SIXTEEN

The Drug Bank

Nugan Hand liked to brag about its banking relationships with the rich and famous in order to attract new depositors. But there was at least one prominent Australian figure—a former Olympic hero and police official—whose banking relationship was something the firm didn't much talk about with outsiders.

He was Murray Stewart Riley, and his status as a customer made big headlines when it was discovered after Frank Nugan's death. Riley, a rower on Australia's 1952 and 1956 Olympic teams (he won a bronze medal in 1956), and then a detective, had seen his fame turn to disgrace in a police corruption scandal in the 1960s. It was discovered that he had been protecting the business interests of Abe Saffron, the Sydney vicelord. He lost his job.

Riley was tied to half a dozen illegal gambling casinos and was eventually convicted of bribing a policeman. He was jailed for nine months, then went back to the vice industry, specializing in the narcotics trade. He was arrested in 1978 in a luridly publicized case when he greedily overloaded a boat, the *Anoa,* which he used to bring "Buddha sticks"—a concentrated form of marijuana—in from Hong Kong. Unable to reach its intended port, the multimillion-dollar cargo sailed into the hands of police. Riley was jailed for ten years, and nine others were jailed with him. The ensuing investigation established that Riley was also importing about a hundred pounds of heroin a year, some for use in Australia, the bulk for transhipment to the United States.

"He bought it for several thousand dollars a pound in Thailand,

and sold it for several thousand dollars an ounce in Australia, after being cut [diluted with sugar or another harmless powder] three times," says a police investigator on the case. According to police investigators and the staff of two royal commissions, the heroin Riley brought in was shipped to the United States on freighters that were serviced by stevedoring firms infiltrated by Riley's associates.

In 1980, in the heat of the Nugan Hand collapse, Riley sought to reduce his sentence by confessing some selected sins under oath before a royal commission on drug trafficking. He testified that Nugan Hand had moved his drug money from Australia to Hong Kong. He said it financed his purchase of at least one boat (not the *Anoa*) used in trafficking, and that he had sought out Nugan Hand because it could "transfer funds from Hong Kong to the United States."

With Riley's at times detailed testimony to go on, investigators from the Commonwealth/New South Wales Joint Task Force on Drug Trafficking and the Corporate Affairs Commission were able to find Nugan Hand records documenting some transactions by Riley and his friends. They showed a total of $211,000 in deposits, mostly in Sydney, and $174,000 in withdrawals, mostly in Hong Kong, all between November 1975 and December 1976.

Since the quantities of drugs Riley was handling were worth much more than that, and since Riley continued trafficking until his 1978 disaster and continued to use Nugan Hand, it is assumed there was much more money involved, and that other records were either destroyed or never kept. (When dealing with the surviving records of Nugan Hand, one must constantly be aware that they are fragmentary, selective, and often coded or understated.)

Investigators also found records of transactions for quite a few other dope traders. Prominent among them, of course, was Andrew Lowe, whose standing as one of Australia's leading heroin importers while on the Nugan Hand staff as a "commodities" dealer has already been described.

Other dope dealers named in these records were friends or relatives of George Shaw. As Australian lawmen began interviewing Shaw about this, one acknowledged associate of his was charged with supply and possession of 1,760 pounds of heroin. Shaw's family is said by police to have a record of drug trafficking, though it's hard to trace because of names. Shaw acknowledges that his name is a derivative of an originally Lebanese name; he insists,* however, that he doesn't

*Interview with the author.

remember what his original name was, or what his father's name was or is.

As laid out in the Corporate Affairs Commission and Joint Task Force reports, Nugan Hand's records showed:

—Donald William McKenzie (or MacKenzie), who had eleven criminal convictions relating to drug offenses alone, and an additional history of other crimes, ran at least $36,180 through Nugan Hand in 1975 and 1976. One $20,000 deposit, identified by the task force as the proceeds of drug sales, came a few days after McKenzie was arrested for possession of marijuana. McKenzie dealt mostly with George Shaw.

Shaw, in his initial testimony, tried to minimize his knowledge of McKenzie and assert that he thought McKenzie was interested in the leather business. But Rona Sanchez, Shaw's secretary at Nugan Hand, testified that she thought all along McKenzie was a dope dealer.

"I could tell by the style of Don's living," she said. "He never had a job and yet he drove a new red Mercedes-Benz. He was always smartly dressed and he told me that he had sent his girlfriend on two or three cruises." Besides overhearing conversations about money "obviously . . . from the sale of drugs," she reported that "Don was quite often stoned when he came in to see George."

According to testimony before the Corporate Affairs Commission from narcotics agent Denis Kelly, McKenzie was employed for a while by Jack Rooklyn, an expatriate American who came to Australia to supply slot machines to Saffron's gambling dens on behalf of Bally Corporation. Bally is a major American gambling concern that started under secret Mafia ownership, and was later financed by the Teamsters' Union's corrupt Central States Pension Fund. McKenzie, the dope dealer, was brought onto the staff of Bally's man Rooklyn in the perhaps surprising capacity of tutor for his children.

Like other dollar amounts listed here, McKenzie's deposit total of $36,000 is probably much less than what actually flowed through Nugan Hand on his account. To take his case as an example, George Shaw eventually testified that his own records showed McKenzie actually withdrew $100,000 on a day when Nugan Hand's records show him withdrawing only $1,000.

Commented the Corporate Affairs Commission about this hundredfold discrepancy, "This withdrawal of $100,000, if accurate, indicates both the size of the off-ledger cash kitty facility offered by

Nugan Hand Limited through Mr. Shaw, and the likely origin of some of the funds deposited but not recorded in the official books. . . ."

In fact, the incident could indicate that the figures for Riley and the other Nugan Hand drug clients were also grossly understated. In his own testimony, Riley was conveniently forgetful of details like dollar amounts that might have caused him a tax liability. The enormous amounts of drugs that Riley and other Nugan Hand customers were dealing in likely would have produced and required sums in the millions of dollars.

Other persons whose names were found in Nugan Hand records and listed in the Corporate Affairs Commission and Joint Task Force reports as among the bank's drug clients:

—James Lewis Williams (alias James Arthur Watson), who was arrested in 1981 on what the Corporate Affairs Commission called "drug cultivation related charges" (he was convicted in 1982), deposited $23,000 in Nugan Hand and withdrew $27,000 from July 1976 to June 1978, the available records showed.

—George Chakiro, who has no criminal record but whom the Corporate Affairs Commission identified, based on police and underworld sources, as "deeply involved in hashish importation and distribution," deposited $13,000 and withdrew $15,000 between June 1976 and June 1979, the commission and task force said. Hawaiian records not cited by the official bodies show that a George Chakiro was a big borrower from Nugan Hand's Hawaiian Trust Company bank account as far back as 1974.

—Malcolm Craig Ladd, who (in the commission's words) "was involved in the distribution of drugs since 1972," deposited more than $145,000, according to a reconstruction of records by the commission and task force. According to the task force, Ladd had convictions for possession and use of heroin and marijuana, and admitted selling them, and hashish, on a large scale.

Charles Robertson Beveridge, "a partner of Mr. Ladd in drug trafficking," the commission said, deposited $60,000 and withdrew a like amount between May 1976 and February 1979. The task force said Beveridge also admitted his work as a distributor, and, like Ladd, said that George Chakiro was at times his supplier. Both Beveridge and Ladd admitted to the task force that at least most of their deposits were the proceeds of drug deals, and couldn't cite any other jobs or sources of income.

—Barry Graeme Chittem and Murray Don Newman from February 1978 to May 1979 ran at least $30,000 through Nugan Hand that they conceded was money made from, and reinvested in, marijuana and hashish, the commission said. Newman had been convicted for a marijuana offense. The task force said Chittem and Newman argued in testimony that only part of the money they put in Nugan Hand was from drug sales. But the task force said no other source of income could be found, and that the drug activities were on a scale to produce much more money than the amount Chittem and Newman admitted to.

Furthermore, the task force said, Chittem and Newman admitted withdrawing cash from the Sydney and Singapore offices of Nugan Hand, packing it in their luggage, and smuggling it on to Bangkok and Chiang Mai. Added the task force, "Chittem claimed that he was unaware that Chiang Mai was closely associated with drug production and distribution, which seems somewhat absurd in all the circumstances."

—"W," a man the task force would identify only by this pseudonym, deposited at least $23,000 in Nugan Hand between July 1976 and September 1977. In February 1978, the task force said "W," who already had seven "minor criminal convictions," was sought on a warrant for growing marijuana, and escaped arrest by holding a gun on an undercover policeman. He was later captured and when the task force issued its report he was awaiting trial, apparently inspiring the pseudonymous reference.

—Bruce Alan Smithers, another drug trafficker, deposited $43,000 in late 1977—while he was on bail on charges of cocaine and hashish trafficking. He was convicted, and deported to New Zealand in July 1979.

—James Sweetman, who in the words of the Joint Task Force was "a major drug trafficker in the 1960s and 70s," was apparently a client. Although direct evidence of deposits or withdrawals wasn't found, his name appeared on the client list Frank Nugan carried with him at his death. Sweetman associated with Riley and members of Riley's group. He disappeared after two drug-related arrests in Britain in 1977.

—George Shamoun, a Lebanese, was arrested March 19, 1980, on a charge of trying to import into Australia twenty-two pounds of hashish oil, which police said was worth about $176,000. When he was arrested, Shamoun was carrying a receipt from Yorkville, a Nugan Hand affiliate, for $80,000. It was signed by George Shaw. Some sixteen other Nugan Hand documents were found indicating international transfers by Shamoun of about $200,000, mostly to Singapore.

Shamoun was acquitted at trial on the hashish charge. He explained his Nugan Hand deposits to the task force with "vague details of a gift from his family in Lebanon and of business dealings he claimed to have had in Singapore, Lebanon and Saudi Arabia." Shaw supported this story. Both men said the $80,000 had been a typographical error, and that the actual deposit was $8,000.

But after its investigation, the task force determined "beyond doubt" that Shamoun and Shaw were lying in "an attempt to hide their participation in drug related activity." They eventually admitted as much, after Karen Jones, a Nugan Hand secretary, testified that the Yorkville deposit was $80,000, and that "Shamoun regularly visited Shaw and . . . made other substantial deposits with Shaw."*

During this time, Shamoun was unemployed and on welfare.

—James Blacker, Colin Courtney, Stephen Demos, John Brooking, and John Ceruto all were dope dealers brought to Nugan Hand by Andrew Lowe, the task force said. For most of their transactions no records were kept, the task force said, but it found "reliable information" that Courtney alone deposited about $400,000 cash.

From all this, the Corporate Affairs Commission drew its typically reticent conclusions: "The delegates [commission members] do not assert that Nugan Hand actively pursued the drug trafficking industry for business, although in the case of Mr. Hand this is a possibility. However it seems unlikely that the executives were completely unaware of the activities of certain clients associated with drug trafficking. As with other areas, Nugan Hand was not in the business of refusing funds associated with illicit or questionable activities. . . . Whilst it cannot be stated with confidence that Mr. Shaw was aware of the activities of these drug traffickers, or of the source of their funds, however [*sic*] it is reasonable to infer that he was aware the funds were not the result of normal commercial en-

*Shamoun came clean about the $80,000 figure before the task force, and Shaw testified to it before the Stewart Royal Commission.

terprise and fell within the general description of 'black money.' "

The Joint Task Force was a little more blunt, stating in its conclusions that Shaw's " 'drug' clients . . . were in their early to mid 20s at the time of their dealings with Shaw. In every case," the task force said, "deposits they made were by way of cash, often in quite substantial sums, and frequently no 'official' receipt was issued. . . . With perhaps one or two exceptions, it can be fairly said that in neither their physical appearance nor their mannerisms did they have the appearance of legitimate successful business people. Indeed, one depositor was described by an employee as frequently having the appearance of being affected by drugs on his visits to Nugan Hand offices. Shaw's clients were quite open in their comings and goings. . . . In short, apart from any legal responsibilities Hand and Nugan had towards Shaw as their employee . . . there can be little or no doubt that they were aware of Shaw's procurement of 'drug' money . . . and that their failure to stop it was, if nothing more, an implied acceptance of that practice."

As for war hero and CIA man Mike Hand himself, the task force concluded, "throughout 1976, Hand was knowingly involved in drug activity with the 'Riley' group in that he permitted and even encouraged the use of Nugan Hand facilities for the movement of 'drug' money. . . . By 1977, Nugan Hand was well established in drug activity."

How much did the other executives know? Les Collings, Nugan Hand's Hong Kong representative, offers a perfectly innocent explanation of how he happened to dole out funds to dope dealer Murray Riley. "He was like any other Nugan Hand customer," Collings says. "He was a businessman and he wanted cash put out of Australia. I was told [by the Sydney office] to pay him some money. I was told to wine him and dine him. I didn't know who he was from Adam. Riley could have been anybody. Here was a nice guy coming up and giving Nugan some money."

A fine story—until you analyze it. For one thing, Riley was a wildly notorious character, especially in 1974 when Collings was still living in Sydney. Riley was all over the newspapers that year as a result of hearings by the Moffitt Royal Commission on organized crime activities.

For another thing, the Joint Task Force reported testimony from Collings that in September 1976 he got "urgent instructions" from Mike Hand to have $100,000 in U.S. cash available for Riley, who then dropped by to pick it up, or most of it. The orders were so urgent that Nugan Hand didn't have time to supply the documentation required by Hong Kong banking authorities for large bank withdrawals.

So, Collings told the task force, he had set up an account in his own name to pay Riley—clear evidence that Riley was *not* just "like any other customer." When Mike Hand heard about Collings's special arrangement, he was so alarmed that he shot a memo to Collings saying, "Please hold fire on using this account for pay offs. Some method totally disassociated with you and the company should be employed for payout."

The task force noted that "both Nugan and Hand frequently handled 'black' money, which caused them no particular concern, but these transactions were of particular concern to Hand." In other words, Hand knew that his customers were engaged in dope smuggling, not just routine tax cheating. Strong suspicions, at the least, might likewise be attributed to any Nugan Hand executives who got instructions like the ones Hand gave Collings.

From what it could find of records, the task force also raised the "question" of whether Nugan Hand, rather than just moving money, was lending Riley and his friends their capital, and thus financing the dope trade. Justice Philip Woodward, in his Royal Commission report in 1980, had indulged in the same speculation.

One ground for thinking that Nugan Hand was bankrolling heroin, the task force said, was that much of the money the Hong Kong office shelled out to Riley and his friends "appears never to have been reimbursed"—either through deposits or through money transferred up from Sydney. The task force also noted that Mike Hand had personally ordered the destruction of the Riley records in Hong Kong, and "regarded his relationship with Riley as being so significant that he was prepared to perjure himself in respect of it."

He certainly did perjure himself. Appearing before Woodward's Royal Commission inquiring into drug trafficking, Hand was asked, "Do you know Murray Stewart Riley?" He replied, "I do not recall meeting a person by that name." Hand then flatly denied he knew of any discussion by anyone in the Nugan Hand organization in which Riley's name even came up. He even denied that Nugan Hand ever transferred funds except "through a regular bank."

"It seems highly probable," the task force concluded, "that Hand knew Riley and [his friend Harry] Wainwright were involved in drug trafficking and that their requests for use of the Nugan Hand facilities for the movement of money were in furtherance of that activity. And knowing this, Hand assisted them not only by freely offering them the use of those facilities, but indeed encouraging that use."

One more aspect of the Murray Riley case deserves to be explored before moving on to Nugan Hand's other connections with dope, and murder-for-hire. It involves both the American Mafia and Sir Peter Abeles, that knighted bastion of proper wealth, whose circle of friends kept popping up as benefactors to Bernie Houghton and Michael Hand.

Riley had a pack of expatriate American friends in Australia, with pretty unsavory pasts of their own. There was Harry Wainwright, a New Orleans native who practiced criminal defense law in San Francisco until his disbarment, and began going to Australia in 1968. Wainwright became a naturalized Australian citizen in 1973, thus escaping extradition; he was indicted that year on federal tax charges in San Francisco.

According to Justice Woodward, writing in his Royal Commission's 1980 report on drug trafficking, "Information received from the United States authorities alleges that he [Wainwright] was, while practicing as a lawyer . . . , an associate of known 'Mafia' leaders. Despite his denials, I am satisfied by the evidence . . . that there is substance in this allegation." Justice Woodward also reported that he had received "some evidence" that Wainwright got his Australian citizenship in ways that were "highly suspicious and obviously call for further investigation by the appropriate authorities."

In Australia, Wainwright, like Riley, became a client of Nugan Hand. Les Collings remembers wining and dining and paying Wainwright money several times in Hong Kong—but, of course, noticed nothing suspicious about him.

Justice Woodward wrote that "Wainwright came to the attention of the Commission principally because he travelled through Wings Travel Pty. Ltd.," whose services were relied on by the dope syndicate Riley was part of. Wings was owned by William Sinclair, a Labor Party politician working for a city council that deposited its money with Nugan Hand, and who was jailed in Bangkok for heroin possession. According to the Joint Task Force, Wings was "a significant vehicle for the secretion of travel movements by those involved in all levels of the drug trafficking trade."

Another Wings traveler was Kenneth Derley, a henchman of Riley's. Derley appears in Justice Woodward's catalogue of characters "who have strong links with drug trafficking." He also appears, through an alias, on the list of Nugan Hand clients found on Frank Nugan's body at his death.*

Tracking a courier who was "bringing back white powder from Manila," Justice Woodward wrote, led the commission to another friend of Riley's, Danny Stein, or Steinberg, an illegal gambling figure who was visiting from Las Vegas.

"New South Wales police received information which they regarded as reliable that the purpose of Stein's visit to Australia at that time [1975] was to organize importation of drugs from the 'Golden Triangle' for transshipment to the United States," Justice Woodward went on. (Woodward's commission on organized crime should not be confused with the more criticized Stewart Royal Commission on Nugan Hand.)

Other Riley friends included George ("Duke") Countis, who from the late 1940s or early 1950s had been an illegal bookmaker and otherwise business agent in the operations of Mafia leader Aladena ("Jimmy the Weasel") Fratianno.** Fratianno, a racketeer and hit man with at least two dozen murders to his credit, traveled in the glitzy Las Vegas show business world. His most famous photograph published in *Life* magazine, shows him bringing together Frank Sinatra and the late Boss of Bosses, Carlo Gambino. Finally, in the 1970s, boxed in by the FBI, he became a highly effective government witness.

Countis's love of casinos led him to the Abe Saffron quadrant of Sydney. There, inevitably, he got to know Murray Riley. According to the Joint Task Force,† it was Countis who first introduced Riley and Harry Wainwright to Frank Nugan and Mike Hand. That was in 1975 or early 1976.

Justice Woodward reported that Wainwright not only "dealt with Frank Nugan" but "became a friend of his. They played chess together. Nugan handled the transfers of money to Hong Kong" for

*The name on the list was Ken Dooley, and the amount by his name was "$19,267." It is widely assumed—the Joint Task Force flat-out states—that "Ken Dooley" is Ken Derley. The change may have been a crude code, or may just have resulted from Frank Nugan's slapdash accounting system. Either way, it was typical of Nugan.

**The Joint Task Force Report, volume two, at page 317, calls Countis "one of Fratianno's illegal bookmaking agents." There are other police documents to support the association, as does Fratianno's memoir, *The Last Mafioso,* written with Ovid Demaris.

†Citing testimony from Stephen Hill, among other things.

Wainwright and Riley, Woodward said, and did so without the knowledge or consent of the Australian Reserve Bank—in other words, illegally.

The Woodward Commission's report went on to speculate about the source of this money: "I think," Justice Woodward wrote, "that the costs involved in importing . . . would have been beyond the unaided financial resources of Riley and his group. I am convinced that there was a financier or financiers behind the importation . . . and that his or their identity is known to . . . Riley" and his associates. "They have kept their secret, motivated, no doubt, by fear of the consequences of disclosure. . . . Some information came into my possession implicating the Americans Wainwright and Stein in financing the *Anoa* venture, using the facilities of Nugan Hand. It has not been possible to verify this information. The records of Nugan Hand are in complete disarray and many of them are missing."

The Joint Task Force reported that in June 1976, at the very time Wainwright and Riley were importing a big load of heroin from Asia, "Wainwright held a lavish function at his Darling Point [an exclusive waterfront section of Sydney] penthouse. It was attended by Nugan, Hand, Hill and other Sydney-based employes of Nugan Hand, Clive [Les] Collings the then manager of the Hong Kong office, and a number of other people not identified. The attendance of these Nugan Hand people at this party certainly demonstrates a considerable degree of familiarity with Wainwright, greater than one would reasonably expect if the client was not a major one."

Riley, the task force reported, became a social friend of Mike Hand's. In fact, it said, "Hand's decision to establish offices in Thailand was substantially influenced by discussions he had with Riley, and perhaps Wainwright, during the latter half of 1976."

Riley and Fratianno's man "Duke" Countis even approached Mike Hand about financing a $23 million Las Vegas casino project. Hand was interested, but the deal died. In his memoir, *The Last Mafioso*, written with Ovid Demaris, Fratianno described his attempt in December 1976 to launder Mafia funds through "foreign banks . . . any tax-haven bank" to build the casino, but said it never came off.

There was a far stranger deal that *did* come off, however, between Fratianno and his Australian connections. Riley and Wainwright, according to various accounts, were working with Jimmy the Weasel (Fratianno) on a plan to farm a purportedly new strain of marijuana, and were looking for a plot in Australia to do it. They had become friends of a man named Bela Cseidi, who, although the protégé of a wealthy Sydney industrialist, had himself become something of a playboy, involved in quick stock promotions, horse racing, and other gambling.

Cseidi says Riley and Wainwright approached him to use some of his land for the marijuana farm, and made the approach through their banker—Michael Hand. On a flight back to Sydney from Hong Kong, where Wainwright and Riley had introduced him to Hand, Cseidi says Hand "proposed a serious criminal venture. Wainwright had told him I was the only one who could solve their problem."

Cseidi says he agreed to sell some land to Wainwright, but never participated in the marijuana farm—which is why he is so upset that he had to serve three years in prison for it, especially since Wainwright went free. (The courts decided it was still Cseidi's land.)*

But the interesting part of the story is the effect all this had on Cseidi's mentor, the wealthy industrialist who had taken him under his wing almost as a son when Cseidi was a boy, It was Sir Peter Abeles.

As a familiar credit-card commercial might put it: "Do you know me? I am one of Australia's wealthiest tycoons, the boss of a worldwide shipping empire that rakes in $1.5 billion a year and has at least eighteen subsidiaries in the United States alone."

Sir Peter Abeles is chairman of Thomas Nationwide Transport—TNT, as it's commonly called in Australia. Queen Elizabeth knows him—she knighted him in 1972. Rupert Murdoch, owner of Fox Television in the United States and publisher of the *New York Post* and other publications, knows him; the two men are good friends and business partners in several Australian ventures.

Sir Paul Strasser knows Sir Peter. Sir Paul, who picked up a purportedly penniless, just-arrived Bernie Houghton and got him going in Australia, is a card-playing best-buddy of Sir Peter's.

*The Joint Task Force, following up on the openly declared suspicions of the Woodward Royal Commission, found in its published report that Wainwright was "involved in the financing of the" marijuana venture. The published report doesn't mention Fratianno by name in connection with this particular venture, though it cites him on the casino deal. The task force's detailed account of the Cseidi marijuana venture is contained in a volume of its report that has never been made public. It is said to cite Fratianno.

The Woodward commission, in 1980, came upon the Wainwright involvement too late to cause Wainwright criminal problems in the five-year-old case; several others had been convicted in 1977. But the Joint Task Force flatly declared that Wainwright was prominent in a ring of "known or reputed drug traffickers" who dealt with Nugan Hand, and both the Corporate Affairs Commission and the Stewart Royal Commission accepted this judgment.

Fred Millar also knows Sir Peter. Millar, manager of the real estate business that picked up a just-arrived discharged G.I., Michael Hand, and got him going in Australia, is general counsel for TNT. He is Sir Peter's right-hand man.

It so happened that while Cseidi was getting to know Wainwright and Riley, Sir Peter was trying to expand his shipping and trucking empire to the United States, and was encountering problems with the Teamsters Union. Among these problems, according to a memo from the executive who was sent over to run the American operations, were "wildcat strikes, bombings, burnings, shootings and pickets at all terminals."*

At Wainwright's house one day in 1974, Sir Peter's friend Cseidi met Wainwright's friend from the San Francisco crime scene, Rudy Tham, head of the West Coast Teamsters. Tham—who in 1979 was sent to jail for embezzling union funds—was a friend of Jimmy the Weasel; they even owned a clothing boutique together. On that same trip to Australia, Tham also visited Sir Peter and saw the TNT transport facility.

Tham won't discuss what happened. Cseidi won't divulge all the details, either. But in 1975, he says, Sir Peter asked him to intercede in TNT's business problems. "Ever since I was a young boy I've been a close friend of Sir Peter Abeles, and he said there was this thing he couldn't quite handle, and would I go and handle it. He didn't quite know what he was getting into," Cseidi says.

Sir Peter and Cseidi (together or separately) went to California and New York in early 1975, and met Fratianno (the Weasel) and Tham. Tham and possibly Fratianno suggested that some friends of theirs could probably solve Sir Peter's Teamster problems. The friends turned out to be associates of Frank ("Funzi") Tieri, head of the former Vito Genovese crime family and at the time probably the most powerful Mafia leader in the United States. Among the new advisors Sir Peter was thus introduced to were another professional hit man called "Little Ralph," a character known as "Benny Eggs," and a dock boss who was a cousin of Frank Sinatra.

Sir Peter says that "by this time we knew Tham fairly well," and so he agreed to welcome a couple of the proposed advisors up to his hotel room. "They said, 'We are looking for profitable opportunities,'" Sir Peter recalls. Next thing he knew, Sir Peter, Jimmy the

*The memo was uncovered and published by Marian Wilkinson in Australia's *National Times*.

Weasel, Benny Eggs, and some others were trooping up to the Westchester Premier Theater in Westchester County, New York, a mob-connected theater that later collapsed in a bankruptcy scandal that resulted in several federal convictions. Sinatra sang there in an apparent effort to help out the mob owners.

Sir Peter says he politely turned down the men's suggestions that he buy the theater. But he ultimately agreed to another deal designed to bring labor peace. He paid $700,000 for a little trucking business his new advisors owned, and gave them a 20 percent stake in his U.S. operations. He hired Benny Eggs and Sinatra's cousin as consultants at $50,000 a year, with the money to be paid into a series of small Cayman Island and U.S. corporations his consultants designated. So important was this arrangement that each year, Sir Peter, head of a vast international air, land, and sea transportation enterprise, took time out from his other duties to personally write out the payment vouchers and currency exchange forms for the consultants' fees.

Eventually the Justice Department charged the consultants with hiding their income from the Internal Revenue Service. But when Sir Peter refused to come to the United States to testify at the trial, the judge threw out the charges for lack of evidence that the money from the foreign corporations he paid had gone to the consultants.

Sir Peter says he was treated fairly by Tham and the others, and that all his dealings were legitimate. Cseidi says his dealings, too, were legitimate, though he's not so happy about his treatment. "I had nothing to do with drugs," he insists over an expense-account-breaking lunch topped off with *Cordon Bleu* cognac at his private club before heading to the track. But he had tried the same line on an Australian jury, and it had chosen instead to send him to prison for three years.

CHAPTER SEVENTEEN

The "Mr. Asia" Murders

The Stewart Royal Commission said it agreed with the conclusions of the Joint Task Force and Corporate Affairs Commission about the role Nugan Hand played in the drug business. Then it proceeded to misstate those conclusions. The Stewart commission referred to "allegations of drug trafficking in Australia," and then said the Joint Task Force and Corporate Affairs Commission had found "that the allegations were not correct except to the extent that drug funds were being deposited with [Nugan Hand affiliates] from time to time."

That statement was seized upon by former Nugan Hand staffers, and government officials interested in papering over the embarrassing facts, as evidence that Nugan Hand was clean on the drug issue. In fact, both the Joint Task Force and the Corporate Affairs Commission had placed Nugan Hand in the critical role of surreptitiously transferring drug income overseas, where it obviously could be reinvested in more illegal drugs.

The Stewart commission itself, in its text, accepted that Nugan Hand performed exactly this function. Moreover, it agreed that Michael Hand and George Shaw, at least, knew very well that they were handling dope money. But the commission didn't seem to want to face the implications of this.

As it did in several sections to make its investigation appear more thorough than it was, the Stewart commission devoted a lot of space to shooting down fringe allegations that had little credibility to start with—for example, a charge that Nugan Hand officials had attended a farewell luncheon for a dope dealer and later gave $25,000 to his wife. (The luncheon, reported only in the Communist newspaper *Tribune*, probably never took place, and the $25,000 went to another woman with a similar name.)

After devoting seven paragraphs to repeating and analyzing these two shaggy-dog stories, the Stewart commission tossed off in a mere two paragraphs Nugan Hand's undisputed involvement with a group of people so vile they make Murray Riley look angelic by comparison: The "Mr. Asia" gang.

Early on a Monday afternoon, March 26, 1979—while Admiral Yates was hopping continents seeking deals as president of the Nugan Hand Bank, and General Cocke was lending his luster to the office Nugan Hand would occupy in Washington, and General Black was fishing for business in the Pacific Basin, and U.S. intelligence veterans Mike Hand, Dale Holmgren, Doug Sapper, and George Farris were baiting their own hooks here and there—the telephone rang on the desk of George Shaw at Nugan Hand headquarters in Sydney.

The caller was John Aston, a Sydney lawyer who specialized in criminal defense work, particularly drug cases, and who was a frequent Nugan Hand client himself. By his own admission,* Aston let his office be used frequently by Nugan Hand as a pick-up point for various parcels. He says his law clients wanted to protect their confidentiality, and so didn't themselves want to be seen in Nugan Hand's office. Therefore, he says, they left the parcels with him for pick-up by Nugan Hand. But Aston says he was never aware of the contents of the parcels, including the ones of March 26, 1979.

Shaw has testified under a grant of immunity from prosecution** that the parcels Aston asked him to pick up that March 26 were two overnight bags, containing about $300,000 cash. A cousin of Shaw's and another man, a Nugan Hand client, both have testified that they drove with Shaw to Aston's office, where Shaw entered alone, then returned with the two bags.

Shaw testified that Aston told him, "I have some clients who want some money moved overseas without any fuss. There is $285,000 in

*Interviews with the author.

**In various proceedings, including before the Joint Task Force and Corporate Affairs Commission.

those bags, plus some extra to cover your costs. We don't want this money to show up anywhere on the records."

According to Shaw's testimony, Aston told him to cable instructions to Nugan Hand's Singapore office that a man named Choo Cheng Kui be authorized to pick up the $285,000. Choo was to identify himself with his passport, with a given number.* Helping Shaw carry the money-laden bags to the car was Aston's law partner** Brian Alexander—the same lawyer police found with Ken Nugan at Frank Nugan's house the night Frank Nugan died.

Shaw drove the bags back to the Nugan Hand office, where he met Steve Hill, who also testified, providing additional verification for the story from this point. Both men say they opened the bags and counted Australian bills in $10, $20, and $50 denominations. But they were disconcerted to see that a lot of the money was marked with purple dye, and they remarked to each other that this meant it might have come from a bank robbery. They immediately reported this to Frank Nugan, who they say told them not to worry about it. Nugan ordered the money put in the safe—routine procedure when clients brought in cash deposits.

The next day, there was more routine procedure. Frank Nugan had bought a soft-drink distribution company called Orange Spot, and he used its heavy daily flow of small-bill cash to launder funds that came in to the bank. That's what he did with the Aston money.

Calls were made to the Orange Spot manager, and to an armored car service. Shaw then delivered the money from the Aston pick-up to the Orange Spot office, where it was turned over to the armored car service as if it were soft-drink receipts. The armored car service gave its check to Shaw in exchange. Thus the funds were laundered—accounted for as legitimate business receipts.†

*Originally, the money was to be picked up by Choo half in Singapore and the other half in Germany, but this part of the plan later changed.

**By American terminology, Alexander was effectively an associate in the firm Aston & Alexander, of which Aston was effectively the sole partner. They were the only two professionals in the firm. In Australia, Alexander was what is known as Aston's "law clerk." That term has a very different meaning in the United States, however, referring to an intern who cannot represent clients in court and who often has not even passed the bar examination. Alexander was a fully licensed solicitor.

†The careful reader may detect an apparent flaw in this system. By recording the money as income to Orange Spot, Frank Nugan would appear to have acquired a substantial income tax liability. This was solved, however, by having Orange Spot then issue a check to Yorkville Nominees, the Nugan Hand affiliate, with a concocted explanation for the payment that would allow it to be deducted as a business expense to Orange Spot. In the end, the money just wended its way back to Nugan Hand without ever having shown up as income to anyone.

The trail then leads to Singapore. Telexes have been found from Frank Nugan in Sydney to Mike Hand in Singapore, directing Hand to pay out the $285,000 to Choo when he showed up with the passport that Aston had described. As in most Nugan Hand telexes, the message was conveyed in the code Mike Hand had devised. But with the help of employe manuals, the code has been broken. The telex identified the payer of the money as "our friendly solicitor John," which authorities have taken as a reference to John Aston.

The next day, March 28, 1979, the money was laundered again. Mike Hand instructed Wing-On Bank in Hong Kong to forward $300,000 from Nugan Hand's account there to its account at Irving Trust Company in New York. The next day, Irving Trust was instructed to transfer the money to Nugan Hand's bank in Singapore, Inter-Alpha Asia (Singapore) Ltd.

On April 12, Inter-Alpha was told to transfer the funds from its Nugan Hand account to an account in the name of Dong Xaoi Ltd., a Singapore company controlled by Nugan Hand. Its name may be familiar: Dong Xaoi was the name of the Vietnamese town where Mike Hand in 1965 won his Distinguished Service Cross for bravery. A mere fourteen years later it had been transformed into the name of the company he used to launder drug money.

Hand's assistant in the Singapore office, Tan Choon Seng, was signatory on the Dong Xaoi account. On what he has testified were Hand's orders, he wrote out five checks in Singapore dollars, on April 12, 1979, in amounts totaling $285,000 in U.S. currency. It was the exact amount Shaw had picked up at the Aston & Alexander law office, except for Nugan Hand's fee.

That same day, April 12, Michael Hand delivered the checks to Choo. Documents found later in Nugan Hand's Singapore office completely corroborate Shaw's testimony about this. Mike Hand had even made Choo sign a statement that "receipt of these funds by me does not constitute any breach of law or illegal activity in any country."

The original $285,000 apparently never left Sydney. Exchange control authorities weren't ever notified. The money being paid out to dope-dealer Choo in Singapore was money that unsuspecting

---

Yorkville's only apparent purpose was to disguise the source and destination of the millions of dollars that flowed through it every month. A myriad of phony loan accounts veiled the passage of money from Yorkville to Nugan Hand and back. All this is confirmed by the records of the companies involved, and by the testimony of those concerned, including the Orange Spot manager.

depositors had left with the Nugan Hand Bank in Hong Kong—Admiral Earl Yates, president.

All this might have appeared to be one more routine Nugan Hand money-laundering deal had it not been for a coincidence that occurred halfway around the world. Because of that coincidence, Australian police were able to see a terrible significance in George Shaw's story about the $285,000.

Six months after Choo picked up the $285,000 from Hand, a man named Errol Hincksman was arrested for drunk driving in the county of Lancashire, England. While booking Hincksman, the bobbies of Lancashire found in his pocket a passport in the name of Choo Cheng Kui. The bobbies, of course, didn't know Choo from Adam. But why, they demanded to know, was the drunken Hincksman carrying the passport of some other person—a Chinese?

Well, Hincksman explained, he was on his way to meet Choo at the home of a mutual friend. And who was the mutual friend? Terry Clark.

The police pursued the matter to the house where Clark was staying, and hauled him in, but it was still a while before they realized that in Clark they had their hands on one of the most wanted men on earth. Terence John Clark, a native New Zealander, was believed to be the number two man in the "Mr. Asia" heroin syndicate, one of the world's biggest. Actually, he had become the lead man in the syndicate—having one week earlier successfully plotted the murder of Christopher Martin Johnstone, the man known as "Mr. Asia."

For several days, though they didn't know it, the police had also had their hands on Johnstone himself, or most of him, in the form of an unidentified corpse that had been found in a quarry. Terry Clark had taken every precaution he could think of to prevent the identification of Johnstone's body. Johnstone's hands had been cut off, his teeth smashed and his guts ripped open. A multinational burial was arranged; Johnstone's severed hand would eventually be found in the Almond River in Scotland, and fingerprinted.

So slow were police to recognize what they had that they allowed Choo to pick up his passport and proceed back to Singapore. It took some time for Johnstone's body to be pieced together and identified by forensic experts. Eventually, some members of the syndicate were persuaded to testify for the Crown, against their colleagues, and in 1981, a trial was finally held.

It came out that Johnstone had been attracting so much international newspaper publicity with his colorful "Mr. Asia" alias that Clark and others in the syndicate feared their business was being endangered. It was a business that brought in hundreds of millions of dollars. So they killed Johnstone. (The testimony that the gang had been endangered by constant publicity is further evidence, if any is needed, that Nugan Hand had every reason to be aware of who and what it was dealing with when it washed money for the "Mr. Asia" gang.)

Clark and several others were sentenced to life imprisonment for Johnstone's murder. Hincksman was sentenced to ten years' imprisonment on various drug charges.

British police couldn't touch Choo, who was back in Singapore. But they filed a report on the affair stating that "during our enquiries, it has become clear that Choo, known as 'Jack,' was responsible for running the Singapore end of (Clark's) business." They also said Choo's passport showed he had been in Sydney March 16 through 25, 1979—right up to the day before Shaw picked up the $285,000 from the Aston & Alexander office.

Given all this evidence, it would certainly appear that Nugan Hand was consciously laundering $285,000 in money used for drug purchases. Because the "Mr. Asia" syndicate dealt with Aston & Alexander for a much longer period, and Nugan Hand executives regularly laundered money picked up at the Aston & Alexander office, one might legitimately assume that Nugan Hand laundered far more than just the $285,000 Shaw picked up on March 26. Of course, Aston says he didn't know there was money in all the parcels he routinely laid out for Nugan Hand pick-up. But Nugan Hand certainly found out what was in them, and to whom they were going.

Nugan Hand dealt in dope money, all right. But there is still more evidence, and it points to worse conclusions even than that.

In May 1978, almost a year before the $285,000 Aston pick-up, two couriers from the "Mr. Asia" syndicate had been arrested in separate incidents at Sydney Airport. One, known as "Pommy Harry" Lewis ("Pommy" is a mildly derogatory reference to a Britisher), had some marijuana on him. The other, Duncan William Robb, was carrying an airgun and traveling under an assumed name; when police searched his home, they found heroin.

Both Lewis and Robb were subjected to long questioning by narcotics agents. Both broke down. Both mentioned the names of Johnstone and Clark, and provided other names and details.

They didn't know that the Sydney narcotics bureau was a den of corruption. They didn't know that the two narcotics officers who were hearing their stories were also in regular contact with the Aston & Alexander law office, which seemed to quickly find out everything the narcotics bureau did.

Two members of the "Mr. Asia" syndicate, including the woman Terry Clark lived with, later testified for prosecutors in England and Australia, and said the syndicate got its information about the narcotics bureau from Brian Alexander—Aston's law partner and the lawyer who was in Frank Nugan's house the night he died.

The witnesses from inside the syndicate testified that Clark had told them that a senior Australian narcotics official was on retainer to the "Mr. Asia" group for $22,000 a year. They testified that Clark instructed various other syndicate members to get information about drug enforcement activities from Alexander, and that these syndicate members were given code names to use when calling Alexander. The code names they remembered matched names found in the Aston & Alexander telephone logs.

One of the witnesses, Allison Dine, Clark's common law wife, testified* that Alexander's source in the narcotics bureau "had access to a computer which was daily fed with information such as people the Narcotics Bureau knew were involved with the importation and trafficking of narcotics. . . . When any information came up that involved Terry Clark or any of the people who were said to be known associates of his . . . the narcotics officer would then pass this information on to Brian Alexander and Brian would ring Terry to tell him that he had information."

At any rate, the syndicate knew within hours what Pommy Harry Lewis and Duncan Robb had told the police. Dine, Clark's common law wife, testified that Clark was in Singapore at the time of the Harry Lewis arrest, and ordered another syndicate member, Wayne Shrimpton, to go to Sydney to bail Lewis out.

Shrimpton testified, "I was told by Terry that I was to ask [at the court building] for Brian Alexander and he would know what I was there for. . . . Alexander came out and asked me how much money

*The testimony quoted here from Dine and from Wayne Shrimpton, another syndicate member, was given at the coroner's inquest into the deaths of Douglas and Isobel Wilson. That case will be discussed later in the text, as it comes up chronologically; the inquest took place in Melbourne, Australia, in August 1980. The testimony, however, is consistent with testimony Dine and Shrimpton gave at various other proceedings in England and Australia.

I had. I had a briefcase with the money in it in bundles. I opened the briefcase to show him and he said to me to close it up. He basically said, 'Don't let anybody see it.' "

Alexander then instructed Shrimpton to use a false name in filing the bail, according to Shrimpton's testimony, which was accepted as fact by the Woodward Royal Commission on Drugs. Shrimpton bailed Lewis out under a false name and immediately delivered him to Terry Clark, who within hours murdered Lewis, cut off his hands, bashed in his teeth and hid his body.

Unaware of all this, Robb began telling *his* story, begging the narcotics officer he was talking to for assurances that the story wouldn't get back to other members of the syndicate. According to the testimony of Allison Dine, Clark's common law wife, the story was delivered to Clark *the very next day*—May 29, 1978. Dine said she and Clark flew to Sydney, and Clark telephoned Alexander from the airport.

"The lawyer told Terry that it was urgent that Terry went to see him, that he had some information for Terry," Dine testified. "We caught a taxi into town, into the city. . . . After speaking to the lawyer, Terry came back to the taxi with the news that Duncan Robb had been leaking information about the organization and naming people in it to the police. . . Terry said, 'I think we'll have to teach him a lesson.' "

Dine testified that the "information cost Terry $10,000, which Brian Alexander split with the narcotics officers."

Why Clark didn't eliminate Robb as thoroughly as he did his other victims isn't known. But Clark and two others in the syndicate settled for beating Robb unconscious with ball bats. Robb was found and treated at a hospital for several broken bones and multiple bruises.

Soon afterward, two other syndicate members, Douglas and Isobel Wilson, were arrested in Queensland, Australia. The Wilsons were a married couple who carried drugs for the group. In doing so they had become regular users of heroin themselves. In the deteriorating mental state that heroin reliance induces, the Wilsons broke down and gave long, tape-recorded interviews, telling the police all they knew. Included was the fact that Terry Clark had murdered Harry Lewis.

The Wilsons were released—and nothing happened. Apparently no one had gotten around to bribing the narcotics office in distant Queensland. The office was so lethargic, perhaps no one had seen a need to. The Wilson tapes apparently were left sitting on a shelf for the better part of a year, and no one paid any attention to them.

Then, on March 15, 1979, Pommy Harry Lewis's mutilated body was identified in New South Wales. The Australian press was extravagant with lurid details about his heroin dealings and murder. (This is still more evidence that eleven days later, when the money was picked up, Nugan Hand management was well advised of its clients' narcotics trafficking.) Reading the papers, and apparently realizing the importance of what they had, the Queensland cops suddenly turned over the nine-month-old Wilson tapes to the New South Wales police, who were investigating Lewis's murder.

Within a week, the confidentiality of the tapes had been so widely shattered that their contents was in the hands of the press. Newspapers, eager for ways to follow up on the juicy Harry Lewis murder, ran accounts of the tapes in great detail in the editions of March 25. The stories didn't contain the Wilsons' names; apparently the cops who leaked the tapes thought they could protect the Wilsons by concealing their identity. But there was plenty enough detail in the stories for Terry Clark and those close to him to make an educated guess about who the mystery squealers were.

The next day, March 26, was when George Shaw picked up the $285,000 at the Aston & Alexander office. That was in the afternoon. Aston's calender for that day, eventually confiscated by police, showed a mid-morning appointment with Jim Shepherd, "Mr. Asia" 's principal Australian heroin dealer.*

Allison Dine and Wayne Shrimpton, the two witnesses from inside the "Mr. Asia" syndicate, testified that at that time, Clark received actual copies of the Wilson tapes. Dine said he bought them for about $275,000.** "I assume he got them through Alexander," she testified. "The tapes were long, two hours or so, apparently describing everything Doug knew," she went on. "Terry mentioned to me

*When the calendar was seized in a police raid in March 1980, the March 26 page was mysteriously cut out. But police, using scientific means, showed by impressions on the page under the missing March 26 page that Shepherd's name had been written there in Aston's handwriting.

**The amount that Allison Dine said Clark had paid for the tapes was 250,000 Australian dollars—about $275,000 in U.S. currency at then-current exchange rates. Shaw reported picking up 260,000 Australian dollars, plus an undefined fee, from the Aston & Alexander office. For convenience and clarity, this sum has been converted in this book to a rounded-off $285,000 in U.S. money, at then-current exchange rates. The reader can judge how easy or difficult it would be for Dine to have confused the numbers 250,000 and 260,000.

several times that he could not believe Doug had talked. . . . It was the obvious reason why he purchased the tapes, to satisfy himself that they had talked."

Dine also testified that Clark told her he paid the same amount to a hit man to kill the Wilsons. It is possible Dine confused the two, or that Clark, in talking to his moll, simply noted how much the Wilson episode had cost him in sum total, and was inconsistent or imprecise about exactly how the expenses were allocated between the tapes and the murder. In other words, there is a real possibility that the money Shaw picked up on March 26, and that Mike Hand paid out in Singapore April 12, wasn't dope money, but blood money.

On about April 13, 1979, Clark lured the Wilsons to Melbourne from Brisbane, Queensland, where they had been in a drug drying out program. They were met by a hit man, who took them to a house and shot them to death. According to Allison Dine, the hit man had promised "that there would be no traces of their bodies ever found because he was going to put them through a mincer."

The hit man had lied. A month after the killing, on May 18, 1979, a meat inspector taking his dog for a walk stumbled on the Wilsons' poorly buried bodies in a vacant lot.

Later, already in jail for the Johnstone murder, Clark himself talked to a Detective Piper of the Lancashire, England, police. He admitted that he had bought the Wilson tapes, though he was less precise than Dine and Shrimpton had been in their testimony.

"They have a narcotics squad out there," Clark explained in reference to Australia. "I have my contacts amongst them. They have got computers and telex machines which I have got on tap."

Asked why the Wilsons were murdered, he replied, "They were grassing. They even said I had murdered Harry Lewis. They made a tape to the police."

"How do you know that?" asked Detective Piper.

"I've had the tape," Clark replied.

"Who was the contact?"

"No names, I just paid the money."

Piper then asked him directly about Alexander, his solicitor. Clark replied, "Jeeze, the money I've paid him. That shit. He was doing well out of me."

"So if any of your people got into trouble, he would act for them?" Piper asked.

"Yeah, that's right. He would let me know what was going on."

Alexander was called to testify at the inquest into the Wilsons' murder in August 1980. He refused, on the ground that his testimony might incriminate him.

The coroner accused Clark and "persons unknown" of the murders, and said he was "satisfied" that Alexander, had he testified, could have named other guilty parties. Without such testimony, however, and with Clark's only life already under sentence for another murder, no charges were filed in the Wilson case.

At the inquest, Aston testified that neither he nor Alexander had ever had clients named Terry Clark or Jim Shepherd. Asked how Shepherd's name came to appear in Aston's own handwriting in Aston's diary, Aston replied, "I have no idea in the world how that came there." He said that despite all, he trusted Alexander "implicitly."

The coroner said in his findings, "The answers given by Mr. Aston are not accepted by this court. Notwithstanding the serious allegation made against Alexander, Aston has made no effort to inquire into the truth of the matter raised." He also ridiculed Aston's attempt to reconcile Alexander's meager salary of $118 to $145 a week with his duties as "a first-class criminal lawyer." The implication was that Alexander was maintaining his handsome lifestyle with money derived from other means.

Alexander and the two narcotics officers who interviewed Lewis and Robb—Wayne John Brindle and Richard John Spencer—were charged with conspiring with Clark to obstruct the course of justice. Magistrate C. A. Gilmore in the Court of Petty Sessions, Sydney, ruled, in May 1980, that there wasn't even enough evidence to bring the charges to trial, and threw them out. His decision was, at least, controversial.

J. R. ("Rod") Hall, the Victoria police commissioner, had been appointed by the federal minister in charge of the narcotics bureau to investigate the case. Hall publicly vented fury at Magistrate Gilmore's decision. "It was obvious Clark was tied up with Aston and Alexander," Hall says. "Could people remain naive about Aston and Alexander? I'd be surprised."

Hall notes that three times—on June 21, 1978 (shortly after the Lewis and Robb arrests and the Lewis murder), and on March 28 and March 30, 1979 (the week the Wilson tapes were turned over to Clark)—$11,000 was withdrawn from John Aston's account at a private bank and deposited there in another account, opened in the name of Spencer, the senior narcotics bureau official charged in the case.

The bank in which these transactions occurred was Nugan Hand.

"One of the things we couldn't understand," says Hall, "was that if the narcotics people had been getting money, what were they doing with the money. Then we found out that Spencer was depositing the money in Nugan Hand."

Aston said he thought the withdrawals from his account were to pay for some real estate that Nugan Hand was helping him buy. He acknowledged that Spencer, the narcotics officer, was a client "in several matters," but says he didn't know how Spencer's name got on the accounts. Spencer said he didn't know either, and denied receiving the $33,000. Still, the names of Spencer and Brindle, the other narcotics officer charged, appear copiously in Alexander's diary.

Aston stresses* that except for the one diary entry for Jim Shepherd, all connections with the dope dealers were through Alexander. "Not one of those persons have said they ever met me," he insists. "I gave Shaw one briefcase at the request of Frank Nugan. I never looked inside it. Nugan was in the habit of having things dropped at my office for delivery to him. I would phone him when they arrived. Of course, they could have contained money. I didn't look."

Justice Donald Stewart, the same man who later headed the Stewart Royal Commission on Nugan Hand, in 1983 headed another royal commission into drug trafficking and the "Mr. Asia" affair. That commission looked long and harshly at the way the Alexander-Brindle-Spencer obstruction of justice case had been dismissed.

Over several pages, Stewart laid out the prosecution case in a favorable light. He went out of his way to cite strange dealings between Spencer and Brindle on the one hand and the Wilsons on the other, and said Spencer had intentionally given false information to other officers in an apparent effort to exonerate Clark in the Harry Lewis murder.

Echoing charges made earlier by Police Commissioner Hall, Justice Stewart said several of Spencer's and Brindle's colleagues in the narcotics bureau changed their previous testimony during the hearing before Magistrate Gilmore. These other officers had stunned the prosecution by suddenly declaring that information given by informants to Spencer and Brindle had been discussed at a meeting in the bureau. This meant that others, not just Spencer and Brindle, might have leaked the names of the squealers. Stewart expressed doubt that such a meeting really took place.

*Interview with the author.

Faced with these new assertions that the leaks could have come from anywhere, and not yet knowing about the Nugan Hand account in Spencer's name, Magistrate Gilmore was justified in freeing Brindle and Spencer, Stewart said. But he made plain that he believed crimes had gone unpunished.

"The evidence points strongly to Spencer being one source" for the leaks, Stewart declared. "After Spencer took over the Clark . . . investigation a great deal of information appears to have been passed on to Clark and associates through Alexander." He also accused Spencer and Brindle of a "lack of concern" for the welfare of informants. "The Commission has evidence that Spencer rang Alexander's office on 12 April 1979 and said he was coming over. On 13 April 1979, Good Friday, the Wilsons travelled to Melbourne where they were murdered," Stewart wrote.

The Alexander case, he said, was worse. Here, the magistrate had based the dismissal on his belief that testimony from Dine and Shrimpton, the two "Mr. Asia" group members, was unbelievable. Magistrate Gilmore declared that Dine "is an evil woman" and that Shrimpton's word "is suspect, if not worthless."

Said Stewart, "The Commission doubts that the decision" by Gilmore "was a proper exercise of magisterial function in a committal hearing. Unfortunately it would appear that at times the magistrate lost control of his own court."

Though Aston and Alexander had asserted they never heard of Clark, and couldn't identify photographs of Clark that were shown to them, Stewart noted that Alexander's own *mother* had testified that her son and Clark were associated, and that Clark sometimes picked Alexander up late at night for mysterious trips.

Brian Alexander, who was supposedly employed by Aston at a salary that finally peaked at $9,500 a year, had upped his bank deposits from $5,100 in 1975 to $70,000 in 1978. The next year, he shelled out $121,000 cash for a new house. That, too, is subject to a possible innocent explanation, but no such explanation has been forthcoming.

In December 1981, Alexander disappeared. Authorities presume he was murdered, though a body hasn't been found—or at least identified.

In July 1979, shortly after the Wilson murders, Aston and a friend traveled to Hawaii. Their hotel reservations were made, and the $1,600 bill paid, by General Edwin F. Black, U. S. Army, retired.

General Black said* he didn't remember Aston, and must have paid the bill on instructions from Sydney. It was paid from the Nugan Hand Hawaii bank account, on which General Black was sole signatory.

*Interview with the author.

CHAPTER EIGHTEEN

Bernie of Arabia

When you are living a lie, you are living in constant fear of exposure. This was true for others at Nugan Hand, of course, but Frank Nugan was the only senior figure who would have no place to flee when the lie was exposed. Hand and any other Americans involved could go home someday. Nugan *was* home. The lie was his whole life, not just a chapter of it. As he entered his last year, Frank Nugan was losing his grip on himself.

The beginning of the end was probably the burgeoning family fruit company scandal. Until 1973, ownership of the company lay entirely with the family. But then Frank's brother Ken had raised $700,000 for a new cannery by selling shares of stock in the company. In the stock sale, several large insurance companies acquired a 40 percent interest.

As noted in Chapter 4, the disappearance of an anti-drug campaigner in the Nugans' home town of Griffith in July 1977 led to investigations. These investigations turned up records of cash payments from the Nugan Group fruit company to various people. One was Antonio Sergi, the reputed head of the local Mafia. Another was Sergi's friend and alleged Mafia colleague Robert Trimbole. (Though officials didn't know it then, Trimbole, under the alias "Australian Bob," was also working with the "Mr. Asia" heroin syndicate.)

Ken Nugan explained that the various cash payments had really been made to fruit farmers who wanted to remain anonymous for tax reasons. He said that the names Sergi and Trimbole on his company's books were just pseudonyms for the anonymous farmers.

But the insurance-company shareholders and the fruit company's auditors wouldn't let it go at that. Although they never figured out who actually received the cash payments, they decided that money was missing, and complained that Ken Nugan had been diverting funds that belonged to the shareholders.

So Ken Nugan did what any entrepreneur would like to do in such a situation. He kicked the insurance company representatives off his company's board of directors, and fired the auditors.

He managed all this at two rowdy shareholders' meetings in the fall of 1977. Minority shareholders were guaranteed certain protections by law and contract, but Ken Nugan overcame these protections by turning the voting procedures topsy-turvy.

Under Australian shareholder law, meeting procedures may be voted on at the spur of the moment, with one vote for each shareholder present, rather than one vote for each share. So the hall was packed with drunks and thugs, who had been given newly issued certificates for ten shares of stock each. They railroaded through some motions Ken Nugan proposed, changing procedures to accomplish his ends.

The minority shareholders screamed, of course. And the Corporate Affairs Commission—the equivalent of the U.S. Securities and Exchange Commission—backed them up. The attorney general of New South Wales pressed criminal fraud and obstruction of justice charges against Ken Nugan and several people who had helped him pack the meeting. Ken Nugan was also charged with, in effect, embezzling large sums of cash from the company for his personal use.

Among the accomplices charged with corporate fraud was his lawyer, who was said to have devised the meeting-packing scheme—Ken's brother, Frank Nugan.

In Parliament, members rose in public session, taking advantage of the scandal to vent anti-Nugan outrage they had long suppressed. One parliamentarian, John Dowd, revealed that the auditors had "been subjected to personal pressure. Certain persons have called at their homes, and the circumstances of the visits are such as to raise the greatest concern among the citizens of the state and the attorney general."

After Frank Nugan died it was discovered that he had then offered financial support to several people if they would run against the outspoken Dowd for Parliament. It was also discovered, from his files, that he had forged the signature of the attorney general, Frank Walker, on a letter to a Swiss bank, opening an account in Walker's name. The only apparent reason for writing such a letter would be to try to frame Walker, to embarrass or blackmail him. But Walker says he never heard about it until the letter was found after Nugan's death.*

Criminal proceedings against the Nugan brothers progressed throughout 1978 and 1979. So did tangled lawsuits over the future of the fruit company. But Frank Nugan assured everyone that things were all right. Both General Edwin Black and Admiral Earl Yates backed him up.

General Black attended court hearings on the case in Australia and declared his continued faith. Admiral Yates went to Sydney in May 1978 (according to newspaper accounts at the time), and assured the press that the charges against Frank Nugan "relate solely to his position as a solicitor advising his client. In this, he acted in conjunction with three legal firms in Sydney and with two Queen's Counsels."

The newspapers quoted Admiral Yates as saying, "None of the charges relate to money or assets. The legal argument is a technical one, centering around the splitting of company shares. In Australia, Nugan Hand banking activities have in no way been affected. . . . In fact, the deposit base has increased as a result of new deposits which have been received from customers showing their strong support for the banking group."

Les Collings sent out the clippings with a "Dear Customers & Friends" cover letter, apparently to anyone who had expressed doubts. Admiral Yates had insisted that Nugan Hand was "in no way" involved in the court action against the Nugan brothers and the fruit company, and that "there are no financial connections between the two."

But Frank Nugan, at least, knew otherwise. Through a series of loans, concealed by intermediary companies like Yorkville, Frank Nugan was using Nugan Hand money to pay mounting legal and

*The Swiss bank Nugan used to set up a phony Frank Walker account was the Union Bank of Switzerland. Bernie Houghton was well acquainted with a traveling official of the Union Bank, and had brought him around to Nugan Hand representatives in Asia to make introductions. Union Bank was also central in the Gough Whitlam affair; a package of fake documents that was used to start a political scandal over the obtaining of Arab loans through a shady middleman (see Chapter 9) was sent off with a Union Bank cover letter. By the time the opposition parliamentarians who received the package had turned its contents over to the press, the signature had been torn off the letter. Even though the documents were later exposed as bogus, their publication helped weaken and ultimately destroy the Whitlam government. All this may or may not be coincidence.

other bills for himself, his brother, and the fruit company. By liquidator John O'Brien's assessment, about $1.5 million was diverted during the fruit company affair.

Frank Nugan had already used more than $1 million in Nugan Hand money to buy and improve his lavish waterfront home. His expenditures on worldwide first-class jet fares and hotel accommodations were relentless. Hand, Yates, Black, and others were also jet-hopping.

A lot of money was certainly coming in to Nugan Hand. Its $1 billion-a-year publicity figure may have been exaggerated, but hundreds of millions was likely. Most of the money, however, was just going right back out again, laundered. How much Nugan Hand was collecting in laundering fees is not on record. But the bank certainly wasn't making any money in the banking business, as it told outsiders it was.

At some point, Frank Nugan must have realized that ends weren't going to meet, and that the pressures of the criminal investigation against him were hastening the denouement.

"He was helping his brother, but the bank was getting a bad reputation," explains his friend Paul Lincoln Smith. "I remember Frank telling me that some big overseas customer had canceled a big deal because of those involvements," Smith says.

The big Bank of New South Wales, which had earlier given vital references to Nugan Hand, issued a negative recommendation in July 1979, based on the fruit company case. Jerry Gilder, the sales staff manager, sent a copy to Mike Hand. Who else knew about it isn't clear, but Frank Nugan certainly did.

For some time now, he had started his whiskey consumption in the morning. His secretary added water to the bottles to try to slow the pace. He put on weight.

He told people that Mike Hand, the Christian Scientist, had advised him to lean on religion in times of trouble, so he began going to church a couple of times a day. He picked one that was particularly mystical and revivalist, and became nearly a fanatic about it. A Bible was always in his pocket, except when he took it out to consult or jot notes in.

Ken Nugan remembers Mike Hand telling him, "Frank was almost atheistic and I brought him back to religion."

But the religion didn't make him any easier to live with. In the summer of 1979, his wife Lee returned to her parents in Nashville, taking their two children. She denies she left him and says she moved only because he was traveling most of the time and could visit her more easily in Tennessee. Records of her Nugan Hand-paid American Express card show she charged off $21,200 before the year was out. She says most of this was legitimate business expense.

She told the *Nashville Tennessean*, "My marriage was an extremely happy one. There was never a moment's thought about leaving him. . . . It was a terrific relationship."

Close friends of Frank Nugan say he was beside himself wanting her back. He went on the wagon and shed fifty pounds in six months. He continued to spend money in manic style, including about $500,000 to add still more luxury to their home, hoping to entice her to return to it.

The bank didn't stop operating during this time. Rather, it expanded.

Probably its most brazen fraud of all was being carried out during 1979 and 1980 in Saudi Arabia. The man who ran the fraud was Bernie Houghton, the barkeep with all the military intelligence connections. Houghton himself has admitted taking $5 million in Nugan Hand deposits out of Saudi Arabia, mostly from American civilians and servicemen.

Steve Hill has recalled Mike Hand saying at one point that $6 million had been raked in from the Saudi venture. The various investigating authorities in Sydney and Hong Kong say the total easily could have exceeded $10 million. Of course, the money was never repaid to the victims—or, as they were known in those days, "investors."

Houghton, typically, has clouded the origins of the Saudi venture. The Corporate Affairs Commission, which interviewed Houghton, reported, "Admiral Yates suggested to him the prospect of expansion into Saudi Arabia."

To the Joint Task Force, Houghton said Yates had merely spent several days in the fall of 1978 persuading him to join Nugan Hand—as Mike Hand had been doing for some time—and that he came up with the Saudi idea independently while on a mission for Hand. He said Hand had sent him to Germany that fall to "review" the operations of a small private bank in Hamburg that Nugan Hand had recently boasted of acquiring, the F. A. Neubauer Bank. Houghton said he had protested that he "neither spoke German nor knew the banking business . . . in Germany," but that Hand had told him "that my logic and judgment were what he wanted."

He told the task force that on the way back to Australia, he visited his native Texas and stopped in Dallas at the office of the Henry C.

Beck Company, a large engineering and construction firm that does a lot of work overseas.

Houghton told the Joint Task Force that he had been asked by Frank Nugan to visit "a senior executive" of Beck for whom Nugan had done some "legal work." He said he didn't remember the executive's name. He told the Stewart Royal Commission, however, that it may not have been Nugan who sent him to Beck, but rather Admiral Yates.*

Houghton said the executive began describing the Saudi project Beck was undertaking, and then (as the Corporate Affairs Commission reported it) "requested Mr. Houghton to impress on Messrs. F. J. Nugan and Hand the amount of business potential in Saudi Arabia." This Houghton said he did, and on Admiral Yates as well, and soon he was on his way to the Middle East.

Houghton's story is further clouded by evidence that he, Admiral Yates, the Beck Company, and Nugan Hand may already have been involved together for several years.

The evidence comes from Douglas Schlachter, the witness the Joint Task Force has identified only as "J," a former aide to Edwin Wilson, the renegade CIA and naval intelligence agent. Both the Joint Task Force and Corporate Affairs Commission said they found "J"—Schlachter—highly believable.

Schlachter told the task force that in late 1976 or early 1977, while he was working for Wilson in Libya, he visited Wilson in Washington at a cover office Wilson had set up for Navy Task Force 157. As Australian investigators reported it, Schlachter "accompanied Wilson to an office in that city and met Admiral Earl P. Yates. At the time, Yates was in the company of another retired senior U.S. Armed Services officer whose identity is not known. The office referred to by 'J' is believed to have been that of retired Brigadier General Erle Cocke [which later served as Nugan Hand's U.S. office]."

"The meeting," the task force reported, "is said to have dealt with the possibility of Nugan Hand involvement in port construction then being undertaken in Libya and in which Wilson was involved. One of the companies involved in that construction work with Wilson was the Dallas, Texas, based company Henry C. Beck." The task force said "nothing is believed to have eventuated" from the discussions.

*The Stewart commission, which didn't mention the inconsistencies with Houghton's prior testimony, identified the executive as James Wheeler, apparently on Houghton's word. Beck says Wheeler left the company in 1980, and that it doesn't know how to locate him.

After reading that, Yates wrote the task force protesting that he never attended "such a meeting with Wilson," and that "J" "must have mistaken some other person for me." As proof, Yates noted that "J" said the meeting took place no later than February 1977; Yates insisted that "I did not work for Nugan Hand until June of 1977 and would not have had authority for such discussions even then."

The Joint Task Force has since said that the date "1977" had been a typographical error, and that the end-date Schlachter gave for the meeting had been February 1978. Even so, however, there are many grounds for questioning what Yates says.

The U.S. mission in Hong Kong, in its report to the U.S. Commerce Department on Nugan Hand dated April 1977, says (as cited earlier) that Yates was Nugan Hand's U.S. representative. Moreover, the context of the report doesn't suggest that this was any kind of new development. Houghton, who was working liaison between Nugan Hand and Wilson at the time, has testified that he had been a good friend of Yates "and his family" since the early 1970s.

Based on interviews with Yates and Houghton, the task force said Yates was invited on board "in early 1977." Reporter Maxine Cheshire in the *Washington Post* has quoted unnamed "sources" as saying Yates began running the Washington office of Nugan Hand in February 1977.

Perhaps most telling, Frank Nugan introduced Yates at a formal, tape-recorded speech in October 1979 as having been "perhaps our most important counsellor for the last two years and ten months," putting the beginning date in either December 1976 or January 1977. Yates responded by describing his recruiting work for the bank as going on "for almost three years now," and a new officer followed by saying Yates had toured him around the Nugan Hand empire "over two-and-a-half years ago." All these descriptions time Yates's association with Nugan Hand well before the June 1977 date Yates stated in his letter to the task force, and well within the time frame described by Schlachter.

The Stewart Royal Commission, however, didn't deal with any of this contrary information. Its report made no reference to "J" as a source of information, or to Schlachter, or to any effort to investigate the situation. The commission apparently wasn't even impressed by its own new evidence—a Nugan Hand document setting out Yates's employment terms, dated January 24, 1977. Stewart merely said, without explanation, "The Commission has found no evidence to support the allegations and accepts the denial made by Admiral Yates."

Houghton testified at least twice that Beck sponsored him in Saudi Arabia. The task force concluded that it did. A Beck spokesman denies that.*

But victims of the swindle say they, too, thought Beck was sponsoring Houghton. L. L. Bass of Portland, Oregon, was working for a Saudi Arabian firm in June 1979 when he deposited $10,000 with Houghton—"all I had," he describes it. "Houghton was introduced to me I think by the Beck resident manager—I'm sure Beck was closely associated with Houghton," he says.

A call to Beck in Dallas produces Bill—not William—Millican, who identifies himself as a director of the company. Asked about Houghton, Millican replies, "Yeah, I've heard of him." Where? "Just conversation." Conversation with whom? "A number of people. I'm not prepared to talk about it." Does Beck ever do any work for the CIA? "Not that I know of. It would have been without our knowledge."

Later, Millican called back to say that he had talked to Beck's "man in Saudi Arabia," and learned that many Beck employes had "lost lots of money" because of Houghton. They had tried to hold Beck responsible, on the ground it had recommended him. But Millican said that Beck had been "advised by counsel" that the employes had "no case."

Indeed, everyone seems to have escaped responsibility for the Nugan Hand Saudi mess. It would be hard to think of a bigger fraud in which all the principals were known and none had been prosecuted.

Houghton went to Saudi Arabia for a week in November 1978, to check it out. In January 1979, he returned with some assistants, rented a villa, and started making the rounds of American workplaces. He was armed with tools Michael Hand had given him: blank international certificates of deposit, identification cards signed by Hand detailing the benefits of being a Nugan Hand client, and sample money market securities to show clients how their money would supposedly be invested.

Houghton told the Joint Task Force he continued to consider his Nugan Hand employment temporary during a couple of month-long trips to Saudi Arabia, just to set things up. He said at Mike Hand's urging he then agreed to stay on permanently, on condition that he take orders only from his friend Hand, never from the increasingly

*To the Corporate Affairs Commission and in an interview with the author.

disagreeable Frank Nugan, for whom Houghton evinced much less respect.

(Ron Pulger-Frame, the courier, told the Stewart Royal Commission that he had gone to Nugan after being stopped and searched for drugs in Hong Kong in late 1977. Nugan, he said, had taken him to Houghton, and had "literally sat at his [Houghton's] feet" and asked for help. Thereupon Houghton, in the commission's words, "said he, with his connections in the United States, would get to the bottom of the matter and there was nothing to be concerned about.")

Houghton told the task force he insisted on reporting only to Hand because he wanted it clear he was working not for the Sydney company, but for the Nugan Hand Bank of the Cayman Islands, the entity Admiral Yates was president of. He said the bank, unlike the Sydney company, was owned entirely by Mike Hand—though by the other evidence, this wasn't correct.

"Did you have any previous experience in banking?" a member of the Corporate Affairs Commission asked Houghton.

"Just borrowing," he replied.

But he joined the industry at the height of OPEC's power, the year of the biggest oil price increase ever. Saudi Arabia had been awash with money since the first oil price jump in 1973, and now a vast new flood of money was pouring in. The Saudi government ordered all kinds of construction projects. Whole new cities were planned, and thousands of American professionals and managers were arriving to supervise the hundreds of thousands of Asian laborers who were also arriving.

To get their services, Saudi Arabia had to offer much higher salaries than either the Americans or the Asians could earn back home. Most of the Americans were going over for a couple of years, prepared to suffer the isolated, liquorless, sexless, joyless Moslem austerity in exchange for the big nest eggs they would have when they returned to the U.S.

When they got to Saudi Arabia, they faced a problem, however. Every week or two, they got paid, in cash, American or Saudi. And because Moslem law forbids the paying or collecting of interest, there were no banks in the Western sense of the word.

So what to do with all that money?

As described in a claim letter from Tom Rahill, an American working in Dhahran, Saudi Arabia, "Mr. Houghton's representatives would visit Aramco [Arabian American Oil Company] construction camps in Saudi Arabia shortly after each monthly payday. We 'investors' would turn over Saudi riyals to be converted at the prevailing dollar exchange rate, and receive a Nugan Hand dollar certificate. . . . The monies, we were told, were to be deposited in the Nugan Hand Hong Kong branch for investments in various 'secured' government bonds."

Another claim letter, from a group of seventy American workers in Saudi Arabia who among them lost $1.5 million, says that was their understanding as well.

Not only Aramco and Beck, but other large U.S. concerns are said by investors to have boosted Nugan Hand, and let salesmen hold meetings on company property and use company bulletin boards. Among them were Bechtel, the giant international construction firm then guided by George Shultz and Caspar Weinberger, and University Industries, Inc. of San Diego.

"The companies were passing down to their employes that this man was being made available, and they could put their money in and get 18 percent" interest, says Linda Geyer, now of San Diego. When she lived in Saudi Arabia, in 1979, she and her husband (who died of cancer in 1982) invested and lost $41,481 with Nugan Hand. Her son, John H. Geyer, invested and lost another $32,500. Both men worked as plumbers with University Industries on a construction job dominated by the Beck company. (Her husband was also a project manager.)

Mrs. Geyer is another victim who asserts that Beck sponsored Houghton. That, she says, is what gave him credibility. "Everybody said, Well, Beck, they're not going in with just any old guy," she says.

For its part, University Industries doesn't deny that any of this happened. "It sounds like you've got a real story," a spokesman says, after checking with a company employe in Saudi Arabia, who "basically confirmed everything you said."

Mrs. Geyer says Houghton "only worked in cash. He left Beck, Bechtel, and Aramco with so much money he could barely even carry the case," she says. "One time he had to have two briefcases. He used to brag about it. Some people I know lost $100,000 or $200,000, easy." Others remember Houghton actually using plastic garbage bags to tote away the loot.

Once he was established, with branch offices in Jeddah and Al Khobar, he could travel less. "The people, they'd come into the house from five o'clock in the morning until midnight," he told the Corporate Affairs Commission. "It was kind of like being open on a twenty-four-hour basis, because they work shifts. Strangers would come and knock on the door. As soon as one from a new company had approached you, you would suddenly get a lot of people."

By his own admission, Houghton toted off the intended savings not only of private-contract American employes, but also of U.S. Air Force personnel stationed in Saudi Arabia. In fact, the record shows, Houghton quickly made contact with two colonels, apparently air force, whom he had known from Vietnam war days. One of them, R. Marshall Inglebeck, "showed Mr. Houghton around, introduced him and explained that Mr. Houghton was a banker looking for business for Nugan Hand Bank," the Corporate Affairs Commission reported.

The other was Colonel Billy Prim. There has been speculation that Colonel Prim was the air force colonel mentioned earlier who picked up Houghton in Sydney in March 1975 and went with him to Iran, to "assist" in some business; the trip coincided with the trip to Iran of Edwin Wilson, then working for Naval Task Force 157, and the sale through him of a U.S. Navy spy vessel to Iran. According to the testimony of Bernie Houghton to the Joint Task Force, Prim had served on Yates's staff at the Pacific Command, and had introduced Houghton to Yates back in the early 1970s.

The air force won't disclose Prim's or Inglebeck's whereabouts now, though it did agree to forward letters to them asking for comment; they haven't responded. One victimized American in Saudi Arabia, Robert Speer, testified before the Corporate Affairs Commission that Prim and Inglebeck had introduced him to Houghton as a longtime friend. Other than that, Prim's activities with Houghton in both Iran and Saudi Arabia remain a mystery—all the more a mystery because on Nugan Hand's internal staff list for January 1980 appears the name William Prim, with the communications code number 517.

Houghton is highly critical of normal banking channels. "The banks were just impossible. You'd go and you'd have to spend the entire day there," Houghton told the Corporate Affairs Commission. So, instead, he set up his own system for getting the money to Singapore. It involved a local money changer named "El Raji." "He was very quick," Houghton said.

Just that quick, El Raji would change the cash Houghton brought him for Thomas Cook traveler's checks in $1,000 denominations. He or his agent would sign them and make them payable to Nugan Hand Bank. Then they would bundle up the checks, along with deposit records, and send the packages via DHL air courier to Mike Hand in Singapore—holding back, according to Houghton's testimony, enough cash to pay expenses for the Saudi operation.

Houghton denies responsibility for what became of the money

after he sent it to Singapore, of course. According to his testimony, he just knew that he got a 1.5 percent commission off the top on all the money he collected. This, if true, would be small potatoes for the kind of work he was doing; mutual fund salesmen routinely get 8 percent. On the other hand, legitimate bankers get salaries, not chunks of depositors' money. Anyway, Houghton said most of the money he earned was applied to repay a large loan he had received from Yorkville, the Nugan Hand affiliate, for purchase of his swank waterfront condominium.

Later, he told the Corporate Affairs Commission, he complained about the low wages. So Nugan and Hand agreed to pay him a $100,000-a-year salary and forgive his loan. But, he insisted—in testimony to the commissioners who could have demanded he give back his ill-gotten earnings—not a penny was ever actually paid him.

The claim letter from the group of seventy investors who lost $1.5 million says, "We were greatly influenced by the number of retired admirals, generals and colonels working for Nugan Hand."

Indeed, there is a strain that seemed to have run through a lot of investors' minds that Nugan Hand had some kind of secret government affiliation, possibly through the CIA. This would not be an unnatural feeling for an American in Saudi Arabia. Anyone would assume there was a good deal of CIA activity going on there then.

One man who inspired such thoughts was Houghton's chief assistant in Saudi Arabia, Michael Murphy. Murphy had been born in Jessup, Georgia, in 1949, and somehow landed in Australia after finishing college in the United States. He lived in Houghton's apartment, worked for the restaurants, and eventually helped manage them.

After a few years Murphy went back to the United States. By some accounts he fought in Rhodesia, but he stayed in touch with Houghton. He returned to Australia on his honeymoon, the Stewart commission said, paid for, it said, by Houghton, as a wedding present. Houghton then offered him the job in Saudi Arabia.

"We were suspicious about him," Linda Geyer says. She remembers her husband's remarking more than once, "I get the strangest impression sometimes that he's working fo the government."

That impression about the whole Nugan Hand operation in Saudi Arabia was only strengthened by the way it all ended, in April 1980, as the bank went into bankruptcy in Sydney and Hong Kong.

Houghton had returned to Australia after Frank Nugan's death in January 1980 and stayed several weeks. Mike Hand then sent him back to Saudi Arabia—to resume supervision of the deposit-taking,

Houghton testified. But Houghton only stayed a short while, then returned to Australia with a briefcase containing files relating to his Saudi activities, which he turned over to Mike Hand. Then he headed for the Washington, D.C., area where Yates lived and worked.

Meanwhile, Mike Murphy also flew to Singapore. He testified before the Corporate Affairs Commission that Hand admonished him about "the need for secrecy and confidentiality in the private banking records of Nugan Hand Bank maintained in Saudi Arabia." On Hand's instructions, he testified, he returned to Saudi Arabia, destroyed all the records kept there, and refrained from keeping more.

On April 12, 1980, a Middle East newspaper carried a Hong Kong report that the Nugan Hand office there was no longer redeeming deposits. At this point, the stories Murphy and Houghton told to the various investigators diverge. Murphy told the Corporate Affairs Commission that on seeing the story he called Houghton and Hand in Singapore, and was told not to worry.

But he says he was also told that any Saudi withdrawals should be from funds on hand there, as money couldn't be removed from Hong Kong. Murphy said he was suspicious about that, and called Houghton's aide in Sydney, Robert W. Gehring, the American Vietnam veteran. Gehring, he said, told him to get the whole Nugan Hand crew out of Saudi Arabia immediately, which he did.

Houghton, on the other hand, told the Joint Task Force that Murphy called him in Washington and "asked me what he should do. I suggested he contact Mike Hand," Houghton testified, "and also I stated that if it were I, I would probably leave the area. In Saudi Arabia there is a debtors' prison policy, and the likelihood would be that Mike Murphy and his employes could remain in prison until the debt is paid, which could be for life." Although the task force interrogators didn't press him on the point, Houghton thus tacitly admitted his awareness that the depositors' funds had been dissipated, even as he tried until the last second to get more deposits.

Murphy, Houghton testified, then called Hand, who confirmed that Nugan Hand was in receivership, and also that Murphy should get out. "At the same time," Houghton testified, "depositors of the [Al Khobar] branch began demanding their money. All money on hand was disbursed to the depositors. The situation became somewhat violent and Mike Murphy and his employe, whose name I cannot recall, then abandoned the—." Houghton broke off in midsentence, and resumed, "It is my understanding that the premises in which the bank branch was located was severely damaged by the depositors after Mike Murphy left the premises."

Murphy's own story was that he booked flights for the staff out of Saudi Arabia using depositors' funds to pay for the tickets. While two staffers left on an early flight, Murphy and K. Rex Shannon used $40,000 remaining to hold off fifty or sixty depositors who had showed up. Then they ducked out to take a 3:00 A.M. British Airways flight to London. When they learned it was delayed, they took a domestic flight to Jeddah and boarded a Saudi flight to London—a lucky thing, because, Murphy testified, Saudi police were already after them and stopped and searched the British Airways flight they had been booked on.

Murphy went to Hamburg, Germany, and closed out his own account at Nugan Hand's Neubauer bank there. Then Murphy, the biggest banker in Saudi Arabia, returned to Sydney, where Gehring arranged for him to live in Houghton's penthouse condo and work as night manager at the Bourbon and Beefsteak bar.

One American depositor in Saudi Arabia was Jesse J. Defore, then a faculty member at the University of Petroleum and Minerals in Dhahran. He remembers the bank's collapse this way: "The Nugan Hand offices here were dismantled during the night hours, in one night, and . . . Murphy has not been seen again."

But then Defore tells an amazing story: "After Murphy left," he says, "there were for several days a group of American military personnel, supposedly personal friends of Murphy, staying in the house that Nugan Hand had occupied. These men assured all comers that 'Mike has gone to see what's the problem. . . . He'll be back. . . . Don't you worry. . . . We've got a lot of money in this thing, too, and we don't worry.' "

Eventually, the Joint Task Force heard about this U.S. military protection that covered Nugan Hand's escape from Saudi Arabia. The investigators went back to Houghton, who hadn't mentioned anything about this in his original description of the violent flight of Murphy. When the story was called to his attention, he replied, "I can only rely on what Murphy has told me. The air force men were on the same baseball team that Murphy was captain of. They were there socially and certainly in no official capacity."

The task force didn't buy that for a minute. Its official report concludes the Saudi chapter thus: "Whilst it might be that the military knew Murphy well, it seems unlikely that they would have compromised either their military or civil position in Saudi Arabia by acting as unofficial guards in a situation described by Houghton as being violent.

"For the reality is, [based] on Defore's account, that over several days and nights they either deliberately acted on behalf of Nugan Hand and lied to inquiring victim-clients, or had been deliberately lied to themselves by Murphy, which information they then passed on in good faith. The latter seems unlikely in view of the background of Houghton, Murphy, Hand and other former military personnel who were involved with Nugan Hand at that time [and, one might add, in view of the ridiculousness of such a story in the face of the already announced bankruptcy and other obvious facts]. In considering this, it is perhaps worthwhile reiterating the observation of some seventy U.S. clients in Saudi Arabia: 'We were greatly influenced by the number of retired admirals, generals, and colonels working for Nugan Hand.' "

The Stewart Royal Commission did not address this situation, or, based on its report, do any independent investigation of the Saudi affair. Astoundingly, it simply accepted what Houghton told it, and reported as fact that "No payments other than expenses were received by Mr. Houghton. . . . Millions of dollars (Mr. Houghton roughly estimated the total as US$5 million) in deposits were taken, but these were ultimately transmitted to the Singapore office for investment on the Asian Currency unit market at low interest rates or were otherwise squandered in the operations of the Group as a whole."

There seems to have been no consideration by the commission, in its one-paragraph treatment of the Saudi branch, or the two other paragraphs dealing with Saudi Arabia in a biographical sketch it prepared of Houghton, that any money might have been stolen. Or that Houghton might have had a motive not to tell the truth in his testimony.

The commission's report offered no evidence that any money had been legitimately invested as Houghton suggested, and no evidence that the commission had talked to any of the victims.

Houghton did tell the commission he had received $364,000 in expenses over the eighteen months he was a bank executive. But apparently expense money is not subject to taxes—or to recall by the bilked depositors.

CHAPTER NINETEEN

The Admiral's Colors

"A former Admiral commands our Private Bank," blared the headline of a full-page ad in the *Far Eastern Economic Review*—the most prestigious business publication in the region, which is partly owned by the publishers of the *Wall Street Journal.* Below the headline was a photograph of Admiral Earl ("Buddy") Yates, occupying most of the top half of the page.

The text of the ad says:

> When Rear Admiral Yates exchanged the gold stripes of an Admiral for the pin stripes of a banker, he brought added strength to NUGAN HAND INTERNATIONAL–PRIVATE BANKERS. He brought the experience of a man who administered the office that controls a powerful Navy. He brought the executive experience of a man that controlled the careers of tens of thousands of men. The financial expertise of a man who has controlled multi-billion dollar budgets and programs. The business experience of a man who has dealt with the largest engineering and construction firms in the world. All this and, in corporate terms, against the toughest competition in the world. 'Bud' Yates, like all NUGAN HAND executives, gets out and sees his clients on their own ground, face to face. He says, 'That's where you find the clients' problems and that's where you will find the solutions.'

But because Admiral Yates's activities were more scattershot than Frank Nugan's or Bernie Houghton's, and seem to have involved politically sensitive matters, there is no thorough catalog of them.

One strange and elusive piece of business he sought for Nugan Hand was to create and run a central banking system for Brunei, a sultanate the size of Delaware, located on the north coast of Borneo. Brunei has been self-governing since 1971, though until 1983 its foreign affairs remained linked to those of its colonizer, Britain. Brunei is a tiny spot, but it was a valuable listening post near the volatile Malaysian-Indonesian border. And life for its 220,000 souls, almost all of them pledged to Allah, had been considerably improved by the discovery of oil.

Many interests covertly sought the sultan's ear as the rich little nation emerged. One was the United States Government. Just how much intimacy the United States achieved was suggested in December 1986, when it was revealed that the sultan had secretly helped the Reagan administration evade a Congressional ban on aid to the Contra rebels fighting to overthrow the Government of Nicaragua.

In Congressional investigations of the affair, it was revealed that the sultan had agreed to donate $10 million to the Contras at the State Department's urging. Ironically, it was also revealed that U.S. operatives had lost the whole $10 million while trying to transfer it to the "private" Contra arms network being run by Bernie Houghton's old friend, "retired" air force General Richard Secord. National Security Council staff member Oliver North gave Assistant Secretary of State Elliott Abrams the wrong Swiss bank account number, and the sultan's $10 million wound up in the pocket of a Swiss businessman who was no doubt delighted with his windfall. In May 1987, after a five-month search, the geniuses who run the U.S. Government finally located the businessman, and went to court to try to get the money back from him.

Still unresolved was the possibly more important mystery of just what the United States had done to induce the sultan toward such generosity in the first place. Nugan Hand's involvement with the sultan certainly reveals he had long been inclined towards secret business dealings with allegedly private concerns that had links to the U.S. Government and promised under-the-table benefits. What he sought from Nugan Hand was assurance that if he were chucked out of office, either by his subjects or by one of his country's large neighbors, he could take Brunei's public treasury along with him as a retirement benefit.

In March 1978, Brunei's state finance officer, Pehin John Lee, and an advisor to the sultan, Pehin Dato Isa, agreed to a deal under which Nugan Hand was to "submit . . . an initial draft of an enactment to be known as 'The Central Bank of Brunei Enactment of 1978,' " and then would become the central bank's management advisor. Nugan Hand also sought the personal accounts of the sultan and other top officials.

Financial officer Lee was assured in a letter from Nugan Hand representative Graham Steer, who worked directly under Michael Hand in Singapore, that "we are presently advisers to and are acting for a number of Government and semi-Government bodies throughout the world." These weren't specified.

On May 19, 1978, according to surviving bank records, Admiral Yates was dispatched to Brunei to meet with His Highness the Sultan about the bank and about something referred to as Admiral Yates's "own 'project.' "* This "project" was apparently too sensitive to describe in Admiral Yates's marching orders from Steer, a copy of which was found in Nugan Hand's remaining files even though the orders are headed "CONFIDENTIAL" and "Please Destroy After Perusal." But from the context, the "project" seems to have more to do with intelligence about future political alignments in the region than with banking.

The memo leaves little doubt about Nugan Hand's main selling point, noting, "We would provide his Highness the Sultan a Bank structure and Depository system which he alone can control should any change of Government take place, together with top security for deposits held in Nugan Hand Bank to ensure confidentiality in all matters."

Regarding financial officer Lee, the instructions to Admiral Yates say, "It would seem that we would have to run one more conversation with him of private personal advantage to him." The memo does not clarify whether this means a bribe.

"As to your own 'project,' " the memo continues, "you will notice from the recent press release that both Malaysia and Indonesia are taking more than a close look at Brunei, and we were advised that the [result of the] closed session between the prime minister of Malaysia and the president of Indonesia was that Indonesia would not

*On May 17, 1987, a Sunday and the day before the already type-set galleys of this book were to be sent to the printing and binding plant for the last time, Admiral Yates responded to five years of queries, the latest request having been mailed to him in January, 1987, when, he says, he was on a boat trip from which he just returned. Several specific discrepancies are footnoted.

Admiral Yates says he never went to Brunei. "I remember some discussion of it. I was interested in it. I don't remember the details of it," he says. He says he doesn't remember why he didn't go, or whether someone else from Nugan Hand went in his stead.

stand in the way of Malaysia should it wish to incorporate this State in their own federation. There is no doubt about it that the oil is the attraction for both Malaysia and Indonesia."

How Nugan Hand learned the contents of a closed meeting between the Malaysian and Indonesian heads of state is not told. But the memo notes that "under the above political circumstances surrounding Brunei, your own proposed 'project' should be warmly received not only by the British High Commission but also by the Sultan, and in particular his advisor."

No known files reveal what came out of Yates's trip to Brunei. It may have failed, or it may have succeeded so well that the results were among the records that Admiral Yates and other Nugan Hand managers saw fit to remove from the office in the week after Frank Nugan's death. The Stewart Royal Commission didn't look into it.

But Yates continued to travel for the cause. John Owen, the Nugan Hand representative in Bangkok, remembers Yates arriving there, pulling a flask of brandy out of his pocket and adding it to his morning coffee.* Others remember Yates talking about a big petroleum reprocessing deal, but nothing like that eventuated.

Some correspondence found in Nugan Hand's own files indicates that Yates went to Beirut for the bank in 1979—and was searched by customs on his arrival into Washington. On the continuing flight, he wrote angrily to Mike Hand back in Singapore, "They stopped me, pulled me out of line, searched me from head to toe and questioned me about my banking activity dealing with overseas banks." From the context, Yates had been in Beirut on behalf of a Nugan Hand client in the Far East, but the specifics weren't disclosed.

The note from Yates was found in the files with a memo attached, carrying Mike Hand's handwritten reaction. "Adverse news preceded Buddy to Washington," it said, noting that the bank's client was very unhappy over losing money on Yates's mission. Yates had paid several thousand dollars on the client's behalf, the memo says, though it doesn't say what for.

An official of the Hong Kong liquidator's office says that from what he can tell from the surviving records, "Yates was off trying to make deals with big shots that never came off. He stayed away from day-to-day operations. The thing was actually run by Hand and Nugan, and later Hand and Houghton."

As long as the question of Nugan Hand's relationship to the U.S. Government stays open, however, one has to question whether

*Yates says he never drinks spirits.

Yates's seemingly fruitless journeys can all be chalked up to foolishness and incompetence. Brunei, Beirut, and Southeast Asia were all war zones or prospective war zones. What Yates could have been doing is open to the imagination, but if he were running government missions, or government-approved missions, under cover of a private company, he would hardly have been the first person to do so.

Nugan Hand's valued friends at the ANZ Bank certainly suspected Nugan Hand did CIA business. A memo in ANZ's files says an ANZ officer brought the matter up in conversation with the owner of a large Hong Kong bank, General S. K. Yee, former head of Chiang Kai-shek's Kuomintang army. The memo says that General Yee, who might be expected to know a thing or two about CIA connections, and who had just been talking to Admiral Yates about the possible sale of his bank to Nugan Hand, assured the ANZ officer that the connections were real.

One project Admiral Yates worked on intensely with Mike Hand throughout 1979 and even into 1980 was, at least ostensibly, the transfer of thousands of Indochinese refugees from Asia to the Caribbean. It was hoped to obtain millions of dollars in grants from the United Nations High Commission on Refugees, and perhaps other quasi-government funding, which would flow through Nugan Hand—although everyone who discussed the project insisted that it was motivated by charitable, not profit, impulses.

But the whole idea seems a bit bizarre, and it was pursued through some curious channels. There have been official and unofficial suggestions that an ulterior motive lay behind the refugee project. Some even involved plans for a coup d'état in Haiti. Moreover, there are discrepancies in the accounts that have been given of the affair.

Discussing it later, Admiral Yates has attributed the project to Mike Hand's long-standing humanitarian concern for the fate of the allies who loyally fought alongside him in Vietnam. That raises the question, however, of why for counsel on the project Yates decided to turn immediately to Mitchell WerBell III, of Powder Springs, Georgia, who is not a man best known for his charitable pursuits. WerBell is, rather, better known as a longtime trainer of terrorists, and inventor and seller of mini-machine guns and other terrorist equipment, on contract to, among others, the CIA.

Admiral Yates gave this explanation to the Joint Task Force for his choice of consultants: "As I recall, WerBell had extensive experience in Central America, according to the information [we] had. At the time we were involved in trying to get refugees housed into various western hemisphere countries and we thought that WerBell might be able to help us with some insights into getting them accepted."

When a task force investigator asked who arranged the WerBell contact, Yates said, "I don't know. It might have been Roy Manor," the Nugan Hand general who was an expert in guerrilla warfare. (Manor, for his part, says he met WerBell through Yates, though he says he's seen WerBell since then.) "I was aware that WerBell was in the soldier-of-fortune business," Yates explained to the task force.

And, boy, was he—with a lust for fighting communism that was actually nurtured in the Russian Revolution! This is how the task force summed up WerBell's incredible career:

> A U.S. citizen born 8 March 1918, WerBell is the son of a white Russian emigré who served in the U.S. as the Czar's liaison officer. WerBell graduated in 1938 from Fork Union Military Academy in Virginia and served with the Office of Strategic Services (O.S.S.) in China during World War II.
>
> He retired as a lieutenant colonel and . . . commenced his own public relations firm offering 'geopolitical p.r.' to such people as the Dominican Republic's then president Hector Bienvenido Trujillo Molina and Cuba's Fulgencio Batista [two dictators the United States Government supported, with continuing unpleasant repercussions]. Following the rise to power of Fidel Castro, WerBell led anti-Castro missions, his teams comprising for the most part . . . exiled Cubans and former U.S. military personnel. . . .
>
> During the early 1960s WerBell was active in the Southeast Asian conflict and served as a training advisor to the Special Forces in Vietnam. . . .
>
> WerBell has been and still is involved in a number of U.S. companies which under the descriptions of 'defence' and 'physical security' offer advice on guerrilla warfare [the task force reported]. He is a former licensed firearms dealer and has been reputedly involved in the sale of arms to anticommunist or anti-left wing forces. . . .
>
> In December 1974 U.S. authorities seized a large quantity of weapons owned by one of WerBell's companies. Subsequently his son and an associate were indicted on charges of conspiring to sell 2,000 submachine guns and 1,000 silencers. . . . All charges were dismissed. . . .
>
> Since the late 1970s WerBell has owned and operated a private training facility for counter-terrorism and counter-

> insurgency in Powder Springs, Georgia. . . . Facilities at the center . . . include a gun laboratory, two firing ranges, high-speed driver training track and a parade ground. Attendees have included serving U.S. military and enforcement/secret service personnel, private individuals and foreign nationals. . . .
>
> WerBell is credited with the design of the world's smallest submachine gun, the Ingram and the Ingram silencer.

Finally, the task force said, "WerBell is widely accepted as having been since the 1950s through the 1970s until possibly the present day, a contract agent for the CIA and many of his actions have been carried out on their behalf, though neither the precise nature of that relationship nor extent of his sanctioned actions is known."

Asked about this, WerBell says, "Not so! I never worked for 'em. I've worked *with* the CIA, but I never got paid by 'em." Does that mean he did it for free? No, he says, he got paid. But the money came from "a group of well-minded private citizens" he would prefer not to identify.

The task force also provided, by way of exhibit, an advertising brochure for his training camp that lists twenty-six major covert actions WerBell has been associated with—including General Manor's raid on the Sontay prison camp in 1970. "I have no idea where the hell that came from," WerBell says; "it certainly didn't come from here." Manor says WerBell "had zero to do with Sontay."

Why would Admiral Yates, whether or not on General Manor's advice, consult a man like WerBell about a refugee-aid project? Well, the answer may be that the refugee project wasn't the real, or at least the only, reason they were meeting.

Whereas Yates told the task force that his chat with WerBell was arranged by someone else, possibly Manor, and "was my one and only meeting and discussion with him," according to the task force, WerBell "said that he knew Yates through their connection with the U.S. Armed Services."

Then WerBell told the task force that he and Yates actually discussed promoting a possible revolution in Haiti. WerBell had some experience with Haitian revolutions. In 1967, WerBell had been indicted by a Miami, Florida, federal grand jury for his involvement in an attempt by Haitians, Cuban exiles, and others to mount an invasion of Haiti from Florida.

The indictment was dropped, which, WerBell says,* shows that

*This is what he told the task force, and repeated in an interview with the author.

the U.S. Government sanctioned the operation. He says the invasion he organized wasn't intended to really happen, but was a ruse to bluff Haitian dictator François ("Papa Doc") Duvalier into a more moderate course, and to test Fidel Castro's responses.

The task force, after interviewing WerBell on June 12, 1982, reported, "Yates indicated that he wished to meet with WerBell as there were some matters affecting Haiti which could be to their mutual benefit. . . . Within a short period of time, WerBell met with Yates, 'some other U.S. military personnel' whom WerBell declined to name, and Clemard Charles,* an exiled Haitian."

Charles had been a banker and bagman for Haitian dictator Duvalier, until one day the mercurial Duvalier decided Charles had been overrewarding himself, and so seized the bank and jailed Charles. After some years, Charles was released and exiled, but his animosity toward the Haitian leadership continued, even after Duvalier died and his son, Jean-Claude ("Baby Doc") Duvalier, took over. WerBell, on the other hand, in the wake of his bluffed invasion of Haiti, claimed to have maintained such good relations that Baby Doc had hired him to train his private security force.

Now, in 1979, WerBell answered Yates's call and flew to Washington. Nugan Hand covered his expenses. (The canceled check Yates wrote to WerBell led the task force to discover the incident.) According to the task force, Yates proposed a plan to move Mike Hand's former Vietnamese comrades, now refugees, to an island in the bay of Port-au-Prince, Haiti. There they would be set up in a fishing village.

"Because of WerBell's knowledge of Haiti and the fact that he knew 'Baby Doc,' " the task force reported, "they [Yates, Charles, and the other, unnamed, military men] wanted WerBell to go to Haiti with the plan and to add to it the threat that if 'Baby Doc' did not grant them the island camp there would be an attempt made to oust him and to have [Charles] installed as president by 'popular vote.' In return for his efforts, if 'Baby Doc' granted them the island, WerBell was to have been given the contract for providing a security force for the island. If 'Baby Doc' refused, WerBell was to have been responsible for the takeover of Haiti and the subsequent security of the whole of Haiti.

*The task force reported the name as Charles Clement, possibly because that was the way WerBell remembered it. Some research into Haitian politics, and a phone call to a Charles ally in New York, left no doubt in this author's mind as to who was being talked about.

"WerBell discussed the proposals over the two days he was in Washington," the task force went on, "but said that from the outset (the time of Yates's telephone call) he thought it was an unrealistic proposition, largely because he did not see it as the type of action that would have any support from the U.S. Government. WerBell turned down the offer."

Yates, needless to say, was sorely distressed to read the task force's findings. He quickly went to WerBell, got a signed statement conforming to yet another version of the events, and presented that account in a letter to the task force. Under this version, Mike Hand had met with Charles and devised a plan whereby Charles would borrow $250,000 from Nugan Hand for the refugee project. Yates called WerBell to Washington to obtain an independent opinion as to Charles's qualifications.

Then, the new Yates-WerBell story goes, WerBell flew on to New York alone, where Charles—not Yates—proposed the plan about overthrowing the Haitian government. WerBell decided the proposal was impractical, and returned to Washington with this news. Yates took his advice, paid him, and saw no more of WerBell or Charles—if you accept this new version of events.

But that's still not the end of it.

About the same time, the fall of 1979, Frank Nugan, Mike Hand, and Admiral Yates were also pursuing what they said was a plan to move the refugees to the Turks and Caicos Islands—thirty dots of British-owned land, six of them inhabited, near the Bahamas. The main exports are salt, crayfish, conch shells, and cocaine.

Nugan and Hand were in Geneva regularly to try to wheedle money out of the U.N. refugee commission for the move. They also wanted help from Washington. There, they and Yates took advantage of an ally who was already on board, in a sense: General Cocke, the native Georgian, who was not reticent about letting potential public relations clients know who else in town shared his home state: the president and all his cronies.

"Admiral Yates wanted to meet somebody in the White House because he wanted to talk about a refugee program," General Cocke recalls.* So Cocke introduced Yates to John G. Golden, the former

*A desire for White House influence doesn't comment one way or the other on what possible continuing links Nugan Hand may have had to U.S. intelligence. Plenty of people in government seek such influence to promote their special projects. A real mover like Edwin Wilson constantly plied prominent senators and White House staffers to help strengthen his hand while he was a career officer both at the

college roommate and, in the words of the *Washington Post*, "favorite partying companion" of Hamilton Jordan, who, in turn, was the closest advisor of the President of the United States. Through Golden, then a "consultant," Yates and Nugan each bought $1,000 tickets to a Democratic fund-raising dinner. Golden seated them at his table and, Maxine Cheshire reported in the *Post*, was so eager to satisfy Nugan's wish to meet Jimmy Carter that he spilled a bottle of wine on the table while introducing them.

Another evening, Yates, Nugan, Cocke, and Golden dined at the Four Seasons Hotel in Washington with some other men; Yates told Cheshire he "doesn't remember" their names, and "doesn't recall" what was discussed. But Cheshire found "another source who was present" who recalled that Nugan wanted Golden to help Nugan Hand in Panama, where Hamilton Jordan had been conducting negotiations over the Panama Canal and other matters with dictator General Omar Torrijos.

According to this source, "He [Golden] bragged about Hamilton's connections with Torrijos. He said General Torrijos would do anything for Hamilton—they're very, very good friends."

Asked about this, Cocke says, "I might have been there. I'd hardly say it was a major dinner. It was one of those things where people went in and out all evening." He does remember, however, that Nugan Hand "wanted to salvage military equipment on the islands."

Yates told the task force that the U.S. Navy was closing its base on Grand Turk Island on March 31, 1980, and that Nugan Hand wanted to use the base for its refugee settlement. Others recall that Nugan Hand wanted the navy to leave behind as much equipment as possible, for use or salvage. Wilf Gregory, George Shaw, and General Black all remembered Yates pursuing the deal energetically, but said they didn't understand how it would make money.

Nugan Hand signed a preliminary agreement with the Turks and Caicos Government in early 1980. In exchange for rights to the soon-to-be-abandoned navy base, the bank pledged to provide at least $1 million capital for maintaining the base's airport and port facilities, improving the deep-water harbor, building roads, and so forth. The bank collapse made the agreement null almost before the ink was dry.

All this prompted considerable speculation from the task force, which said Nugan Hand probably couldn't have raised the necessary capital for the port improvements and that the islands lacked enough food and water even for their present populations.

Central Intelligence Agency and in the Office of Naval Intelligence.

"The above considerations pose the question of the existence of hidden motives for the project," the task force declared.

> One possibility is that Hand/Nugan Hand envisaged the future use of the Turks and Caicos Islands as a tax haven. . . . Another possibility is that they expected [an] influx of government . . . United Nations and private funds following the commencement of the program and from which funds they would be able to benefit either by way of commissions or manipulation. A third option is that it was simply a wild scheme with little real possibility of ever eventuating.

"There is, however, a fourth and far more sinister option," the task force wrote.

> The proximity of the Caribbean and Central America to a number of South American drug source countries makes them a natural transit point for illicit drug shipments destined to the North American market. The Turks and Caicos Islands are a significant transshipment point along the line of route. Drugs are usually transported in small, private aircrafts or seagoing vessels, which put into the islands in order to refuel or to change the drugs over to another courier method. Lack of habitation on some islands enables aircraft to land and ships to unload or load in secret. Traffic is organized primarily by Colombians and North Americans, though a number of local individuals are also involved.

In 1985, several senior officials of the Turks and Caicos Government were convicted in U.S. federal courts of taking bribes from major cocaine syndicates to allow refueling and storage rights.

No final conclusion is available to the task force" [it said.]

> But one option the task force feels it can reject is that put forward by the friends of Hand, that it was a project based on Hand's humanitarian concern for the refugees of Southeast Asia. Certainly there is no evidence in the past activities of Hand or in the WerBell/Haitian episode . . . that reflect[s] for Hand a humanitarian image. The deception of employes by Nugan and Hand has been previously referred to and it should be stressed here that the task force makes no assertion whatsoever against Yates in relation to drugs or proposed drug-related activity.

Another possibility is that the United States Government, having dragooned the Montagnards into a hopeless twenty-year fight, having left many of them dead and more of them abandoned, genuinely felt an obligation to do something to help the rest—and at the same time saw the possibility of using them further. An analogy might be the

Cuban Bay of Pigs veterans who were later hired on in great numbers by Uncle Sam to work on all sorts of secret and not-so-secret projects here and abroad.

A nearby colony of a similar Third World group who were orphaned of their own country by their dedication to fighting communism might have appealed to certain minds at the CIA and Pentagon, or even at the White House. That idea might have met the desire of a private bank with strong government connections to make some money and put itself on the map. The men in government and their career colleagues at the bank might have made a secret deal to cooperate, each being mindful of the goals of the other.

The private company helps the government pursue policy goals, and the government helps the private company make money. Such deals are routine procedure—note the case of Paul Helliwell's companies, already described in these pages, or the constant cooperation between the CIA and international banks, airlines, and big and little military equipment manufacturers. Note also many arrangements revealed in the Iran-Contra arms scandal of 1986–87.

If such secret cooperation occurred in the Nugan Hand refugee affair, it certainly would not constitute an oddity. But without a public investigation, we'll never know. The Stewart Royal Commission, which took its testimony in secret, didn't report on it.

The same possibility of secret cooperation could have applied to many Nugan Hand ventures. For example, the company maintained an interest in the international arms business through its last year, though solid evidence of completed sales hasn't turned up. Correspondence was found in surviving files showing that Mike Hand was working with Prince Panya Souvanna Phouma, America's longstanding hope to take over the Laotian throne once occupied by his father.

Prince Panya kept himself busy running an arms company that sought Hand's help in finding customers. Among products Prince Panya listed in his correspondence with Hand are Hughes helicopters, various Italian-made handguns and machine guns, French combat aircraft, British armored vehicles, Chrysler tanks, and "missiles of various types."

A Washington man named Joseph Judge has asserted to several newspaper reporters that Nugan Hand financed numerous arms sales Judge helped arrange while working with the Central Intelligence Agency. Unable or unwilling to supply documentation to support this, Judge might be passed off as a totally unreliable source—except for two things. First, he clearly was working for a U.S. Government-sponsored front company set up by Edwin Wilson during Wilson's CIA/Naval Intelligence days. And second, he knows too much about Mike Hand and Bernie Houghton to have invented his acquaintanceship with them.*

"We were told to use Nugan Hand as international bankers for various deals," Judge asserts, but then says he can't reveal the details because "it would be against the law. I was with the agency then." He remains one more unfittable piece in the Nugan Hand puzzle.**

Judge has also contended that Nugan Hand, working with Wilson and with the blessing of the CIA, helped move some of the Shah of Iran's money to safe havens in the late 1970s. He describes deals in which road-building materials were sold to the Iranian Government at grossly inflated prices, so that hundreds of millions of Iranian Government dollars could be diverted to Swiss accounts. But, again, Judge is unable or unwilling to supply documentation.

Again, however, there is just enough independent evidence to keep the curiosity afloat. In its investigation, the Corporate Affairs Commission came across correspondence and even eyewitness accounts verifying that Nugan Hand—Iranian discussions were held throughout the second half of 1978 and into early 1979, the year the Shah was chased from power.

These discussions were carried out at first with a Swiss financial broker, Peter Busse, who claimed access to the Shah's funds. Also participating was a purported Iranian princess named Madame Nambah. Later, telexes refer to a mysterious "Mr. X" whose identity and bona fides as an Iranian contact seemed to be known to and accepted by Michael Hand. The negotiations were carried out by Karl Schuller, an Australian who had earlier been a partner in a financial planning business with Wilf Gregory, Nugan Hand's Manila representative. Schuller himself had worked briefly for Nugan Hand.

The deal involved a series of loans that would launder funds in

*Admiral Yates says he met Judge through a friend and that Judge *was* with the CIA, but only before Nugan Hand existed. So, he says, Judge couldn't have been told to use Nugan Hand on CIA deals.

**For what it's worth, Judge fits a profile also fit by several other people in this book—Peter Wilcox and Neil Evans, for example. They are men who have had an intelligence connection, whether or not by chance, and who arrive at the scene of scandals involving the CIA, poisoning press accounts with exaggerated and undocumentable claims. Doing this, they invariably make a legitimate story appear "kookie." That such characters may be evidence of conscious efforts by the CIA to defuse problems in this manner is purely speculation on the part of the author. There are other entirely plausible explanations for their remarks, and the truth about Judge or any of them is something I can't provide.

the hundreds of millions, in some cases even billions, of dollars—sums so large that the negotiations might seem ludicrous if they hadn't involved so much of Mike Hand's attention.

The financial world is always awash with brokers claiming access to the most famous fortunes of the day, and many of these brokers turn out to be schemers or dreamers who fail to produce any money when called on. Nugan Hand's Iranian negotiations may have been just such a bubble.

On the other hand, the Corporate Affairs Commission found telexes into 1980 indicating that Mike Hand was making serious efforts to unload large amounts of Iranian currency. There was also a telex dated June 22, 1979, from General Black with copies to Frank Nugan, Mike Hand, and Admiral Yates, stating that Black's wife was "arranging special dinner our house" the next day for Charles El Chidiac, a Middle Eastern financier, "and Gen. Moinzadeh, senior member Shah's staff."*

Concluded the commission, "Whether these telexes relate to the above Iranian fund venture remains an open question."

*A lawyer for El Chidiac, who now resides in Hawaii, denies on behalf of El Chidiac and Mrs. Black that such a dinner ever took place. The telex was disclosed in the Corporate Affairs Commission report of 1983, after the author's interview with Black and shortly before his death. To the best of my knowledge, he was never asked about it.

CHAPTER TWENTY

Men of Substance

During the summer of 1979, as Bernie Houghton hauled away bags of cash from U.S. civilians and servicemen in Saudi Arabia, and police around the world struggled to solve the "Mr. Asia" dope murders, four extremely heavy hitters from the United States intelligence community got involved with Nugan Hand.

They began coming on board about the time of an international conference in Manila June 24–29. Called the International Congress on New Enterprise, or ICONE, the conference was supposedly privately organized. But it bore the clear fingerprints of the U.S. Government, and it allowed Nugan Hand extraordinary prominence and promotional leverage.

The organizer, William McCrea, was identified as an American businessman. But before he began the business of organizing ICONE, he had been working under contract to the State Department arranging trade with developing countries. Before *that,* he had worked for the National Aeronautics and Space Administration, and before that for the engineering department of Pratt & Whitney, a major defense contractor. In other words, his career was entirely consistent with that of a well-regarded CIA officer, though, of course, he may not have been one.*

For ICONE, McCrea obtained financial sponsorship from the World Bank and a few affiliated regional banks dominated by the

*Attempts to locate him failed.

United States Government. Original co-sponsors included several U.S. Government agencies, the Philippine Government, two otherwise unidentified private sources, and Control Data Corporation.

At the conference, to this rather exclusive group of co-sponsors was added the name Nugan Hand. And the five hundred businessmen who shelled out $995 each to attend couldn't have overlooked the company's presence. Frank Nugan and other executives from the group were featured on panels. Nugan Hand hired Mercedes cars to ferry dignitaries around, rented a lavish penthouse suite, and held cocktail receptions graced by Marcos family members—in fact, Imelda Marcos is said by some to have attended, although that is denied by others.

Also among the participants in the conference was Guy Pauker, one of the most important foreign policy advisors the U.S. Government has had over the past thirty years. Pauker says he came to the conference at the suggestion of his old friend Admiral Yates, whom he used to advise while Yates was on active duty in charge of planning for the U.S. Pacific Command.

Pauker told the Stewart commission that Yates had introduced him to Bernie Houghton in the early 1970s, and that Houghton had "displayed kindness in inviting him to use the facilities of his penthouse and dine at the Bourbon and Beefsteak." In Hawaii in 1977, Yates introduced Pauker to Frank Nugan and Mike Hand. Two years later, on the eve of ICONE, Pauker says Yates again wanted him to meet the two owners of Yates's bank. Indeed, the bank was a heavy presence in the official program.

The list of participants in the ICONE conference session of June 25 begins with the names Earl Yates, Guy Pauker, and Donald Beazley—a Florida banker who was also destined soon to join Nugan Hand. Interviewed in 1982,* Pauker at first denied he had ever worked as a consultant for Nugan Hand. When some of his own tape-recorded statements from 1979 were read back to him, however, he agreed that his words would justify the assertion that he was a Nugan Hand consultant. "I didn't know they had recorded this," he explained.

Pauker has also denied over and over that he works for the CIA. To pursue the question, as some journalists have, is to be a little naive about how intelligence relationships work. Pauker doesn't deny get-

*By the author.

ting paid for dealing in secret information with people in the military and foreign policy apparatus. His career has been that of a professor at the University of California and a staff member at Rand Corporation, a think tank heavily relied on by the government (and vice versa). Whether or not Rand is a CIA cover for Pauker is significant only for Rand's bookkeeping purposes.

Pauker, friends say, had frequent personal access to White House National Security Advisors Henry Kissinger and Zbigniew Brzezinski. He is one of the government's leading experts on many matters, particularly Southeast Asia. Before the fall of Saigon in 1975, Pauker has acknowledged spending a lot of time in Vietnam, Laos, and Cambodia.

His best known expertise, however, is with Indonesia—going back to the 1950s, when the United States organized covert military operations to overthrow the socialist government of President Sukarno there. Although an amphibious Bay of Pigs-style invasion we organized in 1958 failed, in 1965 we succeeded in having installed in Indonesia a military regime under President Suharto that, with U.S. counsel, massacred hundreds of thousands of Indonesian citizens.

Admiral Yates told the Stewart commission, it said, "that Dr. Pauker . . . had been involved in Indonesia when President Suharto succeeded President Sukarno." For his part, Pauker has openly boasted that the head of the CIA's Asia section "became a very dear friend of mine," who later thanked Pauker for saving him "many millions of dollars" in some unexplained way.

Fletcher Prouty, a longtime military intelligence official who served as the Pentagon's liaison to the CIA during some of the Indonesian operations, and has since quit in disgust, says he remembers Pauker serving as a diplomatic missionary to cover for the military operations. "I worked with Pauker a lot in my job as CIA liaison officer," Prouty told the Australian *Financial Review,* adding, "There is no question in my mind that he worked for the agency with Rand as a cover."

Whatever the case, one can certainly say that Pauker has—to use Mitchell WerBell's distinction—worked *with* the CIA if not for it.

Pauker himself says he got to know Yates years ago "in connection with my normal duty, consulting the Pacific Command. Buddy Yates and I are friends. We've stayed in each other's houses." Yates, he says, is the one who invited him to speak at ICONE—further indication of the close connection Nugan Hand had with the planning of the conference.

There in Manila, Yates re-introduced Pauker to Frank Nugan, and they evidently made quite an impression on each other. Yates (or maybe it was General Manor, Pauker says) told Pauker that Frank Nugan "was the most brilliant young tax lawyer in Australia." Nugan was impressed that Pauker knew "everybody in Southeast Asia." One of the people Pauker knew was Australian Prime Minister Malcolm Fraser, who later acknowledged in Parliament that he had met Pauker on several occasions going back many years.

After the ICONE conference was over in Manila, Nugan tagged along with Pauker to an energy conference in Bali, Indonesia, where Pauker had also been invited to speak. Soon Pauker was assigned his own secret code number on the Nugan Hand staff. (After the debacle, he maintained that he never authorized that.)

At the conference in Bali, Pauker introduced Nugan to another man he calls his "good friend," Walter McDonald, a career CIA officer since 1952. By his own account, McDonald has served the agency in some forty countries. He rose to head the economic research branch, occupying one of the deputy director jobs that are the second-highest in the CIA, reporting straight to the director, then James R. Schlesinger.

When Schlesinger left government in 1979 to pursue big bucks at Lehman Brothers, a Wall Street investment firm, McDonald decided it was time for him, too, to branch out on his own. He declared himself "Consultant and Lecturer on International, Economic and Energy Affairs." Nugan Hand became his first and biggest client. By his own account, he spent most of his time with Nugan Hand. He traveled the United States and Europe with Frank Nugan and talked to him daily, if not in person then by telephone. It was McDonald, along with Yates, who arranged for a former CIA director, William Colby, to become legal counsel to Nugan Hand.

Pauker remembers going home and getting a "very excited" call from McDonald, saying the former CIA economic division chief had stopped off in Sydney on the way back at Nugan's invitation, and decided to accept a job representing the bank in Washington.

"They had a big office, three stories in a high-rise next to the Sydney Opera House," McDonald says. "It looked like any brokerage house that you go into, very up and up, lots of busy-looking people doing lots of things." McDonald says he went from office to office of the bank to see how it was run. "It really looked like a real viable bank. I was surprised as anyone to see it go down the tubes."

In an interview with the *Wall Street Journal* March 15, 1982,

McDonald said he hadn't heard rumors about Nugan Hand's being involved with drugs until after Frank Nugan died. He also said he was unaware of Hand's CIA connections. "He certainly wasn't the type," McDonald said of Hand. "Where he made a lot of money, he and Frank invested in real estate."

But eighteen months earlier, in a September 30, 1980, interview with *Inquiry* magazine, McDonald said he *had* been aware of both the drug and CIA matters.* He said Frank Nugan had showed him legal files on the drug allegations, and offered to open the bank up to him and show him any other records "to disprove this sort of thing. He was very forthcoming," McDonald said. Moreover, McDonald said he had checked with two banks, both of which told him Nugan Hand was "sound and responsible."

As for the CIA connection, McDonald revealed to *Inquiry* that he was well aware Hand and Nugan had handled money for Air America pilots during the Vietnam War. And he told the Stewart commission that Pauker had "vouched for the credibility of the Nugan Hand operation."

McDonald signed an employment contract giving him $120,000 a year, use of company credit cards, and office expenses of up to $40,000 a year. Pauker told the Stewart commission that shortly afterwards, McDonald called him and reported taking his old boss, Bill Colby, out sailing on his boat with Frank Nugan, during which time it was decided Colby would represent Nugan Hand.

(Colby remembers talking at about the same time to Admiral Yates, who also knew him from Vietnam War days. But he thinks McDonald approached him first. For that matter, General Black also knew Colby from the Vietnam campaign.)

Colby's bills show that he, McDonald, Hand, Nugan, and Bud Yates spent a lot of time meeting on the Caribbean refugee resettlement project, on negotiations to purchase a bank in Homestead, Florida, and on the tax consequences Nugan would face if he resettled in the United States. The bills also refer to unspecified work Colby's firm, Reid & Priest, did for Nugan Hand in Panama.

Like McDonald, Colby says all his work for the bank was straightforward and businesslike. He acknowledges he had heard stories

*The *Inquiry* editor who interviewed McDonald, and later wrote the first solid account of the Nugan Hand mess to appear in the United States, was Jonathan Marshall. I have known and admired Marshall as a reporter, writer, and editor since 1982. He is meticulous about detail, and I trust his work. He has shared with me his original interview notes. Obviously, I did the McDonald interview for the *Wall Street Journal.*

about the bank's involvement in the drug traffic, but says he checked one or two references who thought the bank was reliable, and discounted the stories.

The fourth major U.S. intelligence figure Nugan Hand linked up with in 1979 was Theodore G. Shackley, who may have had as much to do with U.S. covert operations in the Cold War as any man alive. Before he announced his retirement from the CIA after thirty years' service in September 1979, Shackley had led the secret war against Cuba and the secret war in Laos. Later, as station chief in Saigon at the height of the Vietnam War, he commanded CIA activities throughout the region. Finally, he became number two man running the clandestine services division worldwide, at CIA headquarters in Langley, Virginia.

Looking at the list of disasters Shackley has presided over during his career, one might even conclude that on the day the CIA hired Shackley it might have done better hiring a KGB agent; a Soviet mole probably could not have done as much damage to the national security of the United States with all his wile as Shackley did with the most patriotic of intentions.

Between Shackley's Cuban and Indochinese campaigns, more dope dealers were probably put onto the payroll of the United States Government, and protected and encouraged in their activities, than if the government had simply gone out and hired the Mafia—which, in the case of the Cuban campaign, it did.

Shackley was the CIA officer Edwin Wilson gave reports to during his service with Naval Task Force 157, and afterwards, when he was supplying arms and terrorist equipment to Muammar Qaddafi. It was Shackley who almost torpedoed Kevin Mulcahy's attempt to blow the whistle on Wilson. And Shackley was also the CIA officer who on November 8, 1975, notified the Australian Security Intelligence Organization that the CIA was gravely concerned about the actions of Australian Prime Minister Gough Whitlam; three days later, Whitlam was removed from office.

Despite the announcement of Shackley's retirement in September 1979, he stayed active enough to play a critical role in the Iran-Contra affair. In November 1984, he met in West Germany with two Iranians who had been important officials in SAVAK, the Shah's secret police, and yet who were influential with the Ayatollah Ruhollah Khomeini's government as well.

They were General Manucher Hashemi and Manuchehr Ghorbanifar, and they used Shackley to relay to the White House the cockamamie notion that President Reagan could prevent Iran from falling into the Soviet camp by delivering sophisticated U.S. missiles to "moderates" in Iran—people like Hashemi and Ghorbanifar, for example. They even suggested that they had contacts through which the U.S. could ransom for cash and weapons the American hostages, including CIA station chief William Buckley, who had been seized by Palestinian groups in Lebanon.

Shackley first took this news to the State Department and got no positive response. He tried General Vernon Walters, the Top-secret U.S. national security emissary and later United Nations ambassador; there still was no positive response. He continued to meet with the Iranians. Finally, in May and June 1985, Shackley got their message through to consultant Michael Ledeen and Lieutenant Colonel Oliver North in the White House.

The rest is history. Shackley also worked as consultant to a company that General Richard Secord used to aid the Contras with White House help in defiance of an act of Congress.

Against this background, we return to the fall of 1979, immediately after Shackley's resignation from the CIA, to find him hobnobbing with Michael Hand—apparently an old friend, or at least acquaintance.

"Dear Ted," Hand wrote to Shackley on November 27, 1979, "I finally returned home on Saturday the 24th, in the morning and after greeting my wife who thought I was a stranger, settled down to try and catch up on my sleep and at long last feel alive and well again. The opportunity of meeting you again on different terms was very enjoyable and I sincerely trust that something worthwhile businesswise may surface and be profitable for both of us."

Meeting you again on different terms?

"I just checked with Dale Holmgren," Hand went on, throwing out a name Shackley probably had known in CIA days, "with regard to the equipment query which you gave me, and [am] on-forwarding by telex. He advised me that some of the items could be supplied from Taiwan and he has already forwarded a catalogue to you.

"If there is anything else which we may be able to exchange ideas on, or any avenues in S.E. Asia which we may be of assistance to you on, please feel free to call or write. I would be very happy to get something worthwhile going. Maybe next time I am in Washington, we may be able to have the opportunity to sit down and have a bit of lunch together with Bernie Houghton."

Houghton is not otherwise identified to Shackley; apparently, he didn't need to be.

Did Hand somehow hear that Shackley was loose from the agency and on the trail to make some money, then get in touch with him? Did the veiled reference to a change in relationship mean something else? There is no further evidence of how they got together.

Could Shackley have been dealing with Michael Hand for years the same way he dealt with Ed Wilson, after Wilson went off into private business? If so, was his relationship ordered by, approved by, or even known by anyone else in the CIA? Did it even need to be? Despite much bandying about in the courts and the press, we still don't know the answer to those questions in regard to Shackley's relationship with Wilson. In regard to his relationship with Hand, apparently no one in position to ask Shackley under oath about it has thought to do so.

On December 10, Shackley wrote back to Hand in a way that provides no real clues. "Dear Mike," he began, "I enjoyed our Washington discussion and look forward to seeing you again, either here or out in your part of the world." Shackley wrote that he had already exchanged telexes with Dale Holmgren, and referred to a "Mexican oil deal" he had obviously discussed with Hand, which he did not otherwise explain.

Shackley declines to talk about this episode in his life. He wasn't accused of any illegal activity by Australian investigators, though the Joint Task Force listed him as one of the leading characters whose "background is relevant to a proper understanding of the activities of the Nugan Hand group and people associated with that group." Much of his connection to Nugan Hand involves Europe, and a discussion of that requires the introduction of yet another character, the last major new figure in the Nugan Hand saga.

Donald E. Beazley was born in 1942, and, according to his biography as generally given*, went through military school and Virginia Polytechnical Institute. After, the army, he began a banking career in a not extraordinary way, as an examiner for the U.S. Federal Reserve Bank in Virginia.

He became a junior officer at the First National Bank of Atlanta in the early 1970s, then vice-president with Flagship Banks, a Florida chain. His big break came in 1977.

Beazley somehow caught the eye of Marvin Warner, a big, fast-

*Though Beazley agreed to telephone interviews with the *Wall Street Journal* in 1982, he hung up when approached with questions for this book.

rising bank wheeler-dealer who liked to hobnob with the politically powerful and was able to contribute enough money to the Democratic Party to do so. President Carter, the object of much of Warner's political munificence, appointed him ambassador to Switzerland. And while Warner was away, he needed someone to watch his bank chain, then known as American Bancshares, now as Great American Banks.

So Beazley became president of Great American, a big Florida-based company whose shares were traded on the New York Stock Exchange. "When I left, he assumed the position," Warner says. "I don't recall the transitions or what he was offered, but we considered him to be a good banker, a very responsible, able fellow. I have a lot of respect for Don."

But, of course, not so much respect that when Warner returned from Switzerland he didn't want his old job back. So in 1979, Beazley needed another chair. And maybe just as well; barely a year after he left, Great American Banks was caught up in a drug-money-laundering scandal involving a big Colombian cocaine cartel that brought in bags of cash and came away with cashier's checks in the U.S. or overseas, much as the Mr. Asia syndicate did at Nugan Hand. The bank chain and some officers (not Beazley or Warner) were indicted for conspiring to defraud the government by not filing, or falsely filing, required reports of currency transactions totaling some $97 million.The bank paid a fine of $500,000.

In 1987, Warner himself was convicted in state court, Cincinnati, of banking and securities violations in connection with the 1985 collapse of his Home State Savings Bank; that collapse had caused a run on savings and loan institutions throughout Ohio.

As for Beazley, after leaving Warner's Great American Banks he tried consulting, then joined Nugan Hand. Admiral Yates once said that his daughter had worked for Beazley awhile. Beazley says Admiral Yates, acting on behalf of Nugan Hand, had approached him back in 1977 to buy a Great American subsidiary, the Second National Bank of Homestead, Florida, location of a major U.S. Air Force base. Negotiations are said to have dragged on stubbornly and unsuccessfully for two years.

Though it's difficult to confirm after many ownership changes, the Second National Bank of Homestead is said by some to have been an interest, years ago, of none other than Paul Helliwell, the career CIA man whose supposedly private business, Sea Supply Corporation, ran guns and dope for the CIA in Thailand, and whose other supposedly private business, Castle Bank, was involved in fraud and political money movement in the Bahamas. Helliwell had also been paymaster for the Bay of Pigs operation.

Beazley says he's never knowingly worked for U.S. intelligence, or for anyone he knew was involved with U.S. intelligence.

In early 1977, shortly after Yates approached Beazley about buying the Homestead bank, he took Beazley to Sydney to meet Frank Nugan and Mike Hand. Then the admiral escorted Beazley on a tour of other Nugan Hand offices—quite a treatment for a stranger from Florida who already had a good job. Beazley says he was pursued off and on for two years by Yates and Frank Nugan to sell the Homestead bank and come to work for Nugan Hand. He assures everyone he avoided any association.

But among the undestroyed records of Nugan Hand, authorities found a June 1978 list of commissions paid to representatives who solicited deposits. Most of the names on the list are those of full-time staffers, like Jerry Gilder, Graham Steer, John McArthur, and John Owen. But one name stands out: "Mr. Donald Beazley . . . $5,000."

"The payment," commented the Corporate Affairs Commission in its report, "indicates a much earlier association in which he [Beazley] obviously introduced depositors to Nugan Hand Bank and received a commission."

And sometime by October 1979, Beazley had agreed to become president and chief executive of Nugan Hand—the first real banker the organization had ever had. It was widely agreed that one was needed.

It may have been put best by Jill Lovatt, the office manager in Hong Kong who now describes herself as "only a secretary," although Nugan Hand literature described her as a "Monetary Specialist . . . with a strong background gained from working with a Hong Kong finance house. . . ." As to why Nugan Hand needed Beazley, she says, "They felt they should have someone in with qualifications, instead of having it run by people like me with no qualifications."

CHAPTER TWENTY-ONE

What the Tape Recorder Heard

Beazley was introduced to the staff in grand style at a big conference for several dozen Nugan Hand executives from around the empire. At an estimated cost of $500,000, they were flown to Sydney, stashed at a good hotel, and wined and dined for several days, October 13–15, 1979.

Beazley and Yates have used that conference to try to belittle their affiliation with Nugan Hand. In effect, they have put themselves on opposite sides of the same coin. Beazley says Yates persuaded him to come to the conference and look around. "I was just there on an interim basis," he says. "I said I'd go in there and see if I liked what I'd find. They were going to produce a consolidated financial statement. They never were able to produce one." So, he says, he walked out and isn't responsible for what happened later.

Yates, on the other hand, says he resigned at the conference and that Beazley came on board to replace him. "I introduced my relief," Yates says, in admirals' lingo. So, by this explanation, he also isn't responsible for what happened later.

Fortunately for the truth, the conference was secretly tape-recorded, and the tapes have been found. They make clear that Beazley had agreed to be president of the Nugan Hand holding company, in charge of daily operations. Mike Hand and Frank Nugan were going to be co-chairmen, in general oversight positions.

And there was no indication that Yates intended to do anything other than stay on as president of the Nugan Hand Bank; certainly there were plenty of plans for his activities with Nugan Hand in the coming months. The Stewart Royal Commission said Yates was made vice-chairman of the group, and that his salary was soon increased to $100,000 a year.

Frank Nugan began the conference by telling the group, "Admiral Earl P. Yates . . . who has been perhaps our most important counsellor for the last two years and ten months has gone to a great deal of difficulty and effort in guiding us and in himself assisting in recruiting a very fine new president."

There followed a long, rambling discourse, in which Nugan jumped between past, present, and future, began anecdotes he didn't complete, and generally gave every indication of owning a mind three months away from suicide. But at the same time he promised "a new day and a new firm." He concluded, "We are handsome, we are lucky and we are winners, and we intend to be the most successful Asian banking firm there is."

Hand, too, gave a long, rambling speech, not at all the kind that would lead one to believe he could run a large international bank. His speech seemed to have no beginning, middle, or end, and at times to contradict itself. A sample:

> "We have a reality to face today, and since you people are all in the seniority of this organization we must deal with trying to effectively develop a better system. We seriously need to take a very agonizing appraisal of this word called lack of communication. It does exist at all levels of this organization. At the top, the side, the middle, the bottom and everywhere else. I would like to wipe over the situation by saying, oh, heck, it's just a matter that there's not enough time for everybody to do it. But we've all got to set down guidelines in all of our areas, be it legal, trade, finance, administration, to deal with keeping the other people totally and unequivocally informed of developments which may affect them, and I underline which may affect them. We also because of the very nature of our business as private bankers cannot and will not and do not feel it's practical to expose every situation to every employee, to have what we would classify as secrets, which we deal with on a need to know basis. Compartmentation is important for our clients, be it a trade matter, a legal matter, a financial matter—so please exercise discretion upon receipt of information—passing information through to the next person—and also on a standardized basis informing other people who may somehow become affected by your situation as to what you're doing. . . .

And so on. Eventually he turned to religion for some quotes, and ended with a plea to "please love one another." Then he introduced Yates, "the toughest guy we know."

Yates introduced Beazley, who, he said, "has been courted consistently by this firm for almost three years now." He was lavish in his praise, even asserting that the U.S. Federal Reserve Board had described Beazley as "the finest banker in the United States under the age of thirty-five."

Then Beazley—who now says he never really joined Nugan Hand at all—told how impressed he had been during his first visit to Nugan Hand early in 1977. "Watching the company grow, then I became even more impressed," he said. "Listening to Buddy and Frank and Mike over a period of two to two and a half years I was able to make the decision that I would want to be associated with this group. It was an opportunity and a challenge that I think is probably one of the best ones I've ever made, decision-wise. . . . I am looking forward to a long and fruitful relationship. . . . It is a privilege and an honor for me to be president [of] this company."

He said that he and "people like Walt McDonald who are going to assist me will be meeting with you privately, and discussing and getting your honest opinions of where you think the company should be." Then Beazley shoveled out some really appalling misinformation about Nugan Hand's money-market operation—which existed only as a small, money-losing front for what the bank was really doing—and about the tax law background of Frank Nugan, whose tax advice was in fact little more than counsel to commit fraud. Beazley told the assemblage:

"You're fortunate to have probably one of the best money-market operators that I've ever seen, and certainly one of the highest qualified desk tax departments or divisions of firms that I've ever seen. . . . Having the size group which we have here, and having the expertise available is a rarity, and it gives us a competitive advantage." It is hard to believe that a major bank executive, or even a banker of modest skills, could be so fooled about things like that. Why he said it can only be speculated on.

He announced plans for Nugan Hand to try to acquire commercial banks, particularly in Asia and Miami, and concluded by asking the group "to give me the same type of loyalty and dedication that you were able to give to Mike and Frank, and confide in me, call me and talk with me. . . . It's a privilege and an honor working with you and I hope to know each one of you better shortly."*

The assemblage was also treated to blunt admissions that Nugan Hand branches in Singapore, Malaysia, and Taiwan were operating illegally as banks.

Tan Choon Seng, the administrator in Singapore, complained that other Nugan Hand offices were risking exposure by giving him "as little as two days to raise U.S. hundred thousand. And we have no choice but to raise it in small notes, and when—if you can just imagine what it comes to, ten dollar bills, hundred thousand dollars would come out in a big basket. So if all of you could help us, try to eliminate having pay-outs to clients in cash, because it's really risky business. And it's also not very good for us to do so in Singapore, since we don't have banking status. . . .

"Now, in terms of deposits," Tan said, "that's even a more sensitive issue, because we literally . . . function like a bank, though we try to do as much [by] legal methods as possible." He urged his colleagues to strive to arrange for deposits to be made in local Singapore currency as much as possible. In all this, he seemed oblivious to the fact that the illegal part of the operation was what was attracting the clientele.

As he continued to wash this laundry, Tan was interrupted by a strange bit of byplay. In response to something going on in the room, he broke off, saying, "That's got to be the signal for me to stop." There followed general laughter, and an unidentified voice saying, "That's ASIO telling you, not—." This, too, was followed by general laughter, indicating that everyone was familiar with the acronym of the Australian Security Intelligence Organization. Tan then continued his talk.

Graham Steer, the Malaysian representative, referred to "our present, non-official banking activities. . . . We're only registered there as a trade service company. . . . We cannot have the term banker on our door, or our letterheads or business cards." In a question period, someone asked, "Do you feel, I mean, are you personally uncomfortable about it?" And he conceded that "naturally it does create a lot

*Beazley's prepared remarks were later printed and circulated to the entire Nugan Hand staff. They began: "As the newly installed President and Chief Executive officer of the Nugan Hand Group of Companies it is my privilege and pleasure to join with Frank and Mike in welcoming you to this management conference. . . . In addition to the formal program, Walter McDonald and I plan to meet most of you privately to discuss both individual and company concerns."

of uneasiness when you are presenting a case, particularly first up." It is hard to interpret such remarks, however euphemistic, as other than a frank admission that Steer was soliciting illegal deposits.

Dale Holmgren, the CIA veteran running the office in Taiwan, bluntly noted that "it is illegal to take money from Taiwan," while also noting that he had just talked to his wife by telephone and learned that she had just sold a $15,000 certificate of deposit on the Nugan Hand Bank, whose headquarters, everyone knew, was in the Cayman Islands. Holmgren said Nugan Hand had just moved into a new, 3,000-square-foot office on Taiwan, and employed seven people.

John Charody, the East European immigrant who was close to Sir Paul Strasser, also spoke. He was identified as a consultant to Nugan Hand, like Walt McDonald and Guy Pauker. (Only his innocuous opening and closing remarks were recorded; his substance, if any, was lost while someone changed the tape.)

Then came General Manor—most of whose remarks have already been summarized (see Chapter 12). He urged the group to form a stricter organizational chart. He encouraged more planning, as opposed to the prevailing philosophy of "you know, if we throw enough mud against the wall some of it will stick." He cited his extensive contacts in the Philippines, said he hoped he would make more, and added, "I can assure you that I will contribute in any way that I can. You have an extremely challenging mission. You're dynamic. You're growing."

His partner in the Manila office, Wilf Gregory, emphasized the need for secrecy. In the Philippines, he said, under his friends the Marcoses, "the telephone is monitored, the telex is monitored, the mail that leaves our office—90 percent of it is opened when it goes overseas. Practically every piece of paper that comes into my office from overseas is opened. . . . I cannot put things down on paper because I'm afraid when that paper goes overseas that somebody is going to open it and read it." He recommended a better in-house courier service.

Frank Nugan, introducing Guy Pauker, minced no words about the fact that his work on Indonesia and Southeast Asia "has been supported by the United States Government," and that the Rand Corporation that employed him "advises only components of the U.S. Government or acts otherwise in the public interest. . . . I introduce to you one of the major intellectual and data banks of the United States, that is at the present time a consultant to your firm, Dr. Guy Pauker."

Pauker, who has since denied he was a consultant to Nugan

Hand, didn't deny it then. Instead, he said, "I am really thrilled to be here, and I have first of all to express my gratitude to Buddy Yates who first introduced me to Frank and Mike. . . . Now, I really hope to be able to be useful to your group."

In his mostly mundane discussion of Nugan Hand's possible future agenda, he repeatedly mentioned his links to the U.S. Government. Advocating Nugan Hand participation in an ethanol-from-sweet-potatoes project in Sumatra, he noted that he was executive director of the Asia Pacific Energy Studies Consultative Group, formed by about fifteen countries including the United States. The group, he said, had sponsored a series of workshops in which "my good friend Walt McDonald, at that time still a high U.S. Government official, participated."

In advocating a Pacific Basin free-trade zone modeled on the European Economic Community, he noted, "The State Department [is] very much interested in this, and, off the record, having sent some quite senior officials throughout the area just a few weeks ago to explore this with the interested countries, wants a major conference to be held on this topic some time in late 1980. And I've been asked together with two or three other people to prepare this conference."

As for Indonesia, his specialty, he said, it might be ready for a political transition. "One of the ways in which I could be useful to the group is to help you be more successful than the U.S. Government seems to be in dealing with the problems of transitions in the countries in which it has influence," Pauker said, adding, "They are not very good at that."

On the subject of his dedication to Nugan Hand, Pauker concluded, "Nothing would give me more personal pleasure than to have the phone ring in the middle of the night, wherever I happen to be, in California or elsewhere, and somebody saying, you know, this is on my mind, do you have anything to say which will be of use. . . . I may not have the answer right away if somebody cares to call me in the middle of the night, but I might be able to come back a couple of weeks later with something."

Another day during the conference, Pauker was called back for a more detailed lecture on Indonesia. What transpired was a rambling, sometimes contradictory diatribe in which Pauker sounded more as if he should be advising the Politburo than the world's strongest democracy. Displaying the cynicism that all too often underlies U.S. policy in the Third World, he announced himself, four-square for continued military dictatorship in Indonesia—a dictatorship he, after all, had helped establish.

"I have very, very little respect for Indonesian politicians," he said. "I certainly believe that the United States of America [and] Australia should be democracies," Pauker assured everyone. "But we have a very different tradition, a very different history, a very different background. In Indonesia under the Dutch there was no opportunity to learn how to manage civilian party-controlled politics, and the politicians are really pretty worthless characters. They have no experience," Pauker said.

"They"—the potential civilian leaders of Indonesia—"have not got much civic commitment," Pauker complained to this gathering of executives of a company engaged in heroin financing, tax fraud, investor fraud, and indirectly, by much evidence, contract murder—a company to which Pauker, despite his later protests, had now become a consultant of almost boundless zeal.

Pauker, the trusted advisor to Kissinger and Brzezinski, even justified the system of bribery and corruption by which the military establishment has effectively controlled the Indonesian economy for two decades, enforcing their own monopoly on many industries, insisting on ownership shares in other businesses, suffocating free enterprise and keeping the Indonesian population impoverished.*

"I have considerable respect for them," Pauker said of the ruling generals. Military pay was only a few hundred dollars a month. "I cannot expect a man who has served his country for thirty years and more, who has risen to the rank of general officer, or an admiral, or an air marshall, to live like a coolie." So Pauker evidently didn't begrudge the military men the chance to extort tribute from economically productive citizens.

"What they have," Pauker said, apparently keeping a straight face as he said it, "is what they call a system of *extra budgetary revenue* [emphasis added]. This is not visible to the naked eye, but the pattern is a well-understood one, and a fairly orderly one. . . . They consider themselves very bluntly the guardians of the nationhood of Indonesia. And they have done an incredibly good job in my opinion."

So much for bribery.

Pauker then revealed an opinion of free enterprise that equalled his opinion of democracy. "Ninety percent of the Indonesian economy is really state-controlled," he commented enthusiastically. And more might be better, judging from his praise of the state-monopoly

*Once again, the author must refer readers who doubt such sweeping statements to *Endless Enemies* for documentation.

oil company and airline, and the state-run plantations. No objections were heard from the U.S. flag officers and CIA men.

Pauker on racism: "Anybody who knows the country realizes that when a Chinese gets a credit from the state bank he will plow every penny . . . into developing his business, and the Indonesian will consider that not as a credit, but as a gift from heaven and go out and buy himself a home, buy himself a Mercedes, and take his wife on a trip to Europe, or to Hong Kong at least. And he will assume that he will never have to pay this money back."

Pauker on influence-peddling: "I first went to Indonesia not knowing where the heck that it was on the map in 1954–55. I was either lucky or had good taste in selecting my friends. My friends are running the country today, and this is true both on the military side and on the civilian side, especially the so-called Berkeley Mafia. . . . I talked them into coming to Berkeley because I was the chairman of the Center for Southeast Asian Studies at Berkeley, and these were bright, young Indonesians and fun to have around. Now these are the people who are today the deputy prime minister, the minister for economic affairs, the minister for finance, the minister of trade, et cetera, et cetera." Apparently Pauker didn't mind having just a few "worthless politicians" as friends.

"I have pretty good connections in Indonesia," he summed up, "and as I said before, anybody who needs anything specific about Indonesia is welcome to call me at any hour of the day or night and I'll be really pleased to be of service."

Somehow Pauker sang a different tune when the Stewart Royal Commission asked him about whether he had helped Nugan Hand get involved in the Indonesian oil business as Frank Nugan requested. "Dr. Pauker told the Commission that as an employee of the Rand Corp. and as a matter of principle he regarded it as improper to use his friendship and influence with government officials in such a way," Stewart reported.

Then, revealing as clearly as ever what his investigation was made of, Stewart wrote, "The Commission accepts Dr. Pauker's evidence in this regard." If the commission bothered to check the readily available transcripts of Pauker's remarks at the 1979 conference, it made no mention of that in its report.

Furthermore, the Stewart report says, "Dr. Pauker . . . told the Commission that the Rand Corp. is not linked to the CIA. There is no evidence before the Commission which contradicts Dr. Pauker's evidence concerning these allegations and the Commission accepts Dr. Pauker's evidence."

During the speech introducing Walt McDonald, apparently by Jerry Gilder* the CIA situation came up. "I hope Walt can help you in understanding how to deal with allegations about the connection with the CIA," Gilder said. "The CIA has got a damn sight better people, as he can tell you, to use for its purposes. . . . They hardly have any occasion where they could get some assistance from us. We would be honored to do anything for them, and I think that's the approach, but I hardly think they'll ever ask."

McDonald did not deny his CIA connection. He did assure everyone that he and Pauker were friends of James Schlesinger, Henry Kissinger, and Zbigniew Brzezinski. "Guy [Pauker] could walk in the White House . . . any time he wanted and talk to those guys, and they wanted to hear what he had to say," McDonald added.

Then he told how, of late, he had been spending most of his own time on Nugan Hand. Frank Nugan, he said, had gone into "his American period, where he decided to spend most of his time in America, so I had the pleasure of our boss every day—flying here and there, London, Connecticut, and what have you."

McDonald spent most of his time discussing the world oil situation—expounding the scenario advertised by his old CIA branch, that Soviet oil production was decreasing, which would cause ever higher oil prices and maybe war in the Middle East. (The CIA later reversed its assessment of Soviet oil production, and oil prices have nosedived.)

Speakers spent much time glorifying each other. Jerry Gilder introduced Admiral Yates as "a very remarkable human being. . . . His physical capability is that of Clark Kent." The admiral passed the favor on to Pauker, calling him his favored advisor while Yates was vice chief-of-staff of the U.S. Pacific forces. "The people in Washington, at the CIA and the State Department, shared those views," he said—thus admitting a knowledge of the CIA and State Department that he would later deny.

"Guy, it is a real pleasure for me to be serving with you again," said one man to the other, each of whom would later deny he was serving at all.

Of General Manor, Admiral Yates said, "He's recognized as a leading U.S. military authority on internal insurgency, and, I might add, insurgency and strike operations"—certainly unusual talents to bring to what is supposedly a banking group.

*The Corporate Affairs Commission identified the speaker as Gilder. The author's copy of the transcript doesn't identify the person giving the introduction.

Yates praised Walt McDonald's advancement through the ranks of the CIA, "one of the toughest bureaucracies in the world." He said that although many people weren't aware of the CIA's economic division, which McDonald headed, it was—in a curious phrase—"acknowledged in this world of grass politics, drug events and battles, and it starts generally in the area where Walt is going."

Finally, Yates got around to his work. He disclosed that he had been working with the Overseas Private Investment Corporation, a $700 million U.S. Government agency designed to finance small and medium U.S. companies in foreign ventures. He said that with Nugan Hand paying his fare, he had traveled with OPIC leaders "to tour all of Southeast Asia . . . and make a report to the president on any type of business in Australia."

He also talked of consulting with Robert McNamara, then head of the World Bank, and Mike Hand's idea of sponsoring a think tank on investment. To be known as Foreign Investment Development Research Program, or FINDER, it would have a blue-ribbon board of representatives of big U.S. corporations who would "identify the opportunities, the products, and technologies in these Asian countries and develop these internationally."

All Yates's grandiose efforts died with Nugan Hand.

At one point, Yates checked to see if his time was up. A voice from the audience seemed to leave no doubt about whether Yates had surrendered command to Beazley: "You're president of Nugan Hand Bank," the voice said, and Yates continued.

Frank Nugan's second speech was so disjointed it's difficult to imagine anyone in attendance taking him seriously. The Corporate Affairs Commission commented, "Based on the transcript only, Mr. F. J. Nugan did not appear to be coherent at this point." The session ended with Admiral Yates calling for all the papers left around to be locked up while everyone went to lunch.

There were announcements about developments in the branches. In Manila, an unidentified woman had deposited $1 million. In Germany, Nugan Hand had acquired the small-but-licensed F. A. Neubauer Bank, which would issue a new kind of international certificates of deposits, for worldwide sale, backed by the Deposit Security Fund of the Federal Association of German Banks.

One representative after another got up over the several days and told about the millions, or tens of millions, of dollars his branch had brought in. Then Bernie Houghton got up and told the assemblage about the gold mine in Saudi Arabia. "One of our clients approached us on a $70 million contract and was apologetic because it wasn't more," he said, as if serious.

"It's a totally cash society," he added. "We get garbage bags full of money over there." Since the largest-denomination riyal note is worth only $30, he said, "they take these big, black garbage bags, the plastic ones, and they'll come in and dump these bags on you. Very common in Saudi for the people to draw a million dollars at a time in cash out of the banks. . . . Under the Islamic law . . . if they catch anybody stealing, they'll cut their hands off. . . . There's not supposed to be any liquor over there, but I guarantee you in Nugan Hand's house over there, it's got a closet full."

Houghton also gave his listeners a hint why he didn't feel any remorse for all the money he was stealing: "I don't think Saudi Arabia is going to last that long," he said. "It's totally surrounded by the Russians and the Russians are creating as much strife as they can in that area. You've lost Iran, which basically means that it's pro-Russian. If they are not with you, they are against you. Pakistan and Afghanistan have also gone. On the southern tip of Saudi Arabia in Yemen, well there's a big Russian Navy base there." Houghton continued to paint a bleak geopolitical picture. He said the Saudis were basically giving up and sending all their money out of the country anyway.

Then he gave a lesson on how he became Nugan Hand's most successful representative so fast—a Houghton primer on theft, as it were: "You can't talk quickly to people when you're going to take their money," Houghton explained. "In every movie and play that you've seen, the city slicker comes in and begins talking rapidly and trying to thrust a pen in somebody's hand. So you need to take a little backward attitude I think . . . speak softly and slowly, repeat what you're saying maybe three or four times, so you're sure it's penetrating, because they don't listen all the time."

"I always repeat the same pitch maybe from three or four different angles," Houghton said. "Each time I see them, and generally two or three times during approaching them, and telling them the advantages. And if they ask me can they lose their money, I say of course you can lose your money. I say I don't see how you can, because we basically deal in commercial bills. They are bank-endorsed. We take those commercial bills that are bank-endorsed, and they're guaranteed by the central banks in each of the three countries that we used the money market operations in. So basically, you've got a central bank that guarantees the bill, plus its member bank, and of course our bank, which is international. So the fact is, that you can't lose any money. We don't deal in the commodities exchange. We don't take any equity positions in anything. So basically we're not at risk. We state that we earn our fees from accounting services, from legal fees, and maybe one or two percent on certificates of deposit. So basically we do a lot of business, but make small funds, but we're readily liquidable. . . ."

And on and on.

Don Beazley, who later said he just came to investigate, explained to the group from a more technical standpoint how Nugan Hand made its money on the money market. "The money market situation is nothing more than the past ten years of experience that Frank [Nugan] and Steve [Hill] and Mike [Hand] have in taking advantage of different interest rate movements in the money market. And it's been very successful, extremely successful. That is a hidden asset. It doesn't show up on any balance sheet. It doesn't show up in anywhere else. You couldn't place a dollar figure for it. That, along with the volume of transactions that takes place in the money market, I think you do between a billion and two billion dollars worth, or three billion dollars worth of book transactions a year—it really gives you some kick. As the number of deposits increase, your importance in the money market increases also," so that Nugan Hand could make a profit from what Beazley called "volume discount."

There had to be money somewhere, because Beazley was certainly planning on spending some of it, as he got the hang of the operation: "I'd like to go to Hong Kong at the end of this week," he said, "and then I have some obligations to my former employer [Great American Banks] that I have to go back to first, to the United States for a short period of time, then I would like to come out and in the first part of next month to visit your operation over in Germany and also London again, and then come back over and spend about a month going around—we'll be taking people with us—Walt and Buddy and some other people. . . ."

Dale Holmgren then asked where the funds were coming from to pay the expense accounts. "We have, Dale, made a great deal of money out of tax avoidance," Mike Hand answered, adding that money market profits and legal fees were also important.

Mike Hand certainly knew that the tooth fairy would be as reliable a source of income as Nugan Hand's profits from legitimate business. How many of the other people in the room shared his knowledge, and to what degree they shared it, can only be presumed.

CHAPTER TWENTY-TWO

The Wilson Connection

A month after the meeting in Sydney, according to the Joint Task Force report, Admiral Yates attended a meeting in a London hotel; with him was Frank Terpil, former CIA officer and the partner of Edwin Wilson in the sale of U.S. military equipment, including plastic explosives, to Libya. Also present, the task force says, were the source known as "J"—a Wilson employee named Douglas Schlachter—and another retired senior U.S. military officer, unnamed.

"Discussions, at times between Yates and 'J,' centered around the possibility of Nugan Hand becoming involved in the financing and handling of finances for Libyan airport shelters and hangars," the task force said. "The contract potential for this construction work was three to four hundred million dollars. 'J' is not aware if there were other meetings between Yates, the unnamed officer and/or Terpil, or precisely how the above described meeting came about. He is aware, however, that the unnamed officer and Yates knew one another previously, and from the conversations that took place, [he] formed the view that Yates and Terpil had at least met one another before. It was not long after this meeting that Terpil was arrested when he attempted to import the machine guns to South America," the task force said.

After reading the task force report, Yates exploded with denials. In reference to the November 1979 meeting "J" described, he wrote the task force, "I attended no such meeting, do not know Terpil, and discussed no involvement of Nugan Hand in financing such activity." His very next sentence, however, may indicate his state of truthfulness at the time of writing: "I resigned from Nugan Hand officially on October 12, 1979, and had no authority whatsoever to discuss such matters."

At the time he wrote, the admiral was evidently unaware of the tape recordings of himself, and of others in his presence, at the Nugan Hand executive meetings, which took place October 13, 14 and 15, 1979. Obviously, neither Yates nor anyone else talked of his resigning. To the contrary, Yates and everyone else talked of the many tasks he would work on in the months ahead, including setting up a Nugan Hand-sponsored think tank to encourage industry in the Pacific, and touring Don Beazley around the empire.

In January, two months after the alleged meeting with Terpil, Yates flew to Sydney on Frank Nugan's death. Steve Hill has testified that Yates was still a director of the company when it went into bankruptcy. Even the accepting Stewart commission, which seemed to take on blind faith almost anything else Yates told it, found that he was vice-chairman of the company into 1980.

Yates's attempt to move up the date of his departure from Nugan Hand appears to parallel his attempt, already discussed, to say he didn't join Nugan Hand until June 1977, when there is abundant evidence he joined much earlier. One must remember these statements when evaluating his further denial to the task force: "I do not know Wilson nor Terpil, have never done business with them, and to my knowledge have never even met them."

Schlachter, in a 1987 interview, says that for years he held onto the business card, which he vividly recalls Yates gave him at the meeting with Terpil.

Whatever conclusion one may come to about whether Yates met Terpil that November, there were certainly many other meetings in Europe over the winter of 1979–80 between Nugan Hand's senior managers—including Bernie Houghton—and associates of Edwin Wilson. Among those associates was Ted Shackley, who the task force said was meeting occasionally with Michael Hand in Washington. Shackley had just retired as CIA deputy director of operations; and had stayed in regular contact with Wilson after Wilson left the CIA.

Shackley had gone to work for a new company called A.P.I. Distributors, Inc., based in Houston, founded by Thomas Clines, a CIA official who had worked directly under Shackley (on the anti-Cuban campaign, among other things), and who had taken his CIA retirement a few months earlier. Clines founded A.P.I. with a large loan provided by Wilson, the task force said. (Reporters Edward T. Pound and Walter S. Mossberg had already reported in the *Wall Street Journal* that Wilson had arranged a $500,000 loan from a Swiss source to an intermediary company in Bermuda that funneled money to Clines.)

Clines and Bernie Houghton knew each other independent of Shackley. They had been brought together by Major General Richard V. Secord, then still serving with the U.S. Air Force.

SECORD: Operational head of the covert "private" arms network created from 1984 to 1986 under the aegis of CIA Director William Casey and National Security Council operative Oliver North. The object of the network was to try to keep Congress and the public from finding out about arms sales to Iran and the Nicaraguan Contras, since some sales were contrary to policy and others to law.

Secord, a 1955 West Point graduate, has been involved in intelligence-type work since the war in Indochina. He commanded the U.S. military mission to Iran from 1975 to 1978, then directed all U.S. military sales worldwide, from the Pentagon. In the first few months of 1980—while his friends Clines, Shackley, Wilson, and Houghton were discussing various business deals to exploit what remained of Nugan Hand—Secord was involved in planning the disastrous mission to rescue U.S. hostages in Iran, and was deputy commander of a second rescue plan which was never implemented. His longtime friend and eventual business partner in the Iran-Contra deals, Albert Hakim, worked on the mission from inside Iran, according to the published account of the National Security Archive. Hakim later hired Wilson and Shackley in his private business.

From 1981 to 1983, Secord served as deputy assistant secretary of defense for Africa, the Middle East, and Central Asia. He left that job in a scandal involving his relationships with Wilson and Clines in which he was the subject of a prolonged investigation by federal prosecutors. Wilson, Clines, Secord, Shackley, and another Pentagon official had met over a deal to make substantial money hauling U.S. military material to Egypt. Secord and the other official directed the shipments as part of their Pentagon jobs; the goods were carried by a company Clines owned in partnership with an Egyptian, and which he founded with Wilson's money. The Pentagon paid $71 million.

Correspondence between Wilson, his lawyer, and Clines's lawyer—first unearthed by Peter Maas for his book *Manhunt*—shows that Wilson expected a cut of the action. A January 18, 1979, memo from his lawyer says stock will be owned by a foreign corporation—apparently to be controlled by Wilson—and four "individual U.S. citizens." Wilson, his bookkeeper-girlfriend, and a woman friend of Mr. Clines's offered testimony that the four citizens were Clines, Secord, Shackley, and the other

Pentagon official, and that they planned to share in the profits. But prosecutors were uncertain that these witnesses had sufficient character to stand up to the denials of prominent officials. Since the scandal seemed to have terminally stained the remaining public careers of those involved—at least until the Iran-Contra affair—personal indictments weren't sought.

In an agreement to end the investigation, Clines, on behalf of his company, pleaded guilty to filing $8 million in phony invoices to the Defense Department, and was identified as part of a criminal scheme. The holding company Clines was associated with paid a $10,000 fine and $100,000 in civil settlements, and the operational company he had formerly been co-owner of repaid $3 million of the illegal profits. Some investigators in the case still think justice was subverted.

In Congressional testimony in May 1987, Secord said that in 1984, soon after his Pentagon retirement, Colonel North asked him to start forming the covert arms network. Secord testified that he knew so little about the market for small weapons that he immediately brought Tom Clines in as his deputy; he knew Clines as an expert in the field and as "a very close associate of mine from CIA days," he testified.

Secord testified that when the U.S. Congress forced the CIA to pull out of the Contra war in 1984, the Contras were left "in dire straits . . . starting from scratch" without trained logistics or supply or maintenance officers—indicating that the operation had been more American than Nicaraguan from the start. He, his business partner Hakim, Clines, and some other recently retired military officers set up companies designed to earn a 20 to 30 percent profit, he testified, filling the Contras' needs. When the Iranian opening came, they were given that assignment, too.

The arms were shipped from allied countries like Portugal, and even Communist countries like Poland and Rumania. To persuade these foreign governments to allow the shipments, without disclosing that the weapons were going to the Contras in defiance of Congress, the Secord-Clines companies submitted forged documents making it look as if the arms were going elsewhere. (They may have relied on Clines's experience filing phony documents with the Pentagon for profit in the Egyptian arms case Secord was involved in.)

The Secord-Clines operation bought airplanes. It hired pilots, mechanics, and cargo-handlers, mostly veterans of other U.S. clandestine operations, to move the weapons. Secord received a coded communications device by which he could talk securely to North at the White House or to the CIA station chief in Costa Rica, where part of the Contra effort was being organized.

Clines helped North obtain a ship, the *Erria*, that not only ferried arms but also was used in a vain attempt to ransom the hostages in Lebanon with funds from data processing tycoon H. Ross Perot; according to the *Los Angeles Times,* Clines went along on board the *Erria* for the mission.

When Clines was due in court in Virginia in a civil matter in 1986, someone from the National Security Council called to excuse him by saying he was on assignment with the government.

When the first planeload of U.S. weapons was delivered to Iran, Secord flew with the mission to the Middle East, though he remained behind in Israel to monitor the situation while National Security advisor Robert ("Bud") McFarlane, who came over with him, continued on to Tehran with the missiles, a cake, and a Bible inscribed by President Reagan. Secord was also put in charge of the Swiss bank accounts through which the money flowed.

Secord told the Joint Task Force in Australia that he had met Houghton in 1972, at the home of Colonel William Prim. Prim, as has been noted, *(a)* was a former member of Yates's military staff, *(b)* was the air force officer whom Houghton contacted in Saudi Arabia, *(c)* is believed by some to be the officer Houghton flew to Tehran with in 1975 in connection with the sale of a spy ship to Iran, and *(d)* was listed on a Nugan Hand internal document as a staff member in January 1980. (He has not responded to a letter the air force agreed to forward to him.)

The task force reported that Secord saw Houghton occasionally and socially in Washington, D.C., Saudi Arabia, and the Netherlands throughout the middle and late 1970s. Secord said Houghton had talked about Nugan Hand, and in 1979 brought him together with Clines.

By that time, the general was close enough to Edwin Wilson to regularly use Wilson's twin-engined Beechcraft free of charge. Clines sold Secord an investment property in Washington, and when it flopped Wilson bailed the deal out with cash. (Secord's lawyer told the *Wall Street Journal*, which exposed all this, that his client was totally innocent of any wrongdoing. Lawyers for Clines and Shackley told the *Journal* their clients hadn't done anything wrong, either, but wouldn't let them be interviewed.)

General Secord having made the introduction, Clines and Houghton met repeatedly with Shackley in Washington, which eventually led to a deal with A.P.I. to sell Philippine-made jeeps to Egypt. Apparently, the deal never produced any sales.

Houghton was also meeting often with Edwin Wilson in Geneva during the fall and winter of 1979–80 to discuss some financial laundering work regarding military sales. Libya had given Wilson a $22 million letter of credit, but the document specifically identified certain military hardware that was forbidden to Libya under U.S. law.

So it was proposed that Nugan Hand would issue small letters of credit, naming textiles and other goods as the items of purchase to mask the military purchases. But despite what the task force said was several days of discussions with Clines and others, there was no evidence the letter-of-credit matter was ever resolved. Houghton tried to minimize these dealings, and denied that Wilson was a Nugan Hand client. But the task force said Houghton was being "deliberately misleading" in saying that, and the Corporate Affairs Commission said it didn't believe Houghton, either.

In the Stewart commission, however, Houghton finally found a mark. The commission simply said it "accepts the evidence [testimony] of Mr. Houghton that the negotiations were unsuccessful'-'—as it also accepted his testimony that he didn't keep any of the money he carried off in Saudi Arabia (except "expenses").

Houghton said he was introduced to Wilson by a lawyer representing Wilson in Geneva, whom he had been told to see by either Mike Hand or Frank Nugan. If the commission bothered to ask him who the lawyer was, or how Hand or Nugan found out about the deal, it did not record the question or answer in its report.

In addressing the question of Nugan Hand's involvement in arms dealings, the Stewart commission again adopted the technique of meticulously shooting down some bizarre rumors, without doing any real research on the more likely leads. Sources of serious allegations were never called to account under oath. There is no mention, for example, of Prince Panya, or Doug Schlachter, or John Owen's detailed military reports.

The Stewart report does note an "allegation" in the *Wall Street Journal* that "Nugan Hand files show that Nugan Hand worked on big international arms deals, although it is not clear what, if anything, was shipped." It dismisses the "allegation" as "vague and imprecise," and says it was "based at least in part on information given to that newspaper by Mr. J. D. Owen," who it earlier noted had left Nugan Hand in a nasty salary dispute. Actually, the *Journal*'s evidence consisted mostly of documents found in Sydney, which Owen hadn't mentioned in an interview.*

"The Commission has found no evidence to support allegations that the Nugan Hand Group had been involved in arms dealing," the Stewart report says, though it later acknowledges that Nugan Hand tried to be.

*The *Journal* stories were researched and written by the author of this book.

Houghton was playing with large amounts of cash in the winter of 1979–80, as he flitted back and forth between Europe and Saudi Arabia. His explanations of how he got it were not very believable. There was, for example, a puzzling journal entry in the Nugan Hand records—"funds in Switzerland, $465,000,"* with a reference to Houghton. When the Joint Task Force asked Houghton about it, he explained, "A gentleman delivered it to me in the hotel. . . . The man gave me no documentation to sign and did not identify himself. He just says, 'Are you Bernie Houghton?' And I say, 'yes.' And he handed me the envelope"—which contained $465,000.

An easy way to make a living, it sounds.

Houghton testified that he assumed the man was a law client of Frank Nugan's. He said he took the money to a bank and telexed it to Singapore.

There was another witness who reported seeing him take several hundred thousand dollars in U.S. $100 bills out of a safety deposit box, bundle it up in his coat, and walk casually to a nearby bank to deposit it and telex it. It isn't known whether it was the same money.

Hand and Nugan also appeared in Switzerland at about this time. They rendezvoused with Houghton, who says their mission was to see the United Nations High Commissioner for Refugees in regard to the Caribbean project. But Hand, at least, also met with some of the Wilson men. Houghton recalls meeting both Nugan and Hand in Geneva within the week preceding Nugan's death.

One other deal that brought all the Nugan Handers to Europe was the planned acquisition of a bank there, London Capital Securities Ltd., which became available for purchase after its former owner, a onetime British member of Parliament named John Stonehouse, defalcated. Perhaps lacking Frank Nugan's true grit, Stonehouse only faked his suicide; he was found alive and well in Australia, and was returned to England and jailed.

Ernest C. L. Wong, a former Nugan Hand executive who says he worked on the deal, claims Nugan Hand was to be reorganized around a legitimate international commercial bank like the one in London, then sold to another old CIA and Pentagon pal, ex-president Somoza of Nicaragua, who was in and out of Miami back then. Wong says the Somoza deal was set to go in June 1980; no one else has said anything about it.

Beazley, Hand, and Nugan negotiated a tentative purchase agree-

*420,000 Australian, as roughly converted to U.S. dollars at then-current rates.

ment for the London bank, but the deal crumbled—because of Frank Nugan's death, Beazley said. Houghton, on the other hand, told the Corporate Affairs Commission that "Frank and the gentleman over there, whose name I forget, had a big argument and the fellow said he would not do business with Frank Nugan."

Houghton also said that after Nugan died, "Mike says, well, he couldn't go ahead with it because they couldn't afford to lose the capital. So I says, 'Well, what if one of my clients withdraws his funds and buys the bank? . . . Then you could still manage the bank.' "

According to Houghton, Hand replied that the idea of using a behind-the-scenes money man to make the purchase "was acceptable to him. . . . It was to be purchased in the name of Don Beazley, who was going to be the head of it."

But the client Houghton put forward as the behind-the-scenes man turned out to be another CIA operative, Ricardo Chavez. According to what Beazley told the task force, Houghton did not disclose Chavez's true identity. Beazley said Houghton told him that "Chavez was a wealthy Mexican who wanted to diversify his assets out of Mexico, largely because of an anticipated peso devaluation."

Ricardo Chavez was no Mexican. He was Cuban. He had been a CIA contract agent off and on since 1961 when he worked on the Bay of Pigs invasion. His case officer on that operation: Thomas Clines, the CIA officer who ran the illegal Egyptian arms deal with Edwin Wilson's money.

Another Chavez associate and CIA operative was Rafael ("Chi-Chi") Quintero.

QUINTERO: A Cuban-American veteran of the Bay of Pigs who became a protégé of Clines in the CIA's long, clandestine war against the Cuban Government, conducting sabotage and terror misions. In 1976 he signed on with Edwin Wilson to assassinate international terrorists, and in particular a political opponant of Libyan dictator Muammar Qaddafi, who, along with U.S. Navel Intelligence, was employing Wilson; Quintero later explained that he thought the missions were sanctioned by the CIA (and who, really, can be sure they weren't?), and that he ultimately didn't carry them out.

When Clines was hired by General Richard Secord to be his deputy in the Iran-Contra covert arms network, which was being run under the aegis of the CIA and White House through National Security Council staffer Oliver North, Clines brought Quintero on as *his* deputy. Quintero was based in Coral Gables, Florida, but spent much of his time in Central America, hiring, paying, and directing pilots and flight crews for the Contras.

About the time of Frank Nugan's death, Clines and Quintero happened to drop by Wilson's Geneva office. According to task force witnesses, they found a travel bag full of documents left by Bernie Houghton. Clines and Quintero rifled Houghton's bag, found a document concerning General Secord, and removed it, the task force reported.

"We've got to keep Dick's [presumably General Secord's] name out of this," Clines said, according to the task force report. (Assistant U.S. Attorney Lawrence Barcella in Washington, who supervised the prosecution of Edwin Wilson, confirms the gist of this story.)

About a year later, General Secord was appointed by President Reagan to be deputy assistant secretary of defense—chief weapons advisor for Caspar Weinberger for the Middle East and south Asia. About the time he was due to get his third star, though, the Wilson scandal caught up with him and forced his resignation. What his reputation had been doing several years earlier in Bernie Houghton's travel bag has never been explained.

In early March 1980, Houghton delivered about $300,000 to the Britisher who was selling London Capital Securities after the Stonehouse debacle. The money was to pay for a 50 percent interest.

Most of the $300,000 was in the form of Thomas Cook traveler's checks, the kind Houghton learned to use in Saudi Arabia. Houghton told the Corporate Affairs Commission he just didn't remember where he had bought the traveler's checks. "The delegates do not accept Mr. Houghton's recollection," the commission report said. "One would envisage that a transaction of this magnitude soon after the death of Mr. F. J. Nugan would be indelibly imprinted on the mind of the participant." The commission determined that Nugan Hand's general funds were used to buy the London bank.

The commission found records of a $100,000 advance to Beazley at about this time, which he has said was used for the bank deal. The commission reported that while it was "not able to state positively that the funds were applied in the acquisition of the London bank," it inferred from the ledger entry that the money was intended to be used that way.

Dennis Mosselson, the British businessman who was selling the bank, told the London police that over the next few months Houghton cashed $57,000 in traveler's checks at the bank, all with the approval of Beazley, whom Mosselson said he called in Washington.

Beazley told the task force he flew back and forth to London, talked occasionally with Chavez, and met him once at the Miami airport. But he said he resigned his position at London Capital Securities in October 1980. He said the bank wasn't profitable enough to justify the work and travel, and besides, he had just been offered another job—as president of Gulfstream Bank, Boca Raton, Florida, a bank big enough that its shares were traded on the New York Stock Exchange.*

That was the job he held when the task force interviewed him—in the United States and not under oath—March 12, 1982. However big a banker Beazley was, the task force didn't think much of him as a witness. "Beazley appeared to be vague and distant from those matters which one would reasonably expect a person of his profession to be conversant and particularly familiar with," it said. "There appears to have been a distinct lack of formality and background knowledge which one tends to expect from conservative bank administrators. . . . Whether this is a deliberate attempt to minimise his own role in the matter or whether it is simply the nature of Beazley, the Task Force has not and need not determine.[*sic*]"

The task force also didn't believe the story about Chavez's buying the bank with funds from his Saudi Arabian account. "Task Force inquiries in the U.S. reveal that Chavez had no known connections, commercial or otherwise, in Saudi Arabia and is most unlikely to have had sufficient funds of his own to purchase the bank," the task force reported. It noted that Clines, Quintero, and Chavez had "a close relationship . . . and generally the view is that many of the business partnerships and dealings so far as Quintero and Chavez were concerned were little more than nominee situations [fronts] for Clines.

"It is thought that quite possibly this was the case in the London Capital Securities purchase. Obviously one of the reasons that Houghton misled authorities in respect of the London bank and in particular his connection with Chavez, was to hide his connections with Clines and Wilson."

People very close to the intelligence apparatus of the United States were trying to hide something. Whether it was money Wilson was taking illegally out of Libya, or money Bernie Houghton was taking illegally out of Saudi Arabia, or both, was a mystery the task force wanted to solve. (Considering Clines's importance to U.S. policy in the 1980s, one would think American investigators might be interested, too.)

The task force talked to two business associates of Wilson and

*The shares were traded through its one-bank holding company, of which Beazley was executive vice-president and chief administrative officer.

Clines, whose names it didn't disclose, who said they had been told that Clines had put close to $1 million (several million, by one account) in Nugan Hand. But there was no way to find out.

The Corporate Affairs Commission also expressed frustration at not knowing the source of Chavez's alleged $325,000 account with Nugan Hand, or the significance of the Chavez-Houghton-Hand-Wilson associations, or the truth of the contention that Nugan Hand was going to be turned over to Somoza.

None of these items "has been sufficiently investigated to finally report," the commission said. "It is difficult to imagine that this could be done without enquiries in England and the U.S.A."

That such inquiries haven't come about may well be the result, at least in part, of the incredible influence Bernie Houghton continued to wield. John Walker, the CIA station chief, remembers Houghton hosting a visiting contingent from the Army War College. In January 1980, just a couple of weeks before Frank Nugan's death, Houghton was opening his barroom doors to a five-man delegation (and their wives) from the U.S. House of Representatives Armed Services Committee, out on a tour of U.S. military installations.

Representative Bob Wilson of California, then the ranking Republican on the committee, says he had met Houghton on a previous trip to Australia several years earlier. He says he had been urged to drop in and see the barkeep by a friend of his wife's, who owned a Sydney hairdressing salon. The Wilsons, along with another member of the Armed Services Committee, had lunch with Houghton at his Texas Tavern in the Sydney honky-tonk zone, he says.

They evidently liked it, because they returned, Representative Wilson says. And when Houghton then invited the whole contingent of ten or twelve members of the committee, and their staffs, to dinner at the Bourbon and Beefsteak, well, how could they refuse?

So, Wilson, Richard Ichord (a Missouri Democrat and then chairman of the Research and Development Subcommittee of the Armed Services Committee), and three other committee members flew into Sydney late on the afternoon of January 7, 1980. After they were greeted by officials from the American Embassy and whisked to the local Hilton, it was just natural for them to head on down to the Bourbon and Beefsteak—despite having to run the gauntlet of prostitutes and sex-show barkers.

"It wasn't odd," Representative Wilson says. "It was our first night in Sydney and nothing had been scheduled. Also a lot of people were out of town due to holidays."

Wilson says he was on the House intelligence subcommittee for twenty-six years. "I usually tried to interview on my own any operatives" he found in the places he visited, he says. "But I didn't know any in Australia." So he settled for Houghton.

"Bernie is a kind of typical Texas bullshitter," Representative Wilson confides. "All he talked about was his business. He didn't talk of military or defense."

But he did talk of Michael Hand over dinner. "He said, 'If you stop off in Singapore, you should meet my associate,' " the congressman remembers.*

On January 11, the committee delegation's first day in Singapore, Representative Wilson was introduced to Mike Hand by a U.S. consul. The next night Wilson, one other congressman, and their wives dined with Mike and Helen Hand at a restaurant. Wilson says they talked of business, not public affairs, and that he invited Hand to visit him on his next trip to the United States.

That trip turned out to be a quick one, on the occasion of Frank Nugan's death. And on the *next* trip, Hand had good reason to pass up the Wilsons' kind invitation. That trip was in June 1980, and Hand was by then a fugitive from justice, traveling under a false passport.

Perhaps the final blow to Nugan Hand came in the fall of 1979, from Price Waterhouse & Company, the Big Eight accounting firm that had given Nugan Hand its cachet. Robert Moyle, the Price Waterhouse auditor who signed the Nugan Hand Bank's books for the year ended June 1977, had left.** His successor, Richard Harris, who had worked on the '77 books and then signed off on the June 1978 books himself, suddenly started balking.

Although Nugan Hand advertised that the bank's books were audited by Price Waterhouse, the actual balance sheets and income statements were seldom shown. They might have looked suspicious. Considering the big sums of cash that were flowing in and out of Nugan Hand, the actual asset and liability figures certified by its auditors, including Pollard & Brincat in Sydney, were relatively small.

*This quote, beginning with the words, "He said," and the "It wasn't odd" quote originally appeared in *The Australian* of August 16–17, 1980, and were confirmed by me in my own interview with Wilson, June 17, 1982, whence derived the other quotes.

**Moyle, now working for another firm, declines to comment, citing "pending litigation."

For example, a balance sheet from Pollard and Brincat for the Sydney holding company, dated January 31, 1979, shows assets of $13.7 million and a net worth of $2.3 million. The assets shown consist almost entirely of top-grade securities: $9.2 million in commercial bills of exchange, $3.2 million in negotiable certificates of deposit, and some government bonds. Other balance sheets have been found showing assets of more than $27 million.

There isn't any indication on any of the balance sheets of what had really happened—that the securities originally bought had been traded in, the money taken, and the securities replaced in the company's vaults by IOUs from the affiliated companies that Frank Nugan and Mike Hand and their associates had set up.

Steve Hill has testified that he routinely rewrote his books before giving them to the auditors. Hill added or subtracted $4 or $5 million at a stroke, merely on Frank Nugan's word that certain accounts had been paid, or certain assets were on hand. To clean the bank's books at year's end, accounts were sometimes assigned to Nugan Hand, Inc. Panama, which Hill has testified was mostly a reservoir for phony accounts needed to balance the books. Phony assets—usually IOU notes from companies that were secretly affiliated with Nugan Hand—were supplied as needed, and sometimes altered, to even the numbers. Price Waterhouse apparently just took all this down and signed it.

The Corporate Affairs Commission found documents showing, for example, that on August 5, 1978, Price Waterhouse requested confirmation from the Sydney office that $4.7 million in securities were really held by that office on behalf of the Hong Kong and Cayman-based Nugan Hand Bank. On August 9 and 11, 1978, Frank Nugan and Mike Hand telexed Price Waterhouse that the securities were indeed there, collateralizing a debt owed by Nugan Hand, Inc. Panama—and so the matter appeared on the audit that Price Waterhouse signed.

On October 10, 1978, the commission reported, Price Waterhouse telexed Sydney for more details on the debts allegedly owned to Nugan Hand Bank by Nugan Hand, Inc. Panama. Hill replied by telex two days later that Nugan Hand Bank had a claim on securities held by Nugan Hand Ltd. for Nugan Hand Panama. Hill, the commission reported, "stated the matter had been discussed in full the previous year with Messrs. Harris and Moyle of Price Waterhouse. He stated the basis of the scheme was to ensure profitability and security for Nugan Hand Bank."

That explained nothing. Commented the commission, "To the reader today, the reply appears not particularly helpful from the perspective of supplying an answer to the request for information from Price Waterhouse." Nevertheless, the commission reports, "Price Waterhouse accepted the explanation of Mr. Hill." A year earlier, the commission noted, Frank Nugan himself had given the assurances.

Admiral Yates went to the Caymans to sign the 1977 and 1978 audits, according to Hill. Clive Jennings of Price Waterhouse (an associate who was assigned to help Harris on the 1979 audit)—who answers questions hesitantly, after long pauses—says the same. Yates told the Stewart Royal Commission, it said, that he "thought that he had only signed the 1977 accounts," leaving the 1978 situation uncertain. Hill told the Stewart commission that in his opinion the admiral would have been "totally unaware" the books were phony.

The Corporate Affairs Commission also reported doing its own audit of the securities listed by Hill. The results, it said, showed that the securities held by Nugan Hand Ltd. weren't assets at all, but had already been pledged against debts owed to those corporate Nugan Hand depositors who demanded and got collateral for their accounts.

The commission found other inaccuracies and obvious inconsistencies in the figures that Price Waterhouse had accepted. But the commission—rather shockingly—admitted it never interviewed the Price Waterhouse auditors. "They may well have been misled in circumstances of which the investigation is uninformed," the commission said.

Trevor Gorman, senior partner at Price Waterhouse, says* no one from the firm is aware of any discrepancies in the 1977 or 1978 audits. "No one has ever questioned our audits of those years," he insists.

The Stewart Royal Commission did more than just question the audits—it flat-out states that "the accounts of Nugan Hand Ltd. in no way presented a true and fair view of the financial state of the company."

The commission took expert testimony on "the duties of an auditor, with particular regard to the auditor's duty to detect fraud." And the commission reported finding "little or no consensus of opinion in relation to this aspect of an auditor's duty. . . . The distinction seems to be whether the auditor is under a duty to detect fraud, that is, to specifically search for fraud, or whether, on the other hand, it is enough for the auditor to plan his audit so that he has a reasonable

*Interview with the author, who also talked to Harris (who referred queries to Clive Jennings), and to Jennings.

expectation of detecting material misstatements," the commission said.

It found that "the latter view appears to be echoed in this country" by auditing professionals, while client companies and businessmen who wanted to rely on audited financial statements believed they were getting more protection. "In the view of the Commission there is a need for the legislature to define precisely the auditor's duty to detect fraud," the report said.

(A similar dispute is raging in the United States, where, under pressure from the courts and Congress, the accounting profession is trying to strengthen standards to increase the auditor's role in detecting fraud.)

The men at Price Waterhouse—Gorman, Harris, and Jennings—contend that they raised new questions in 1979 because there were wholly different circumstances from those surrounding the 1977 and 1978 audits. To an outsider, it is hard to understand what those different circumstances may have been, except possibly the introduction of a skeptical Clive Jennings.

Hill has said that he thinks the auditors became more skeptical in 1979 because of the bad publicity Nugan Hand was receiving over the Nugan Fruit Group scandal in Australia, though he didn't account for how the news might have reached the Caribbean.

Jennings, for his part, asserts, "There were significant gaps in the records" that Hill brought with him for the October 1979 auditing session—as if this were a stunning new development. "He said he'd been rushed when he came," Jennings says. So Jennings gave Hill a list of items that would be required to satisfy the auditors. "And that was the last I ever heard from him" except for telexes, Jennings says.

Hill has testified that the queries dealt with the receipt and payment of funds from Nugan Hand Panama, and that he telexed Frank Nugan for information but got no satisfactory answers. Hill has also testified that Yates joined him and his wife at the October 1979 audit, too. "Mr. [*sic*] Yates was present during all the discussions with the auditors," he said, specifically referring to Clive Jennings.

In January 1980, Frank Nugan himself showed up. He "said he would handle it personally," Jennings says. But on January 15, when the auditors appeared at Nugan's hotel room, they were told, "You'll never guess what's happened. I came all the way from Australia with the answers to your questions, but then I left the file back in Australia."

Nugan made a show of phoning his secretary and telling her to send the file. Jennings and Gorman say Nugan stayed two nights, then left on a morning flight. Jennings and Harris talked hours with Nugan, had dinner with him. What was said? Jennings seems very reluctant to be specific.

What information was being sought?

"Routine questions that any auditor asks his client."

For instance?

"I don't think that's appropriate."

But, Jennings says, "An inspector had told him it [the bank] would be decertified if he didn't produce the accounts. I think that's what prompted his visit here."

Indeed there was evidence that Singapore banking authorities had been giving deadlines for certification of the books, and that Hong Kong authorities might be waking up to the problem, too. "He seemed worried about decertification," Jennings said. But when Nugan flew out, "his attitude was that all the information we needed to our satisfaction would be forthcoming."

Two weeks later he was dead.

CHAPTER TWENTY-THREE

The Explosion

Lee Nugan returned to Australia over Christmas 1979—the ostensible occasion being Steve Hill's wedding. Her husband had spent several hundred thousand dollars of the depositors' money refurbishing their already resplendent waterfront home. By several accounts, she wasn't pleased with his taste.

Guy Pauker, of all people, brought his wife and son to spend the Christmas and New Year's holidays visiting the Nugans. He told the Stewart commission, "Nugan and his wife seemed to be not on very good terms, and he was definitely clearly depressed. . . . He would bounce that little girl of theirs on his knees very wistfully and talk to the little boy. . . . The way he was talking to those children, in particular, almost in retrospect of course, looked as if he was saying goodbye to them."

(Lee Nugan denies what Pauker said, and says her husband was just nervous because of Pauker. "Frank did not want him there," she says. "He asked him, but then he changed his mind.")

On January 7, 1980—the day Bernie Houghton was entertaining the Republican head of the House Armed Services Committee—Nugan walked into a store, and with speed that startled the store-owner, bought a rifle. To anyone's recollection, it was the only gun he'd ever owned.

Two days later, Nugan flew back to the United States with his wife. But then he was off alone to Florida, the Caymans, and Switzerland. He apparently visited Colby in the United States, and made plans to see the former CIA director in Asia the next month. He told people he was moving to the United States, and entered negotiations to buy a Florida condominium.

He was back in Sydney January 25. Bernie Houghton told police he stopped by Nugan's office to say hello that day—a bit odd, considering Houghton's outspoken distaste for Nugan—and saw nothing untoward. Hill says he and his boss had a confrontation over the audit that night—that Nugan tried to tell him everything had been taken care of at Price Waterhouse, and that Hill didn't believe it. Hill says he resigned, which certainly looks good for Hill; there's no way to prove it, and Hill was back at work when the disaster hit the next week.

On Saturday, January 26, Nugan agreed to purchase a $2.2 million country estate he had been dickering over with the owner. The estate contained 828 landscaped acres and a mansion. It was, he told the prospective seller, "the finest in Australia." He agreed to close on it the next day.

Instead of keeping the appointment, he put the rifle in his Mercedes and made his trip to Lithgow.

Pat Swan, Frank's secretary, has said she got a call about noon on Sunday, January 27, from Ken Nugan. Steve Hill has testified that Pat Swan called him that day.* Bernie Houghton says Hill woke him up with a phone call, "told me that Frank was dead and that I should get the people out of Saudi Arabia." Houghton did, though soon they all went back.

The next day, Monday, was a legal holiday. By the available evidence, Hill, Swan, Ken Nugan, and perhaps others went into the office and began removing files.

On Tuesday, Houghton seemed to take over. Hand and Yates were due in from the United States, and Shaw from the Philippines. Houghton brought Mike Moloney, his lawyer with the checkered past, to the airport for the big homecoming—"to handle the press," Houghton has testified. But as soon as everyone got to the office, Moloney—whom Hill and others in the organization had never seen before—began barking orders.

Houghton introduced Moloney to the crowd, saying, "He is a good guy, and will help us." Then Hand declared that Moloney was operating with Hand's express authority. Hand seemed to be taking signals from Houghton, who, for his part, recalls, "It was bedlam

*The Stewart commission says instead he was called by Ken Nugan, at 4 P.M.

down there, everybody crying and wringing their hands, and the phones were ringing."

Hill and Shaw have recalled being startled by Moloney's sudden ascendancy, especially when the lawyer began leveling his heavy-handed threats that their wives might be cut up in little pieces and returned to them in boxes if they didn't cooperate. Hill also wondered at how Moloney had suddenly become so thoroughly aware of Nugan Hand's entire business, as his remarks revealed him to be.

Hill testified before the Corporate Affairs Commission, "Mr. Moloney moved into our office and was conducting his legal practice for all intent and purpose from our office. From that time onwards, Mr. Moloney took over the management of the company, which included issuing instructions to the staff."

As for the man who had recently been vice-commander of the combined air, sea, and land might of the United States Armed Forces over more than one-third the world, Admiral Yates contends he just sort of stood around, as if nothing unusual were happening. Moloney, however, says he and Yates "were great mates," and that the admiral concurred with the decision to remove the files and helped carry them.

"Frank had been making loans to everyone without recording it on the books—just his handwritten notes," Moloney says. "And people on the staff were removing this and removing that. If I had an IOU for $50,000 in there, I would have been the first one to it."

At the decision-making meetings the rest of the week, the same pecking order continued. Houghton recalled to the police that some staffers objected to his taking part in the meetings because he wasn't officially on the board of Nugan Hand. But Houghton said he sat in anyway, because Mike Hand wanted him to.

Tuesday night, the Stewart commission reported, Admiral Yates met at Hill's house with Hill, his wife, and the two Australian auditors, Pollard and Brincat—further evidence that Yates was actively involved in events and certainly aware of them.* Under questioning from the auditors, Hill revealed that Nugan Hand owed $20 million overseas with "hardly anything" there to pay, and $1.5 million to unsecured depositors in Australia with $50,000 in the bank. The debts, of course, were just those Hill was aware of; Hand, Nugan, Houghton, and Shaw, and possibly others, kept records of their own deals.

*The commission said Yates "did not recall attending this meeting but said that he could have been there." The commission reported it as fact, however, based on Pollard's write-up of the events in his diary and other accounts.

According to the Stewart commission, "Reference was made by Mr. Hill to the possibility of fraud on the part of Messrs. Hill and Brincat, and Mr. Pollard suggested that Mr. Hill should see a lawyer."

Next morning at the office, Hand, Houghton, Yates, Shaw, Hill, and Jerry Gilder heard Brincat announce that Nugan Hand's worth was overstated by $5 million because of the internal IOUs that were passing for assets. He urged bankruptcy proceedings. "This was strongly resisted by Michael Hand and Michael Moloney, who suggested bringing in funds from overseas," Hill testified before the Corporate Affairs Commission.

The search for funds of all kinds certainly never stopped. And funds were found. They were not, however, applied to Nugan Hand's solvency problem. Everyone seemed out to protect himself, and it was clear there were two classes of clients. Some privileged ones were getting their money out, while others were being recruited afresh, with new lies, to replenish the coffers.

More than $1 million—no one knows for sure how much more—was handed out in the week after Nugan's death to clients brought in by George Shaw. Many of these clients identified themselves by nothing more than Shaw's word that they were owed the money. No records had been kept. Some $1.3 million, all unsecured deposits, were retrieved at the same time by the owner of a food store chain who had dealt with Steve Hill.

One dentist was paid off, Shaw testified,* after a third party, representing the dentist, summoned Shaw and Nugan Hand staff lawyer Graham Edelsten to a hotel lobby. The middleman slugged Edelsten a couple of times, Shaw testified, and announced "that he had a pistol in the glove box of his car that he was not afraid to use, and if we did not compensate Dr. Shalhoub within five days that our lives would be at stake." The dentist was paid.

Two brothers who had deposited money with Nugan Hand visited Shaw's house and left him a threatening note, Shaw testified. They were paid. Some clients of a Nugan Hand representative named Andrew Wong were paid through Moloney, after death threats were issued against Wong, according to the liquidator John O'Brien.

According to Shaw, threats were flying almost indiscriminately. Immediately after Frank Nugan died, he testified, "There were pressures applied by Michael Hand, Michael Moloney and others that I should go to the Philippines with great haste, so as to make myself

*Before the Corporate Affairs Commission.

unavailable for any interviews by investigators. I was threatened [by Hand] and warned, and with great pressure applied involving injuries . . . not only to myself . . . but to my family, that under no circumstances" would Shaw identify any clients to authorities.

Hand even called Shaw's wife, Shaw testified. Houghton's name was used to underscore the danger. "Arrangements can be made through his [Houghton's] connections," Shaw quoted Hand as saying.

Claiming that he felt "bewildered" and "apprehensive" about all this, Shaw said he sought legal representation. But of all the lawyers in Sydney he could have gone to, he picked John Aston, the lawyer for the "Mr. Asia" heroin syndicate. According to Shaw, Aston said he couldn't represent Shaw because it would be a conflict of interest.

Aston, Shaw testified, then volunteered some startling advice. As the task force summed it up, Aston said that Frank Nugan "had been involved in a number of questionable dealings, that he had been involved with people of questionable background, and that no one should ever know about the cash transferred to Singapore because should that eventuate the lives of Mr. Shaw and his family would be in danger."

"Shaw maintained that he took this statement to be intimidation in the form of a death threat," the task force reported—not an unreasonable interpretation. Shaw said Aston specifically told him to destroy all files "relating to his, Aston's, transactions and those of Richard Spencer," the narcotics officer Aston dealt with—or give them to Aston for destruction.

Added the task force, "After cautioning Shaw about his responsibilities as a director, Aston advised him to give as little information concerning the affairs of Nugan Hand or its clients as possible if questioned by the authorities."

Bob Gehring, Houghton's employee and friend, remembers driving Mike Hand to Shaw's house once during this period. (Gehring eventually testified before the task force, in exchange for a grant of immunity from prosecution for his own actions. By the time he testified, both Hand and Houghton had long since fled Australia.) Gehring said that Hand had declared, "Shaw is getting pretty nervous. I'm just going to calm him down." The two of them went to a basement room alone for ten minutes or so, Gehring testified.

When they emerged, Gehring said he remembered Shaw pleading, "What am I going to do?" and Hand saying, "You are a mess. You should see a doctor." Shaw said he had been to a doctor.

"I have never seen anyone so emotionally upset," Gehring recalled. "I remember him mentioning that he had changed his phone and got a silent [unlisted] number, and he was still getting calls." As Gehring and Hand prepared to go, Gehring testified, "George Shaw . . . came out to our car, he was crying and hanging onto Michael Hand, and then we left."

The politically powerful local organizations that had invested with Nugan Hand, such as the football leagues clubs and town councils, by and large got their money out before the bankruptcy filing.

As late as mid-March, at least two other depositors were able to reclaim their funds—Elizabeth Marcos, sister of Philippine President Ferdinand Marcos, and her husband Ludwig Peter Rocka. Elizabeth Marcos was also the appointed governor of a large province in the Philippines. Between them, she and her husband had deposited a total of $3.5 million, according to records Wilf Gregory slipped to Mike Hand by personal courier March 17, 1980, on the eve of a visit to Sydney by Rocka to retrieve the money. For whatever reason, the missive from Gregory was left around for authorities to find.

Meanwhile, Bernie Houghton, having seen how easy the pickings were in Saudi Arabia, couldn't resist raising some money the same way when he got back to Australia. He persuaded a police sergeant with the Victoria Police Force, of all people, to withdraw $80,000 from his pension account on January 22, just five days before Frank Nugan died.

The sergeant had answered a newspaper advertisement for gold bullion investments placed by a former employee of Houghton's, and wound up talking to Houghton. Unfortunately for him, he decided he preferred the security of a Nugan Hand deposit to the vagaries of the bullion market. He started out small, with a few thousand dollars, and cleverly tested the system on a trip to Asia. As he had been promised he could, he withdrew $500 in Hong Kong from Jill Lovatt, and $500 more in Manila from General Manor.

Thus convinced of the soundness of the scheme, he went home and put in his whole stake. He lost every penny. The paperwork from his big deposit was still being processed as George Brincat, the accountant, declared Nugan Hand was insolvent. It was shortly after that that the sergeant's money went into an account in the name of a corporation whose directors were Bernie Houghton and Robert Gehring, Houghton's employee and friend.

Nationality was no barrier for Houghton. Tucker T. Coon was a fellow American, working temporarily in Melbourne. He had an account with the same commodities dealer the police sergeant had contacted, and also decided to make the change to Nugan Hand. On January 31, the day after Brincat had declared Nugan Hand insolvent, Coon liquidated his commodities account, which brought him $23,000.

But, as earlier suggested by Houghton and the commodities dealer, instead of cashing his check he merely endorsed it over for deposit in Nugan Hand—only, for reasons he was told had to do with foreign exchange, he endorsed the check directly to a company called Arnim Proprietary Ltd., the signatories on whose account were Houghton and Gehring.

Houghton was so unscrupulous that, according to the Corporate Affairs Commission, he even cheated Dr. Tom Wall, a $300,000 loser in Nugan Hand, by misappropriating a $25,000 check sent to Dr. Wall through Nugan Hand by a bank in Singapore. Houghton deposited the check to the account of a corporation he controlled, with an endorsement that Dr. Wall says is forged.

Houghton told the Corporate Affairs Commission that Nugan Hand had given him the check made out to Dr. Wall as repayment of an alleged loan Houghton had given Nugan Hand. He said he assumed Dr. Wall's signature on the back was genuine. In fact, Houghton admitted he took several deposits intended for Nugan Hand and put the money in corporate accounts he controlled—but said he did so because Mike Hand had warned him that Nugan Hand might fold!

Mike Hand was telling different things to different people. In early February, just about the time Houghton was protecting Dr. Wall's check by stealing it, Dr. Wall tried to withdraw his funds from Nugan Hand, he told the commission. But he was informed by Mike Hand "that the whole bank had closed down, that the funds had been frozen."

Dr. John K. Ogden, who lost more than $600,000, says he flew to Sydney as soon as he heard Nugan had died. "Mike Hand kept reassuring me that all was well, and there was no reason to take my money back. Hand and Beazley, they both reassured me that there was absolutely no reason to worry about my deposit."

But perhaps the most imaginative stalling tactic Hand devised was this: On March 11, 1980, a depositor named Ah Chuan Liau, of the town of Carlingford in New South Wales, wrote asking to borrow $30,000 against his much larger deposit. In reply, he got a letter from Hand, stating, "On occasion, clients of our bank, as we are sure happens with clients of other banks, make requests to prematurely break deposits or to borrow against their deposits. Each transaction is studied on an individual basis.

"At present we are in a period of extreme escalating interest rates," Hand went on, "and are viewing a market fall in the price of precious metals, such as gold and silver. It would not be prudent of us to advance low-interest-rate loans at the time when money could be laid off throughout the world at extremely high rates of interest."

However, Hand went on, "we are prepared to allow you to benefit by the increased interest rates in existence throughout the world." So, Hand informed him, the interest rate on his deposit would be increased from 11 percent to 16 percent from March 28 until its maturity in June. There is no record of whether Ah Chuan Liau was satisfied with this offer.

Some other people did get money out of Nugan Hand, however. John McArthur, then managing the Hong Kong office, reports that on orders from Hand and Beazley he sent $200,000 to an account in Florida in the name of DEB/NHI, and $400,000 to a German bank. There was a notation by the $200,000, "Pay out to Bernie Houghton's clients in the U.S."

Beazley, whose initials are D.E.B., says some money was sent to him for purchase of a Florida bank, and that he returned it when the deal didn't work out. Liquidators in Sydney and Hong Kong say there is no record of his return of the money. (Beazley hung up when a reporter called to ask if he had proof he returned the money.)

Like Beazley, Houghton denies receiving any improper payments. McArthur, however, says Houghton took $50,000 in expense money in October 1979, and $150,000 more in February 1980.

McArthur says another American banker Beazley hired to assist him left Hong Kong with $94,000 in expense money and some documents. In a rare recorded case of FBI cooperation with Australian-Asian authorities investigating Nugan Hand, the FBI found the missing banker and retrieved the documents—but not the money, which the banker denied he took.

McArthur says that even after bankruptcy papers were filed in April, Hand continued to instruct him to transfer hundreds of thousands of dollars out of the legally frozen accounts; McArthur says he drew the line then, and refused.

McArthur says Shaw, like Houghton, was still soliciting deposits after the pay-outs had stopped. So was General Manor, though Manor says that up in Manila he wasn't aware of the pay-out problem.

On March 17, 1980, a Hong Kong company named Anchor

Promotions Ltd. sued Nugan Hand for about $800,000 that it claimed it had deposited, and that the bank, as of February 7, refused to pay back. Anchor said Frank Nugan had agreed a year earlier to make the payments to an affiliated company in Australia, and had already paid out more than $350,000 there, the latest chunk being $130,000 paid on January 15, 1980. Three weeks later, the suit alleged, Nugan Hand had refused to recognize Anchor's deposit in Hong Kong.

Anchor asked the court to appoint a receiver for Nugan Hand, which caused a furor in the Hong Kong financial press. The suit became the lead item for a local scandal sheet called *Target Financial Service. Target* continued to headline Nugan Hand's troubles in exposé fashion the rest of the spring.

On March 25, Elizabeth Thomson, the in-house counsel at Nugan Hand's Hong Kong office, tried to deal with the situation in a staff memo, claiming the problem was just "a legal technicality," and "a normal part of commercial business." Her memo urged staffers not to talk to the press about the matter, since it was in litigation.

Nevertheless, more lawsuits followed from other depositors who were unable to recover their money. On April 28, the Hong Kong Financial Secretary appointed Peat, Marwick, Mitchell & Company to investigate Nugan Hand's affairs, and one day later Peat, Marwick reported back that it believed the company was insolvent.

No wonder. "Six million was cleaned out of [the Nugan Hand account at] Irving Trust in the last two weeks" before the bankruptcy proceedings, Moloney says now. In fact, he says, he personally supervised the importation of $2 million from Hong Kong into Australia on the Tuesday after Frank Nugan died.

Les Collings says he thinks Hand and Houghton raided the bank after Nugan died. "That Houghton is still tending bar, I think it's criminal," Collings says, adding that less than a month before the bankruptcy, Hand and Houghton had been falsely reassuring him, too, about the bank's rosy future. They "were up here telling me that Nugan had been undergoing treatment for cancer" before his suicide, Collings says.

In bankruptcy cases, a receiver, or trustee, takes over management of a company during a period of investigation and negotiations aimed at an amicable settlement between the company and its creditors. When the court determines that further negotiation is fruitless, and that the company should be liquidated and the assets distributed to creditors, a liquidator is appointed. In Hong Kong, all these functions are performed by a government office.

In Australia, as in the United States, receivers are private professionals, and the person filing the bankruptcy petition often influences the court as to who is appointed. In the case of Nugan Hand in Australia, Moloney filed the papers. His and Mike Hand's choice of receiver (or "provisional liquidator" as it was called) was the accounting firm B. O. Smith & Company. Moloney was retained as attorney for routine work, while courtroom representation was entrusted to the business partner of a right-wing Parliament member Frank Nugan knew and had supported financially.

In an initial report in the Hong Kong court, the Hong Kong receivers said they had met with Smith, the Australian receiver, and "were not very satisfied with his attitude, which seemed to be to reach an early settlement by selling off available assets rather than pursuing claims to recover assets." In other words, Hand and Moloney were trying to wrap the case up without an effort to trace the missing money and recover it for the depositors. Furthermore, the Hong Kong receivers reported, "the lawyers in the Cayman Islands acting for Nugan Hand (Bruce Campbell & Company) are not cooperating voluntarily."

Steve Hill has testified that Mike Moloney received more than $96,000 in fees from Nugan Hand between February 1 and April 16. "On several occasions I endeavoured to determine what was the basis of payments made to Mr. Moloney, without success," he testified. He also testified that Moloney, in Hand's presence, lied about the location of company records to investigators from the Corporate Affairs Commission, who were on the case by mid-February.

So cowed were the investigators that Moloney was able to stall them, and sometimes literally fight them off. Months passed before it was publicly known that the fraud was not just a minor or technical one.

To protect his wife from angry creditors, he said, Michael Hand secretly moved into some unoccupied rooms over Bob Gehring's butcher store, where the company records were also secluded. Gehring was fully trusted by Hand and Houghton, as a nominee (or front man) of Houghton's companies, Gehring sometimes had signing power over Houghton's money.

According to Michael Moloney, Gehring had even applied to the CIA, and used to tell a story about it. The marine from Dayton "had no academic credentials," Moloney relates, but the CIA "liked his attitude. 'The world is full of commie bastards and all I wanted to do at that time was kill, kill, kill,' " Moloney quotes Gehring as having said.

"They told him to report to a place in California. But he heard first from Bernie. This was in the late '60s. Bernie didn't say what it was, but Gehring said he decided to come to Sydney because it was quiet." While waiting for his CIA appointment, Moloney says, Gehring had taken up reading in the library on Guam, and even developed a habit of quoting a lot from Shakespeare. (This account, of course, begs the question of whether Houghton might have *been* Gehring's CIA appointment.)

Gehring had done all he could for his friends through the crisis after Nugan's death. As he remembered it in his task force interview (which he gave in exchange for immunity from prosecution, and only after Hand and Houghton were long out of the country), Hand had walked into the Bourbon and Beefsteak bar and asked Gehring's help in storing the records. "I said I'd only be too happy to help him."

That very night, Gehring testified, he, Bernie Houghton, George Shaw, and a butcher-shop employee moved the records in the meat van to the butcher shop, from a temporary office location where they had been stored. "There were files in manila folders, there were cash books, journals, and ledger-type books," Gehring said. Later, "with the assistance of all my employees," he said, he moved the files again, for convenience's sake, scattering them among a couple of nearby locations he owned for his meat and provisions businesses.

Eventually, Hand and Houghton turned to Gehring again, this time entrusting him with their plots to escape Australia.

Houghton left with a blue-ribbon escort on his getaway flight. The task force found out about it when the detectives happened to interview a Houghton associate, Gerard W. J. Matheson. Matheson recalled he was having a drink at the Bourbon and Beefsteak June 1 or 2, when Gehring "announced that he had to go to the airport to meet someone."

As the task force related it, "Matheson accompanied him and there they met an American who Matheson described but could not name. The three went from the airport to the Bourbon and Beefsteak, where they met Houghton a short time later. Matheson said that from the tenor of the conversation that was had, he formed the view that this man was connected with U.S. intelligence and/or the military. There was also mention of arms sales.

At Houghton's request, Matheson then made inquiries about the availability of seats on a flight to the Philippines. He believes that that evening or the following day, Houghton and the unnamed man departed Australia together for the Philippines.

"From the description supplied by Matheson and an examination of airline and immigration records," the task force reported, "the unnamed American has been identified as being Thomas Clines."

Former senior CIA official Tom Clines was a principal figure in the White House approved Iran-Contra arms transfers of the mid-1980s.

During his Acapulco interview in June, 1981, Houghton told the task force he had spent his year abroad traveling on a business deal "involving an American company and the sale of jeeps to Egypt." He refused to identify his associates. But at exactly this time, a company owned by Clines, who had been working with Ted Shackley after borrowing seed money from Ed Wilson, was reaping a tidy $71.4 million from the U.S. Treasury, in commissions as shipping agent for the sale of jets, tanks, missiles, and other arms to Egypt.

As already noted, at least $8 million of those billings, approved under the Supervision of General Richard Secord, were phony. Houghton's name never publicly surfaced in the investigation, and it isn't known exactly what role he played.

Houghton having departed Australia in the company of President Reagan's eventual weapons maneuverer, Clines, Hand was left in Sydney. Houghton had been inquiring about false passports in Europe, but apparently didn't find one for Hand. Hand told Gehring "there was a 'stop' on him at the airport and he needed a passport in another name," according to Gehring's testimony.

In investigating this, the task force found several irregularities in the way Hand had obtained his original Australian passport in 1973. For one thing, he hadn't been forced to turn in his U.S. passport. The task force also found that a folio had been mysteriously "torn away from the Sydney file" on Hand's application, indicating that some information may have been unlawfully removed. Finally, the task force observed, the application had been approved by the same immigration officer who had granted citizenship to Harry Wainwright, the lawyer and dope trafficker.

The Nugan Hand people were no strangers to tampering with the customs and immigration process, but now that Hand's back was against the wall, his efforts weren't working. "Mike . . . told me he was attempting to get an Australian passport in another name . . . but everything failed," Gehring said. "The situation was becoming impossible, and I felt he had to get out of the country because of the threats he was getting."

Gehring said Hand had told him about at least two death threats from depositors. "Even if he sorted out the problems in Australia, the newspapers suggested he would be extradited to Singapore," Gehring added. "I decided to help him by getting a passport in the name of one of my employees who was about his age and had the same color hair.

"So I got some birth certificates of my employees by telling them I needed them for the superannuation [pension] scheme," Gehring said. From these, he chose a butcher named Alan Glen Winter as fitting the age and hair requirements. He obtained the application forms for Australian passports, while Hand had pictures taken of himself with a beard, mustache, and different-style hair.

Then Gehring went to a trusted travel agent and bought a round-trip ticket from Brisbane to Fiji and then on to Canada. On June 5, as an accommodation to a customer, the travel agent applied for, and soon afterwards he got, the passport for Hand.

But Michael Hand had not entrusted his departure to amateurs. At the time of the passport application, Gehring was introduced to the mastermind of the scheme, an American identified to him only as "Charlie." All Gehring knew about the name was that it was "not his correct name. . . . Mike Hand said he knew him from the army or somewhere like that," and "told me that Charlie had come out to help him get out of the country."

It was Charlie who provided the false beard and mustache, and Charlie who took the photographs. And it was Charlie who got on the train from Sydney to Brisbane with Hand, and left the country with him.

"I only saw him about five times. They acted very secretively," Gehring said. "I wasn't told where he was staying, and he appeared as if he didn't wish to be seen in company with Michael Hand."

Two days before they departed, Hand visited Gehring at the butcher shop. "He came in and shook my hand, and said, 'I won't see you anymore.' He told me that he intended going to Fiji, flying into Canada and then traveling by land from Canada into the United States. . . . He wouldn't require a visa to enter America from Canada."

Hand left at the beginning of a three-day weekend in June, Gehring said, "and every day for about a week I would put fresh food in the fridge, wet down his sox and toothbrush, flush the toilet, run the shower for a while and stomp around and bang some doors for the benefit of the neighbors. . . . Ultimately Michael Moloney rang me and said he wanted to contact Hand in relation to some court case. Hand had told me to tell no one about his disappearance, and I told Moloney I hadn't seen him for a couple of days, and I told him I would leave a note on his mirror in the bathroom. I did this. Michael Moloney kept ringing each day, and I put two or three notes on the mirror."

Eventually, Gehring returned a call to Moloney but got someone else at the Nugan Hand office. He left the message that Hand hadn't been seen for over a week. Before Moloney returned, the person Gehring had talked to had passed the news on to one of the journalists who was besieging Nugan Hand, and, as Gehring testified, "the rest is history."

Hand immediately took on the usual "missing-man" celebrity. "Missing Banker In Rio, Says Interpol," screamed a headline in the Sunday *Telegraph* (which also reported that its "efforts yesterday to locate him [there] were unsuccessful"). "Missing Banker Feared Murdered," read another headline. And there was even, based on an optimistic forecast from a lawyer Moloney was working with, "Michael Hand May Return."

Target Financial Service, the gossipy Hong Kong newsletter that claimed to have first exposed the Nugan Hand affair, led its November 17, 1980, issue with an "EXCLUSIVE" report that not only was Michael Hand living in South America, helped there by his "friends"—former CIA employees—but that Frank Nugan was living in South America, too.

The late Mr. Nugan was occasionally the subject of reports that he had been seen in bars in places like Atlanta and Kansas City. Suspicion grew so wild that in February 1981, officials ordered Nugan's body exhumed, just to put everyone's mind at ease. There was grisly television and newspaper coverage.

The headline over the top of the front page of *The Australian,* the next day, said, "Body Was Nugan's, But How Did He Die?" Reporter Nicholas Rothwell wrote, "The nation looked on through the lenses of countless press and television cameras as the investigators who dogged international banker Frank Nugan until January 26, 1980, the date his death was recorded, pursued him to the grave."

The exhumation took three hours, the stench occasionally driving back the crowd. A "police scientific expert" was lowered into the reopened grave to examine the coffin before it was hauled up.

"Some are dry, some are wet," one weary gravedigger told interviewers by way of complaining that Nugan was "wet," and therefore "very messy." A dentist finally identified his remains.

That same month, February 1981, Gehring spoke again with Michael Hand. "I went to America and visited my mother and my brother, who both live in Dayton, Ohio," he has testified. "Eventually

I got a phone call from my brother when I was in San Francisco. He gave me a telephone number and the name Charlie, and told me that Charlie wanted me to contact him urgently. . . . I looked up the area code and it was somewhere in Wyoming."

"I asked for a man named Charlie," Gehring testified, "and the person on the phone said, 'There is no Charlie here.' There was a pause, and he said, 'Wait a minute,' and the man Charlie came to the phone," Gehring said, adding that he recognized Charlie's voice from their meeting in Sydney.

"Charlie said that Michael Hand wanted to talk to me, and asked for a phone number. . . . I told him I was leaving from the San Francisco airport." Charlie took the number of the pay telephone Gehring was using, and moments later Hand called.

"He was looking for news about himself, and the investigation over here [in Australia]. He also asked me about Helen, his wife, and also if I had gotten into any trouble over the false passport. He also asked me if I had seen Bernie Houghton [who was also on the lam then], and I told him I had.

"I asked him how he was doing, and he said he was doing a bit better, and getting it together," Gehring said. But he said Hand didn't reveal where he was, or what he was doing—except to report that he was no longer relying on the alias of Alan Winter.

In March 1983, the task force reported:

"Inquiries have revealed that "Charlie" is identical with James Oswald Spencer, a U.S. citizen born 22 September 1940, presently resident in Arizona. Spencer is a former member of the U.S. Special Forces, and like Hand was loaned to the Central Intelligence Agency during the latter half of the 1960s for operations in the Southeast Asian conflict. Hand and Spencer became close at that time."

Obviously they still were. In applying for a visa at the Australian consulate in Los Angeles before going to rescue Hand, Spencer had listed his purpose as "sightseeing" and "medical treatment." For a contact address, he listed "H. Boreland, P.O. Box 2045, G.P.O., Sydney." That box was rented out to Helen Boreland, who was also Mrs. Michael Hand.

Spencer arrived in Australia May 14, 1980, and left June 14, on the same Fiji-bound flight as Michael Hand, traveling under the name Alan Winter.

While task force investigators were in the United States in November 1982, they persuaded the FBI to interview Spencer. Besides apprehending the American banker who had taken some documents out of the Hong Kong office, the interview with Spencer was the only instance of cooperation that Australian or Asian authorities have received from the FBI in the investigation of Nugan Hand. (A Justice Department prosecutor, Lawrence Barcella, who put Edwin Wilson in jail, did arrange for the task force investigators to talk to "J," and other witnesses against Wilson, many of whom were sequestered in protective custody.)

Spencer told the FBI he had last seen Hand "several years ago when Hand was in the CIA." He denied helping Hand leave Australia, refused to say whether or not he had ever been to Australia, and otherwise declined to answer any questions "regarding when, where or under what circumstances he last saw Michael Hand." Spencer couldn't be located by reporters.

Concluded the task force, "Taking into account all the available information, the Task Force rejects outright Spencer's denial, and concludes that Spencer is 'Charlie.' "

The task force also listed the whole "Charlie" episode among various pieces of evidence that "suggest that Hand retained his U.S. intelligence ties—whatever they might have been—throughout the 1970s and probably into the 1980s."

And where is Michael Hand? Says Wilf Gregory, who ran the Manila office with General Manor, "All I can imagine is that Mike Hand has been transferred to another CIA operation and he's taken the money with him."

CHAPTER TWENTY-FOUR

Thwarting the Investigators

Some dedicated people have worked years trying to solve the Nugan Hand mystery. The staff of the Joint Task Force, and Geoffrey Nicholson, the independent counsel eventually hired by the Corporate Affairs Commission to produce its two-volume report, are obviously among them. So are the Hong Kong liquidators' office and John O'Brien, the outside liquidator finally appointed by the Australian courts in July 1980.

No one was more clever or persevering or did more to inform the public about both the truth and the mystery of Nugan Hand than Marian Wilkinson, reporter for the *National Times* in Sydney. Rising above the sensationalism of many of her colleagues, she was consistently accurate and kept the heat on the official investigators.

But there was only so much all these people could do against a well-coordinated cover-up—particularly since they lacked authority to compel sworn testimony from the many suspects who weren't Australian. Even Bernie Houghton, who was making his home in Australia, never had to testify under oath.

The initial inspectors sent out by the Corporate Affairs Commission after Frank Nugan's death were ridiculously inept. They allowed themselves to be shoved around and intimidated by Michael Hand and Michael Moloney until the evidence was dissipated.

For example, the commission's report describes how one afternoon the inspectors cooled their heels for four hours, fruitlessly waiting to be admitted to see documents and mumbling threats of legal action. Then, the report says, "Mr. Moloney removed a large envelope containing documents, stating he would have it photocopied prior to production. Neither the records or photocopies of them were subsequently produced to the delegates."

When the investigators finally did get their invitation to enter, they seemed surprised to find many of the file drawers empty. They came across a box of check stubs and deposit slips from Yorkville Nominees' bank account; according to the report, Pat Swan, Nugan's private secretary, initially allowed them access to the box, but Moloney immediately took it from them.

For an American, used to FBI efficiency, it is hard to imagine cops so spineless that they let criminal suspects carry evidence away right under their noses, while waiting for permission to examine it.

Geoff Nicholson was brought in to put the commission's investigation on a professional setting. He eventually did manage to reconstruct a balance sheet for the Nugan Hand holding company, but the document wasn't worth much. It showed $17.2 million in assets, of which $16.8 million consisted of "Inter-group companies' accounts." (Actually, there was about $1 million in honest assets by the commission's reckoning, but much of this was offset by a $746,000 checking account overdraft.)

The unpaid and unpayable claims appeared to approach $50 million. It was assumed that a great deal more money had been lost by people who had too much to hide to file a claim. This was the money not just of drug dealers and obvious criminals. One of Nugan Hand's main lures was helping people avoid their countries' foreign exchange control laws. Filing a claim for money that had been illegally sent out of the country in the first place would be asking for heavy trouble in Malaysia, Indonesia, Thailand, the Philippines, Taiwan, and a lot of other places—even Australia.

Also, early seekers got no hopeful responses that might have encouraged others to write in. Those who wrote Admiral Yates's Nugan Hand Bank in the Cayman Islands got replies from a Bruce Campbell & Company, whose address was a box number there, saying it merely acted as "the registered office" for Nugan Hand and had no meaningful information. The liquidators in Sydney and Hong Kong offered little cheer either, as they faced years of investigation with few assets in sight.

The Corporate Affairs Commission's effort to apply normal accounting methods to the corpse of Nugan Hand was futile. In Singapore, Tan Choon Seng, who supposedly kept books there for the Cayman bank, explained that he had got his job through George

Brincat, the totally manipulated accountant in Sydney. Tan Choon Seng said he had learned his bookkeeping methods from—of all people—Brincat and Steve Hill, who have testified that they routinely altered their figures as Frank Nugan or Mike Hand told them to—the accounting equivalent of "Hello, Sweetheart, get me rewrite."

The commission found there was no control register listing the bank's international certificates of deposit in order of serial number. "Mr. Brincat agreed under examination . . . that in the absence of such a register it was quite possible that a representative accepting a deposit and issuing an International Certificate . . . could simply pocket the deposit if it had been made in cash," the commission reported.

Though the point wasn't raised, the deposit also could be pocketed by having the client make out the check to a separate corporate front, as Houghton did at times. "Mr. Brincat could not recall ever seeing a reconciliation between deposits accepted and International Certificates of Deposit issued," the commission said.

John O'Brien was able to raise $1.2 million from the sale of Frank and Lee Nugan's house, which had clearly been bought and refurbished with depositors' funds. He also raised about $40,000 from the sale of various furniture. But, as is the case in many bankruptcies, the fees for the investigation ate up much of the money the investigation produced.

O'Brien drew a whole list of people and companies that appeared to owe Nugan Hand money as a result of receiving loans from Nugan Hand. But as O'Brien well knew, and acknowledged in private, these "borrowers" weren't really borrowers at all—just people having their "deposits" returned to them in a way Frank Nugan said would mean they didn't have to pay taxes on the money. Instead of taxes, they paid Nugan Hand a fee, often as high as 22 percent.

Collection proved next to impossible. People denied they received the loans—and there was no evidence to prove they had, except for some notation, often cryptic, that O'Brien had found among Nugan Hand's records.

Moreover, many of these "borrowers" were suddenly represented by counsel of a curious sort—John Aston, and his new partner, Alex Lee. In some ways, Lee could be considered a Nugan Hand insider. He was the husband of councilwoman Yolanda Lee, who had arranged government deposits for Nugan Hand. Soon Lee joined Aston's law firm, and also became a director of the Nugan fruit and vegetable group.

Dr. Ogden, the $600,000 loser, also went to Lee for advice, but in his case, he says, Lee "just told me not to try to get anything back, that it was useless."

In some cases, corporations had been created as fronts, to help people borrow back their money anonymously. But when O'Brien tried to collect on these corporate loans, he could never get anyone to admit to any continuing involvement with the corporation that borrowed the money. Often, the address of these front companies was care of some lawyer or accountant, who would respond that he no longer worked for the company and didn't know who did.

Pollard and Brincat, the accountants for Nugan Hand itself, were involved in representing these front companies. They would respond to O'Brien's formal demand letters with, for example: "Further to your letter dated 8th August, 1980, we advise that we no longer act in any capacity at all for Garcia Hardware Proprietary Limited. Yours faithfully, Pollard & Brincat."

What was O'Brien to do? Money had been turned over to Garcia Hardware, but Garcia Hardware was nowhere around. The money in all likelihood had flowed to some person for whom Garcia was a front, but how was O'Brien to prove it did, or find out who the person was?

Another problem that stymied the liquidators was the conflict of jurisdictions. O'Brien was liquidating seven Nugan Hand-related companies domiciled in Australia, while the Hong Kong liquidators' office was handling companies based there. Hong Kong and the Cayman Islands both claimed jurisdiction over the Nugan Hand Bank.

So O'Brien refused to accept many claims from depositors who thought their money was being supervised by Nugan Hand in Sydney, but who could not prove that their money ever actually arrived in Australia. One Filipino depositor who was in this bind hired Peat, Marwick's Sydney office to represent him. Peat, Marwick wrote O'Brien that "representatives of the Nugan Hand group in the Philippines assured him that the certificates of deposit were guaranteed by a counter deposit with the Bank of New South Wales."

The Filipino was turned down. So was an American who wrote a poignant letter arguing that since Hand and Houghton took the money, and they were in Australia, O'Brien ought to be able to lay hands on them. Even some Australian depositors were refused, on the ground that because they had received international certificates of deposit on the Nugan Hand Bank, their money had gone to the

Cayman Islands and they had no claim against the companies O'Brien was liquidating. The one consolation for such people, if you can call it that, was that O'Brien didn't have enough money in the till to pay them anything meaningful even if their claims had been ruled valid.

An unfortunate chill developed between the two liquidators' offices. Seeking official authority to question Irving Trust Company, the U.S. correspondent bank for Nugan Hand, O'Brien says he asked M.D.M. (Mike) Woollard, a lawyer in the Hong Kong liquidators' office, for permission to become co-liquidator of the Cayman bank. "And he basically told me to go to hell," O'Brien says.

The Hong Kong liquidators say they are duty-bound to protect only the creditors of those entities they are liquidating. "The duty a banker has toward customers to confidentiality does not cease when the bank goes into liquidation," one asserted. And the Hong Kong authorities complained in their internal memos that the Corporate Affairs Commission in Australia had stonewalled them on requests for information.

The Hong Kong office began making formal demands of O'-Brien. The books of Nugan Hand Bank in Singapore showed $6 million had been transferred to the parent company, whose own books, of course, showed that the money hadn't been received. "The view we take is that the Singapore books are substantially correct," a Hong Kong liquidator says. So, despite the fact that those books were subject to the same totally arbitrary rewriting as the Australian books were, basically by the same people, Hong Kong was demanding that O'Brien send back the $6 million—which, of course, he didn't have.

Hong Kong also demanded that O'Brien account for 500,000 shares of stock in one of the Hong Kong companies, saying that no capital investment had ever been paid in to obtain the stock. Of course, Frank Nugan and Mike Hand apparently never paid in genuine capital for any of their companies. For the liquidators to be arguing over who owned the stock to this or that subsidiary, and whether the stock had been legitimately obtained, seems ludicrous. All the Nugan Hand companies were a tangled interlock of lies.

Despite the mishandling of the investigation in Australia, and the conflicts with Hong Kong, the most frustrating impediment to a solution of the Nugan Hand case has been the refusal of American authorities to cooperate.

The Australian investigative teams were absorbed with the American role almost from the beginning. One prosecutor working on the Nugan Hand case in Sydney had eleven books on the shelf by his desk the day a reporter stopped in. *Three* of them were related to the CIA and American politics: Philip Agee's *CIA Diary,* Edward Epstein's *Legend,* and John Stockwell's *In Search of Enemies.*

If that was the concern of the Australian *Government,* one can imagine the concern of the Australian *press.* The *National Times* petitioned the FBI under the U.S. Freedom of Information Act for information it had on Nugan Hand. The newspaper was told that of some 151 pages of material in the FBI files, it could see seventy-one.

But when the papers arrived, they resembled a collection of Rorschach tests, with page after page blacked out in heavy ink and bearing the notation "B-1," indicating that disclosure would endanger U.S. "national defense or foreign policy." What was left was a few pages of more or less routine information, such as the incorporation papers of Nugan Hand's Hawaii branch.

The Joint Task Force, the Corporate Affairs Commission, and the official liquidators all tried the same thing and got the same result. Mike Woollard, lawyer for the Hong Kong receiver, wrote a four-page, single-spaced plea to the legal liaison office of the American consulate in Hong Kong. In painstaking detail, Woollard enumerated the many reasons for suspecting that the U.S. Government had, or certainly should have had, important information about Nugan Hand that it wasn't disclosing.

After noting that the bank operated branches in the United States, and that many extremely high-ranking U.S. military and intelligence personnel were involved in its management, Woollard's letter assailed the withholding of FBI material.

> It is clear from my investigation to date" [Woollard wrote], "that NHB [Nugan Hand Bank] and Nugan Hand's companies in general conducted the following activities in which I would expect the Federal Bureau of Investigation to take an interest:
>
> 1) They dealt with persons having known or suspected connections in dealings with drugs, and they are known to have assisted in making funds available for such persons in various jurisdictions in a way which makes the payees and recipients of those funds difficult to identify.
>
> 2) They maintained an active interest in banking in Florida and in particular in Dade County. They employed as their adviser and later chief executive a person who had been a president of a banking group centered on Dade County. They maintained an account with a bank which in February 1981 was the subject of a raid by officials of the Revenue, Drugs Task Force and Customs services.
>
> 3) They engaged in transactions having the effect of transfer-

> ring funds from one jurisdiction to another under conditions of some secrecy.
>
> 4) They were actively involved in negotiations relating to the supply of military equipment to various countries and persons who might have difficulty in openly acquiring such equipment.
>
> In addition to the above indications of Federal Bureau of Investigation interest in NHB, there is also evidence both circumstantial and to an extent direct of Central Intelligence Agency or other U.S. intelligence agencies' involvement with NHB.

Woollard then listed ten examples, from the one-time CIA personnel on the Nugan Hand staff to the intelligence community veterans Nugan Hand dealt with on the outside.

"I should make it clear that as liquidator I have no interest in the activities of U.S. agencies except in so far as they assist in my primary task of locating assets," Woollard wrote. "Accordingly, the above connections both known and circumstantial are not the result of any systematical investigation by me of U.S. Government involvement in NHB. They have merely come to my attention as part of my general investigation of NHB affairs."

Saying he expected the Nugan Hand liquidation to go on for years, Woollard offered to negotiate with the American Government to get the facts he wanted under terms that would protect the U.S. desire for secrecy.

He was flatly turned down.

John O'Brien, Woollard's counterpart in Sydney, has been even more frustrated. "There's lots of questions to be answered," he says. "I wrote to the prime minister's office, the Commonwealth police, the American embassy here in Canberra," trying to obtain U.S. Government cooperation, he says. "But they don't want to answer my letters. The Americans, after prodding, said they had lost my letter. Then they had to send back to the U.S. for instructions."

Finally, in April 1982, more than a year after O'Brien (as well as the task force, Corporate Affairs Commission, and others) had begun requesting cooperation, the State Department sent a two-man FBI delegation to Sydney. But the G-men just stonewalled everyone, saying the FBI had already given its information to an appropriate Australian agency. They wouldn't say which agency they had dealt with, and they wouldn't re-release the information.

Both the Australian federal police and New South Wales police—each of which participated in the Joint Task Force—say they've never received the information. The only other likely recipient would appear to be ASIO, the secret counterspy group with close ties to the CIA.

Asked if it was ASIO, Stephen King, a senior officer responding for that organization, will say only, "I can't imagine anyone in ASIO having authority to request information on Nugan Hand of the FBI." ASIO deals only in "sabotage, espionage and related areas," King says. "There is no law enforcement" function.

Says O'Brien, "They sent the FBI out here to tell me there was nothing doing. I still can't understand why they sent them here to tell me that."

One of the FBI agents who came was John Grant, who was serving as legal attaché at the U.S. Embassy in Manila. On the mostly blacked-out documents that the FBI had supplied to Australian investigators, about the only thing left visible was a notation that some of them had been prepared by the legal attaché in Manila. The other agent, O'Brien recalls, was named Leahy.

"It was a very hot day and Leahy had on a wool coat and vest and wouldn't take them off," O'Brien remembers. "John Grant was most emphatic that all the FBI had done was make inquiries at the request of the Australian and Hong Kong police and that 'all information has been given to the Australian police, ask them.' " In fact, O'Brien had already written to the commissioner of the Commonwealth police for the alleged FBI dossier; the letter back stated, "If such a file exists, then the Australian Federal Police certainly does not have a copy."

O'Brien was amazed by the FBI men's lack of curiosity about information O'Brien tried to offer *them.* After Grant said he wouldn't supply O'Brien any information, O'Brien says he tried to show Grant a letter from William Colby describing work Colby did for Nugan Hand, as evidence of American involvement in a criminal endeavor.

"Grant refused to look at it," O'Brien says. "I finally just tossed it on the desk, but he still wouldn't look at it. Neither Hand nor Houghton is sought by the U.S. The FBI has no interest in investigating. I believe that the FBI got themselves in the middle of something political. It has obvious overtones that someone is covering something up.

"I can't understand what the problem is about answering my simple questions," O'Brien says. "If you ask a simple question and they don't want to answer it, you begin to think it's not a simple question. Then, if you push and push and push and they give you a simple answer, you begin to wonder if you can believe the answer."

O'Brien's colleagues at the Corporate Affairs Commission were fairly scathing in their final report. "That there is a Nugan Hand file maintained by the United States Department of Justice . . . is beyond dispute," began the section of the report on U.S. cooperation. Commenting on the U.S. refusal to turn the file over on grounds of national defense or foreign policy, the commission said, "Without access to the material actually deleted it is difficult if not impossible to conceive the reason for the classification and deletion of the subject material."

The commission disclosed that Hong Kong police had tried to investigate Nugan Hand's drug connections, but had been refused cooperation by the U.S. Government. A U.S. Treasury agent had said his office was "interested in the activities of Nugan Hand," but that prosecution was unlikely because "they were too careful. Much of the money is carried by couriers and even if the couriers are apprehended, it would still prove impossible to tie them to Nugan Hand." Impossible? The Australians had already done it.

"It does not seem unreasonable," the Corporate Affairs Commission concluded, "that the United States Government be requested to supply all information known to it or its agencies concerning Nugan Hand to an Australian Government-appointed investigation."

Privately, an official at the top of the commission's investigation was livid. "There's supposed to be intelligence cooperation between the countries," he said. "There's an alliance. We want to know if it [Nugan Hand] was a way of giving money to operatives. That doesn't mean we're trying to identify operatives. We're not.

"It's very hard for me to understand how a request for information from Hong Kong is of national security importance for the United States. Or from Australia. Or the activities of an American in Australia—unless, of course, he had a link with the security agencies. At least, that's the inference I draw. How can the activities of private individuals acting privately outside the United States of America possibly relate to American national security?"

Of course, as the Iran-Contra affair showed again in 1987, the acts of "private individuals" roaming the world certainly *can* relate to American national security, at least as Washington views it. But that is precisely the point. As the theory of perpetual covert action is exercised, our national security is perpetually in the hands of criminals.

The Joint Task Force, in the introduction to its report, said, "It will be seen from the report that at times those links [to U.S. intelligence organizations] appear to have been an intrinsic part of the then ongoing activity and have the appearance of the direct involvement of the U.S. intelligence community itself. . . . Because of the links disclosed and the nature of some allegations, the task force forwarded a request through normal channels to the U.S. Government seeking information from the Central Intelligence Agency, the Drug Enforcement Agency (as it then was), the Federal Bureau of Investigation and more generally from 'any agency or bureau within that country which might have information of assistance.'

"No replies were received," the task force said, "and in mid-1982 a further request seeking urgent replies was forwarded. . . . To date, no reply has been received. . . ."

Federal prosecutor Lawrence Barcella, who put Edwin Wilson in jail, objects to this characterization. Barcella says he did arrange for the task force to meet some witnesses he knew about relating to Wilson, and that he even supplied an FBI agent to help the Australians. But while this example of cooperation is a valid footnote to the Australian complaints, it is too isolated and minimal to rebut them. Barcella's own upstream struggle to bring some measure of justice to the Wilson case against a powerful current flowing from other forces in government is testimony to the tendency toward cover-up that the Australians were complaining about.

A *Wall Street Journal* reporter* was treated no better.

Reporters and law enforcement officers often swap information on crime stories where confidential sources aren't involved. Each side believes it can further its own end this way, and if things are proper their ends are not incompatible. In investigating the Nugan Hand affair, the *Journal* reporter found his relationship with Australian officials typical of that spirit—in marked contrast with the hostility accorded by American officials.

The U.S. Drug Enforcement Administration (since merged into the FBI) provided a helpful briefing in Washington on the Asian drug situation in general as the project started. But as for Nugan Hand, John J. O'Neill, Far East regional director of the DEA, insisted, "That bank has never come under any scrutiny by us as a result of any investigation we have done."

Yet, overseas, the reporter encountered foreign nationals who said they had been interviewed by DEA agents about Nugan Hand. When the overseas DEA agents whose names and phone numbers

*Obviously, the author.

were given to the reporter by O'Neill's office were approached, they refused to talk on any terms.

James Wilkie, the senior U.S. Customs investigator in Hong Kong, agreed to meet. His was the only U.S. law enforcement agency that acknowledges it even briefly looked into Nugan Hand (despite considerable evidence that others did, too).

But as Wilkie waved the reporter in for the scheduled interview, on his desk was a shredding machine, and beside him was a large carton of papers bearing a red horizontal strip, outlining the white letters "C-L-A-S-S-I-F-I-E-D."

Wilkie was calmly feeding the documents into the shredder as he spoke, taking each batch of shreddings out and putting them through a second time.

"We can't comment on anything that's under investigation or might be under investigation," he said.

Was Nugan Hand under investigation?

"There wasn't an investigation. We did make some inquiries. We can't comment," he said.

The reporter asked what was being shredded.

"It's none of your business what's being shredded," Wilkie replied.

In Bangkok, Richard Virden, a press attaché with the International Communications Agency of the State Department, instructed the DEA men in Thailand not to cooperate with the *Journal* reporter. But he did much more than that. First, Virden went out of his way to prevent a consul at the embassy from issuing a routine credential the consul had agreed to provide to help the reporter deal with the Thai Government. (Later, Virden issued the credential, after causing much delay and inconvenience in a tight reporting schedule.)

Then, Virden thwarted what might have been a real breakthrough.

When the reporter went to Chiang Mai, Thailand, the financial capital of the Golden Triangle drug center, DEA agents seemed genuinely enthusiastic about getting a list of Thai citizens who were alleged in Australia to have invested drug money in Nugan Hand. The agents offered to swap their own information on these people, to the extent it wasn't confidential.

The agents were well aware Nugan Hand had occupied virtually the same office suite as the DEA in Chiang Mai. One, who identified himself only as "Connie," said, "It always seemed like such a coincidence that all the way up here they would wind up so close to us."

Another agent, Greg Korniloff, said he thought the DEA and the reporter could help each other, but first he had to clear it with Bangkok.

But when the reporter returned with the Nugan Hand depositor list, there was bad news. Virden had issued instructions not to talk with the reporter, Agent Korniloff said with apparent disappointment.

"I had hoped we could work something out," he said, "but Bangkok specifically ordered me not to talk to you." He said the orders had been delivered by David Knight, an embassy official in Bangkok, but had come from the press attaché—Virden.

Asked if he was aware of this, Knight replied, "I might be, but I am not willing to talk to you about it."

In Manila, the reporter called up John Grant, the FBI agent and legal attaché who had visited Australia with the FBI's stonewall message for Australian investigators. "I'm a very nice guy and a friendly person," Grant said. "But I can't do it [discuss Nugan Hand]. Nothing will make me change my mind, so please don't insult my intelligence by giving me some arguments to make me think I should."

So the reporter tried Michael Armacost, the U.S. ambassador, who has since become one of the highest State Department officials, under secretary of state for political affairs. A press liaison said Armacost was too busy to see the reporter. So the reporter wrote a long impassioned plea to Armacost, saying that although the ambassador was new to his post, and might not be familiar with Nugan Hand, his embassy contained information about an organization run largely by American citizens that had committed a series of crimes against other American citizens, as well as foreigners.

The reporter's letter mentioned the names, the heroin, the contract murders, the investment fraud against Americans, and the cover-up. "I have asked John Grant to talk to me about the bank and he has refused, those being his instructions," the letter said. "Can you, as his supervisor, re-evaluate that policy?"

There was no reply.

The reporter did talk to the one U.S. official who has acknowledged looking into Nugan Hand, Victor J. Renaghan, Jr., a customs officer once stationed in Hong Kong. "It was one of those things where you knew something was going on, but there was no evidence of violation of a U.S. law," Renaghan said. "I was trying to find out all I could about an organization that was extremely suspect. It would have taken more men and time than I had. Only the FBI would be geared up to do something like this."

Could he start out now?

"With the principal witness dead and the other two guys pretty tough characters, I don't know how much you could hope to get on them. Black is a general and Yates is an admiral, and this implies a certain degree of sophistication. The CIA is not a monolithic organization. I would love to go out and interview these guys," Renaghan said.

But he didn't.

In addition to the refusal of the U.S. Government to cooperate, some strange things were happening in Australia.

For example, in December 1980, there was a bizarre night break-in at the investigative section of the Australian Tax Department. The burglars struck the exact spot where some recovered Nugan Hand records and other materials from the Nugan Hand investigations were being analyzed to see what back taxes the department might levy. Supposedly, only a few dozen people knew the documents were there. Though the papers appeared to have been left intact, what may have been removed or altered couldn't really be determined.

News of the break-in was restricted. The investigation was carried out secretly by ASIO, the intelligence service, and by the federal police (which, under Conservative Party leadership, was far less inquisitive about Nugan Hand than was the Labor-controlled New South Wales government, whose Corporate Affairs Commission was kept in the dark about the break-in for several weeks).

One large newspaper, the *Sun-Herald*, reported that the ASIO and federal police investigators had refused requests by Tax Department officers to take fingerprints from file folders, leading to "speculation . . . that the break-in may have been the work of intelligence agencies themselves." The case was never solved.

Then O'Brien learned something that gave him a chill, and made him (he says) wonder if he was growing paranoid—or if, perhaps, paranoia was justified. Shortly after O'Brien's firm, Pegler, Ellis & Company, had started handling the Nugan Hand liquidation, an accountant he knew in Melbourne recommended an associate to help in the investigation. O'Brien accepted, and the accountant switched firms.

A year or so went by before O'Brien accidentally discovered something the new accountant hadn't told him in all that time—that the accountant was a former Australian intelligence officer, had served in Vietnam and *had known Michael Hand there.* O'Brien tried to be very careful after that in monitoring what information his aide received.

Still, that was nothing compared to what O'Brien found out in 1982. An official of the government-run telephone company disclosed to him that spring that Frank Nugan's telephone conversations had been secretly recorded the last two years of his life, by a device installed at the telephone company. The phone company's cooperation almost certainly meant that a government agency was behind the taping.

O'Brien says the official—whom he declines to identify—told him that the recorded tapes, which might solve a lot of the Nugan Hand mysteries, aren't at the company anymore. Wiretap authority is tightly restricted in Australia. The federal police can get a warrant from a judge to wiretap only in connection with drug offenses. The federal police say they don't know anything about a wiretap on Frank Nugan—as do New South Wales state police, who are never allowed to wiretap under Australian law anyway.

There is, of course, an exception to these restrictions—the same exception that applies to the United States' careful wiretapping laws: national security. In Australia, the federal attorney general is authorized to issue wiretap warrants for ASIO on national security grounds.

Asked* if he authorized such a wiretap, Attorney General Peter Durack issued this statement through a spokesman: "The only agency the attorney general is responsible for in this context is ASIO. It has been a longstanding practice by attorneys general not to disclose any of the activities of ASIO, including details of phone tapping or information received by the organization. I do not intend to depart from that practice."

Nothing more is known about the Nugan tapes, where they are, or what was on them—except to any government agents who took them.

So worried had many Australians become by 1982 that the opposition Labor Party leader in Parliament, Bill Hayden, rose to demand that a royal commission be appointed. He said he wanted the commission to look into "all activities of the Nugan Hand Bank, and persons or organizations associated with it, including drug trafficking, arms trafficking, laundering of money, involvement in organized crime,

*By the author.

and the relationship between Nugan Hand and the operations of foreign intelligence agencies in or through Australia."

Prime Minister Malcolm Fraser replied that he believed the current investigation was "wide enough."

When Vice-president George Bush visited Australia in April 1982, Labor Party leader Hayden used his thirty-minute meeting with Bush mostly to press for the release of details in the Nugan Hand and Gough Whitlam affairs. Bush would only give his personal assurances that the CIA wasn't involved in either matter. Bush, in 1976, had succeeded Colby as Director of Central Intelligence.

Finally, the CIA was pushed to issue a statement: "The agency rarely comments on such allegations," the statement said, "but in this case we emphatically deny the charges. The CIA has not engaged in operations against the Australian Government, had no ties with the Nugan Hand Bank, and does not involve itself in drug trafficking."

Obviously, the CIA did engage in operations designed to alter the course of Australian domestic affairs; the Chris Boyce spy case established that. Even more obviously, the CIA for more than thirty-five years has involved itself in drug trafficking. If that is not a policy ever officially approved by a Director of Central Intelligence, it is still a practice so widely known that it can be considered an approved policy by the mere fact that no director has put a stop to it. The fact that the CIA probably happened onto its drug connections by coincidence rather than intent doesn't make the connections any less momentous, or less outrageous.

In the face of that, the CIA's Nugan Hand denial can be taken for whatever it's worth.

And if you accept it, how then do you explain Nugan Hand—a thoroughly corrupt and fraudulent organization staffed by all those generals, admirals, and intelligence officers?

"What you're left with," says an official in charge of one of the major Australian investigations, "is saying, here are all these patriots who have served their country faithfully for years, suddenly saying, 'Let's all become criminals. Let's forget our war service, our heroism, and go out and commit crimes against the very country we've been working for.' "

CHAPTER TWENTY-FIVE

"Everybody Left Alive Is Innocent"

Donald Beazley, working to resurrect his respectable American banking career, continued to try to disassociate himself from the scandal. He told the *Wall Street Journal** that Nugan Hand's only U.S. business was arranging mergers and acquisitions, and that he had quit the bank because "the merger and acquisition market went to hell." The *Journal,* at that early stage, was unaware of the American deposit-taking.

George Farris, the Nugan Hand Washington representative who was reached in 1982 through the switchboard at Fort Bragg, North Carolina, where he was on secret assignment for the army, remembered Beazley in charge of the company. "After Frank Nugan's death, all things came out over Beazley's signature," Farris said. This lasted "at least through March [of 1980]."

According to the Stewart Royal Commission, Nugan Hand employe Andrew Wong talked February 4 in Hong Kong with Beazley, "who gave him the impression that the Nugan Hand Group was financially stable and that there was no need for concern about the future of the organization." The Stewart commission said that "in order to forestall any run on the bank following Mr. Nugan's death Mr. Beazley had made public statements in Hong Kong to the effect that the bank was sound." But it accepted his word that he was dissatisfied with the information available in Sydney, gave Hand his resignation, and left Australia February 13, 1980.

*Reporters E. S. ("Jim") Browning and Chris Pritchard.

Says George Farris, "I know he said he submitted his resignation, but I know when he came to town [Washington] at the end of February he was still assuming his role as the big shot, reassuring me that everything was all right. Nugan Hand was still going to go on to great things." Questioned about what Farris said, Beazley acknowledges it is "possible."*

In August 1982, Beazley left his job as president of Gulfstream Banks and became president of City National Bank of Miami. City National was once one of Miami's largest banks, though it had begun to fade. The bank's new owner, who hired Beazley, was Alberto Duque, a Colombian coffee heir. Duque's, and the bank's, lawyer happened to be Stephen W. Arky, son-in-law of Marvin Warner, Beazley's old boss and benefactor at Great American Banks.

But a year after Beazley went to work for the Colombian, Duque's empire was in collapse as banks and other creditors sued him for fraud. He had pledged nonexistent coffee as collateral for some very big loans. In 1986, Duque was convicted in federal court, Miami, of sixty counts of fraud and conspiracy involving $108 million; he was sentenced to fifteen years in prison.

Beazley found himself once more defending a besieged institution. "City National Bank is a strong, solid financial institution," he insisted to the press (as quoted by reporter Mike Langberg of the *Fort Lauderdale News/Sun-Sentinel* in August 1983). Duque might lose his controlling interest, Beazley asserted, but the bank would do fine. Would the scandal cost Beazley yet another job? "It depends on who buys the bank," he replied.

Meanwhile, as late as March 1984, Stephen Arky's law firm continued to represent Beazley in threatening a libel action against a *Wall Street Journal* reporter** for articles published in that newspaper. Arky told the *Journal* it could mitigate damages by retracting the articles. The articles weren't retracted, and the suit wasn't brought.

General LeRoy Manor wouldn't cooperate with the *Journal* reporter while a series of stories was being prepared in 1982. He asserted that he never had anything to do with Nugan Hand. But nine months after that series of articles, when the reporter was preparing

*My interviews with Farris and Beazley on this point came prior to the Stewart commission's interviews. John McArthur also told me that Beazley had telephoned him in Hong Kong from the United States on Nugan Hand business as late as March 21, 1980, still acting as if in control.

**The author.

another series based on the work of the Australian Joint Task Force, the general changed his stance.

Howard Landau, a retired colonel who, in the air force, had been Manor's personal public relations man, invited the reporter to meet the general at the general's comfortable but not palatial home in the Virginia suburbs of Washington. Sitting himself amidst a veritable museum of memorabilia attesting to a career as a fighter ace and honored commander, Manor ruminated that "It's demoralizing to have five months of your life really destroy a lot of that."

He recalled that he and Admiral Yates had worked and played tennis together in the military. He described conversations in which Yates seduced him into Nugan Hand. He told how impressed he was by the Nugan Hand offices, and by the October 1979 conference. He insisted he was never paid more than expense money.

He praised Wilf Gregory, his colleague in Manila, and Beazley, "a very highly respected individual in the banking business. I said, 'Don, you have very fine credentials. You know what my background is. Would I be over my head?' He said, 'No, give it a try.' He said, 'Even at your age there's a possibility of moving up in an organization like this, because we're going to expand. And if I didn't think that way I wouldn't be in it."

Manor told how he tried to work on commercial deals for Nugan Hand—a Swedish knitting mill, a Chinese plastic toy business, an Australian coconut oil sale—none of which ever came off. He insisted that soliciting deposits was "a very minor part of it. We weren't told to push that."

He says people like Colonel H. Kirby Smith and Colonel Jimmy Maturo, whose deposits he took, *volunteered* to invest, after hearing him talk about the bank. Why did he continue taking deposits after the bank was in collapse? The night he learned of Frank Nugan's death, he said, "I sat up late at night talking with Gregory, who assured me everything had to be okay." Still, General Manor said, he vowed not to do any business "till I got an explanation." He said he met Beazley in Bangkok, and Beazley told him, "I'm sure everything's all right, but I'm going to Australia and find out. And I'll come back and tell you."

Instead, Manor said, Beazley sent his regrets and went on to England. Mike Hand came instead, and said, "Let me assure you that our books have been examined. We have the backing of large financial institutions in Australia. As far as liquidity is concerned, you have no problems."

So, Manor said, he told Colonel Maturo it was okay to put in some more money in March 1980—the general added an "unfortunately" after recalling this fact. But he insisted that by the same token, his caution had protected the money of a pilot who served in the C-130 wing that Maturo commanded. Because he suspected trouble, Manor said, he had warned the pilot against making a deposit, and the pilot didn't.

"Nobody told Jimmy to invest," he said of Maturo. "I told him I had confidence in it. You can invest in stocks and lose everything, too."

Wilf Gregory says General Manor left the Philippines on the advice of William Quasha, their lawyer. Quasha, who calls himself an "old friend" of Manor, declines to comment on that statement, citing the attorney-client privilege. Manor, at his home, said he didn't flee at all. He said he went to the United States on leave, intending to return, but was prevented from doing so when he got the assignment to investigate the Iranian rescue mission.

"I just wish I hadn't been involved with it at all," he said of Nugan Hand. "But I can see why I made the decision. It looked good. Until Frank Nugan died, I enjoyed the work."

How could a three-star general not be smart enough to see through a fraud as thinly veneered as this one, he was asked. "I've asked myself that question a lot of times," Manor replied.

What does he think of Admiral Yates now? "I think he was taken in as I was. He's an honest individual. A hard worker. I don't think he was the kind of person painted in that [the *Wall Street Journal*'s] article. He's very capable."

The admiral himself, president of the Nugan Hand Bank, told one reporter, "I was just an employe." "They never let me know what was going on," he told another. He said he didn't trust reporters enough to talk to them further. One time he said he didn't have time to talk because he wanted to take his wife sailing on Chesapeake Bay. But he stuck to his story that he had resigned effective with Beazley's appearance.

The Nugan Hand suite in a largely U.S. Government-occupied building by Manila Bay stayed open under the name International Planning & Development Corporation. Wilf Gregory kept his old office and ran it. An office in the suite was occupied by International Planning & Development Corp.'s chairman, Ludwig Peter Rocka, who also happened to be Ferdinand Marcos's brother-in-law.

"I took the office over because they owed me money," Gregory said in 1982. "We [International Planning] get involved in some of the things Nugan Hand used to be involved in." Asked to say what that might be, Gregory replied, "That's private information. I'd get in trouble."

A year after Manor welcomed the reporter into his home, his client, Colonel Smith was still trying to get his $20,000 back. On May 7, 1984, he wrote Manor, praising the accuracy of stories that had appeared in the *Wall Street Journal,* and again asking for his money:

> I invested with you after your "pitch" for Nugan Hand Bank during your speech as the guest speaker before the PACAF/JAG [Pacific Air Force, Judge Advocate General, or military law] Conference at Hickam Air Force Base Officers' Club in December of 1979. My wife and I invested with you because I had been taught through the years and at the Air Command and Staff College as well as the Air War College that general officers obtain their respected rank based on hard work, intelligence, honesty, integrity, etc. . . .
>
> As my investment broker at that time for Nugan Hand Bank, you owed me, my wife and all your other investors a fiduciary relationship to reveal Frank Nugan's murder/suicide as quickly as possible. You knew of Nugan's death when you gave me Nugan Hand Bank's International Certificate of Deposit for $20,000 at the Visiting General Officers Quarters at Clark Air Base in February of 1980! . . . Why didn't you tell me?

Colonel Smith went on to recall that Manor "departed Manila quickly in late April," and later sent Colonel Smith a letter asking him to contact other depositors about sums exceeding $100,000. The letter, Colonel Smith said, was written "23 June 1980 from the Bolling Air Force Base, D.C., while you were heading up the Iranian Rescue Debacle Investigation."

The reply to Colonel Smith's letter came from a lawyer named Donald G. Smith, of Fairfax, Virginia. The lawyer said, "I represent Lieutenant General LeRoy Manor. . . . The charges that you have made in your letter are unfounded and may be libelous. Your insinuation that General Manor is less than an honorable man must be retracted immediately. Your request for payment of $20,000 is ludicrous and will not be made in whole or in part."

Colonel Smith wrote the lawyer back a more detailed and blistering letter, containing some labels for Manor that almost certainly *were* libelous, if they were not true. The next day he wrote the *Journal* reporter, complaining bitterly about the disinclination of the air force to respond to his complaints, and the difficulties under international law of trying to bring suit about a deposit taken in the Philippines, even if the deposit was suggested at a U.S. air base during a military function. He also said he thought the CIA was "probably" involved in covering the matter up.

And he seemed especially bitter that General Manor, having completed his report on the Iranian rescue mission, had been made executive vice-president—the full-time staff head—of the Retired Officers' Association, a prestigious armed forces alumni group that carries considerable political weight.

Colonel Smith enclosed a copy of Manor's message to the association's membership upon assuming office. "During recent years . . . we have witnessed a trend of diminishing respect and support for our military establishment," the message said. "This trend must be reversed . . . if our nation is to remain strong and continue a meaningful leadership role among the other nations of the free world."

Les Collings, the Nugan Hand Hong Kong representative, went to work for a company there that claimed to have perfected an engine that would burn grass. "It's a company that's about to be very big and well-known," Collings declared in 1982.

Kevin Shirlaw, a representative of the Australian provisional liquidator B. O. Smith, visited Hawaii a month after the bankruptcy. He later wrote a report of what he had found.

His first stop was to see Douglas Philpotts, Nugan Hand's account supervisor at Hawaiian Trust Company (as well as vice-president and treasurer of Hawaiian Trust). Shirlaw learned from Philpotts that the financial data for Nugan Hand Hawaii was prepared under the same standard George Brincat and Steve Hill had used. Regardless of the money actually paid and owed by the Hawaiian unit, Shirlaw's report said, in preparing the financial statements "he [Philpotts] and his associates had followed instructions from Frank Nugan."

Then Shirlaw visited poor Colonel Maturo. He reported telling Maturo "that there was little that I could do as it would appear that he is a creditor of Nugan Hand Cayman Islands Bank and should therefore contact the authorities" in the Caymans—who were already reported to be not cooperating.

The liquidator then went to General Black, old pal of Allen Dulles and Richard Helms, undercover agent against the Chinese, military advisor to the National Security Council, commander of all

U.S. forces in Thailand during the Vietnam War, and executive director of the Freedoms Foundation.

Black "asked me who he should direct the depositors to contact," Shirlaw reported, and again Shirlaw suggested the Cayman Islands. Black "then advised me that it was his understanding that all deposits which had been taken were invested in commercial paper in Australia. . . . I advised him that the provisional liquidators had not come across any short-term paper."

"He expressed some surprise at this," Shirlaw reported.

Two years later, at an outdoor lunch with the *Journal* reporter in the garden of the general's private club, Black declared his conscience was clean. The reporter brought up a letter written to Black by Edward F. Pietro, who said he had served with Black in the European Theater in World War II. After seeing a brochure with Black's picture in it as a representative of the bank, Pietro had deposited and lost $4,900 in Saudi Arabia April 8, 1980—more than two months after Nugan's death. "We need some help, General. Can you shed any light on the situation?" the letter said.

General Black had sent Pietro a handwritten note expressing his regrets over the bank's demise, and saying Black would forward Pietro's letter to the liquidators, which he did.

To the reporter, General Black replied, "Nobody I know ever gave me any money. I never took any deposits. Some soldier who served with me in Vietnam may have read my name and deposited money in the Philippines. But my name isn't well enough known around the world to convince many people. They were putting their money in to get higher interest and avoid tax. If somebody had given me money and this happened, I'd feel personally liable to pay them back, if it was a friend of mine. But I don't feel guilty that because of me some guy got swindled."

CHAPTER TWENTY-SIX

The Agency's Assets

In June 1985, Royal Commissioner D. G. Stewart completed more than two years of work on Nugan Hand by submitting his two-volume report to the governor-general of Australia. That his effort would fail to solve the Nugan Hand mystery was predictable almost from the start. Stewart had rejected the help of investigators like Geoffrey Nicholson of the Corporate Affairs Commission and Clive Small of the Joint Task Force, who had carried the ball halfway downfield and knew the yardage still to be covered. Stewart preferred his own neophyte staff.

Even so, the thoroughness of the failure was astonishing. There was an almost total lack of investigative effort to resolve major issues raised by the earlier investigations. Stewart apparently never tried to compel publicly accountable testimony from Douglas Schlachter, or William Prim, or the many people who had observed Bernie Houghton in Southeast Asia or who helped him leap to wealth and influence almost overnight in Australia—just to name a few obvious examples.

Stewart's report was full of elementary factual errors. Mike Hand was credited with a degree from Syracuse University he never got. Ed Wilson, the merchant of death, was identified as a U.S. Congressman. General Black, who had been dead two years, was described as "currently engaged as a consultant." There were dating errors of a kind unlikely to have been typographical, and other mistakes, some of which have already been noted.

More important was the whitewashing of various CIA connections. Long-identified CIA operatives like Ricardo Chavez were referred to without identification, as if they were ordinary businessmen. Dale Holmgren was said to have "managed all in-flight services for a group named Civil Air Transport," without any indication that Civil Air Transport was a wholly owned proprietary company of the CIA. William Colby was said to have gone to Vietnam for the State Department with the rank of ambassador; no doubt that was an effective cover for his real work in the 1960s, but to maintain that cover story in print in light of what is now known is absurd.

Frank Terpil, the CIA veteran who has been shown in and out of court to have reaped a fortune supplying all sorts of weapons to such lunatic dictators as Idi Amin and Muammar Qaddafi, was identified only as "a reputed arms dealer." Although Stewart claimed that his commission received full cooperation from the U.S. Government, he reported, "Whether Mr. Hand's assertions that he was employed by the CIA are true, the Commission has no way of knowing." Identifying Thomas Clines and Edwin Wilson (in a different section from the one identifying him as a congressman), the commission says they "are alleged to have been CIA agents."

The commission certainly lashed out at Nugan Hand as a corporate entity, which at least countered the continuing efforts of some right-wing groups in the United States to defend the bank. One such organization, called Accuracy In Media, asserted that Nugan Hand was really an honest but hard-luck banking organization that had been maligned by an anti-military press.

Said Stewart, Nugan Hand "depended upon a multitude of frauds and deceptions the like of which may not have been seen before, in this country [Australia] at any rate. . . . The . . . audited accounts were nothing other than gross untruths published year after year from the very first set of accounts as at 30 June 1974 to the last finalized set as at 30 June 1979. . . . Nugan Hand Ltd. was at all times insolvent (and in all probability so were all the other Australian companies within the group).

"The group simply flouted the provisions of the legislation as it then stood in that large volumes of currency were moved in and out of Australia," the commission said. In Hong Kong, it said, "activity was recognized, even by the employees of the company, as being a blatant breach of the Banking Ordinance, in that Nugan Hand (Hong Kong) and the Nugan Hand Bank were carrying on a banking business in Hong Kong. . . .

"It is evident that at least until March 1977 the staff of Nugan Hand (Hong Kong) were involved in activities which were in breach of the local Securities Ordinance. . . . There is also evidence that Mr. Collings sent information concerning deposits to the company direct to Mr. Nugan for the purpose of rewriting" the accounts.

In general, however, the commission made shocking little effort to try to fix any blame except on men who were beyond the reach of legal action. It allowed Yates, Houghton, and McDonald to go on record, unchallenged, blaming Nugan for the fall of the bank. Contrary to all previous investigations, but apparently not based on any new evidence, it singled out the missing Mike Hand as "responsible for the shredding of documents . . ., the instruction of others to shred documents and the concealment of records. . . ."

The commission freely laid blame on Hill and Shaw, who had already made their deal with authorities and testified, and on Brincat, who the commission said might be unprosecutable because of flaws it said needed to be remedied in the law regarding accountants. But other characters were allowed to claim that they simply believed what Hand and Nugan told them. While the commission didn't always say it believed them, neither did it marshal challenges.

The commission did write a section on who it thought should be prosecuted for violating the laws of Australia or New South Wales. The section consisted of 208 paragraphs. All but the first two introductory paragraphs were deleted from the report as released to the public.

On the subject of the CIA, the commission simply gave up the game by default. "It is difficult to imagine that a professional group such as the CIA would use or even think of using such a Group [as Nugan Hand] without first making a thorough check of its bona fides," Stewart wrote. "Even a cursory check would have revealed shortcomings which would undoubtedly make the CIA shy away from having anything at all to do with such a Group."

The commission never attempted to resolve the double standard by which it said the CIA would have recognized Nugan Hand's shortcomings as obvious from "a cursory check," while all the former CIA and Pentagon bosses who were engaged in promoting Nugan Hand were allowed to plead ignorance.

On the issue of whether the CIA used Nugan Hand, the commission quotes Admiral Yates saying, "It was too small for one thing, it was too visible for another . . . and if the CIA had been involved in it they certainly would not have let it fail." It quotes General Black saying that the CIA wouldn't use "a little fly-by-night operation like Nugan and Hand's bank."

"The Commission accepts the evidence of these witnesses," Stewart wrote. "None of these witnesses is contradicted by any credible evidence."

Apparently the commission hadn't heard of Paul Helliwell's Castle Bank—or of the Hawaiian investment banking firm of Bishop, Baldwin, Rewald, Dillingham & Wong.

In 1976, Ronald R. Rewald, who would become chairman of Bishop, Baldwin, Rewald, Dillingham & Wong, was convicted in state court, Wausau, Wisconsin, of theft and the illegal sale of franchises. Essentially, Rewald and an associate had conned two high school teachers into investing in a sporting goods business under false pretenses.

Rewald was ordered to pay $2,000 restitution and spend a year on probation. In 1978, both the sporting goods business and Rewald personally were declared bankrupt in federal court, Milwaukee. He had personal debts of $224,987.93 against assets of $1,429.50, and his company had debts of $126,559.19 against assets of $27,326, the court records show.

That same year, 1978, Rewald opened an investment concern in Honolulu. And the United States Central Intelligence Agency helped pay his office expenses and gave him work as a message relay station and a cover for covert operatives. His investment concern was originally called CMI Investments, but soon changed its name to Bishop, Baldwin.

And by 1983 it was thick with CIA and other intelligence men—one of them working on its payroll in his retirement. A couple of air force generals bearing a total of seven stars graced its roster of backers. That was the year Bishop, Baldwin, like the sporting goods business before it—and like Nugan Hand three years earlier—went into bankruptcy.

This time more than a hundred investors lost a total of more than $23 million. Most were Americans. Many were suckered in by the presence of so many military/intelligence heroes, just as the victims were at Nugan Hand. Once again, as at Nugan Hand, there were blatant lies, false financial statements, and gross theft of customer funds.

This time, however, there was no question that the CIA was involved with Rewald's business—though to what degree is still in debate. Rewald claims that Bishop, Baldwin was created and run by the CIA, and that everything he did at Bishop, Baldwin was on CIA orders. That is very unlikely, and as a defense it certainly failed to keep Rewald from being convicted of fraud. He was found guilty in federal court, Honolulu, in 1985, and sentenced to eighty years in prison.

But many boxes of records from the Rewald case were sealed at the CIA's request for national security reasons. And still, enough got on the public record to make a strong case that the CIA gave Rewald the credibility he needed to run his big fraud, and that the CIA knew or should have known what was going on.

Rewald says he was recruited by the CIA in the 1960s while a student at MIT: on questioning, that turns out to be the *Milwaukee* Institute of Technology, a two-year school from which he failed to graduate. He says he was hired to spy on campus war protesters, which the CIA was indeed doing then. The dean who Rewald says introduced him to the CIA flatly denies having done so, and Rewald has lied so much his word is worthless.

But if Rewald is lying about being a CIA man on campus in the 1960s, he told the same lie to friends and relatives back at the time. Rewald says that when he decided to relocate to Honolulu, his CIA contacts from those early days arranged for him to meet Eugene J. Welch, chief of the CIA office in Hawaii.

At Rewald's trial, Welch testified that Rewald called out-of-the-blue to the CIA's listed phone number in Honolulu in 1978 and volunteered his services. Of course, the word of Welch and other CIA men may not be worth any more than that of Rewald; Welch also testified that he thought his CIA secrecy oath protected him from prosecution for perjury if he lied in court. (Among other things, he also testified that the CIA hadn't reported on student dissidents in the United States, which it had, and that he had never heard of covert operatives being provided with false background credentials, which they have been.)

However the initial contact was made, Rewald wound up lunching with CIA chief Welch, welcoming Welch and his wife to his house for dinner, and meeting Welch's replacement, John C. (Jack) Kindschi. Rewald, new CIA chief Kindschi, and their wives became very close. Kindschi testified that from the fall of 1978, when they came to Hawaii, to 1983, the Kindschis were together socially with the Rewalds an average of two or three times a month.

"The [Rewald] children looked upon us sort of as almost grandparents," Kindschi testified. He participated with the Rewald family in backyard basketball and tennis games, he said.

Meanwhile, Rewald was put to work for his country. Welch testified that the CIA's Hawaii office wasn't a covert station, such as existed overseas, but rather a field office such as existed in cities around the United States to collect data volunteered by American citizens traveling abroad. The office was supposed to be "discreet, perhaps, but not secret."

Rewald and his growing staff at Bishop, Baldwin were jet-hopping the globe, seeking investors and trade deals—often involving arms—from Argentina to India to the Philippines. So Welch, Kindschi, and Rewald made a deal whereby the Bishop, Baldwin staff would collect intelligence for the CIA. They would get questions, sometimes in writing, from Kindschi before leaving, then return with lengthy reports.

Welch testified that he asked CIA headquarters in Langley, Virginia, for a name check on Rewald, seeking derogatory information. Despite the criminal conviction and bankruptcies, Welch said nothing showed up, and a CIA file card on Rewald shows that he was approved for a "secret" security clearance in September 1978, and continued with it until the Bishop, Baldwin bankruptcy five years later.

Welch made no bones about the CIA's limited criteria for trustworthiness: he testified that the purpose of the name check was to make sure there was "no derogatory information on file—he is not a Communist, in other words." Mitchell P. Lawrence, Jr., the CIA's deputy director for personnel security and investigation, a thirty-year veteran of both undercover and administrative posts, testified that "based on the volume of work" the FBI didn't like to search criminal records for the CIA unless it was given a fingerprint card, and so normally checked only "what we referred to as the subversive files."

Theft, never mind.

Rewald's clearance meant he could participate in discussions of information classified as "confidential" or "secret," but not "top secret." Kindschi testified that when CIA headquarters asked him to provide a cover for covert operatives in Asia, he suggested Rewald; and headquarters approved the choice on November 6, 1978.

A phony company was established in Rewald's office, with telex and telephone. The CIA paid the bill. Messages could be passed back and forth, and whenever someone called to check on an agent's bona fides, Rewald and his staff would give a positive response.

Then in May 1979, Rewald got involved with the foreign resources section of the CIA, whose job is to recruit foreign nationals visiting the United States to spy on their own countries for the CIA when they go home. Charles Richardson, chief of the foreign resources section in the western United States, asked the CIA for a substantial international company to serve as cover employer for his attempts to persuade foreign nationals. Kindschi was asked for a suggestion, and volunteered Rewald. This time, instead of a phony company, the cover was to be CMI, the actual Rewald investment concern, which became Bishop, Baldwin.

This was a still more sensitive assignment, and the CIA dispatched John H. Mason, a twenty-five-year veteran formerly in the clandestine services, now assigned to headquarters, to check Rewald and his company out. Kindschi forwarded a glowing report, falsely asserting such nonsense as that "Former clients have ranged from Elvis Presley to professional athletes and millionaires."

A new security check was done. This time, the FBI evidently wasn't too busy to cooperate, and the franchise violation was discovered (though apparently not the theft or bankruptcy cases). Moreover, Rewald told Mason and other CIA officials that he had worked for the CIA as a student spy. In fact, he said that so much bad publicity had come upon him when the student spying operation was exposed that he wanted the CIA to forgo the usual questioning of his former neighbors while doing this new check. And the CIA men testified that they agreed!

Deputy Director Lawrence testified that CIA files were checked and showed that Rewald *hadn't,* as he said, spied for the agency as a student. Despite that discrepancy, despite the criminal record, and despite such easily checkable lies on Rewald's résumé as that he graduated from Marquette University and played football for the Cleveland Browns (neither of which was remotely true), the CIA renewed his secret clearance and okayed him for the new, more sensitive work.

As for CMI, the only checking that the officials of the free world's greatest spy agency said they did was to order a Dun & Bradstreet report. They relied on it, even though veteran agent Mason agreed that a typical D & B report "only reflects what the individual company submits to D & B."

Testified Deputy Director Lawrence, "We had to weigh what we had against the need for Mr. Rewald." The work, he testified, was "very important." Agent Mason had argued that the cover was "needed badly."

So much for the contention that the CIA would not have needed Nugan Hand because larger companies were available! Nugan Hand may not have been Chase Manhattan, but it was big enough to dwarf Rewald's operation. And yet Rewald's Hawaiian company had been "needed badly."

Mason introduced Rewald to secret agent Richardson, who was using the alias Richard Cavanaugh. Rewald evidently met other covert operatives, but Kindschi, not having a need to know, testified that he didn't get further involved with that.

While covering for agents and taking in millions from duped investors, Rewald was hardly living in the obscurity that people like Royal Commissioner Stewart say they expect of the CIA. Rewald spent about $400,000 a month to keep lavish offices around the world and a high-salaried staff of prominent Hawaiians, including lawyers and CPAs. He spent $250,000 a month to please himself and his family.

He owned a fleet of twelve limousines and other luxury cars worth up to $50,000 each (an Excalibur, a Jaguar, two Mercedes, a Rolls, a Continental, and three Cadillacs, among others), and he hired chauffeurs not just for himself but also to take his five children to baseball practice, or to lessons with their $9,000-a-month private tutors.

He owned ranches, and polo clubs, and an oceanfront villa with its own lagoon and gardens. He displayed fine art and antiques, threw eye-popping parties, and surrounded himself with gorgeous women, some of whom were supplied with their own Mercedeses.

His CIA contacts didn't seem to be dummies. Welch had joined the CIA in 1952, and spent a career procuring and managing overseas safe-houses and running several domestic intelligence collection offices. Kindschi had been a State Department foreign service officer in Moscow and Cairo, then entered the CIA's clandestine services branch in 1957, and stayed there until he got the Honolulu job for his last two years before retirement. (He also testified that he was forced out of the clandestine services in part because CIA turncoat Philip Agee exposed him as a CIA man.)

When retirement came, in 1980, Kindschi became a $60-an-hour consultant for Bishop, Baldwin, with an office in the firm's luxury suite and plenty of expense-account travel. Eventually he began receiving a $4,000-a-month salary on top of the consultant's fees. He brought an old friend from his CIA days in Stockholm onto the staff as a business consultant, too.

Kindschi's replacement as head of the Hawaii CIA office, Jack W. Rardin, went into the CIA immediately upon graduation from the prestigious Georgetown University School of Foreign Service in 1950. He worked first in foreign broadcast operations, then in the domestic collection division. From the time he arrived in Hawaii, he was frequently seen in the swank Bishop, Baldwin office, conferring with Rewald.

Among other matters, they discussed the influential millionaire businessmen Rewald was soliciting investments from in Indonesia, the Philippines, and elsewhere—men Rewald would also milk for political gossip. They also discussed the arms deals Rewald was trying to finance in India and Taiwan, apparently without success.

On official reports, Rardin rated Rewald "from good to excellent" as a source, and on what he acknowledged was "a number of occasions" he called Rewald's information "excellent." For example, about the time of the British-Argentine war over the Falklands in 1982, Rewald visited Argentina armed with a list of CIA questions. Under the guise of Bishop, Baldwin business, he queried Argentine bankers about their financial plans.

Rewald also reported to a CIA man identified in court only as "John Doe 5" at a "Far East location." More than a dozen CIA "John Does" were involved in the Rewald trial.

As time passed, several other Bishop, Baldwin staffers were referred for security clearances to the "secret" level. Some of them, it turned out, already *had* it. Rardin testified that when he applied for clearance for Captain Edwin Davis Avary, retired chief pilot of Pan American World Airways, and now a Bishop, Baldwin consultant, he was told that Avary was already in a relationship with the agency. Avary* gives a sly no-comment on whether he did CIA work at Pan Am. But he says he and others wrote "damned good reports" for the CIA while on trips for Bishop, Baldwin. (He cites an analysis he did of German election prospects.) He also worked on the Taiwanese arms deal.

Sue Wilson, Rewald's blond executive assistant (with check-writing authority), had—after being a semifinalist in the Miss Teenage America pageant—served nine years with the National Security Agency (the CIA's high-technology twin) in Washington and Honolulu before joining Bishop, Baldwin. Her résumé shows she handled highly sensitive cryptoanalysis, missile trajectory data, and space data.

One lawyer on the Bishop, Baldwin staff, Lieutenant Clarence Gunderson, was a reserve air force intelligence officer. On the investment firm's collapse, he was quickly back in uniform, giving

*Interview with the author.

intelligence briefings to the commander-in-chief of the air force's Pacific Command, and dealing in highly classified Soviet data.*

One commander Gunderson briefed was three-star General Arnold Braswell, who was widely identified as among Rewald's circle of allies. Braswell acknowledges** he was weighing going to work for Bishop, Baldwin when he retired from the air force. He filed a six-figure claim in bankruptcy court for loss of his savings, which he said he had invested with the firm.

A prior air force Pacific Commander, four-star General Hunter Harris, the highest-ranking officer in Hawaii, was close to Rewald and frequently in his office. Through Harris, Rewald met an aide of Lieutenant Colonel James ("Bo") Gritz, who was raising money with Pentagon help for a secret expedition into Laos to look for U.S. prisoners of war Gritz believed were still being held there; the mission was highly publicized after it failed.

General Harris and the Gritz aide say Rewald merely donated $2,000 of Bishop, Baldwin money to the cause. Rewald told investors and potential investors that he was financing the Gritz mission, and they were impressed when they read about the mission in the newspapers months after Rewald had confided to them that it was going to occur.

Clients who lost fortunes in the Bishop, Baldwin fraud say Rewald would call them aside privately, either in his office or at his lavish parties at the private polo club he bought, and would point out the high government officials around. He would single out CIA and FBI personnel for particular attention. He would note that Bishop, Baldwin was part of the CIA, though cautioning the clients never to repeat it.

The CIA connection proved their money was safe, he assured them. "If you can't trust the government, who can you trust?" they recall him saying.

His parties were attended not only by federal officials, but by Governor and Mrs. George Ariyoshi and other Hawaiian dignitaries. The office of then Lieutenant Governor, now Governor John Waihee, has acknowledged that Waihee received a $10,000 canceled check to him that Rewald has shown around. (The governor's staff says the check was a down payment on a business transaction that

*Author interviews with Gunderson and others in Hawaii.

**Interview with the author.

was never completed, and that the money was returned to Rewald.)

Were all these officials and service leaders suckered in by Rewald's fraud? As with Nugan Hand, that explanation requires one to believe that people who are supposed to be experts in intelligence, who are charged with protecting the United States from the deceptive practices of the Kremlin, are pretty easily led.

For example, while operating for three years directly in the eye of CIA officials, Rewald advertised that Bishop, Baldwin's deposits were protected by the Federal Deposit Insurance Corporation for up to $150,000 for each depositor. The FDIC, of course, insures only banks, not private investment firms like Bishop, Baldwin, and its limit was $100,000 for each depositor, as any bank advertisement would have revealed.

Kindschi recalled at the trial that he had asked Rewald about this, and was told, "Well, we have a special relationship with the banks to increase it to $150,000." Kindschi acknowledged that after that, he had reassured Bishop, Baldwin clients who asked about the FDIC limit. Kindschi testified that he didn't question Rewald further because "I trusted him."

This was the same fearless and resourceful covert operative who also told the jury, "When you serve overseas under deep cover, you do not have the full force of the United States behind you. . . . You are on your own. So if things had gone a-cropper in places where I served, I would have been left to get out of that situation with my own wits, and I understood that."

Kindschi, employing those wits at Bishop, Baldwin for $60 an hour, eventually helped prepare brochures containing some of the more outrageous Rewald lies. Though the CIA men knew Rewald had just come to Hawaii in 1978, Kindschi acknowledged that he "edited" a brochure calling Bishop, Baldwin "one of the oldest and largest privately held international investment and consulting firms in Hawaii. . . . Over the last two decades we have served the investment and consulting community with an average return to our clients of 26% a year."

Merely the name of the firm was a gross deception. Bishop, Baldwin, and Dillingham are old-line aristocratic names in Hawaii, as almost everyone there knew. It was as if someone had started a firm in New York City with the name "Rockefeller, Vanderbilt, Rewald, Roosevelt & Mellon."

Kindschi testified that he believed Rewald's explanation that somehow Bishop, Baldwin "came directly from the bowels of the old Bishop Investment Company."

Asked why he wrote, "The brick and mortar foundation of Bishop, Baldwin, Rewald, Dillingham & Wong has been deeply rooted in Hawaii for more than four decades," he testified, "It could have been just a typographical error."

He wrote—or "edited"—that the company's clients had an average worth of $4 million, and that 90 percent of those who tried to invest with the firm were turned down. (Rewald made it seem a personal favor to people, done out of friendship, to take their mere five-figure investments.) Bishop, Baldwin "has served the last four national administrations as White House consultants on subjects ranging from small business matters to the complex international relations of Asia," the brochure Kindschi edited said.

He told the jury he simply accepted Rewald's word for all this. He also testified that he was aware by 1979 that Rewald had a court record in Wisconsin for franchise violations. And he acknowledged that the brochures he helped prepare showed CIA agent Richardson as a Bishop, Baldwin consultant.

Bishop, Baldwin also advertised widely that its investment accounts "have been available since Territorial days," and that the firm worked for committees of both houses of Congress and "a former president of the United States," all of which was nonsense.

Bishop, Baldwin offered two financial statements with figures differing by one decimal place, apparently geared to differing levels of gullibility. One statement, for example, put accounts receivable at $187.9 million and total assets at $1.42 billion, while another put accounts receivable at $18.7 million and total assets at $142 million. (There hasn't been any evidence that Kindschi helped prepare the financial statements.)

Neither statement had a standard auditor's certification letter; one statement said "audited by Price-Waterhouse" under the figures, and the other just said "audited by a 'Big Eight' accounting firm." Apparently neither Price Waterhouse nor anyone else audited Bishop, Baldwin. The bankruptcy trustee said its checkbook was never even balanced.

Rewald says the CIA ordered the phony statements and approved them; he did produce documentary evidence that the CIA concocted a phony financial statement for the phony company that was set up in Rewald's office to serve as a cover for CIA operatives in the Far East. But the CIA men who testified all denied telling Rewald to do anything fraudulent in connection with Bishop, Baldwin.

Rewald told investors and his adulators in the local press that the company had two dozen offices with multimillion-dollar investments scattered around the world. Captain Avary, who prepared reports for the CIA while on Bishop, Baldwin's staff at $4,000 a month, says he helped establish "mail-drop" offices for Bishop, Baldwin in various cities by hiring an executive "front" firm to collect mail or telephone calls at a prestigious address. CIA documents produced in court show that unspecified Bishop, Baldwin offices overseas were in contact with CIA stations there.

Surely the case of Rewald is enough to disprove the Stewart commission's contention that someone who had real CIA connections would never advertise them. Rewald was the least secret agent imaginable. He cultivated his reputation for being wired into the agency. He acquired title to his first Honolulu home from former Cambodian Prime Minister Lon Nol, and spread the word that the house was really a CIA-owned "safe house." When he moved to his oceanfront villa, he deeded the supposed "safe house" over to Russell Kim, a Bishop, Baldwin consultant from Korea, whom Rewald says is a Korean intelligence agent, and who did receive a security clearance from the CIA up to the "secret" level.

A typical victim, Nella Van Asperen, says her impression that Rewald was an important CIA figure led her and her parents to invest—and lose—$400,000 in the firm, mostly her parents' retirement money. Mrs. Van Asperen—a commercial artist and another gorgeous blonde—had been approached by Rewald to design advertisements for a sporting goods chain he was starting in Honolulu.

Right after the Soviet invasion of Afghanistan, she was introduced to a traveling Afghan jeweler who was desperate to extend his thirty-day visa to the United States so he wouldn't have to return home. Says Mrs. Van Asperen, "Ron had told me he was with the CIA, and I thought if anybody can help he could." Rewald arranged a meeting for the Afghan with "the CIA," under conditions worthy of a Graham Greene spy novel.

"You will walk down this block, you will turn here, you will wait at this place," Mrs. Van Asperen says he told her. She and the Afghan wound up at an outdoor café with Rewald and two strange men. The Afghan, now working in San Diego, says he was asked a lot of questions about his father, an army general, and about the use of chemical weapons and Chinese arms. Then, he says, a "Mr. Anderson" gave him a business card and told him to take it to the U.S. immigration office, where he would be given political asylum. He says the immigration office seemed to recognize the card and gave him a long-term visa, and that he never heard from "Mr. Anderson" again.

"It's hard for me to believe someone would set all this up as a charade," says Mrs. Van Asperen. She saw Rewald all too often after that, as he persuaded her and her father to deposit their cash. Often she and Rewald had lunch, but she says he always excused himself in time to return for what he said was his daily 3:30 P.M. briefing from the CIA. Once, she says, he even invited her to join the CIA, but he later advised her not to because of "the danger." (He did sign up two men, however, administering secrecy oaths to them; the CIA officials who testified at his trial said the oaths and ceremonies were worthless.)

More tragic was the case of Mary Lou McKenna, a blonde former Playboy model who had just moved to Hawaii because of devastating medical problems. Living in Los Angeles, divorced and raising three children, she had undergone cancer surgery. Then her back was broken in two places in a car accident, leading to spinal fusion operations that were only partially successful, and left her hampered in movement and requiring long-term therapy. Finally, she contracted a rare, life-threatening lung disease that required her to live in a warm, non-smoggy climate.

With about $150,000 put together from savings and from the jury award in her accident case, she moved her family to Hawaii, and happened to land in the same apartment building where Jacqueline Vos lived. Vos, a Farrah Fawcett look-alike, was keeping books for Rewald.* Soon, McKenna was being invited to polo parties where Vos and Rewald introduced her to General Harris and Governor Ariyoshi, and pointed out "all these men in dark-looking suits" as being CIA and FBI agents.

Soon, Rewald had Mary Lou McKenna's nest egg. On advice from his legal staff, she sold some property in California, so this, too, could be invested in Bishop, Baldwin. When the firm collapsed, she was forced to move out of her Honolulu apartment, sell her furniture, stop the physical therapy, and take a store clerk's job that caused her severe back pain. She was visibly aching and despondent.

There were scores of other cases.

In 1982, the Internal Revenue Service smelled something fishy and started a criminal investigation of Rewald and his company.

*She says she believed what he said as everyone else did, and she hasn't been charged with a crime.

When Rewald was asked to produce records, Rardin, with Kindschi's help, had the CIA intervene with the IRS to hold up the audit. Rewald told Rardin he had received not only business expense money from the CIA, but also funds for passing to various people around the globe.

Two officers from CIA headquarters in Langley, Virginia, visited Hawaii in January 1983. In front of them, Rewald changed his story, saying that the only money he had received was for business expenses. The flip-flop didn't bother Rardin. The CIA gave Rewald phony cover stories to tell both the IRS and his accountant about the source of the money. Asked at the trial why Rewald's status continued unchanged, Rardin simply testified, "At the time, we trusted Mr. Rewald's integrity."

The CIA says its hold-up of the IRS criminal investigation was merely temporary, to allow time to create a cover story for the small amounts of expense money it gave him. But the fact is that ten months after the IRS had moved to investigate, the investigation was still frozen, and Rewald was still stealing.

At that point, in late July 1983, a local consumer protection agency, troubled by Rewald's FDIC claims, subpoenaed his books and records. Moreover, it leaked its suspicions—along with its discovery of Rewald's bankruptcy record in Wisconsin—to a local TV news reporter. The reporter confronted a Rewald aide with a camera crew and played the embarrassing interview on the air.

That day, Kindschi withdrew $170,000 of what he said was $291,000 that he and his mother had on deposit at Bishop, Baldwin. (The bankruptcy court later forced him to return it. He filed a claim for the money, but the court-appointed trustee filed a counterclaim against him. The trustee argued that almost all the money that Kindschi claimed was still on deposit represented fictitious interest and dividends that Rewald had credited to the Kindschis' accounts, or else was money that Kindschi had in effect already reclaimed through the high fees and salary he was collecting. The case is still pending.)

For his part, Rewald, after hearing about the TV interview, quickly emptied out Bishop, Baldwin's bank account with a $200,000 check to his lawyer, apparently as a defense fund, and sent his wife and children back to Wisconsin. His security guards began removing files from the Bishop, Baldwin office.

Rewald checked into a large Waikiki hotel. The next afternoon, the hotel's assistant manager, making her routine rounds of rooms whose occupants were due to check out but hadn't, found Rewald amidst a lot of blood. His wrists and forearms had been slit by a razor found nearby. Police took him to a hospital, where doctors described the wounds as "superficial" and said no vascular or nerve damage had been done.

He had reacted like a gutless Frank Nugan. He may well have known about Nugan. Remarkably, police later said they never checked to see if the blood found in the room had come from Rewald's body or had been brought there.

As the huge scandal dominated the Hawaiian press, efforts were made to cover up all traces of the CIA. Rardin denied to the police that he even knew Rewald. A federal judge put blanket restrictions on visitors to Rewald in prison, where he was held on an astronomical $10 million bail. The judge issued gag orders barring Rewald's lawyers from repeating what he told them. Case records, normally public information in a criminal matter, were sealed from public view, and Rewald was ordered not to talk about the CIA. The CIA won't comment on whether it disciplined any of its agents.

Most remarkably, the U.S. Attorney in Hawaii, Daniel Bent, turned this, his biggest case, over to a brand new lawyer on his staff, John Peyton. Peyton had come to work at the office just days after Rewald slashed his wrists. Peyton's grand jury investigation of the Rewald case was distinguished by its careful avoidance of any reference to the CIA; Rardin, for example, was identified to the grand jury as just a federal civil servant.

Once you learn Peyton's background, however, none of this seems so strange. From 1976 to early 1981, it turns out, Peyton had been chief of the litigation section of the CIA. After that, he had worked on the government's narcotics task force in Florida, which intelligence community sources say was heavily laced with CIA personnel. Suddenly, then, Peyton decided to seek work as an assistant prosecutor in Hawaii.

Peyton insists that it was just "pure, utter coincidence" that he wound up on the Rewald case.* The U.S. Government's explanation for both the Bishop, Baldwin and Nugan Hand cases, to the extent it has provided one at all, seems to rely in large part on an almost mystical faith in the power of "pure, utter coincidence."

Late in 1986, American citizens got still better evidence of the damage wrought by their government's foreign policy of perpetual covert war. For the second time in eight years, Iran humiliated the United States and crippled a president.

*Interview with the author.

We had given Iranians every reason to want to do that. Back in 1953, at the behest of an oil monopoly, and blinded by a foreign policy that mistakes other countries' independence for communism, the United States overthrew the only even semi-democratically elected government in Iranian history. In its place, we installed a brutal and unpopular dictatorsnip. That all this was done covertly merely kept the American electorate from finding out about it; the Iranians knew damn well that the U.S. was behind the restoration and maintenance of the Shah.

Among those American officials who did the most to help the Shah preserve his regime of repression and torture was General Richard Secord, who headed the U.S. military assistance program there while palling around with the likes of Bernie Houghton and Edwin Wilson. There was a certain delicious irony in the fact that it was Secord who organized and went along on the arms-running mission with national security advisor Bud McFarlane that the Iranians used to entrap President Reagan. But as an American, it's hard to get much satisfaction from it.

From the day he took office President Reagan had preached about the need to isolate "terrorist states," and specifically identified Iran as one of them. We must, he repeated at every opportunity, refuse even to bargain with hostage-takers, let alone pay ransom to them. Then, it turns out, he *arms* them. And with the arrival of the Secord-McFarlane arms shipment, an Iranian-influenced group in Lebanon releases one American hostage while holding on to a half-dozen others. And soon seizes more.

At first the president denied the arms shipments were ransom for hostages. Then he rather acknowledged they could be fairly interpreted that way.

At first he insisted that only a few "spare parts" were involved. Then he acknowledged that we shipped Iran planeloads of "defensive" antiaircraft missiles (which could just as well attack a 747) and antitank missiles (which could just as well attack an American official's bulletproof limousine).

For purposes of deception—not of the Soviets, but of Congress and the American public—the income from these sales and other money was channeled through numbered Swiss bank accounts. Among those deceived, inadvertently, were two of the plotters, Colonel Oliver North and Assistant Secretary of State Elliott Abrams, who lost $10 million by getting the account numbers wrong.

And who was put in charge of the secret Swiss accounts? Why, General Richard Secord, who two years earlier had resigned from the

Pentagon under a cloud for his involvment with Edwin Wilson in what former CIA officer Thomas Clines admitted in federal court was a fraud against the U.S. Government; Clines's various companies paid more than $3 million in fines and penalties for the fraud. And who did Secord hire as his chief aide in the Iran-Contra mission? Why, Thomas Clines, of course—the same Thomas Clines who, in the wake of the Nugan Hand collapse, jetted to Australia and accompanied Bernie Houghton on his flight from the country so he could hide out until the heat was off.

By his own testimony before Congress, Secord (or the company he owned 50–50 with his partner Hakim) collected $30 million from Iran for weapons he simultaneously bought from the U.S. Treasury for $12 million. Of the difference, he testified, only $3.5 million went to help the Contras (some of whom complained they hadn't received a dime). Secord testified that the Contras were desperately short of funds and that Colonel North was scrounging for donations for them; yet he testified that $8 million from the arms sales remained unspent in the Swiss account he controlled (not to mention the $10 million from the Sultan of Brunei that was lost in transit). Why wasn't the $8 million sent to the Contras if Secord and his partner didn't intend to keep it? The question was never satisfactorily answered.

Of even more concern to common decency was the hiring of assassination experts like Chi-Chi Quintero and Luis Posada from Clines's old anti-Cuban campaigns to work in the supply program in Central America. Posada, a CIA operative, had been in jail in Venezuela for blowing up a Cuban civilian airliner in mid-flight over Barbados, killing seventy-three persons. (Venezuelan justice had not seen fit to bring him to trial in nine years, but the evidence against him, including tape-recorded telephone conversations, was substantial.) Though the CIA disclaimed responsibility for that terrorist act, when Posada escaped his Venezuelan jail (apparently through bribery, not derring-do), the CIA, or the Secord Clines network it set in place, hired him back to help kill Nicaraguans.

Meanwhile, evidence was building that the Contra program was supported not just by arms shipments to Iran, but also by dope trafficking. In October 1986, a Contra supply plane crashed in Nicaragua killing most of its crew and leaving one a prisoner in Managua. Reporters found all sorts of links between the plane and the CIA, from its registration to the phone numbers found in the cockpit. They also discovered that it was the same plane that convicted dope dealer Barry Seal had used to fly cocaine in while he was working as part of a federal "sting" operation. Witnesses then placed Seal in the Contra supply program while he was earning a self-declared $50 million running cocaine into the U.S.

Other witnesses reported seeing cocaine stored at a south Florida house where Contra arms were warehoused before being shipped out. One woman reported seeing cocaine being loaded in Colombia onto a Contra supply plane that had dropped off weapons in Central America and was headed back to the U.S. Gerardo Duran, a pilot who ferried arms and personnel around for many Contra groups, was named by Costa Rican and American authorities as a cocaine trafficker. (He wasn't charged in court.)

Costa Rican-based Contras were also involved in a 400-pound cocaine seizure in San Francisco in 1983. Two Nicaraguan natives convicted in the case, Carlo Cabezas and Julio Zavala, who are brothers-in-law, later claimed that at least $500,000 of their drug profits was sent to Contras in Costa Rica. Some $36,000 found by federal agents in Zavala's house—along with cocaine, a military rifle, and a grenade—was seized as drug profits. But amazingly, the money was returned to Zavala by the Justice Department on certification by a Contra group in Costa Rica that the money belonged to it. (And the person whose signature was on the certification later claimed it was a lie. The Contra leader, Vicente Rappacciolli Marquiz, said he falsely certified that he had given the $36,000 to Zavala to help his friend, the dope dealer. This added considerable credibility to Zavala's claims that he donated large drug funds to the Contras.)

The most clear-cut case of all involved a Costa Rica-based Contra group that struck a deal with George Morales, a multimillionaire Colombian-born cocaine kingpin living in Miami, right after Morales was indicted on multiple federal drug charges in 1984. According to both Morales and members of the Contra group, the Contras promised to use their CIA connections to take care of Morales's case if he helped them out.

Federal Aviation Administration and other aviation records confirm that Morales provided the Contras at least two aircraft, one of them costing $264,000 and the other of undetermined value, as well as trained pilots (including Duran). There is some corroboration for his statements that he also provided large amounts of cash, both his own drug money and contributions he solicited in the Miami Cuban community.

Aircraft maintenance receipts show that while Morales awaited trial, and while he continued to bring large amounts of cocaine into the U.S. (according to federal charges he was later convicted on), an airplane he gave to the Contras regularly refueled at Ilopango Air

Force base in El Salvador. The receipts show that the fuel was supplied by the Salvadoran Air Force, though the base is under joint American-Salvadoran security. Ilopango has been a main transshipment point for arms going from the U.S. to the Contra bases in southern Honduras and northern Costa Rica.

In the spring of 1987, a variety of House and Senate committees plunged hastily and at first, at least, ineptly into investigations that might answer some questions about the Contra operations. Somewhere in the files of one such panel, the Senate Intelligence Committee, however, there is probably still a list of other unanswered questions. The author of this book provided the list at the committee's request after a series of articles he wrote about Nugan Hand appeared in the *Wall Street Journal* in 1982.

Robert Simmons, then chief counsel to the committee, praised the list as "extremely valuable" and said it formed the basis for closed-door testimony the committee took from CIA director William Casey and others. "Unfortunately," Simmons explained, "the answers can never be made known to you." They were all secret.

An edited set of the questions is appended on the pages following. Some original questions, whose answers have since been tracked down independently and are published in this book, are deleted from the list.

APPENDIX

The Questions Whose Answers Are Secret

1. Did any U.S. intelligence agency ever have a relationship with Bernie Houghton? What was the nature and duration of the relationship?

2. What were the dates of Michael Hand's employment by any U.S. intelligence agency, whether on a permanent or contract or other ad hoc assignment, and what was his work?

3. Did the CIA ever have a relationship with Frank Nugan? What was the nature and duration of the relationship?

4. Admiral Yates has said that Dale Holmgren, while an officer of Nugan Hand and officially retired from the intelligence service, continued to work actively to develop "a close relationship with the U.S. military forces and the business and government community" on Taiwan. What was the exact nature of Holmgren's relationship with the U.S. military or intelligence community, or the U.S. Government at all, while he worked for Nugan Hand?

5. How and when did Bernie Houghton meet Admiral Yates? What was the nature and duration of their relationship? Did Houghton, as Sir Paul Strasser has said, have letters of recommendation from Admiral Yates and other high-ranking U.S. military officers when he arrived in Australia in 1967? If so, how did this come about?

6. Colonel Allan Parks, U.S. Air Force (ret.), has said that while serving undercover for U.S. intelligence as an official of the U.S.

embassy in Vientiane, Laos, in the 1960s, he became aware that Bernie Houghton was generally known by U.S. intelligence to be transporting contraband such as drugs and gambling devices around Southeast Asia, along with surplus military equipment and other goods. Talks with numerous persons make clear that Houghton had such a reputation. Colonel Parks has said that Houghton's movements were frequently recorded on cable traffic he saw at the embassy, and that General Aderholt was also aware of it. What did the U.S. intelligence agencies do with their information and records on Houghton? Did the United States ever attempt to stop his trafficking in contraband? If so, how? If not, why not? Did the United States make its knowledge of Houghton's trafficking in contraband available to Yates and others who met with him while on active duty, and who later went to work for Nugan Hand?

7. It seems inevitable that U.S. intelligence would have developed further information on Houghton during the years when he was the primary caterer to the social needs of U.S. servicemen on R & R in Sydney. There is abundant evidence that he was well known to various U.S. political, military, and intelligence officials. This period overlapped several years when Houghton was a critical factor in the operation of Nugan Hand, though not yet an officer of it. Were any records kept of his relationships with U.S. officials? If so, what do they reflect, and what use has been made of them? If not, considering his friendships with so many important people—including at least two CIA station chiefs, Milt Wonus and John Walker—why not?

8. What was the nature and duration of the CIA's relationship with Kermit L. ("Bud") King (former Air America pilot)? Does any U.S. Government agency have a file on King's mysterious death during his business association with Michael Hand? If so, does it—or any other intelligence file—reveal participation by Hand in any illegal activities, including but not limited to bringing drugs out of Asia? What use was made of this information? Were U.S. military and intelligence officers who dealt with Hand before and after their retirement informed of this?

9. Does any U.S. intelligence or law enforcement agency have a record of any drug transactions that Hand or Houghton carried on with people from the Asian mainland, including, but not limited to, Khun Sa, the military leader from the Shan States of Burma? Were U.S. military and intelligence officers who dealt with Hand before and after their retirement informed of this?

10. When did U.S. intelligence agencies first become aware that Nugan Hand was soliciting large deposits in violation of the foreign exchange control laws of many countries? That it was moving money for illegal drug dealers? That it was soliciting deposits from U.S. citizens in Saudi Arabia and elsewhere? That it was soliciting deposits from U.S. servicemen, including on U.S. military bases? What use was made of this knowledge?

11. Why was Michael Hand allowed to keep his U.S. passport after he accepted Australian citizenship?

12. Why were the Australian visa problems of Bernie Houghton, a U.S. citizen, in February 1972, solved by the intervention of a top official (Leo Carter) of the Australian Security Intelligence Organization? What do U.S. intelligence agencies know of any relationship that Houghton, or any other Nugan Hand figure, had with ASIO? When and how did U.S. intelligence agencies become aware of this?

13. Has any oversight authority examined records of cable traffic that Christopher Boyce might have seen while working for TRW Corp., to see if the facts might justify his charges that the cable traffic indicated U.S. involvement in Australian political and labor affairs? What records were located, who examined them, and what were the findings? Do records of any cable traffic or other records from any U.S. intelligence organization provide evidence to support charges, made by Boyce, by several officials of the Australian Labor Party, and by others, that the U.S. involved itself in Australian domestic political or labor activities, or provided covert impetus for the removal of Prime Minister Gough Whitlam from office in 1975?

14. Did any U.S. intelligence agency ever have a relationship with, or arrange for money to be paid to or on behalf of, former Australian Governor General John Kerr? If so, please provide details. Did any representative of the U.S. Government communicate, directly or indirectly, with Kerr in the week prior to his dismissal of Gough Whitlam? What was the nature of the communication?

15. People who knew Bernie Houghton well in Australia say that he was given access to U.S. military transport at Richmond Air Base there. Is this true? Why did it happen?

16. Was there any official relationship, on a contract basis or otherwise, between Houghton and the former Australian CIA station chiefs Walker and Wonus?

17. After Hand's tour of duty in Laos with the CIA, did he at any time return to the U.S. for further training or briefing by any U.S. intelligence agency? Did Houghton ever get such training or briefing?

18. During Hand's time in southern Africa or Rhodesia, and during his time in Panama, did he have any contact with, or relationship with, anyone in any U.S. intelligence agency?

19. Did any employe or contract agent of any U.S. intelligence agency ever use the Nugan Hand organization to finance or otherwise arrange arms deals in southern Africa or elsewhere?

20. Did any employe or contract agent of a U.S. intelligence agency ever use Joe Judge to finance or arrange arms deals?

21. Did any U.S. intelligence agency ever use Nugan Hand to make payments to any individual or company for any purpose?

22. Was there any relationship between Patry Loomis and any person associated with Nugan Hand prior to Loomis's retirement from the CIA? Or after? Is there truth to a report in *Foreign Policy* magazine (winter 1982–83) that Loomis, perhaps using another name, was a director of a company in the Nugan Hand group?

23. What was the nature and duration of any relationship between Hand or Houghton and Theodore Shackley before Shackley left the CIA? What do U.S. intelligence agencies know of their relationships with Shackley after he retired from the CIA?

24. When and how did any U.S. intelligence agency become aware of a relationship between Thomas Clines and anyone associated with Nugan Hand, particularly Houghton? What is known about the nature and duration of the relationship? Did it exist before Clines left the CIA? Did Clines have any relationship with any U.S. intelligence agency after his announced retirement from the CIA? When and how did any U.S. intelligence agency become aware that Clines went to Australia shortly after Nugan Hand failed, and left Australia with Houghton? Has anyone looked for records of cable traffic between Clines and anyone involved in Nugan Hand? (Australian authorities say there was cable traffic between Clines and Hand while Clines was still with CIA.) Were any records found? Do any exist? What do they disclose?

25. When and how did any U.S. intelligence agency become aware of a relationship between Ricardo Chavez and anyone associated with Nugan Hand, particularly Houghton? What is

known about the nature and duration of the relationship? Did it exist while Chavez was still a contract agent for the CIA? Did Chavez have any relationship with any U.S. intelligence agency after his service as a CIA contract agent?

26. When and how did any U.S. intelligence agency become aware that Chavez was planning to work with Nugan Hand? What is known about their relationship?

27. Was any instruction given by any employe of any U.S. intelligence agency to any Australian, or to any Australian security agency, about Hand, Houghton, or Nugan Hand in general?

28. How and when did any U.S. intelligence agency first learn the identity of the mysterious "Charlie" who entered Australia and helped Michael Hand leave under a phony identity?

29. Has any U.S. intelligence agency been in contact with Hand since he left Australia in June 1980? When, how, and what happened?

30. When was the last contact that a U.S. intelligence agency had with Houghton? How did it occur, and what happened?

31. Did Naval Task Force 157 ever have representatives in Australia? Who were they and what did they do? Was Edwin Wilson ever one of them?

32. When and how did any U.S. intelligence agency become aware that Wilson and Houghton were meeting? What does U.S. intelligence know about the purpose and content of the meetings?

33. Did U.S. intelligence attempt to warn anyone working for Nugan Hand or any customers of Nugan Hand concerning what it knew about the people involved? Who was warned, and what was the nature and content of the warnings?

34. If any relationship between Houghton and U.S. intelligence or military agencies is denied, what could account for the frequent visits of important U.S. officials to such a seedy spot as the Bourbon and Beefsteak Bar?

35. Why were the FBI's files on Nugan Hand withheld from disclosure, even to Australian law enforcement authorities, on the ground that they would endanger U.S. "national defense or foreign policy"? How would our national defense or foreign policy be endangered by the release of these documents to anyone, particularly

to many properly constituted authorities assigned to investigate and prosecute Nugan Hand's violations of Australian law, specifically: the National Police, the joint state-federal police task force, the Corporate Affairs Commission inquiry under Geoffrey Nicholson, the New South Wales Attorney General's office, and the official liquidator, John O'Brien?

36. Why did FBI agent John Grant refuse to look at evidence of possible violation of U.S. law that John O'Brien, the official Australian liquidator for Nugan Hand, tried to show him?

37. To whom, and at what Australian government agency, does the FBI say it disclosed all its information on Nugan Hand? Why would it not do so to other authorized Australian law enforcement agencies with whom the FBI normally does exchange information on criminal matters?

38. When and how did U.S. intelligence or law enforcement agencies become aware of Nugan Hand's activities in the drug center of Chiang Mai, Thailand? What is known about these activities? Since there is abundant evidence that this activity involved criminal violations, at the very least of the law of Thailand, why has the information not been disclosed? Why did Richard Virden, information officer with the International Communications Agency, intervene to block Drug Enforcement Agency officers in Chiang Mai who were seeking to exchange information about Nugan Hand with a reporter? What information could they have disclosed if Virden had not intervened?

39. When and how did any U.S. intelligence agency become aware that Frank Nugan's telephone calls were being electronically intercepted? What is known about this? Does any U.S. intelligence agency know the contents of any intercepted conversations? Has any inquired?

40. Does any U.S. intelligence agency know any reason why John Owen, a former career British Navy officer working for Nugan Hand in Thailand, would prepare long, detailed reports of military capabilities and troop movements of the various armed factions in Southeast Asia, particularly Cambodia? Has U.S. intelligence ever obtained information from these reports? How?

41. Did any U.S. intelligence service ever receive information from any officer, director, employe, or agent of Nugan Hand on any subject?

42. Has U.S. intelligence had any dealings involving Prince Panya Souvanna Phouma? Has Nugan Hand played a part in any such dealings? Have any U.S. intelligence dealings with Prince Panya involved arms sales, or the possible operation of an air freight service, or a cloud-seeding service?

43. Has any U.S. intelligence agency ever had any dealings with Neil Evans, the Australian who represented Nugan Hand in Chiang Mai? What was the nature and duration of these dealings?

44. Has any U.S. intelligence agency ever had any dealings with Donald Beazley? What was the nature and duration of these dealings?

45. Has any U.S. intelligence agency ever had any dealings with George Shaw, or with relatives of his in Lebanon? What was the nature and duration of these dealings?

46. How did so many employes of Air America and Continental Air Service become shareholders of Australian and Pacific Holdings Ltd., the company Nugan and Hand founded before launching the Nugan Hand group? Did any U.S. Government agency facilitate these investments?

47. Has any U.S. intelligence agency ever had any dealings with Clive ("Les") Collings, Nugan Hand's Hong Kong representative? What was the nature and duration of these dealings?

48. Has any U.S. intelligence agency ever had any dealings with Wilfred Gregory, Nugan Hand's Philippine representative? What was the nature and duration of these dealings?

49. Has any U.S. intelligence agency ever had any dealings with John Needham, a co-founder of Nugan Hand? What was the nature and duration of these dealings?

50. Has any U.S. intelligence agency ever had any dealings with George Farris, a Nugan Hand Washington representative? What was the nature and duration of these dealings?

51. Has any U.S. intelligence agency ever had any dealings with the Wing-On Bank, Nugan Hand's Hong Kong bankers? What was the nature and duration of these dealings?

52. Has any U.S. intelligence agency ever had any dealings with the Inter-Alpha group of banking companies, which handled international accounts for Nugan Hand? What was the nature and duration of these dealings?

53. Has any U.S. intelligence agency ever had any dealings with Elizabeth Thomson, Nugan Hand's lawyer? What was the nature and duration of these dealings?

54. Has any U.S. intelligence agency ever had any dealings with Neil Scrimgeour, a Nugan Hand confidant in Western Australia? What was the nature and duration of these dealings?

55. When and how did U.S. intelligence become aware of Nugan Hand's plan to move Asian refugees to an island in the Caribbean? What thoughts, if any, did it render about this plan?

56. Does the U.S. Government know why millions of dollars were transferred from Nugan Hand accounts in Asia to a Nugan Hand account in Hawaii and then transferred on to Panama? Does the U.S. Government know what use was made of this money?

57. Has any U.S. intelligence agency ever had a relationship with the Hawaiian Trust Company, or Douglas Philpotts, an officer of that bank?

AFTERWORD*

The True Patriots

In his otherwise admirable fight against the scourge of drugs, fraud, illegal arms sales, and abuse of government power, Mr. Kwitny has maliciously maligned and assassinated the character of some truly great American heroes and in so doing has besmirched the reputations of the military and intelligence services of this nation. My purpose here is to defend the honor of those men and the services they represent.

The general comments herein concern only those people for whom I had some measure of responsibility for their involvement in Nugan Hand and for whom I can speak with great confidence. Their names are: General Edwin Black, General Erle Cocke, General LeRoy Manor, Mr. Dale Holmgren, Dr. Guy Pauker, Mr. Donald Beazley, Mr. William Colby, Mr. Walter McDonald, Mr. Robert Jantzen, and Mr. George Farris (hereinafter, THE TRUE PATRIOTS).

I specifically exclude all others, not because I consider them guilty

*PUBLISHER'S NOTE: The assertions and opinions in this afterword do not, obviously, reflect the views of the author. Admiral Yates's rebuttal is included here, at the author's request, because the book contains substantive criticisms of Admiral Yates's role in the Nugan Hand affair, and for five years he had refused to be interviewed by the author. The extraordinary offer of this opportunity to publish his views apparently induced the admiral to read proofs of *The Crimes of Patriots.*

This afterword has not been edited or altered. Mr. Kwitny stands by his account of the doings of Admiral Yates and his colleagues. The reader must decide for himself which version of events stands closer to the truth.

or care any less about their fair treatment, but because I do not have the time, space, or knowledge to defend them against the alleged crimes. I use the word "alleged" advisedly, for as of this date, more than seven years after the collapse of Nugan Hand, no crimes have been proven.

Before addressing the general reader, I direct my first comments to the Nugan Hand employees and investors, who were the principal victims of the bank failure. Each of The True Patriots has expressed to me a most genuine distress for your losses, particularly those of you whom they might have influenced to invest in Nugan Hand. Most of them lost significant sums of their own. For example, I never received any pay due me and personally lost over twenty-five thousand dollars in unreimbursed business expenses. We are, therefore, able to share both your agony and your anger.

Having devoted their lives to the service of their country and having often risked those lives in dangerous missions, The True Patriots highly treasure the morale and reputation of those who are taking the same risks today in our national defense. They are distressed over any damage done to that morale and reputation by such warped and distorted viewpoints as found in this book.

Each of them deplores the injury done to the relationship between the United States and Australia, a long, strong, and mutually important relationship, which the Soviet Union and its KGB Disinformation Service would dearly love to destroy.

For the above reasons they unanimously regret any distress that their association, however innocent, might have contributed to others. I add to these regrets my own remorse for having induced The True Patriots to join Nugan Hand. I must take full responsibility for that. They associated with Nugan Hand largely because of their trust in my assurances that I had gone to extraordinary lengths to determine the integrity of that organization and found no evidence whatsoever of a shortfall.

I informed them that my assurances were based on my personal interviews with a wide range of highly respectable, knowledgeable people and agencies, many of whom had a recognized duty to know the bona fides of Nugan Hand. These included: the managing directors of the two largest banks in Australia, which held Nugan Hand accounts; an agent of the Reserve Bank, which has responsibilities similar to our Federal Reserve Bank; the Premier of New South Wales, whose private office was adjacent to the Nugan Hand offices; two prominent Australian lawyers who had worked closely with Mr. Nugan; an agent of the Australian Tax Department, who was familiar with Mr. Nugan's tax work; the managing director of the Sydney subsidiary of Citicorp, who traded securities with Nugan Hand; a partner of the accounting firm that certified Nugan Hand records; vice-presidents of two large international banks that had accounts with Nugan Hand; the U.S. Consul General in Sydney; the desk officer in the Department of Commerce who publishes financial reports on Australian firms; agents of the Treasury Department; agents of the FBI; some highly satisfied clients of Nugan Hand; and several employees. Of all these, *none* gave any unfavorable information, and most had high praise. General Black and others interviewed similar groups, including prominent newspapers, with comparable results.

In recruiting THE TRUE PATRIOTS, I explained the substance of my lengthy conversations with Mr. Nugan and Mr. Hand about their ultimate objective to build an international "one-stop business shopping-center" organization to make it easier for small businesses to compete in the international marketplace against the multinational cartels. They liked the concept and the opportunity to pursue it. They believed, as I did, that their employment was honorable, that Mr. Nugan and Mr. Hand were honorable, successful, and reliable businessmen, with the highest sense of personal integrity and genuine concern for their clients.

In response to queries about how the firm made money, Mr. Nugan gave me an extensive mathematical dissertation, supported by genuine money market documents, on how to "gross-up" the interest yield on money by buying and selling discounted bills of exchange on the lively Sydney market. He later held a conference of other employees to explain this important aspect of Nugan Hand's money market operation. He further informed me and others that his law practice yielded four to twelve million dollars per year (a false claim, nevertheless substantiated by two other lawyers and a CPA) and that the money was always available as a drawdown to protect our client's deposits.

When I first joined Nugan Hand, I undertook an intensive self-taught accounting and business-law course, at the suggestion of Mr. Nugan, as a first step to better equip myself to make business judgments and eventually assume a position of responsibility and authority in Nugan Hand Bank. In a letter dated 24 January 1977 Mr. Nugan wrote as follows:

> Your title (which may be used on your business cards, letter heads, and in all business contexts) is "President, Swiss Pacific Bank and Trust Company." In this regard you shall be a member

> of the Board of Directors and shall be subject to the Managing Director, (Mr. Hand) and to the Chairman of the Board of Directors (Mr. Nugan) as well as to the Board of Directors meeting as a Board in the normal course. It is contemplated that as of about the time that an interest in the Bank is made available to you, the position of President will be given its full normal powers by the Board to the effect that you shall become the Chief Executive Officer of the Bank at that time.

The title became effective on 6 April 1977 and I resigned officially by letter on 12 October 1979, never having attended a board meeting or been given any executive authority. The cunning delays of Mr. Nugan (which I now believe were contrived to forestall me from gaining the authority and information that should have accompanied my title) prevented me from being able to determine the true financial status of the bank.

For example, in June 1977 Mr. Nugan gave me my first assignment: to call on the presidents of a hundred U.S. banks to tell them about Nugan Hand's guaranteed deposit arrangements. Though it yielded poor results, this four-month project and similar ones, such as the attempted purchases of various banks and the opening of new offices, constituted the major scope of my assigned duties and authorities and served as clever diversions to my efforts toward becoming an executive.

Following my resignation on 12 October 1979, I was placed on a consulting status to Mr. Hand personally, with no Nugan Hand Bank authority whatsoever. I was enrolled in the Harvard University Business School awaiting the scheduled formation of a Nugan Hand international holding company, in which I was promised options on a 20 percent interest and a seat on the board. Nugan Hand collapsed while I was still attending school, and I then learned that several others had been promised options on the same 20 percent.

Throughout my time of observation as president of Nugan Hand Bank, THE TRUE PATRIOTS served honestly and loyally the interests of Nugan Hand and its clients. They had grown up in the military service and spent their lives in the company of gentlemen well known for honesty and honor, where it is commonplace to risk one's life, not just one's money and reputation, based on the word of a colleague. Day-to-day association with that kind of integrity leads military men to trust their fellow man, and it should not be surprising that it led these men to trust me and my judgment. If any fault can be found, it was in this trust of me, for, to my knowledge, not one of them has committed any crime, violated any law, breached any ethical standard, nor performed any act for which they need be ashamed.

Furthermore, notwithstanding Mr. Kwitny's contempt for their findings, the Australian Royal Commission (the highest judicial body established to investigate the Nugan Hand affair) found no credible evidence to charge any of THE TRUE PATRIOTS with wrongdoing. In their investigation, one of the most thorough and widely reported in the history of the country, the commission developed 11,900 pages of testimony from 267 witnesses under oath. They searched the files of the FBI and held conferences with the highest officials in the CIA. They also found no credible evidence of involvement of the CIA. But where findings of the Royal Commission such as this do not fit his fabricated version of events, Mr. Kwitny casts suspicion on the integrity or intelligence of the commission.

It might be easy to say nothing and let the reader believe Mr. Kwitny's suggestion that THE TRUE PATRIOTS were all working for the CIA. To those about whom THE TRUE PATRIOTS care most, working for the CIA is certainly an honorable profession. But hiding behind that shield would be repugnant to each of them and disloyal to the many fine people who are, in fact, working for the CIA.

Mr. Kwitny does not have the benefit of a background in the military or intelligence services, yet he states authoritatively:

> The men this book is mostly concerned with have lived their lives in a world of spying and secrecy. . . . they have been trained to keep the taxpayers from . . . finding out what they do. Compunctions about lying have seldom impeded that effort. They entered their secret world under the cloak of patriotism. . . .

Millions of men and women who have served in the military and intelligence services will easily recognize this as a gross distortion of the truth. They know from first-hand experience that military men and most intelligence officers live remarkably open lives, abhor lying, invite and welcome fair-minded outside attention, and often disguise the depth of patriotism that guides them. This obvious example of distortion is part of a consistent thread of deceit in Mr. Kwitny's descriptions of all the events about which I have first-hand knowledge and leads me to suspect comparable distortions about unfamiliar events throughout his text.

For example, his story that I "raced" to Sydney, Australia, to destroy records is almost totally false. Records of customs, passports, and airlines and other documents readily show this. He even admits to possible error therein, but he nevertheless uses the story to advance the false accusation that I participated in the destruction of vital records. He also fails to note that the records of Nugan Hand Bank (the only Nugan Hand subsidiary in which I might reasonably be expected to have had some personal interest in the records) were located in Singapore, not Sydney.

Furthermore, he recounts minor and irrelevant differences in the accounts of witnesses, apparently to discredit the word of THE TRUE PATRIOTS, yet he fails to note the consistency of the testimonies of those PATRIOTS taken under oath, as was found by the Royal Commission.

He preposterously describes Nugan Hand's relatively small operation as "mammoth." If Nugan Hand was "mammoth," then what word is left to accurately describe Citicorp, a New York banking firm ten thousand (10,000) times the size of Nugan Hand? This sort of distortion pervades his work and makes one wonder about his motives and his efforts to achieve accuracy.

The book also describes an "elaborate code" system used to shield illegal activity. Yet, by any standard, it was the very simplest of codes, far less complicated than pig-latin, used principally to shorten cable messages. It was prominently posted by office telex machines, was widely distributed to employees, and was available to just about anyone who wanted to use it. Only the most unsophisticated and poorly informed would truly believe that this code could have been seriously used to conceal information. To stress on staff personnel a respect for clients' rights to privacy? Perhaps. But to hide from authorities?? One would have to assume that the authorities are stupid, blind, and illiterate, or that Mr. Kwitny merely wished to give a sinister cast to the story.

The book rails against THE TRUE PATRIOTS for failure, as insiders, to uncover and expose the alleged crimes of Nugan Hand, but Mr. Kwitny fails to note that three of the ten PATRIOTS never visited the Australian headquarters, where the alleged crimes were masterminded, directed, and executed; four of them made only one brief trip; and three made only two or three trips. I personally made only four short trips there, none longer than about ten days and two less than four days. None of THE TRUE PATRIOTS were employed by Nugan Hand Ltd. or any other Australian organization. None even knew about the various companies privately owned or controlled by Mr. Nugan and Mr. Hand, through which the alleged crimes were executed, and most certainly were never allowed to examine their records. The book does not reveal that only after three months of intensive analysis by an experienced former U.S. Federal Reserve

Board bank examiner, and a suicide, did the examiner find reason to suspect the true status of Nugan Hand. Even after seven years of study, the liquidating authority, with full access to the records, has been unable to unravel completely the complex accounting and record system which Mr. Nugan had established. To what extent is a prudent man expected to go to establish the integrity of his employer? Should it not suffice to check the certified assurances of reputable accountants, supervising government authorities, clients, business associates, other employees, and the record of past performance?

Through artfully fallacious reasoning, Mr. Kwitny has created criminals out of some noble and unfortunate victims. By reprinting the lies, innuendos, half-truths, loose associations, and distortions of cheap scandal sheets, left-wing newspapers, and communist-fed, anti-American sources, he has, wittingly or unwittingly, served the interests of the Soviet Union and the KGB Disinformation Service.

Finally, even excluding its gross inaccuracies and distortions, this book fails to make a valid case that any of THE TRUE PATRIOTS committed any crime. None were shown to have been involved in or even to have had knowledge of any drug traffic, illegal arms sales, or laundering of money. None of the deposits of their clients violated any currency or banking laws. None of THE TRUE PATRIOTS benefited materially from their association with Nugan Hand, and the only imprudence for which they might be accused is that they trusted a fellow officer.

Earl P. Yates
RADM USN (ret.)

Acknowledgments

This book would not exist without Vicki Barker and Marian Wilkinson. Marian defined the Nugan Hand story. Only her fascination with television left it for someone else to write the book, and she has helped in that immeasurably. Even more important, Vicki defined *me*, and through some terrible times she single-handedly maintained a sense of mission—gave me the reason to be writing at all. She talked about a moral compass; if there is one, she is the magnetic north.

On a somewhat more mundane plane, both Vicki and Marian provided extensive editorial suggestions, as did Robert Sack and Anthony Scaduto. The reader owes much to Starling Lawrence, my editor at Norton, and to Ellen Levine, my agent, for suggesting revisions. In the case of this book, however, I must single out my friend and *Wall Street Journal* colleague John Emshwiller for totally voluntary and herculean work that was primarily responsible for helping me prune out the 20 percent of the original manuscript that was, if not unfit, at least unnecessary for human consumption. Thank you to all, especially John.

John Kelly, editor of the *National Reporter*, was of enormous research help, particularly on the Bishop, Baldwin segment, an episode about which he will probably write a fine book of his own. Jonathan Marshall, editor of the editorial page of the *Oakland* (California) *Tribune*, also played an important part in alerting me to the significance of the Nugan Hand story, and to the work of Marian and her colleague at Australia's *National Times*, Brian Touhey.

For the first time, I have employed researchers to help with detail checking, and they performed sensationally. Vicki Contavespi in the United States was particularly energetic in turning telephone calls that were originally aimed at locating some statistic into interviews that produced unsuspected new information. Both she and Andrew Keenan, of the Sydney *Morning Herald*, in Australia, plumbed court records and bothered numerous people with telephone calls to make sure this book is accurate.

Seth Lipsky, now editor of the editorial page of the *Wall Street Journal/Europe* but then foreign editor of the *Wall Street Journal*, is really the father of this book. It was at his suggestion, having just returned from a stint at the *Journal*'s Hong Kong office in the spring of 1982, that I pulled open the file I had been keeping on Nugan Hand and began probing further. Lipsky had sensed the Nugan Hand story needed to be researched in more depth than the Hong Kong office was staffed for then, and the ensuing series of articles in the *Journal* proved him right.

Stewart Pinkerton, now the *Journal*'s deputy managing editor but then the New York bureau manager, supported the project fully, including signing expense vouchers for some places pretty far from New York. Jack Cooper edited the series in the page-one department. Probably most important of all, Robert Sack lawyered it. And there was important support from a succession of managing editors, including Frederick Taylor (then executive editor, who fended off the Reed Irvine crowd, which, I'm sure he would agree, required far more patience than wit, though Fred has plenty of both), Laurence O'Donnell, and Norman Pearlstine.

A special thanks to Lee Burton, the *Journal*'s accounting reporter, for taking time to apply the tests he considered necessary to ensure that my description of accounting fairly reflects the position of that profession as of the date of his examination.

Thanks to so many people who helped in the concurrent crises: my mother, the Kaplans, Bert and Phyllis Baker, all the Thalers, Tina and Jim Hempstead, Sara Singleton, Tony Scaduto and Stephanie Trudeau, Nancy Enright, Jeane Devlin, Cynthia Jacob, Jill Bullitt, John Emshwiller and Deborah Yaeger, Ellen Levine, Sue-Ann Bennet and Joe Forte, Dick and Arlene Gersh, Don Moffit and Ellen Graham, Ellen Castelluccio, Esther Wender, Sasha Linta, the Plainfield Friends meeting, and maybe most of all my housekeeper, Vicky George. There could never be enough thanks for all they've done.

And lastly a note for readers who may have run across certain other accounts of Nugan Hand that received attention elsewhere, and who may wonder why they are not referred to by me.

One memorable account, which I have noted in the text, was produced by a journalist I previously respected. I couldn't challenge some of it, since her words bore such a stunning resemblance to my own as published in the *Wall Street Journal.* (I have received lavish apologies—and meals—from both of her publishers and consider that matter closed.) Her account is padded out with familiar and undocumented assertions lifted from sources like Neil Evans and the *Covert Action Information Bulletin.*

A second account, written by James A. Nathan, a University of Delaware professor, appeared in *Foreign Policy* magazine, the issue of winter 1982–83. It contained sensational assertions about Nugan Hand and some persons in this book; it stated as fact things that I knew only as rumor or supposition. I eagerly called Professor Nathan to seek documentation, which wasn't provided in the article. Incredibly, he said his only documentation for the daring assertions was press clippings, including some from Communist and other strongly partisan and unreliable publications, and from small-publication journalists I knew to be unreliable. He added that he had "checked it with other people who have agency sources," though he declined to name any. He had not tried to talk to the people involved to hear their denials. Explaining behavior that reporters for any responsible publication would be pilloried for, Nathan said, "Don't get mad at me. I'm not making any of this stuff up. It's all been published. . . . I figure if it was wrong they [the people being written about] would have taken issue with the original source." Many statements in his article can now be proven wrong.

Finally, in the spring of 1987, a Washington group called the International Center for Development Policy held a press conference to distribute portions of a manuscript about Nugan Hand written by Peter Dale Scott, a University of California professor. In his manuscript, Professor Scott made strong assertions about Nugan Hand that will not be found in this book, and everything he says is carefully footnoted. And who is the source for his assertions, if you turn to the fine print and look at the footnotes? Why, Professor Nathan, of course.

And so it goes in academia.

Index